Acclaim for John Gimlette's

AT THE TOMB OF THE INFLATABLE PIG

"Blends travelogue, history and flights of descriptive whimsy to highly tonic effect. . . . For all his mastery of Paraguayan history, it's Gimlette's extravagant prose and unhinged enthusiasm that make the book. . . . You couldn't ask for a more entertaining guide."
—*The Seattle Times*

"Hilarious. . . . What keeps you reading about Paraguay, maybe in spite of yourself, is Gimlette's marvelous wit and eye for character."
—*Pittsburgh Post-Gazette*

"Reading the book is like watching a Komodo dragon eat a tethered goat. Paraguay, as Gimlette portrays it, is . . . completely bizarre. . . . Conquistadores and Nazis, whores and cannibals, all of them rather awful, all of them splendidly rendered. . . . Graham Greene would have approved." —*National Geographic Adventure*

"A glorious travel book . . . in which the country's craziness is portrayed with humor, insight and considerable deftness of touch. . . . As a historian of the absurd [Gimlette] is superlative."
—*The Sunday Times* (London)

"A wildly entertaining read: a raucous blend of history, travelogue, and guide." —*Condé Nast Traveler*

"*At The Tomb of the Inflatable Pig* should be ranked among the very best explorations of its kind: at once a history and a guide to one of the least hospitable nations on earth." —*The Washington Times*

"Irreverent and rambunctious. . . . [A] superior travel book."
—*Foreign Affairs*

"An extraordinary book, part history, part travelogue . . . so vivid that nobody reading it is ever likely to forget the country. . . . A book that sheds fascinating light on a forgotten corner of Latin America' "
—*The Daily Telegraph* (London)

"A richly detailed catalog of oddities and horrors, the kind of eccentricities that flourish in isolation. . . . [Gimlette] spills Paraguay's cruelest, most shameful secrets, but his admiration for the forlorn middle country is real on every page."
—*Outside*

"Howlingly entertaining. . . . There [is] no resisting Gimlette's rollicking account."
—*The San Diego Union-Tribune*

"A truly wonderful exploration of one of the world's most captivating countries. . . . Brilliant."
—*Sunday Express*

"[A] wonderful, wacky book. . . . Filled with the offbeat and the bizarre. Gimlette's narrative attempts to flesh out a country that is as difficult to define as nailing Jell-O to a wall. Vivid, riotous, fascinating and never dull, his book is wildly entertaining."
—*The Tucson Citizen*

"Compelling. . . . Blackly comical. . . . Spicy, exuberant prose."
—*Mail on Sunday* (London)

"Eccentric and richly descriptive. . . . The best travel writers are those with both a sense of history and a sense of humor, and Gimlette qualifies on both counts."
—*Richmond Times-Dispatch*

"[Gimlette] has a firm grasp of the country's intriguing past, and a watchful eye on its perplexing present."
—*Literary Review*

"Terrifically funny. . . . A great book in the noble tradition of British travel writing."
—*Hartford Advocate*

"Perceptive and entertaining."
—*The Times Literary Supplement* (London)

JOHN GIMLETTE

AT THE TOMB OF THE INFLATABLE PIG

John Gimlette is a regular contributor of travel articles and photographs to *Condé Nast Traveller*, as well as numerous journals and newspapers in England. He is a practicing attorney in London, where he lives with his family. This is his first book.

AT THE TOMB OF THE
INFLATABLE PIG

Travels Through Paraguay

—◦◦◦◦—

JOHN GIMLETTE

VINTAGE DEPARTURES
VINTAGE BOOKS
A DIVISION OF RANDOM HOUSE, INC.
NEW YORK

To Jayne

Contents

Illustrations

*Unless otherwise attributed, all the illustrations are from the author's
collection.*

Acknowledgements

I would like to thank the following for their help with this book.

In Paraguay—José and Virginia Franco, Diane and Antonio Espinoza, Robert Eaton, Rodrigo Wood, Dr. Enrique Wood, Margarita Kent, Ysanne Gayet, Stuart Duncan, Arminda Girala de Morales, Bishop Ellison, Beryl Baker, Frank Fragano, Peter and Midi Graham, Jakob and Maria Unger, Geraldo Cadogan, Oscar Centurion Frontanilla, Paula Brown, Eddie and Sonia Mueller, Gundolf Niebuhr, Hein and Maria Braun of Loma Plata, Alberto Yanosky, the Halke family of Nueva Germania, Nancy Cardozo, Ian and June Martin, Angus Martin, Carlos Yegros, Dr. Sergio Burgos, Lucy Yegros, Silvia Caballero, Cord Kelly, Federico Robinson, Dianny Elizeche of Paula's Tours, Brian Condon, José Luis Gadea Miguel (of Spain), Sergio Cáceres Mercado, Guillermo Peroni, Father Feehan and Marcelino Godoy Vera of Nueva Londres.

In Argentina—Michael and Judy Hutton. It was with them that my passion for South America—its people, its landscapes and its wildlife—all began.

In Britain—Eliza Aquino at the Paraguayan Embassy, Andrew Nickson of Birmingham University, John Renfrew, Ian Savile (my uncle), Georgina Capel, Andrew Roberts, Hugh and Lulu Williams, Kate Wykes, Diego de Jesus Flores-Jaime of King's College (London), Bishop Douglas Milmine, Michael Kerr and his colleagues on the *Daily Telegraph* travel desk and Tim Murray-Walker of Journey Latin America. I would also like to thank those who've read through the script and who've offered their own invaluable suggestions and improvements—in particular, Mark Wordsworth and my father, Dr. T. M. D. Gimlette. Perhaps most of all I am indebted to Roger and Maria-Cristina Freeman of the Anglo-Paraguayan Society; although they knew that what I'd write about Paraguay wouldn't always make comfortable reading, they have not hesitated to provide generous support at every stage—whether by means of contacts, literature or advice. Any errors in this book are made in spite of their best efforts to educate me and must therefore be entirely mine.

Some of the episodes in this book first appeared in *The Spectator*.

None of this, however, would have been possible without the support and encouragement of my wife, Jayne. She has indulged me at every stage; seeing this book through several drafts, offering hours of brilliant editing and generally putting up with the "widowhood" that comes of being a writer's spouse. It is to her that this book is dedicated, with all my love.

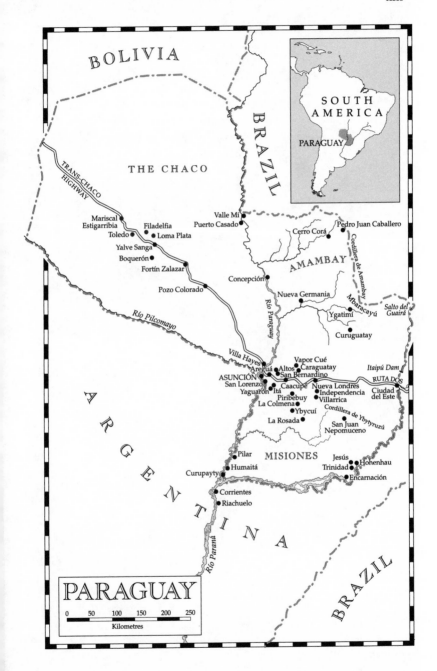

Introduction

"An island surrounded by land," wrote Roa Bastos of his country, Paraguay. For me, it is a remarkable observation not so much because it is true but because it comes from a Paraguayan. Throughout the travels described in this book, I met few Paraguayans who saw their country in relative terms; for most, there was, quite simply, no other world than their own.

As I travelled around Paraguay, I began to appreciate the scale of its insularity. It sits at the heart of a continent but not on the way to anywhere else. Bounded by Brazil, Argentina and Bolivia, it is a country nearly twice the size of the United Kingdom but with only a tenth of its population. This puts it among the most sparsely populated countries in the world. In the outer margins of the country there is virtually no population at all, and these, I suppose, are its oceans. They are even described in the language of the sea, with "islands," "coasts" and "bays."

I set out in all directions from the capital, Asunción, and every journey ended at forbidding natural frontiers: poisonous jungles, boiling rivers, deserts or endless, enervating marshes. In the whole country there are only two all-weather airports and much of what's landed still comes by boat along a great river, the Río Paraguay. Despite thousands of kilometres of frontier there are but a handful of viable entry-points. Paraguay is not merely isolated, it is almost impenetrable. Small wonder that it has become a refuge to Nazis, cannibals, strange sixteenth-century Anabaptists, White Russians and fantastic creatures that ought long ago to have been extinct.

In their more flamboyant moments, the Paraguayans describe their landlocked nation as "South America's Switzerland." In truth, it is its Cinderella. A third of its people live below the poverty line, and until comparatively recently, drinking water was sold from mule carts on the streets, even in Asunción. Only 11 per cent of the roads are paved and the telephone system is so haunted that nowadays there are twice as many mobile phones as there are land lines. It is a young country too; 40 per cent of the population is under fourteen. Few of them will have heard of Switzerland, one in ten of them will get no education at all. Nor are there Alps. At its highest, Paraguay never climbs more than 840 metres out of the savannah. On a sober analysis, the most that Paraguay and Switzerland have in common is a dearth of seawater.

I realised that, for all its difficulties, Paraguay had never ceased to surprise (and sometimes alarm) those around it. I realised too that there was much explaining to be done; isolation has encouraged lively eccentricity. Paraguay is the greatest importer of Scotch per capita in the world and yet few Paraguayans drink it. It is the greatest exporter of electricity and yet a sizeable proportion of its people still live by slash-and-burn. There can be few other countries whose national collections include a Tintoretto (*Iacopo Robusti*) and yet where there are men surviving by the bow and arrow. It is the only country on the continent that still officially speaks the language of its original inhabitants, the Guaraní. Here, perhaps, the Paraguayans are at their most impenetrable. Parents, for example, might speak to each other in Guaraní but will expect their children to address them respectfully—in Spanish.

Less surprisingly, their insularity has given the Paraguayans a powerful sense of intimacy. Although I was always treated with embarrassing kindness, I was seldom regarded as anything other than a curiosity, an outsider. Paraguayan patriotism is about the only commodity that is limitless. Even the word "Guaraní" resonates through society, in the names of boats, buses, hotels, the currency and the national fizzy drink. Sometimes this enthusiasm emerges as ugly nationalism but at other times it is inspirational. Asunción had its own impressionist movement at the turn of the nineteenth century, beautiful but deeply introspective. Its writers, despite their clunky foreign names—Appleton, Appleyard and Thompson—have also given the Paraguayan arts a respectable acquittal (in 1996, Roa Bastos was short-listed for the Nobel Prize for literature). On the sports field too the Paraguayans have bloodied themselves well. Seldom does an international golf or tennis championship take place without some Guaraní heroism. In the FIFA World Cup 2002, Paraguay was seeded ninth (five places above England) and took the fight all the way to the last rounds in Japan, a remarkable achievement for a David amongst so many Goliaths.

A by-product of Paraguay's strong kinship and oral traditions is that no one agrees on anything. History is largely a matter of opinion, which makes this book both harder and easier to write. There isn't even agreement as to what the word "Paraguay" means. Some say it is "the water that flows to the sea" or "the water that is richly adorned." Some think it is derived from the Guaraní for "crown" or the paraquá bird *(Ortolida paraqua),* or from the name of an Indian chieftain. Others, less charitably, say it refers to a group of water-pirates, the Payaguás, who once terrorised the river in their search for good scalps.

Whatever it means, few have any reason to go to Paraguay. Even my own introduction was a matter of chance. In the countdown to the Falklands War, I'd been working on a farm in northern Argentina; Paraguay was my nearest bolt-hole. Although I would often feel excluded, I would come to love this State of Isolation.

As I rummaged through Paraguay's history, I realised that isolation explained much of what was otherwise inexplicable. There seemed few points at which it had connected with the outside world. In the long day of human existence, Paraguay was only noticed in the nanoseconds before midnight. Even then, the *conquista* of 1537 was a very different experience to the genocide endured elsewhere in the Americas. Finding themselves alone at the heart of the continent, the conquistadors bedded down among the savages and a new and peculiar race evolved. In time, the *provincia* of Paraguay, which was momentarily the greatest Spanish holding after Peru, slipped into obscurity.

For centuries, the country had few visitors. Still the only way in was through the hard southern flanks of Argentina and then two months sailing up the Paraná. This long seclusion enabled the Paraguayans to experiment, to try out all the different shapes and sizes of tyranny.

The first was an agricultural tyranny, a land of half-castes herded into work camps or *encomiendas.* Then, from 1609, it was a Jesuit theocracy, ruled by the "sword of the word." However godly and admirable it may have been, Spain eventually saw it for what it was, an empire within an empire, and in 1768 it was dismembered. Independence was then thrust upon the Paraguayans in 1811 (until then they'd never seen the point) and the chance arose for some experiments of their own.

In 1814, God made way for a spindly agnostic in a black frock-coat who is still known as "The Supreme One." For the next twenty-six years, the country was his revolutionary police state. Dr. Francia ruled with genius, madness, ferocious impartiality and scrupulous honesty (he even returned his unspent salary to the treasury). In the course of his experiment, Paraguay was sealed off from the world and the *peninsulares* (those born in Spain) persecuted almost to extinction.

Francia's brand of revolutionary socialism was replaced in 1840 by a period of feudalism under the López dynasty. Though initially there were elements of revolutionary design (the Law of the Womb, 1842, was one of the first moves against slavery in the Americas), by the second generation the family's rule was hopelessly self-serving and often just bizarre. It ended with the bloodiest war modern man has ever known: the War of the Triple Alliance (1865–70).

Ravaged, smashed and isolated, Paraguay could boast no tidy structures in the decades that followed. The worst years were 1910 to 1912, when seven presidents came and went. By this time half the country's land was owned by seventy-nine people. At the moment when it might have recovered, Paraguay was then entangled in another war, the Chaco War (1932–5). It would become the most destructive war of the twentieth-century western hemisphere, a fight with Bolivia over 247,000 square kilometres of desert.

There was then almost a period of fascism. Even the chief of the Asunción police named his son "Adolfo Hirohito" in anticipation of a muscular future, but it never happened. At the last minute, Paraguay changed tack, declared war on Nazi Germany and was admitted to the United Nations.

The last of the experiments began in 1954, when General Stroessner seized power. His own vicious, ill-defined brand of totalitarianism became one of the most enduring the world has known, lasting nearly thirty-five years. By the end, Paraguayans could look back over their history and count only two years of democratic rule of law.

It is not always easy to decide which was the consequence of the other; Paraguay's isolation or its experiments with tyranny. Either way, its relationships with the outside world have always been distant and often tortuous. In the last century and a half, Paraguay has fought all its neigh-bours, on one occasion three at once. It was thrown out of the League of Nations for fighting, and even now there's a tendency to evaluate foreign countries according to their football. It was left out of the Cold War; too self-contained for the communists and too unpredictable for the Americans (Nixon politely declined an offer of Paraguayan help in Vietnam). Its friends have tended to be its benefactors—those who've desperately needed its vote: the Israelis, the Taiwanese and the pre-Mandelan South Africans. Everyone else has left it to its isolation.

Even when relationships have been urged upon it, Paraguay has proved tirelessly exotic. It is the only member of the United Nations to have a flag that is different on each side. Indeed, Asunción had no diplo-mats at all until the arrival of a British consul late in the nineteenth century. Heads of state proved harder to entice; Paraguay only received its first state visit in 1964. It was General de Gaulle, looking more bemused than ever.

How long, I wonder, can Paraguay remain an island surrounded by land? There was once a time when the ripples made by world events took many months to reach Asunción. Now the ripples come faster and faster. At least two Paraguayans were killed in the World Trade Center outrage and the country accuses its most easterly city of being a "focal point for Islamic extremism." The outside world, it seems, can no longer be ignored.

Elsewhere, Paraguayans imagine a union with Brazil, but already this is more real than imagined. Even now, a land bridge extends outwards to Brazil, with 350,000 Brazilians living in the Eastern Border Region, trading in Brazilian *reals* and bargaining in Portuguese. Inevitably, the Paraguay that is described in this book is about to change for ever.

Historically, those who didn't know it tended to refer to Paraguay as "the empty quarter of South America." Those who did brought back fantastical stories, describing a land of lotus-eaters and biddable women, hilarious despots and magnificent wars. These tales were usually too raw for public enjoyment but meat and drink to writers of fiction. Paraguay would crop up time and time again throughout literature, from Voltaire to Graham Greene, sometimes modified, sometimes mutilated.

Originally, I was also going to portray Paraguay in fiction. But, as the history unravelled, I was repeatedly troubled by the same thought: it all seemed so improbable. Was I squandering an opportunity? Would anyone believe me? In the end I decided that it had to be told the way it was and the way I saw it.

Most of the characters in this book therefore appear as they appeared to me and with their own names. A few I've had to change because, even in present-day Paraguay, a view that is safely held today may not be so tomorrow. Others I've changed in deference to their need for privacy. Gareth Llewelyn, for example, comprises several people but one in particular. I hope his family will understand why I've included his unhappy story; he played an important role in my perception of this beautiful and troubled country. Without him, this portrayal is incomplete.

I hope too that Paraguayans will forgive me for telling the story of their politicians with what may sometimes seem like frivolity. It's the only way I know to tell a story that, deep down, makes me feel anger. If my words provoke even a tremor of Paraguayan outrage, I'd be happy. For too long, evil powers have made a scarce commodity of protest. Lassitude, once regarded as endearing, has become a means of survival.

John Gimlette
London, 2002

ASUNCIÓN

I knew nothing of the city, but I believed I would find in Asunción some mingling of the exotic, the dangerous and the Victorian which would appeal . . . How right I would prove to be.

—Graham Greene, *Ways of Escape*

When I first came to Asunción from Spain, I realised that I'd arrived in paradise. The air was warm, the light was tropical and the shuttered colonial houses suggested sensual, tranquil lives. At night we'd go out walking in the streets and I'd be aware of two things; the smell of jasmine and the sound of voices in the dark. But like any paradise, this one had serpents.

—Josefina Plá, Paraguayan poet

My hostess was studying me with renewed interest.

"Did you say," she said slowly, "that he cut the child's hands off with a blowtorch?"

"Well, yes." I fidgeted. "Doesn't anyone remember?"

Down the table everyone shook their head, except the thief.

"I remember it," he said.

Attention swivelled in his direction. The thief was pouring more wine into his Coca-Cola. It was rumoured he'd skinned his own bank and almost got away with it. Overnight, they said, his eyes had turned black like a panda's, and his Dalmatians had run away.

"Didn't they make a film," he piped, "about The Blowtorch Case? With Antoni Opkins and those moths. That was here, wasn't it, Mónica? That was Paraguay?"

There was dissension from the silverware and glass.

The hostess was examining me again. "When did you hear these things, John?"

"When I first came here. About twenty years ago."

Ah, they all said, twenty years ago. Things were different then.

2

Throughout the summer of 1982, Asunción had been gripped by a good murder.

The body of the boy, fourteen years old and horribly mutilated by the blowtorch, had been discovered in a wealthy suburb. The details of the story were happily never very clear and the press had shown a maddening indifference to the whole affair, doubtless on the General's instructions. Perhaps his German priggishness had got the better of him or, more likely, he didn't want his Paraguayans to speculate on the possibility that his police did not have eyes and ears in every home. Starved of details by their *caudillo,* the citizens drank up the trickle of gossip that collected downtown, and suffocated by heat, they made themselves giddy with fantastical tales, each more grotesque than the last.

"They say he's someone in the government—a sadist," I was told by a friend, Reynaldo Gosling. Reynaldo was a few years older than me and was already a student, but he seemed to enjoy our meetings at the

William Shakespeare, feasting on my most mawkish tales from England. One grandfather, he explained, had been a British railway engineer and the other had distinguished himself in the Chaco War of the thirties. Although he'd never been outside Paraguay he affected a familiarity with England and nurtured a fondness for *El Pub Inglés*. "Apparently, he tortured the boy for hours with a blowtorch before strangling him."

"Yes," agreed his pretty Guaraní girlfriend. "And he smashed the boy's face in too. They must have been lovers."

"That's shit," said another man, who'd been munching cornmeal *chipa* at the bar. "He's a Nazi. One of the General's Germans. I heard he did medical experiments in those Jewish camps. Someone's covering for him."

This was dangerous talk and Reynaldo steered us back towards safer ground and the more conventional wisdom. "Look, he's probably just some homosexual."

The police were at their wits' end, and truckloads of constables, old Mauser rifles wedged between their knees, ploughed up and down Independencia. They didn't expect to find the blowtorch killer but they could at least stifle the rumours of their own ineptitude. In a further act of desperation, they took a sniff at the gossip and rounded up all of Asunción's homosexuals. Not knowing what to do with such a large number of patently harmless individuals, they locked them up for a few days and then released them. The citizens were unappeased.

But it wasn't immediately obvious how the rumours thrived or even spread about the city. By day the centre of town was silent and deserted. Baked by the sun, the cobbles shimmered in a heat haze. The windows of the Guaraní-baroque mansions were tightly shuttered against the fierce white light, their vast panelled doors secured shut with bolts the size of ox-bones. Those who had the money had fled the heat by passing the summer on the beaches of Uruguay. A snake of BMWs slithered in and out every season.

It seemed that at these times of day only the beggars stirred in the centre of the city, and they didn't gather to gossip. "Most of them are survivors of the Chaco War," Reynaldo told me. "They got shot up in our war with Bolivia. Then they got amputations and now they hang around on the Plaza de Los Héroes. Actually, they're a nuisance."

They probably wouldn't be for much longer. With limbs so smashed

by explosions and minds so raked by gunfire and *whisky-tipo*, it wouldn't
be long now before old age mercifully carried them off—if the giant Mercedes buses that crashed over the ruts didn't get them first. Each time I
passed them, I wondered if they ever thought of themselves as the lucky
ones, the ones that survived a war so terrible that nearly a third of
Paraguay's fighters perished.

There was a brief moment at the end of each day, that exquisite moment
of dusk that tropical countries earn themselves, when the sun plunged
into the Río Paraguay and the city was suffused with pink light, when
the citizens, those that remained, would emerge from their shuttered
houses, blinking and shaking sleep out of their clothes. Some would
stare blankly into the shop windows at the electrical goods smuggled in
from Panama and the bottles of whisky piled up like ammunition.
Others took their seats under the *lapacho* trees, in the Plaza Uruguaya,
kicked off their shoes and waited for the officious, unofficial curfew to
begin. Perhaps they gossiped, exchanging the latest gothic details on the
blowtorch murder, but most just sat, waiting silently for the end of
the day.

As the light changed from pink to purple, Asunción's only neon sign,
large bright red letters on the pediment of the National Bank, flickered
into life: PEACE, WORK AND WELL-BEING WITH STROESS-
NER. When they saw this, people put their shoes and socks back on and
went home.

For some reason the writ of the curfew never extended to The Lido bar.
As long as you could get yourself there and back, weaving around the
patrols, it seemed as though you could sit there as long as you liked,
sluicing away the dust and diesel with icy pilsen called Antarctica. It
ought to have been the perfect place for the traffic in good stories. It
stood right at the centre of town and had even been described rather
whimsically as lying "at the crossroads of South America." Inside, a great
amphitheatre of tangerine-coloured bar swooped out into a brilliant
white room. It was a room full of air that swirled in through the
windows, was whipped by giant ceiling fans and then hustled out on to
the street again. It was pure 1950s; you pulled upholstered stools up to
the bar and gave your orders to the little duck-hipped ladies in tangerine
aprons and tangerine hats who waddled around in the arena.

Paraguayans enjoyed it, but their enjoyment was reverential and mute. They sat huddled around the counter, inward-looking, facing each other across the gorgeous orange arena; there were the middle-class Hispanics with their brilliantined hair, pig-skin briefcases and buckled alligator shoes; there were *mestizos* and touts, Maká Indians selling bows and arrows and *mercantes* hawking lace as thin and light as cobwebs; there were ruddy, blond immigrants from Latvia, Ukraine and the Balkans spooning up *bori-bori* soup with big, farmers' hands; there were the German settlers pawing over *Neues für Alle*, while their wives, hair-dyed and lacquer-faced, sipped *tereré*, an icy privet-leaf tea; then there were Koreans, newcomers to the scene, who'd set themselves up around the *mercado* and who only occasionally came down to town for acupuncture or lumbago treatment and who stuck to the cold beer. They all ate and sipped and spooned and sucked in silence, while the orange ladies heaved great trays of *parillada* steak and juicy hummocks of steaming maize cake out of the kitchens. The diners stared through them, at each other, wondering, I fancied, who was the police informer, who was the whisky smuggler, who was the Nazi and who could do *that* to a boy so young.

When the silence of the Paraguayans became too much, I would duck across the Plaza and up Calle Chile to the Shakespeare. Although it called itself a pub, it was really just a room above a Korean pharmacy, reached by some musty stairs. It wasn't even particularly English, although it was staffed by two Glaswegians who thought that life in such a place was "better than life on the dole." The young Paraguayans thought it was Paradise, even though there was nothing to drink but Antarctica and the temperature seldom fell below gas mark 3. They liked to hear Rod Stewart roaring out of the tape recorder and they were thrilled to be in a place that could rumble with laughter. Above all they loved the way that you had to shout very loud—in English—to be heard. It allowed them to transport themselves in their imaginations away from the stifling conformity and oppression of Asunción to England, a place hardly any of them had seen, where people had endless fun and sex and danced all night around their palm trees. The illusion was sustained for as long as it took before someone tripped over the plug to the tape deck, throttled Rod Stewart and plunged us all back into silence. During the lull, I was spotted by a girl with a fantastic rick of black hair piled up around her head.

"Are you English, kid?"

"Yes," I admitted. I was terrified; girls at my school hadn't behaved like this. She was sucking the icebergs out of her Antarctica and crunching them up with her teeth. "Are you?"

"Course I'm fucking not. This is Paraguay. I'm fucking Paraguayan." She took a step back and cocked her head, awaiting my reaction. I failed to say anything.

"OK. Look. My father was Japanese and my mother half-Spanish and half fucking English. That makes me fucking Paraguayan."

"You speak good English," I tried.

She'd worked in Liverpool for a while. Now she imported Scotch whisky into Paraguay.

"But only the best. The fucking most expensive. Anyway, what are you doing here?"

I hesitated. "I've come to see President Stroessner."

"Well, he's a fuck-head!" she exploded, and threw her magnificent head back and laughed. "A total fuck-head! You know what he does? He takes people he doesn't like up in planes and flies over the Chaco Desert. And then what? He fucking well throws them out!"

I opened my mouth to protest, but at that moment the music restarted. She pressed her ear up close to my face, which disappeared into an impenetrable thicket of curls and ringlets. Everything went dark and my nose tickled.

"You can't say that here," I muffled. "The *pyragüés* . . ."

The *pyragüés* was the name everybody used for the secret police. It was a Guaraní word which meant—literally—"the hairy-footed ones." It was a cute reminder that their raids were sudden, silent and invariably savage.

"The *pyragüés* don't speak English, you fuck-head. All the police are fuck-heads!" She punched me on the chest and turned and wandered off towards the bar, with her beer bottle raised in salute. "The police are fuck-heads!" The crowd around the bar parted and shrank away.

Reynaldo appeared by my side. "Do you really want to see President Stroessner then?"

"Er, yes." I hadn't considered it before.

"He holds an audience every Tuesday in the Government Palace. That's tomorrow."

*

I zig-zagged back to my *pensión*, the Hispania, on the other side of Los Héroes. It was grizzled baroque and much favoured by Mennonites, the Germanic Anabaptists whose colonies were dotted round the country.

These strange, pale people were the distant fallout of a diaspora that had begun in Switzerland in 1525 when the "left wing of the Reformation" split with Ulrich Zwingli. Self-contained and self-denying, the Mennonites had been jostled around the world ever since, splitting themselves into smaller and smaller fragments. The splinter group that used the Hispania were known as "The Mexicans," for no better reason than that a part of their wanderings had been spent—in conditions of exorbitant misery—in central America. They now padded in and out of Asunción looking for seeds and farm implements.

"We are," said their literature, "*die Stillen in Lande*—the unobtrusive ones." This was only partly true. Certainly, the Mexicans confined themselves to the top floor of the hotel and it was rumoured that they even denied themselves a breeze from the fans lest their elders should hear of such vanity and cast them out from their number. But whenever they went out, they wore strange nineteenth-century costumes of bonnets and black calico. Even in a city of oddities like Asunción, this was hardly unobtrusive.

I had a room on the second floor. It was a vast, mildewed space that might once have been used for dancing classes. It had floor-to-ceiling louvred shutters that were so seized up with drifts of green paint that they'd become petrified in the open position, admitting scalding blasts of dust and roasted corn from the street below. I shared this great green tropical ballroom with two others, for whom it was, in its own way, heavenly. The first was an Englishman called Kevin Pluck who'd come to South America to give some long and careful thought to the question of whether or not he should ever get a job. He had an opening in the car factory at Luton, but the delicious, orange-blossomed lassitude that overwhelmed Asunción ensured that he wasn't going to hurry the decision. He'd at least made up his mind to return to Luton with a suntan and so he spent a lot of time and effort trying to go brown. For some reason his skin remained determinedly cheesy.

The other man was a New Zealander called Eddy Taylor. From the start he declared our room to be a "real beaut," and he dragged us all out to celebrate our good fortune. Eddy was chronically, pathologically happy and I have often wondered since then whether I wasn't somehow infected with his enthusiasm and afflicted with a lifelong and slightly illogical appetite for Asunción. Eddy was unstoppable. He'd been a cow-puncher, a horse-breaker, a sheep-dagger, a dishwasher and a disc jockey. There was no end to the revolting things that he was prepared to find satisfying. He was spattered with freckles and ginger whiskers, and little bits of him—teeth mainly—had been knocked out in fights. He was everything that Kevin wasn't and that Kevin was glad he wasn't.

Although all that we had in common was the fact that we all slept in the same mouldering baroque cavern, we became good friends. We often ate together at the railway station, where—among the belch and hiss of steam engines—the food was the cheapest in the city. Some after-noons, Eddy led us out on illegal bathing parties to the Hotel Guaraní, a hideous concrete pillar built by the General to cope with the tidal wave of tourists that was about to overwhelm Asunción. The hotel was even featured on the bank-notes to guide the tourists home. But the wave never came and the pool attendant was happy to accept that we were all in Room 205, along with two other Eddys that Eddy had picked up in the railway station. Even eighteen years on, I couldn't remember a time when I'd seen a group of tourists in Paraguay larger than our raiding party.

Both Eddy and Kevin were rather older than me, in their mid-twenties, and I considered them to be very wise. When I got back from the Shakespeare, I told them about my discussion with Reynaldo and my plan to visit the President the next day. Eddy immediately became solicitous. "You know he pushes people out of fucking aeroplanes?"

Together we tried to piece together the General. Our guidebooks said that he was born on 3 November 1912. His father was a Bavarian brewer and his mother a Paraguayan beauty. He served in the Paraguayan army during the Chaco War and was a distinguished artillery officer. He seized power in a coup in 1954 and was therefore one of the most endur-ing dictators in the world.

"I also heard the old man's a bit of a randy bastard," added Eddy, but there was nothing in our guidebooks about that. The maps of Paraguay were infested with his name. There was Stroessner Airport, Port Stroess-ner, Fort Stroessner, Camp Stroessner and a street in every town named after either him, his matronly wife Doña Eligia or his father, Hugo Stroessner. His big, saggy face was impressed on all the stamps and coins, and Paraguayans even danced a prim little jig called the General Stroessner Polka. His portrait hung in the hallway of the Hotel Hispania and in every other hotel, bar, shop, office, funeral home and poodle parlour in town. Had we looked closely at the portrait, we might have appreciated his full majesty; he was Generalissimo Alfredo Stroessner, Legion d'Honneur, Knight of the Order of St. Michael and St. George, Order of the Condor of the Andes, Medal of the Inter-American Junta of Defence, Collar of the Order of the Liberator and Grand Cross of the Order of the Sun (with Diamonds).

Anyway, I thought he looked harmless enough, and Graham Greene, writing in *Travels with My Aunt*, had said that he looked like "the amiable well-fed host of a Bavarian *bierstube*." I prepared for my visit.

3

Of course, we didn't know the half of it. Alfredo Stroessner was in the twenty-eighth year of a rule so vile and brutish that it had been given its own ugly name: the *Stronato*. During the Tropical Terror, he'd extorted eight election results from the Paraguayans and plunged the country into a state of siege. Emergency measures were renewed every ninety days. A third of the state budget was diverted into "internal security," or bullies and guns. Several hundred thousand Paraguayans simply fled. Opponents (as everyone was keen to point out) were hurled from aeroplanes or—more economically—simply bound up in wire, mutilated and dumped in the Río Paraguay. The General didn't have to do that many times before the Paraguayans began to realise that the *Stronato* was serious and that it was enduring.

Don Alfredo himself was invincible, the strongman to defend Paraguay against communism and other, rather less specific, dark forces. He invented a new Guaraní doublethink of "elected autocracy" and "guided democracy." Then, from the United States, another useful euphemism was wafted in: the National Security Doctrine ("Get tough, the Commies are under the bed"). Don Alfredo now had all the impressive excuses he needed; Law 294 ("The defence of Democracy") made being a communist illegal, and Law 209 ("The defence of Public Peace and Personal Freedom") made it an offence to foster hatred among Paraguayans. The citizens meanwhile recognised these laws for what they were: the *ley de mbaraté*—the Law of the Jungle. Don Alfredo had all the guns.

Outsiders marvelled at the control that Don Alfredo exercised over his generals. Usually, they were the first to apply a new broom to any president who wavered or faltered (Paraguayans had seen thirty-four presidents swept away in the fifty years before the *Stronato*). The secret was simple: Don Alfredo simply employed the toughest of them on the board of Paraguay Incorporated, which became the greatest smuggling outfit in the world. Surrounded by countries with excruciating import tariffs, the pickings were rich, and Don Alfredo divided the territory up among his General Staff. Engorged with cash, no one would trouble to rock the boat. This easy patronage—known rather quaintly among social scientists as "sultanism"—kept everybody in medals and Scotch for thirty-four years. If Don Alfredo was ever asked about the army's involvement in smuggling, he'd simply shrug. "Ah," he'd say, "that is the price of peace."

Even now, I struggle to understand the scale of this, Paraguay's most productive industry. Suddenly, Asunción had more Mercedes than any other city in South America, and Paraguay became the greatest importer of whisky per capita in the world. In 1977, around 350,000 gallons a year were being sloshed around Paraguay in old Dakotas and army trucks, most of it heading for the borders. By 1993, it was 1,273,000 gallons. By then, however, operations had also expanded to cover heroin for Miami and guns to South Africa.

The Smuggler-in-Chief was General Andrés Rodríguez, who counted among his business associates the French heroin magnate Auguste Ricord. Ricord had a monstrous mansion in Asunción and later had his business success story told in less than reverential terms in *The French Connection*. Rodríguez himself was a man almost as shiny and plump as the President. Their families intermarried and the two cronies grew impressively rich. One American magazine even fêted Don Alfredo— fancifully perhaps—as the ninth richest man in the world.

Whether rolling in it or not, Don Alfredo kept a low profile. There was no presidential Rolls-Royce, and Stroessner took modest, woolly-cardigan holidays in Patagonia. He never gave rallies—because he kept fluffing his speeches—and often just bellowed at people in meetings ("He treated us like twelve-year-olds," one of the country's greatest ranchers later told me). The Old Sultan was at his happiest bantering in Guaraní, the language of his bombardiers. It didn't pay for him to be ostentatious; that might have prompted demands from the boardroom hoods for a greater slice of the action.

For the army's rank and file there were splendid period uniforms of hussars and lancers and the officers were even encouraged to do a little business of their own. Paraguay was in danger of becoming a sort of interactive *Pirates of Penzance,* but with headless corpses bobbing around on the river.

The small problem of an impoverished and potentially complaining populace was taken care of by Pastor Coronel, the head of the *pyragüés.* Whilst he was neither hairy-footed nor even fleet of foot (an Argentine secret agent once described him as "a refrigerator with a tennis ball on top"), he was an enthusiastic interrogator. People were pulled in on the slightest of pretexts. An Australian writer, Gavin Souter, was arrested for taking a photograph of the bullet-riddled lamp-post by the Municipal Theatre, and after a day in the cells found himself in front of Pastor Coronel. He was almost smothered by Coronel's charm. There had been a terrible mistake. He was discharged with all the Inquisitor's warmest blessings and good wishes.

Other guests of the *pyragüés* had a rather different smothering. Pastor Coronel—distinctly less charming on these occasions—liked to conduct his interviews with the subject immersed in the *pileta,* a bath-tub of human excrement. If, after that, they still had wits or dignity, Pastor Coronel's warmest blessings were inserted up their rectums with an electric cattle prod. Some, miraculously, made it home, deaf (like the anthropologist Chase Sardi) or with a mind now permanently scrambled. They, in a sense, were the fortunate ones; Pastor Coronel had the Secretary of the Paraguayan Communist Party torn apart, screaming, with a chainsaw—to the accompaniment of a pretty polka. In order that his master missed none of these noisy details, the entire transaction was relayed to Don Alfredo down the telephone. To most, it became obvious that further resistance was futile, and Terror, in the words of one horrified onlooker, "became internalised."

As if black could get any darker, there was an even blacker side to the *Stronato* which Eddy had accidentally stumbled upon: Don Alfredo had an omnipotent's appetite for exotic sex. For a while, the demands of his liver-spotted, dew-lapped *Burgermeister* body were met by a line-up of women, and Doña Eligia stood dutifully to one side. He even spawned a litter of little priglets, but as the *Stronato* gained awful momentum, Don Alfredo took his adventures to the playground. It was said that he employed a procurer—a child-snatcher on the General Staff. The President liked his girls no riper than fourteen, and after that, well, his official Snatcher could share them out among the crew. There was one lucky exception—a girl that he dandled long into her adulthood, possibly because he enjoyed the irony of her name: Legal.

That night, Kevin and Eddy watched as I prepared for my visit to His Excellency the President. Reynaldo and his friends had advised me to wear the school blazer, the crumpled-up tie and the pair of thick black corduroy trousers that I'd crushed into my luggage. I pulled them out and laid them on the bed and set to work, scouring and scraping at the stains and picking off the bits of fluff. Kevin and Eddy howled with laughter. They doubted that anyone could cross Asunción in that lot without dying of heat. They were still clutching each other and yelping with delight when I set out the next morning, muzzy-headed and leather-mouthed, for the Government Palace. Overnight, the lapels of the blazer, protesting at the soap and mauling of the night before, had curled up like crisps.

"Seriously," said Eddy, his face now deadpan but the tears still dripping off his nose, "don't shake hands with him. He's got something funny about disease. He doesn't like it."

4

Government Palace had been commissioned by newly independent Paraguay's second leader, who also happened to be its second dictator. Carlos Antonio López was born in 1790 to a Creole father and a half-Indian, half-negro mother. In the years before he was appointed to the junta, he practised as a lawyer, accumulating enviable wealth, cunning and girth. By 1844, his chops had begun to roll over his cravat and he'd become too obese and unwieldy to sit on his horse. His physical appearance had become so inflated and hideous that even his colleague on the junta, an old trooper called Alonso, became anxious. When Don Carlos turned on him one day and roared, *"Andante, barbero!"* ("Get out, you dolt!"), Alonso—overwhelmed by the spectacle of a fantastically fat man apparently about to explode—simply fled. Don Carlos then held the cudgels of power for the next eighteen years until he drowned in his own dropsy in 1862.

In power, the President continued to engorge and enlarge. He had a misty idea that Paraguay might one day be an imperial power as great as Napoleonic France, and took to wearing a bicorne hat. This, unsurprisingly, triggered helpless titters among the neighbouring Argentines. Enraptured, they sent their most weasel reporter, Héctor Varela, up the River Paraná to watch "The Monarch of the Jungle" open a theatre.

> One rarely sees a more impressive sight [sniggered Varela] than this great tidal wave of human flesh. He is a veritable mastodon, with a pear-shaped face, narrow forehead and heavy pendulous jowls. During the entire performance, the president ostentatiously wore an enormous, atrocious hat quite appropriate to him and equally suitable for either a museum of curiosities or for the Buenos Aires carnival.

Despite his porcine appearance and the fact that he was only able to conduct affairs of state from a robust armchair, Don Carlos was a surprisingly capable leader. Paraguay became the first country in the Americas to outlaw slavery. Torture was abolished (for a while) and a newspaper was started. Don Carlos even dabbled in a little diplomacy with his neighbours, who until then hadn't been allowed in (or out) of Paraguay for twenty years. He sent to England for surgeons, engineers and mechanics, and among those who came was a builder from Chelsea called Alan Taylor. Don Carlos wanted a Government Palace.

Alan Taylor arrived in Paraguay in 1858 and built himself a house which he fitted with Paraguay's first chimney. It started something of a fashion and soon chimneys were popping up all over Asunción. Once settled, he began work on the palace.

In the excitement, no design was spared, and Don Carlos and his builder incorporated every whimsy of authority: classical pediments, wings like Versailles, an Oval Office like the White House and even a lumpish tower like the Palace of Westminster. Although like all Guaraní-baroque it had been miniaturised, it was to be the culmination of Paraguay's imperial ambition and would trumpet her emergence into the Industrial Age. The American Minister, Mr. Washburn, predicted that the Government Palace would be "the finest building in South America." Captain Richard Burton, who steamed up here many years later—and who, incidentally, loathed Americans and Mr. Washburn in particular—disagreed and thought that the whole building was "an utter absurdity." Although I would come to agree with Burton about Mr.

Washburn, he was wrong about Government Palace; I have always regarded it as an absolute wedding cake, a cool, deliciously iced fantasy on the banks of the steamy Paraguay.

By the time I'd walked this far, rivulets of sweat were trickling down the inside of my shirt and the corduroys were becoming mushy and tangled. I gulped at the air but it was burnt and used up. Little spots were dancing among the cobbles.

Perhaps Carlos' greatest fault was that he died and, in so doing, made room for his son, Francisco Solano López. The gossips said that Francisco wasn't Don Carlos' natural son at all but was the product of his mother's dalliance with a sweaty farmer. Whatever the truth, Francisco inherited from Don Carlos two dangerous traits; the first, his fondness for greasy food (which made him swell up), was inconvenient and vaguely repulsive for those around him, but the second, an obsession with Napoleon, was to prove fatal not only to him but also to Paraguay.

"There are many questions to be settled," gurgled the dying Don Carlos through his dropsy, "but settle them with the pen rather than the sword, particularly with Brazil."

But within three years of his accession (no one challenged this, a second mastodon), Francisco had picked a quarrel with not just one neighbour but three: Brazil, Argentina and Uruguay. Although the fight that followed tore the smile off the face of the Argentines, it was a catastrophe. Paraguay lost a quarter of her territory and up to four-fifths of her population. "Only women, children and *burros* remained," it was reported at the time.

Alan Taylor continued his work on the palace, but by the end, he was forced to work with gangs of six-year-olds. "They were constantly watched," wrote Mr. Washburn, "that they should never idle away a moment . . . They appeared like worn-out slaves, in whom all hope is so utterly extinguished that they never looked up or ceased a moment from their labour." Alan Taylor eventually made it back to Chelsea, utterly broken. He'd been imaginatively tortured, his wife had died of starvation, and their thirteen-year-old son had been conscripted and then executed. Alan Taylor was last heard of, a skeleton, begging the Foreign Office for work. Later, I would come to appreciate how fate came to deal the Paraguayans—and her visitors—such a shocking hand.

By 1870, Paraguay had been dragged down almost as quickly as she'd emerged from her medievalism. She wouldn't resurface again until the twentieth century and then only to be dragged under again by the next catastrophic war, the Chaco War, starting in 1932. The sons of the orphans perished in their thousands, mainly through thirst, and a new generation of orphans emerged.

The Paraguayans who emerged from this war, shattered but, arguably, victorious, dragged a Bolivian tank home with them. They had captured it using only hand grenades. It was placed in the Plaza Independencia, next to the Government Palace, where its rust and diesel oil fanned out like a psoriatic rash. The civic leaders, anxious to deal the final blow, plunged a telegraph pole into the body of the tank, pinioning the whole machine to the concrete and linking the police station up with the military school.

I skirted the plaza, pattering damply down Independencia until I reached the palace grounds, where—as there were no gates—I turned in. Although I could hear my heart drumming in my chest, I felt bloodless and clammy. A truckload of soldiers were parked under a jacaranda tree. They all wore sunglasses and had sinister humps of ammunition bulging around their tureened bellies. I tottered across the palace lawn and their eyes followed like a little nest of crocodiles. One of them, who I presumed was the officer because he had mother-of-pearl grips on his revolvers, stepped out.

"What is it?"

"I've come to see the President," I croaked, and immediately, a heavily built brown suit appeared in the front hallway and, removing his mirrored lenses, waved me inside.

Reynaldo had warned me about this ogre. He was Mario Abdo Benítez, half-Syrian, half-Guaraní and the President's Personal Secretary. Abdo was loyal, obedient and dangerously stupid. He played court jester to Pastor Coronel's chief executioner. Paraguayans told a story about how he once burnt his ear by answering the phone while he was ironing his master's trousers. I can understand how you burnt this ear, the doctor had said afterwards, but how did you burn the other one? "Well," replied Abdo, "I had to phone for an ambulance, didn't I?"

At that moment, I wasn't finding this story amusing. Abdo's face was pressed up against mine like a cartoon bulldog. It was, I noticed, pocked with tiny scars. Suddenly the whole thing sliced itself up into a yellowy smile.

"What exactly do you want?"

Antarctica. The blowtorch man. Nazis and eczema. Your burnt ears. My mind scrambled for an answer but kept alighting on absurdities.

"I've come to pay my respects."

His smile yellowed a little wider. "Follow me please, señor."

I squelched up the red-carpeted stairs behind him. Above us, Carlos and Francisco López, whiskery and bemedalled, scowled down from their gilt frames. I let my trembling knuckles trail along the smooth marble of Alan Taylor's walls and sucked in a few draughts of cool, polish-scented air. At the top of the stairs we came face to face with a bronze statue of another dyspeptic general, snarling fiercely. We turned right and walked along a terrace until we reached the General's office. The Syrian knocked at the door and then entered, closing it behind him.

For a moment I contemplated my reflection in the polished wood and stiffened slightly as I saw the bedraggled and bemused figure peering back at me. I quickly averted my gaze and tried to concentrate on the views beyond the balustrade, towards the sluggish grey river with its tiny bronchitic boats, and beyond, to the distant shore, where the Chaco Desert began. Crushed up against the palace were the *viviendas temporarias*, the slums, run up out of corrugated iron and packing cases. As I watched a stringy cat tiptoe across a sheet of scalding tin, Abdo reappeared. My heart lurched.

"I am sorry, señor, we can't find him anywhere. He must have gone for a walk."

On the way back, I paused at the skewered tank that was bleeding oil and rust. It was of course still dying. The beggars were still dying from the wounds inflicted in the war. For a whole generation of women, family life had choked on the contumelies of widowhood. A whole generation of young men had been so piteously decimated that, for those that remained, there was not the strength or the will power to resist a German immigrant who indulged a fondness for having his opponents filleted and parcelled and yet who could take a Tuesday stroll along the quayside. Paraguayans had become mere caretakers at the tomb of their past, making do as best they could and whispering about what might have been.

But just as there were no bodies at this centuries-long wake, for they were scattered over the Chaco Desert and through the tropical forests of the north, nor was there grief. Doubtless, hot tears had been shed long ago. But now the republic was contracted in constitutional bereavement. Now the children were learning the national anthem in school, *"Paraguayos, República O Muerte"* ("Paraguayans, Republic or Death"), but what they were being offered was not a choice but an epitaph.

Strangely, their neighbours, the Argentines, ever anxious for their own souls, misinterpreted this as a state of contentment. Gustavo Morales was one of the regulars round the pool at the Hotel Guaraní. He was a textile trader who'd been coming to the city for many years, but trying to identify the Paraguayan character left him exasperated.

"They seem so sure of themselves," he said, "but nothing makes sense. You know what these people are buying off me now?" He flung his hand up towards the feverish sun. "Duffel coats! Duffel coats from England!"

His compatriots were often less kind and were wary of the passivity of their ethnically impure Guaraní neighbours at the head of the Paraná, of whom they told stories as purple as any from Paraguay itself.

"You know they come down to Argentina and steal babies," one told me, "and take them away—in truckloads."

5

Naturally, when I told Eddy and Kevin about my visit to the palace, they laughed so much they nearly passed out. I wasn't able to find it quite so funny, because somewhere deep down I felt a little, ill-formed tremble of anger. Still, I wasn't going to let this spoil the fun and so we all went out, to wash down our malaria pills with a good splash of Antarctica.

Then the day came for the boys to leave. Kevin was frustrated by the failure of his skin to react to Asunción's sunlight, and Eddy just had to keep moving. Although our friendship was necessarily transitory and predictably beery, I was sorry to see them go and to have the green dance hall all to myself. Eddy's rucksack was so large and so wide that he had to squeeze himself out of the Hispania sideways, like a crustacean. I never saw them again, but I still laugh when I think of that departure.

By Easter, the citizens had wearied of their own stories of the blow-torch man. Some had even doubted that he existed, although an Anglo-Paraguayan called Virginia Martin told me that she and her boyfriend, Raoul, had some news from the prison.

"Raoul and I go up there every Friday to take dinner for some friends of Raoul's. (They fell out with the government over some land deal and Raoul's friends can't get the right judge. They all want so much now.) We bring these guys food from restaurants all over Asunción but it isn't like home, is it? Anyway, we get all the gossip from them. They say the police have got a lead and they're expecting a breakthrough any day."

And so on. *Asunceños* were spared the next instalment by the war in the Falkland Islands. General Stroessner offered some half-hearted support to the Argentines and I sought the advice of the British Embassy.

"You are only eighteen. You should go home," said the clerk behind the plate-glass. Her coffee was cold in front of her.

"I bet you've been busy since this all started," I teased. She was Anglo-Argentine.

"Yes," she snapped, and took off her glasses and laid them on the desk in front of her. "This morning over one hundred Paraguayans have telephoned in asking if they can fight for the British."

"I presume you told them that that was absolutely fine."

"Don't be ridiculous."

That night the young Paraguayans packed out the Shakespeare and whooped and howled until the rafters shook. I sensed the beginnings of change.

6

I spent Easter Sunday with Virginia's parents in a wealthy suburb of the city. It was a world apart from the crumbling, oven-baked downtown area that I lived in. Here were lawns and sprinklers and shaven-headed Americans chopping tennis balls at each other behind heavy iron railings. There were gleaming brass carriage lamps and doorbells that could chime water music. Most of the mansions up here really were (to borrow Burton's words) "Utter Absurdities." Every architectural whimsy that had ever been conceived was given expression up here—in coloured bricks. There was mock-Georgian, mock-Victorian, both rococo and mock-rococo, Spanish hacienda, Tibetan pagoda (with parking for two Mercedes and a Pontiac Firebird), Swiss Alpine, Swiss cheese, Wild West and igloo. Very often there were combinations of all of them. One house even had "Tudor" half-timbering, a deep straw thatch and a sentry box, all redolent, I supposed, of an English country cottage. I loathed it, and when my Paraguayan friends told me that the whole area was seething with smugglers and Don Alfredo's unsavoury cronies, I made a pointless (and slightly sanctimonious) promise to myself that I would never stay in the area perniciously known as "uptown." It is a promise that I have—broadly speaking—kept to ever since.

When my friends said "seething," they weren't exaggerating. Up here, there was a real and horrible possibility of running into the Whisky Generals or some Serbian neo-Nazis. There were swindlers and robbers from all over the world—the Bartons from Australia and others from Italy, France and America. Don Alfredo's son, Freddie (who was, as it happens, a gibbering cocaine addict), was building himself a full-scale replica of the White House up here, and Georges Watin—one of Frederick Forsyth's anti-heroes (the assassin from *The Day of the Jackal*)— had a little mock-something around the corner. There were countless others.

"Pinochet's got a retirement home in Carmelitas," offered one of the exuberant drinkers at the Shakespeare.

"And Idi Amin's got a plot somewhere," added another.

In the middle of this waxworks of nasties lived Virginia's parents. They must have seemed very incongruous here because it was difficult to imagine nicer people living among such grotesque neighbours. The Martins have, over the years, become a sort of fixed point, a safe harbour in the shifting uncertainties of my Paraguay. They have fed me often enough, and—more recently—Virginia has rescued me from a hotel where, had I stayed a moment longer, I would have been completely consumed by bed-dwelling insects. The first problem, however, was to find them.

I got a taxi up from Plaza de Los Héroes, but once into this ghastly Legoland, we became lost. None of the streets had names and no one, not even a garden-boy clipping a bush, could say exactly where we were. My taxi-driver gave up and abandoned me. Eventually, I got a fat, bald man out of his swimming pool and we both climbed, rather damp, into his oven-like Mercedes. He drove me thirty yards up the road to the Martins' house.

Virginia's father had been kidnapped some years before and I was warned to expect a surprise: his ordeal had turned him completely grey.

The only colour in Ian's face was the red rim around each eye. He introduced himself and said that he'd just purchased a new semi-automatic, so that now a weapon was at hand in every room of his dazzling suburban home. By contrast to him, his wife, June, was brilliantly coppery and vivid. The thought occurred to me that they'd had some sort of colour transfusion.

Over lunch, we discussed the impending crisis in the Falkland Islands and June asked me if I'd been disturbed by the earthquake the night before. I'd been at the Shakespeare.

"No, I didn't hear a thing."

No one ever mentioned the kidnap. It wasn't something the Martins ever discussed. I only came upon it years later when looking through some old Paraguayan newspapers. It's a heartless tale.

7

In August 1973, Señor Ian Duncan Martin was a manager at Liebigs, the meat processing giant, in Asunción. Liebigs made, among other things, Oxo cubes and—in the days before the European Union—lots of money. In the idyllic, frangipani-scented state of Paraguay, where crime was the monopoly of the military, it didn't occur to anyone that a British businessman might be kidnapped. It therefore came as something of a shock when Señor Ian's car was hijacked and he disappeared.

His abductors were clownish first-timers who turned up at the abduction wearing plastic noses and false moustaches. They were also dangerously nervous, and after that, there were no more jokes. Señor Ian was stuffed into the boot of a car and driven out to a deserted farm in the lonely hills that surround Altos. Everywhere they stopped, the kidnappers left little clods of cigarette butts, each smoked down to the filter. They put Señor Ian in an outside shed with some sacks and then set about trying to raise some money. Señor Ian meanwhile was working up a case of pneumonia.

The kidnappers asked for two million American dollars and two million Argentine pesos. Such a sum of money would have been an appreciable fillip to the tiny, wheezy economy of Paraguay. Liebigs were told to gather the money and—a nice touch this—to fly the Union Jack at half-mast over their offices when all was ready. Liebigs had little choice and employed two Pinkerton detectives to courier the money to Paraguay. The Pinkerton boys never got off the plane (they didn't want to put a toe in this mad-dog country), and a man from the meat plant had to go and pick up the purse.

The *pyragüés* hadn't been idle either. Unfortunately, the file was handled by none other than Pastor Coronel himself. He announced that the kidnap was the work of left-wing Argentine terrorists and, with a conspicuous lack of justification (everything about Pastor Coronel was conspicuous), he started to make arrests. He even arrested the Martins' maid and subjected her to unspeakable pain. She survived (and was still working for the Martins many years later), but she will not easily forget her eyeball-to-eyeball encounter with the Grand Inquisitor.

Then things started to fall apart for the kidnappers. Their hideout became known to the police. The official explanation was that an estate agent from Altos had spotted the gang going in and out of a house that should have been empty. Given that Pastor Coronel was later able to appear in the press holding up the clowns' seven plastic noses, this sort of ineptitude was entirely plausible. On 23 August 1973, the gang beat up their weakened captive as the police closed in. Unable to muster the courage to actually kill Señor Ian, the gangsters blasted away at his outhouse. The police meanwhile mowed two of them down like sheep. Three others were caught and two got away.

Señor Ian was free and the money went back to London (less £150,000, which lingered in the police benevolent fund). Pastor Coronel was ticker-taped for his brilliance. Then came the surprise: one of the kidnappers was a Montanaro—a nephew of the Minister of the Interior, Dr. Sabino Augusto Montanaro. The minister was not a man known for indulgence; he'd once been excommunicated for torturing priests.

Everyone smelt a rat and the foreign press went to print. Ed Harriman of *The Sunday Times* raised the awful prospect that Pastor Coronel had set the whole thing up himself—as revenge. He'd fallen out with Dr. Montanaro over an American magazine article (revealing that he and General Rodríguez had just embarked on an enterprising narcotics venture). The Grand Inquisitor blamed Montanaro for the leak and sought to embarrass him. He had little difficulty in persuading the Minister's feckless nephew to join the kidnap jaunt.

The nephew and the other two idiots went to prison. They were released after just less than three years.

8

As the Paraguayan summer drew to a close, the city was frequently sluiced down by hot torrents of rain. At first, these came as something of a respite from the heat but the water that tumbled down the streets was warm, like bathwater, and when the rain stopped, clothes became hot, clammy poultices and my room sprang to life with fresh, luxuriant clumps of mould. During these storms, the shops shuttered themselves against the spray from the buses and an impressive cataract burst through the roof of the Hispania, crashing noisily into the stairwell.

It was in one of these hot, frothy gales that I took refuge in the Strangers' Club. I'd been meaning to avoid this place, as it had the reputation of aspiring to be the British Club. This wasn't a bad aspiration, but there simply weren't enough English people in Asunción to make it a reality, and those there were—the precious few—were far too genteel for candles on beer mats and the Embassy's cast-off copies of *The Times*. For the Americans, the place was just too sordid for words. The Koreans were banned. The Germans had their own place and the owner, Norman Langan, wasn't keen to encourage Paraguayans.

Langan was wringing the water out of his shirt. "Bastard weather," he muttered.

These were his first miserable words to me and the beginning of a series of chance encounters which I hope no one will ever interpret as friendship. He was a lugubrious, basset-like man who sprouted a tuft of crinkly whiskers from each cheek. He'd enjoyed a series of nasty little jobs around the world that usually involved preying on others—his favourite being that of a paparazzi on the Costa del Sol. The strangest thing about him was that he wasn't British at all, but a sort of Austrian-Argentine mongrel called Langer-Strausser. He just happened to have gone to the British school in Buenos Aires and this had left him with the enduring misconception that the British would accept him as one of their own. "That," as the girl with the squall of hair would have said, "makes him fucking Paraguayan."

Langan stamped off to find a dry shirt.

"It's a shit-hole, isn't it?" came a thick Argentine accent. Sitting alone at the bar was a lad of about my own age. He was a big, rangy individual who'd sprawled himself out along the counter in a way that I imagined was designed to irritate Langan. "The Bank of Boston took the snooker table back last week and next week they're coming for the fridge. Bit by bit, they're closing Norm down!"

"Are you Argentine?"

"Nope, Welsh."

"Ah." I scanned his face for traces of mockery. It was open and whiskery, quite incapable of deceit. "What part?"

"Well, I've never actually *been* to Europe." He smiled. "Have you?"

"Yes, I'm from Cheshire."

Gareth Llewelyn shook his head. He didn't know Cheshire. In fact, he'd been born in Paraguay but had never been further than Buenos Aires ("lovely *chicas*"). His father was an engineer from Prestatyn and his mother was from Argentina.

"I went to school in BA. The same one as dick-head here—only thirty years later."

United by the amusement we found in Langan, Gareth and I became allies. We drank six bottles from Langan's dwindling stocks of Antarctica, and I promised that if I ever returned to Paraguay, I would look Gareth up. It now seems strange that in the space of a few minutes—in a place which aspired to be British (and wasn't)—I should have met two individuals who aspired to be British (and weren't) and who would both recur in my life over the next eighteen years. With this unhappy joint being shut down limb by limb, like financial gangrene, the portents for at least one of them were not good.

9

I'd told Gareth that I had one more visit to make before I left Asunción, to see the Bishop of Paraguay. Although he'd been a colleague of my uncle (who was a missionary in Paraguay in the sixties), we were in two minds as to whether or not I should kiss his ring.

"Has he got a palace?"

I said that I didn't think he had; he was an Anglican bishop. Even though I was clear about this, I still half expected him to be swathed in purple and ermine.

The Bishop's palace was in fact a little bungalow in a road off España Street. It wasn't "downtown" but it most definitely wasn't "uptown" either. España belonged to old Paraguay and it therefore fell within the boundaries of my affections. Most of the mansions had been built by Italian merchants at the beginning of the century and were now occupied by minor Latin American embassies, gynaecologists and Chinese restaurants. All day, lines of Mercedes rumbled up and down the street, ferrying the wealthy between their money and their Lego homes. At each of the crossroads were kiosks selling newspapers, General Alfredo lapel-pins and copies of the Paraguayan Constitution. España was the stiffly-asphalted spinal column of the city.

The Bishop's road was a little more modest, and the bungalow sat on a small plot, on the edge of a dainty handkerchief of lawn. There were potted plants around the door and all the woodwork was syrupy varnished. At the back of the bungalow was a banana tree and an even smaller hutch, which housed some Indians that the Bishop had rescued from the Chaco. Because I was five minutes late, he and his wife were already waiting by the door.

We have since talked about this encounter. This delightful, gentle couple remember me as being rather extravagantly polite and I remember them as being rather charmingly apprehensive. There were no rings or ermine. I was led straight through to the kitchen, which was crowded with missionaries and antique appliances, for a solid dinner of mince and noodle pie with tinned peaches.

As I worked my way through several plates of mince and peaches, listening to the missionaries, I began to realise for the first time that there was another Paraguay, far removed from its serene, sensual and slightly snaky capital. To the east was the interior—steeped in forests and feudalism—and to the west the Chaco, a great derelict sea-bed of cactus, Indian black magic and *estancias* big enough to engulf the little republics of Europe. "My country, Paraguay," wrote the author Roa Bastos, "among other strange and unfortunate factors that have marked its destiny—is, in fact, one country divided into three, each one ignorant of the others."

Whilst the missionaries plotted the transfer of water and bibles into these countries within the country, Bishop Milmine busied himself with another pressing concern: Britain was at war with Argentina. We spread a map of the Falklands out among the condiments and planned the campaign. He was a canny tactician, a former bomber pilot of the North African campaign, but it was his wife who was the strategic genius. Ros planned the entire relief operation, mapping it out with pepper-pots and bottles of sauce and an old armadillo shell.

There was nothing odd about the bishop of Paraguay taking such a keen interest in the Falkland Islands. By a quirk of ecclesiastical geography, Paraguay had—until relatively recently—been part of the Diocese of the Falkland Islands. There were still a handful of people in Paraguay who could remember the Bishop of the Falkland Islands steaming up the Paraná to baptise them. Bishop Milmine was simply minding the old parish.

As a final preparation for war, the bishop insisted that I send a telegram to my parents telling them where I was heading: Arica, in Chile. We composed a frugal message and released it into the ether. It reassembled itself in Cheshire as "Safe. Gone Africa." It did very little to allay my parents' now-blossoming concerns.

10

At the end of the Bishop's road, an event had occurred that shook "Freddie"—as the Bishop called the General—to the soles of his ridiculous jackboots. For that reason alone (although it had also been an act of chilling courage), I decided to visit the sites and poke my fingers in the scars.

A few hundred yards uptown of the turning, at number 433 España, there was a dreary, modern orange-brick blob that wasn't really mock-anything. It had industrial gates and a guardhouse and was next door to a rather fluffy pink ice-cream parlour. It was a perfect pied-à-terre for an old confederate of Don Alfredo's: ex-president Anastasio Somoza Debayle of Nicaragua. Somoza was cut from much the same stuff as his Paraguayan friend. After twenty-three years of putting Nicaragua through a mincer of extortion and terror, Somoza finally bade farewell to his bleeding nation in July 1979. As a parting gesture, he bombed six cities and raided the National Bank. His departure was so rapid that all he was able to take with him was an armoury, the bodies of his father and his brother (who'd both been made safe by unhappy subjects some years before), several million dollars in cash and eight tropical parrots from his private zoo.

Somoza arrived in Asunción a month later. There, he found everything to his liking and ploughed around town with his machine-gun posse. Supermarkets had to close whenever he paid a call and he even dallied with a few of Don Alfredo's hand-me-downs. He bought a ranch, and then, fourteen months after his carnival arrival, he himself was smeared all over España.

Whilst there is not really space in my Pantheon of Heroes for terrorists and communists, I have to confess a sneaking regard for the Argentine *Montoneros* who dispatched Somoza. They were veterans of the *La Guerra Sucia*—Argentina's Dirty War—three women and four men. They reasoned that the death of Somoza would send a shock-wave of anxiety through the community of dictators who, at that time, deeply infested South America. "We cannot tolerate the existence of millionaire playboys," one said, "whilst thousands of Latin Americans are dying of hunger. We are perfectly willing to give up our lives for this cause."

The leader of the cadre, code-name "Ramón," who'd cut his teeth blasting his way out of a military prison in Patagonia, led them first to Colombia. There, hidden away in the mountains, he toughened up the team. He'd even brought a little library to toughen up their minds; there was *The Spy Who Came in from the Cold*, *The House on Garibaldi Street* and—rather symmetrically—*The Day of the Jackal*. In a country so deeply bedded in contraband, it wasn't difficult to get their work tools into Asunción. They buried two assault rifles, two automatics, two Ingram sub-machine-guns, an RP-7 bazooka with two rockets and four fragmentation grenades under their rented patio, and awaited their moment.

I walked back along España in the downtown direction. At the junction with Avenida Santísimo Sacramento, some newspaper boys were camped out in front of their kiosk, pawing over some magazines. Back then, one of the terrorists, "Oswaldo," had joined them, disguising himself as a vendor but all the time watching the gates of 433.

Further on, the gang had hired a rather plain-looking mansion that had—since then—been converted into a strangely liver-green Chinese restaurant called La Unión. Their cover story this time was musical; they were in town with Julio Iglesias, making a film about Paraguay. This wasn't such a pantomime excuse as it might seem; Julio Iglesias had already released two songs about Paraguay and the landlady was so steeped in flattery that she held her tongue until the big day, 17 September 1980.

As Somoza and his cavalcade set out, Oswaldo sent a radio signal to the men in the house, who formed up in the front. Somoza's Mercedes purred towards the mansion, and as it passed, the rocket-man pulled the trigger. Nothing happened. Ramón started desperately pumping bullets into the car, and the metallic gale that he unleashed took most of the driver's head off. The Mercedes, now unpiloted, veered into the pavement. The rocket-man extracted the dud projectile, fitted the spare, dropped to one knee and fired.

Even eighteen months on, the asphalt still showed the ripples gouged by the explosion. The Mercedes had opened up like a tin of peaches. Somoza and his rodent lieutenant could count themselves immediately departed, and most of Somoza's economic adviser followed, through many holes torn in the metalwork. The bewildered Nicaraguan primitives in the car behind were firing back, but the *Montoneros* had gone.

Once again, Pastor Coronel's *pyragüés* swung into action. This time, they were barking up the right sort of trees, but too late. All the birds had flown and—with one exception—had made it back to Barcelona, their rendezvous. The one exception was Hugo Irarzún, the rocket-man, who was easily picked out for his blond beard and who died in a blizzard of Paraguayan bullets. The survivors disappeared and never came forward to claim any glory. "I left Paraguay with a bleeding ulcer," wrote one of them in an anonymous memoir many years on. "It took me three months to get it under control. That isn't a romantic experience."

The General hadn't found it an easy experience either. The cabal behaved exactly as the *Montoneros* had hoped they would; they reacted with wibbling funk. All the borders were sealed. No one came in and no one left the country. Nothing moved—not even the *National Geographic* team who'd arrived to put a glossy face on Paraguay. The President started to abandon sleep, and filigrees of eczema began to nibble their way up his arms like a scourge. He took to ringing divisional headquarters in the night, desperately trying to gauge their loyalty. Like Faust, he'd left himself with little room for manoeuvre.

II

Nearly fifteen years passed before I visited Paraguay again, in December 1996. The changes that I'd sensed stirring then had indeed occurred, although not quite in the way that I or anyone else had ever really expected. *Asunceños* had enjoyed a rare moment of pleasure with the

Falklands War, and when, later that year, the Argentines toppled their own general, the Paraguayans began to see that they too didn't need to accommodate a general in the palace. In 1988, marchers took to the streets, and Don Alfredo suddenly found that those who challenged him were too numerous to be bundled out of aeroplanes.

But the crunch came, as so often in Paraguayan politics, from behind. The General, who was now so raddled with nervous afflictions that he could hardly put his bumpkin signature on a warrant, began to make plans for his succession. Freddie Junior had put himself out of the running because his mind only functioned on a spoon of cocaine (eventually, after a particularly heavy scoop, his cardiovascular system simply imploded). That left the other son, Gustavo, who the army loathed partly because he was an air force boy and partly because he was loudly homosexual. That is when Don Alfredo's old buddy, his tippling friend and Minister of Smuggling, General Andrés Rodríguez, saw a chance to make a break.

No two Paraguayans will agree on what had come over Rodríguez. It may be that, by reason of his daughter's marriage to senseless Freddie Junior, he'd felt that he'd acquired some sort of arcane right of succession.

Gareth Llewelyn would have another theory that involved a vicious little dwarf in the cavalry called Colonel Lino Oviedo.

"He put Rodríguez up to it. He put a *granada* to the old boy's face." Gareth was pressing an imaginary hand grenade to his nose. "And he said: 'Either we have a *golpe de estado* or we both fucking well go pop!' That's what happened."

Certainly, Oviedo—"the Bonsai Horseman"—would, from now on, be more than just a little pip on the Paraguayan political landscape, but Gareth's version didn't have that patina of authenticity. I favoured the idea that Rodríguez was seeking beatitude (after all, he had everything else), because only this explains what he did afterwards.

Whatever the reason, Rodríguez cleared it with the two bodies that mattered—the Church and the American Embassy—and then, on 2 February 1989, started letting off the guns.

Don Alfredo was caught—quite literally—with his pants down, round at Miss Legal's love nest. Buckling himself back in, he hurried off to rally his Praetorian guard, and the two generals fought a bad-tempered artillery duel over the city. It was a muddled fight; years of indolence had rendered the leaders incapable of giving sensible orders, and the Praetorian tanks couldn't be deployed because the man who had the keys was with his mistress in the country. By the morning it was all over, and three days later, Don Alfredo was on a plane to exile in Brazil. He must have seen something coming, because he had a private air-strip and a retirement home all ready and waiting for him.

After thirty-four years, Stroessner's tyranny—the most enduring in the western hemisphere—had come to an end. It had been the second-longest dictatorship in the world, outlasted only by that of Kim Il Sung. Now, suddenly, the *Stronato* was over. Or was it?

At first, the signs weren't encouraging. The "General Stroessner Polka" wasn't heard again, but it was replaced by the "Rodríguez Polka" ("God bless you, General Rodríguez and the Armed Forces"). The Rodríguez family then appeared on television, shoulder-to-shoulder with the starry-eyed Freddie Junior; it made the *golpe*—or *coup d'état*—seem like nothing more than the resolution of a family tiff.

But then—extraordinarily—General Rodríguez announced that he'd done what he'd done "to defend democracy, for the respect of human rights and the defence of our Christian religion." What had got into him? Perhaps he'd become a saint—or perhaps he'd felt the sinister nuzzle of his cancer and was trying to buy himself a cooler spot in Purgatory?

Either way, changes began. The President, who'd once been banned from the United States for heroin trafficking, signed a human rights treaty. The death penalty was abolished. Martial law, which had been in force since 1929, was gradually lifted. The intelligent organ of the *pyragüés*—known as *La Técnica*—which for a while had trundled on, gathering files as if nothing had happened, was wound up. After some judicious pruning, the files were made public. They were the work of an admirable bureaucracy; there were files on Indians, files on Nazis, files on informers (including a Catholic bishop) and even files on those who'd died under torture, marked *"empaquetado,"* or "packaged."

To everyone's surprise, Rodríguez instituted some gentle investigations into the activities of the *ancien régime* (though his saintliness fell short of allowing anyone to peer into his own past). The great bulk of Pastor Coronel was rounded up and carted away. The court jester, Abdo, was also arrested, although the circumstances were more peculiar.

He'd been in Brazil when the *golpe* happened and only returned after it was over. To the Paraguayans, this was vintage Abdo.

"Why did you come back?" he was asked.

"Well," Abdo replied, "the boss always told me that if ever there was trouble, I was to head straight for the border."

In the end, only seven of the old cabal went to prison—not a prison with the common criminals, of course, but a pad called "The Special Group," where they could dial out for drinks and pornography.

The greatest surprise of all was that free elections were held. The first was rushed through so quickly that nobody except the General's old party, the Colorado Party, was ready. It was therefore won by the egregious Rodríguez. The second was won by his choice, Juan Wasmosy, who claimed to have been descended from Hungarian aristocracy. Wasmosy was also—blue blood notwithstanding—a civil engineer, and had become suspiciously sumptuous whilst mixing concrete on an expensive dam project. In the end, he too ended up on multiple criminal charges, but for the time being, many old *Stronistas* were surprised— and no doubt delighted—to find that they still had a place in his government.

Graham Greene had ended his travels in the "sad and lovely land" of Paraguay in 1961 by promising himself that he would never return there whilst Stroessner and those that guzzled with him still lived. Sadly, the Stroessner Set all outlived Greene, who died in 1991. I was certainly not capable of assuming such a noble and ambitious resolution as Greene's. Besides, there was the grim prospect that the *Stronato* might, in different guises and new skins, just rumble on for ever. I couldn't wait any longer, and so, at the end of 1996, I returned to Asunción, on a flying visit.

12

I stayed at the Hotel Guaraní. It was not a great success. The hotel flunkies seemed if anything slightly less interested in my contentment now than they had been when I was an intruder. To get across the swimming pool, I now had to nose my way through a froth of flies. Sometimes, I got lost in the gloomy upper floors of the hotel and found myself in rooms that had been abandoned long ago and that were heaped with dirty plates and sheets and dusty scraps of food. Some years later, the hotel was abandoned altogether, and when I next saw it, it was wreathed in soot and was being slowly devoured by tropical succulents.

I paid a visit to my old hotel, the Hispania. The Mennonites had long gone. Appalled at the new liberal order, "Mexicans" tried to avoid Asunción now, and besides, the new Korean owners of the *pensión* had painted it white, like an old bridesmaid, and decorated it with parrot feathers and a large photograph of the docks at Seoul. The Anabaptists had drifted elsewhere.

The rains came early. Hot, bright-red water foamed through the streets. An oil tanker crashed in the Plaza de Los Héroes and a guard was mounted over the wreckage, dressed—I thought—like the Afrika Korps.

I took a bus up to Carmelitas to see the house that General Rodríguez was living in. The bus conductress was wearing tights patterned with elongated tigers, leaping up into her knickers. The rain got hotter and more intense.

Rodríguez's house was a worthy tourist attraction because it was the nearest thing that South America had to a Palace of Versailles. I stood in the long wet grass gaping up at the crenellations and turrets. It had a turquoise roof that had been flown in, tile by tile, from France. When someone once asked the old emir how he could enjoy such lavish *bijoux* on $500 a month, he'd wafted away their impertinence: "I gave up smoking."

Too late, it seems. Cancer was now gnawing its way through the sainted smuggler. Meanwhile, the map of Paraguay had been de-Stroessnered, and Don Alfredo's statue had been chopped up and set in concrete so that now, just one cold bronze eye peeped out, and a finger, harmlessly admonishing the drunks in the new Plaza de los Desaparecidos—the Square of the Disappeared.

Gone too was the Shakespeare. It had served its function and had succumbed to the vagaries of the new order. The Korean pharmacist now used it as a store for his roots and bones and jars of jaguar's paws.

I looked up Reynaldo Gosling and found that he'd made good and moved to Legoland, but I couldn't bear to see him there and so I let our friendship go.

The beggars too had succumbed, as everybody knew they would, to their war wounds and to *whisky-tipo*. The drunks were different now: handsome, russet-faced *mestizos* who babbled merrily in Guaraní.

They railed at the pornography in the Plaza de Los Héroes, and at the plump prostitutes who possessed Uruguaya by night, and at the policemen, taunting them because their rifles were so old and their boots too big.

But the police and the soldiers had yielded power with surprising grace. You could see them, in the police station, rifles slung, among the life-sized nativity scene. There, rubbing shoulders with the Wise Men, they seemed to have found a form of redemption.

There was no denying that they'd fared better than the politicians, for whom the citizens now reserved a special contempt. Everyone seemed to hate Wasmosy, the president that they'd elected, and when I saw "Fuck Wasmosy" scrawled on the wall of the Congress building, I allowed myself to think that the girl with the cloud of black hair had survived the changes intact.

Youth had rallied, too late, to register its protest at the Church, the army and everything. They'd set up a den called the Urban Cave in the merchants' quarter, where they could loose off fusillade after fusillade of rap and self-indulgent anger. But their ideas were thuggish and irrelevant and, worse, they were imported; they wore Tarantino suits and beards and drank purple and green alcopops. No one drank Antarctica any more.

One could only speculate as to what happened to the Nazis. I thought—quite wrongly (as it would turn out)—that I'd probably never encounter an original. I imagined they'd all be dead. One day, a trader approached me with a hardwood presentation box embossed with a knobbly gold swastika.

"Three thousand dollars," he grinned.

Inside was a 9mm Luger and an ivory-handled dagger, inscribed in German: "For long service to the General Staff."

"Where did you get this?" I asked.

"Just some German guy down in Encarnación. He didn't say much about it. I guess he didn't want any trouble with the customs."

13

Many of my old friends were away, having withdrawn to breezy Uruguay for the summer. I did, however, manage to meet up with Gareth at The Lido. The old place was still as tangerine as ever. He limped in, half an hour late, dragging his right leg. I noticed that he too had a Tarantino beard, and that from it a meaty pink scar curled up towards his ear. He was ebullient and threw his arms around me.

"What have you done to yourself?" I asked, when I had extracted myself from his grip.

"Ah, *nada*!" He shrugged expansively. "I was in some Chevy on the way to a party. It came off the *ruta*. The guy driving dropped his ciggie in his . . ." Gareth couldn't think of the word and so he patted his balls ostentatiously. Some of the diners looked over in our direction.

"Boom! We ran into a big tree, a *lapacho*."

"What happened to the driver?"

Gareth shook his head. "No . . ."

The boy had been at the periphery of the Stroessner dynasty. It was unsettling to think of that accursed hand still tickling up trouble in Paraguay.

We talked and drank and slopped up bowls of The Lido's special soup, which was made of vegetables and piranhas. Gareth had been a croupier and a cashier in a finance house that laundered cash. He'd been married and there was a child somewhere, but after the accident, his wife had left him. He'd then begun an epoch as an accountancy student.

I noticed that his English was worse now than when we had met before, and it struck me that he'd started thinking in *castellano*. He still, however, had a strong Argentine accent in whatever language he was speaking.

"I never talk like a *Paraguayo*," he said. "It's just too fucking rough."

I asked him about Langan.

"Langan lost everything, then it came back, and then—*ciao, ciao*—nothing."

The Strangers' Club had died its lingering death. Langan was vehemently penniless and so he'd had a go at setting up "The Asunción International Arms Fair." It flopped. Then he'd found a new and unlikely ally in Lino Oviedo, the Bonsai Horseman. In the muck of the Wasmosy government, the two of them briefly thrived. Oviedo was boosted up from colonel to general and Langan, using Lino Oviedo's money, produced an English-language magazine called *The Guaraní*. It contained little but portraits of the elfin Lino, astride polo ponies and miniature horses rampant. The British community, meanwhile, continued to elude Langan and obstinately neglected to buy his snivelling magazine. Langan had to go back to Lino for more money.

Strictly speaking, the money wasn't Lino's. It was the old story: Lino Oviedo had become a talented extortionist. His black demands made people blanch and crumble ("He took $100,000 from our company each year," a cotton man told me, still gasping years later). There was nothing bonsai about the little man's appetite, and once he'd filled his pockets with money, he wanted power. He wasn't unduly concerned how he got it. He declared that it was time Paraguay was run by the army.

"The trouble started last April," said Gareth.

By April 1996, Lino was head of the army, and when Wasmosy tried to trim him back, Lino threatened to bomb everything. Wasmosy fled to the American Embassy. He offered Lino a job as Minister of Defence and then, when Lino had calmed down, there were hugs and speeches of reconciliation. But when Lino stood for office, Wasmosy snapped him in jankers and had him charged with insurrection and bolshiness.

"There was no coup," said Gareth. It surprised me.

This was, however, what most Paraguayans believed: Lino Oviedo had just popped the President on the head with a whisky glass. Wasmosy had asked for it. The Americans sorted it all out.

"So where's Lino now?"

"In jail, I suppose."

"And Langan?"

Gareth smiled. "Who gives a shit?"

One of the orange ducks waddled by with a dog-fish on a plate. Gareth watched the fish as it passed.

"How's your leg?" I asked.

"I've got a piece of metal here and a piece of metal here. And I've got another one here." He jutted his jaw out at me.

"You know, when I go out dancing, it all vibrates at once. Everything's vibrating. *Todo! Todo!* It's driving me mad, John. I'm going mad."

I didn't think he was mad at all. And then he just disappeared.

14

It had occurred to me, whilst we were sitting in The Lido, that there was another figure on the Paraguayan landscape. He was everywhere. He clustered at every crossroads. He was at the airport and on the bridges that led to Brazil. He nuzzled into his clones, making his bubble-gum-pink rubber body squeak obscenely: the inflatable pig. He'd come from overseas and the citizens had received him, joylessly and yet, it seemed, with fervour. I'd asked Gareth what it all meant.

"Only God knows us," he'd said, enigmatically.

For all their concrete and beards and cocktails, the Paraguayans' mourning was not yet over. The tank was gone but the stones where it had stood were stained red. Some thought it had gone back to Bolivia, but no one could agree on that. But then the wars themselves had a remoteness about them now, as the definition drained away. A painting on Independencia tried to claw back the images of the Chaco War in limpid acrylics; a little aeroplane was neatly trickling bomblets on to a Bolivian position. The bomblets looked like goat droppings. Paraguayans were beginning to forget what it was they were mourning for, and yet still the streets fell quiet at midday and still the diners munched their chicken in silence. Was it for a past that had been lost? Or was it for a future that could only be cheap and brutish and brash?

Now suddenly alone, I gazed out of the window of The Lido, past the Panteón de Los Héroes where Carlos and Francisco López lay among their generals, and into the plaza. At that moment I felt the weariness of incomprehension. A land obsessed with its own demise. A Napoleonic paradise in the age of alcopops. The tomb of the inflatable pig.

15

Three months after I returned to England, General Rodríguez was consumed by his cancer and died.

Because I'd never seen the General in all his flesh, I decided that the next best thing was to go and seek out his mortal remains, and, so when I was next back in Asunción, in spring 2000, I paid a visit to the Cemetery of Recoleta.

At Recoleta, the dead were not entombed within the soil but laid out on the surface, where they had a better view of their heirs. Well-shod, marble-arteried *Asunceños* made their final homes in little mansions not dissimilar to the ones that they'd enjoyed in life. The cemetery was like Asunción in draft. There were Lilliputian palaces, mausoleums scrolled like miniature banks, stuccoed crypts with doors for dwarfs and *panteones* with riveted copper roofs. One sepulchre even had a full set of chimneys and another had squirting fountains and two tiny lily ponds. No stone was left unfrilled.

It was often possible to tell who was at home in each bantam residence. If they'd been famous, the walls would be studded with little brass plaques or *homenajes*. Poets had bunches of copper laurels. National heroes had concrete footballs or clumps of heroic statuary. One *panteón* exuded magic, and so the sick and the dying had taped votives and bouquets of their hair to its walls. "Thank you, Holy Cross!" read their sad and grateful missives.

The necropolis was divided into ghostly neighbourhoods. Here were the dead Russians, next to the Lebanese, and here the police. The Air Force kept their caps in glass cases and went to their deaths with teddy-bears and charms. The army had a heavy steel cross, wittily appliquéd by armour-piercing bullets, and the English had poetry by Tennyson and Keats. There was even an equivalent of Legoland, where the smugglers could get their roasting.

In some places, the streets crumbled away—just like real life—and in others, yew trees had reclaimed the neighbourhood for grasshoppers and birds. Sometimes, the worlds of the living and the dead seemed to merge and intertwine; people taking picnics with their long-gone grandfathers and a palsied, failing child curled up at the gates, a foot in each world. I watched with awful fascination as the twin facets of our fate—existence and non-existence—wrestled and coalesced. In the distance, a barefoot boy, gripping a stolen vacuum-cleaner, was being pursued by policemen in and out of the sepulchres. The mourners hardly looked up from their meat and pickles.

I found the mausoleum I was looking for without much difficulty. It was the largest in the cemetery, something comparable to St. Patrick's in New York, though reluctantly smaller. Curiously, there was only one *homenaje* screwed to its gothic elevations—from the General's friends at his tennis club. I peered through the stained-glass windows. Glittering among the holy sunbeams were brand-new Persian rugs, padded armchairs and a Paraguayan tricolour, tailored from satin.

A grave-digger with a brush scuffed his way in my direction.

"Who's buried here?" I asked. "God?"

The grave-digger grinned. "No," he said. "Much richer. General Rodríguez."

In the next dead street was the tomb of another politician, the cement rather fresher. In its blue-glass, detergent gloom lay all that remained of Professor Luis María Argaña, raised to the high office of vice-president and brought down again by bullets. His death was so mystifying that, in the absence of the impressive *pyragüés*, the Paraguayans had called in Scotland Yard, London.

Paraguayan politics, up until then quaintly Venetian, had become Byzantine.

16

Little Lino had been dangerously busy in my absence. Unable to run for presidency from his prison cell, he got his friend, Cubas, to contest the 1998 election on his behalf. To roars of public approval, Cubas ran on a single ticket: the release of Lino Oviedo. To roars of disapproval, Cubas then released Lino when he won.

Wasmosy left office, to be confined in his own fortress in the suburbs. As his retainers left the presidential palace, they harvested it for every light bulb and every door handle they could carry.

Lino's preening didn't last. There was a shrill voice of protest but it wasn't mistaken for righteousness. It came from Vice-President Argaña, himself suspiciously overnourished. It didn't last either; six months after the election, Argaña was swimming in his innards. On 23 March 1999, three masked and uniformed men jumped out in front of his Mercedes and shredded it with machine-guns. They lobbed two hand grenades into the smoking scraps but they failed to go off. The attackers then vanished.

Asunción over-boiled. On Plaza Independencia, nine harmless demonstrators were cut down by mysterious automatic gunfire. Things were too hot now—even for Lino. He and his lap-dog president, Cubas, fled to Argentina.

That only left a non-entity called González Macchi. A few days later, he took over the presidency by dint of an ancient constitutional blip. The only clever thing that he'd ever done in his life was to marry Miss Paraguay. He now installed a cabinet that included two of Argaña's legitimate sons and one of General Stroessner's little bastards.

Meanwhile, as the fiddlers fiddled, Rome burned. In 1999, the Paraguayan economy simply seized up and wouldn't budge a single per cent. More than half the adult population had no work, and of the little bits of tax collected, only a third made it past government pockets to government coffers. In a country of abundant water supplies, barely a third of its inhabitants had it piped to their homes.

For every old Paraguayan that was carted off to his *panteón*, six piping, pink new ones were bouncing into the world—and an uncertain future. There were now five and a half million Paraguayans. Seventy per cent of them were too young to remember the *Stronato*. There might soon be no one to stop things sliding backwards.

17

It was not always easy to follow all the gossip that was tossed around among the Paraguayans, but over the next few months I assembled an intriguing collection of theories as to who'd assassinated Vice-President Argaña.

The truth was that no one had any idea. Scotland Yard had recognised that there was very little appetite for establishing what had really happened, and the case rapidly became a domestic matter.

Lino Oviedo was the obvious culprit. Having just been released from prison, he was poised to take over the Colorado Party. Argaña brought a court action to eject Lino's mob from the party headquarters, but within a day, he was dead. Lino didn't help his cause by fleeing the country. Then two of his goons were arrested in Buenos Aires and thrown in jail.

All this ought to have been the end of any further interesting speculation. It wasn't. No one seemed very happy with the conclusion that Lino was to blame.

"Lino was too smart for this," people insisted.

"Argaña was no threat to him—and was probably better to him alive than dead."

"Lino was crazy, but he wasn't stupid," said others.

"It was the sons."

Sure enough, the bloated old toad had had eight children. Nelson was now Minister of Defence and Félix was after his father's old job as Vice-President. There was also a massive personal fortune to be soaked up by the heirs. "As your Scotland Yard people say, always look first at those who have the most to gain. It was the sons."

"That's shit!" another would protest. "It was the Colorado Party that got rid of Argaña. He was selling out to the *liberales.*"

"Never!" came another theorist. "It was the government itself. They killed Argaña—to dump Lino Oviedo in the shit and put Macchi in charge!"

This began to sound plausible when it emerged that, within three minutes of the assassination, there were two government ministers on the scene, including the Minister of Public Works.

"Isn't that a bit fishy?"

The theory got another helpful shove when the suspects in the Buenos Aires top-security prison announced that they'd been bribed: "We were told to say that Lino was behind it."

Then they said they'd been tortured.

Then they escaped. In fact, they were the first prisoners ever to have escaped from that prison in all its history. The Argentines were in no doubt that such a feat couldn't have been managed by two yokels from Paraguay and insisted that someone had let them out. They had a point—but who?

A fifth theory emerged. This one needed a few bottles of *caña* to get it up and running, but it was soon all over Asunción like a grass fire: Argaña's death was suicide.

"Argaña had cancer," went the new line. "He knew that he was dying. He staged his own death to achieve immortality and to throw his enemies into permanent chaos."

Was this the famous *pó-caré*—or "twisted hand"—of Guaraní political thinking? It was a concept familiar to the Paraguayans. One writer, Arthur Bray, wrote of the attractions of politics to his fellow-Paraguayans:

> In politics he can give his imagination full rein, also his instinct and art of deceiving and confusing, making of his Twisted Hand an extremely subtle art which consists of overthrowing his adversary and then enjoying the crumbling of the latter's illusions and aspirations. His *né-ñanducá*—the dénouement—constitutes his seventh heaven of happiness . . .

If true, this was surely the ultimate in *pó-caré*; a government collapsed, a president—Cubas—forced into exile, two *Oviedistas* in prison,

Oviedo himself hounded abroad, a demonstration in Plaza Independencia and nine young lives splashed across the tiles.

But even this version wasn't quite good enough in the end. Among educated Paraguayans, I discerned a drift towards a new, a sixth theory: Argaña wasn't shot at all. He was already dead when the gunmen opened fire on his car.

"He died a natural death from cancer," a soil scientist told me. "His family were heard crying the night before the shooting."

"The *Argañistas* then staged the assassination to get rid of Oviedo," said another.

The idea soon gained momentum. "It's true, there was no blood on Argaña's corpse. We all saw the photos in the press. A dead man doesn't bleed, does he?"

"The body was slumped forward," said the soil man. "He'd not been shot up by machine-guns." He paused. "The tragedy was that one of the bodyguards had to die as part of the scam."

"What about Argaña's driver? Did he survive?" I asked.

"He wasn't hit at all."

"So what's happened to him?"

The scientist smiled. "He disappeared. He's never been seen since."

18

I booked into The Gran Hotel, just off España. On the day I arrived, the lobby was heaped with baggage and boxes like an upturned stagecoach. A young American couple were defending it against waiters and porters and other perplexed bystanders.

"We've gotta get out of here," they said. They looked grey and strained, at the very end of their tether. "What are you doing in Paraguay? You're going to hate it."

"I think I like it, actually."

The frontiersmen looked at me sceptically. "We tried to settle."

His wife shuddered. "There's no money, no credit, no drains."

"There's gonna be a catastrophe," said the husband.

"Real soon," said the wife, backing away to swat the bellhops off her bags.

The husband turned on me. "What are you here for?"

"I'm just a tourist . . ."
"There's nothing to see. Go home."

19

I'd arrived back in Asunción in the aftermath of an uprising, the coup of May 2000. It was conceived in Plaza Independencia and aborted two blocks east. I hurried down there, uncertain what I expected to find.

Plaza Independencia had always been one of my favourite places in Asunción. Sometimes it seemed as though I was the only person that felt that way, because it was often deserted and the tree roots were beginning to barge their way up through the chequered paving-tiles. The plinth where the tank had stood was still there—now mounted with a derelict car that was regularly set on fire, stoned and beaten with twigs. It seemed to bear the entire brunt of Asunción's anger.

The square still had a discernibly Parisian air about it. Or rather, it looked as Paris would have looked if it had been overrun by Indians from the plains. The air was often itchy with their wood-smoke.

The gardens had been laid out in the 1870s, when malnourished Napoleonic nostalgia was one of the few things that survived *la Grande Guerra*. There were marble obelisks, frilly iron benches and—rather wistfully—victory columns. In those dark days, López's heroism wasn't fully appreciated and so the lack of statuesque heroes was addressed in an original and—to me—delightful way. The plinths were mounted with innocent creatures—a large bronze frog, a deer and a skinny whippet. Each was stamped *"Rue de Voltaire, Paris"* and inquisitive fingers still fondled and polished their ears and nostrils and enormous balls.

The Indians were camped right up the other end, in front of Congress. They lived in plastic tents that seeped smoke and dissatisfaction. "We are the Dispossessed of Kilometre-70!" said their banners, and that was all that was said. The Indians clustered on the grass in silence—shoeless, landless, hopeless.

But it wasn't an entirely hopeless place. Every now and then, kindly *Asunceños* came down into the plaza and fed the unhappy Indians or treated their callused feet or just stood near them, scowling at the Congress. When all the hairdressers and barbers swooped down on the city's waifs with clippers and combs and soothing powders, I felt my eyes prickle with tiny, hot pins of shame. One of the barbers spotted me and knew immediately: "You're foreign, aren't you?"

A small memorial garden had erupted among the chequered tiles. "Bless the young Martyrs of March 1999! They gave their lives to make us free . . ." Just as their bodies had been scattered across these tiles, so now were their names. It was a smouldering mantra, dashed off in aerosol, seared into wood and deeply cut in plaques of steel. Manfred, Tomás, Henry, Víctor, Armando, Cristóbal . . .

No one had ever been arrested for their deaths. The bullet casings had been gathered up and lost and vital clues were hosed away with all the blood. There was never an inquiry, let alone the penetrating inquisition that the atrocity deserved. "A dead man," wrote Greene thirty years before, in a different age, "makes no trouble for anyone. They don't have coroners in Paraguay."

So, Manfred, Tomás and Henry and friends would drift off to another world with Professor Argaña—who they'd come to mourn—never knowing who'd dispatched them.

The flowers had withered on their little garden and another year had passed before violence bloomed again. This time, however, it would be bloodless and quixotic.

On 18 May 2000, the *Congresso* was hit by a high-velocity tank round.

It had always been a duchess of a building, slightly stooped and eccentrically swagged in brilliant flamingo pinks. An uncouth wild animal had now taken a mouthful from her flanks and poor Alan Taylor's immaculate brickwork looked crumpled and exposed, like a torn bodice. A foxtrot of bullet holes wandered from the cloisters, across the front of the façade and up into the pediment.

There was a lone peanut seller, out to the front, with his barrow.

"What happened?" I asked.

It wasn't going to be that easy. First, he needed to know what country I was from. England. Then there were the usual preliminaries to be established.

"Who paid for your ticket? How is the fog in London?"

I told him that this was business and that the fog had miraculously cleared. He nodded knowingly, as if I'd confirmed what was already rumoured.

"Two months ago," he began, "this little tank came from the Chaco. The government were watching him coming. He crossed the bridge. Nobody stopped him." The peanut man sank his thumbnail into a husk.

"They could have hit him with a bazooka on the bridge but they let him come. He came down into town and rolled into the square over there." He waved his arm in the direction of the frog and whippet.

"He stopped just here," the tank had pulled up next to the peanut barrow, "and just started firing."

"Did you see it?"

"Of course not. It was the middle of the night. I was in bed—with my missus. But we knew this was another *golpe* all right."

"Was it just the tank?"

He shrugged. "There were meant to be others, but they never showed up."

A small dog came over and started licking the *mercante*'s toes. I was feeling rather puzzled.

"So what happened to the tank?"

"It carried on down there. Only two blocks."

"And then?"

"And then it ran out of petrol."

The *golpe* too ran out of puff. All that night, units of the army had come forward to swear their allegiance to the government. By dawn, there were only a handful of rank-and-file constables locked up in their own cells. The Interior Minister—the one who'd sprung from Stroessner's unstoppable loving—began to torture them.

I turned back to the peanut seller. "Was this all Lino's work?"

He grinned. "Lino is in Brazil."

"So who was behind the *golpe*?"

"You're a clever man from England," he said, patting my arm. "You tell me."

20

I was thrilled to be back in Asunción. It didn't matter that there was so much that I didn't understand. I wasn't even sure whether the

Paraguayans understood themselves. I suspected that they were letting on rather more than they actually knew. This in itself simply became another aspect of Paraguay that I just couldn't fathom.

Most of the time, I contented myself with what I could see. It was never difficult to be satisfied. Winter was retreating, taking with it the vicious *pamperos* that had whipped up from Antarctica. The air was becoming warmer and mellifluous and life was slowing to just a few frames per second. Someone had painted "Restless!" along Independencia, but what they really meant was listless. The oranges ripened and flopped thickly into the grass. Carts with rubber wheels carried the heavy fruits away to the *viviendas,* and for the rest of spring, the city's ragged foundlings would look plump and sticky.

There was still that old sense of intimacy. Although there were now well over a million people in Asunción, it had somehow sustained the illusion that everybody knew each other, that there was a commonality of purpose, a quiet confederacy. I suppose I felt like this partly because I couldn't interpret the Paraguayan reserve, the silence on the buses, the absence of rage.

But there was something else as well. Many people lived out their lives on the street and I would see the same people time and time again: watchmen grilling meat, money-changers with satchels of bank-notes, tarot-card readers, shoe-shiners, Maká Indians hawking frail weapons. Somehow, their lives seemed to be so unjustifiably self-contained. They had territories and huddles and days that were rhythmical, almost ritualistic. In the stark light of hindsight, this was perhaps nothing more than a variant of poverty, but their completeness puzzled me. They seemed to have no requirement for interaction and certainly no curiosity for a foreigner—even though there were so few of us. Most of the time, I therefore enjoyed the ghostly and rather satisfying sensation of invisibility.

But best of all, I liked the oddities of Asunción. The buses were known by fractions of numbers, like "30.3," and had long chrome whiskers, as if they were going to feel their way through the traffic. Large packs of dogs took themselves for sober walks in public gardens. The Virgin Mary was a Field Marshal and her statues wore the sash of office. There were no crash helmets, and—on little notices—people were advised not to urinate on plants. It wasn't unusual to see either ice-cream sellers with flutes, or tipper-trucks packed with soldiers of Imperial Prussia. Once, I even saw a man with a large crucifix, festooned with bags of goldfish. What was so odd was that he wasn't even mad.

The policemen shared machine-guns and the City Hall issued rash, intemperate pronouncements: "The public hospital will close!" or "376,000 dogs to be inoculated!" Some dark corners were for lepers and others were for willowy transvestites. All roads—if the signs were to be believed—led to McDonald's. Even the graffiti was consistently impenetrable: "Jump with us! BOING!" or just "We want the end of the world" and a picture of a frog.

Of course there had been a few more changes. The Hotel Guaraní had gone. The Korean pharmacies were disappearing under wreaths of wiring. The statue in Plaza de Los Héroes (angel wrestling with comic-strip hero), previously dedicated to the Anti-Communist League, was re-dedicated to the struggles against the *Stronato*.

There were just as many Mercedes but the pornography had become rather more extravagant. It was even full-frontaled on phone-cards. Oswaldo the Terrorist's kiosk on España now sold magazines about blondes coupled up to donkeys and golden retrievers. I asked the newsboys what they felt about Somoza's assassination nowadays. Oddly, there was no change there.

"It was an outrage. Those Argentines are such fucking whores."

I did make another attempt to try to make sense of the *golpe*. I had tea with a lady who, between great swoops of omelette, told me that the whole thing was a sort of dumb-show put on by the government, though she couldn't think why they would have done that. Another teatime I spent with a very impressive and well-upholstered lawyer who thought that the coup was real enough but half-hearted. The government had allowed the tank to rumble into Asunción; this would bring the opposition out from beneath their stones.

I asked him about Lino Oviedo.

"I met him once," he puffed, "and in my considered opinion, he is somewhat mad."

"Was he behind the coup?"

The lawyer thought he was. Then, soon afterwards, President Macchi was asked if he had himself had head-to-heads with Lino's lieutenants, the so-called *Oviedistas*.

"No. No," the President protested. *"Estuve comiendo un asadito nomás con ellos"* ("I only had a little barbecue with them").

I began to realise that my simple goal—comprehension—was probably unsustainable. Then events took a sinister and slightly surreal turn. The *golpe* detainees complained that they were being regularly beaten with plastic rods, blindfolded with packing tape and hermetically sealed into their cells. Unlike before, however, this time their lawyers were on the move, blasting off writs of habeas corpus and invoking the Magna Carta. It was all vaguely encouraging, I suppose, but far removed from the fishponds of Runnymede.

21

I found Gareth on a mobile number and we arranged to meet at The Bolsi. I would rather have met at The Lido, but then I remembered that its breezy, inward-looking counters had made Gareth fidgety and tense. The Bolsi, on the other hand, was darker and Germanic and the air was slick with vapours of milky coffee and spinach. It was owned by an unctuous little drunk called Tito Valiante, who kept declaring that he was at my disposal. His mother, they say, had been at his; he'd put three bullets in her head and inherited her restaurant.

I arrived before Gareth and threaded through the office girls to find some seats. They were pretty girls with fine, strong cheek-bones, nectarine complexions and manes of twinkly gold. Their clothes were arguably undersized, cupping little breasts upwards and making them taut and teasingly fruitesque. Those who weren't chewing on cigarettes were busying themselves with roasted chickens. Some were working on both.

Gareth was, as before, ebullient, and lurched in grinning and waving. The beard was slightly different and the scars had paled. He looked waxy and exhausted. I was scooped up in an *abrazo* and patted and cuffed. "Hey, John! *Cómo está?*"

He stood back and studied me critically, the tip of his tongue lolling in the corner of his mouth. It was not an expression that I could make sense of. He smelt faintly gingerish.

"Where's your wife?" he asked, and started patting me again as if I kept her in my pocket.

"She had to work."

He was satisfied with this but bitterly disappointed that we still had no children.

"We're happy that way," I protested, but he waved this aside. Every man should have lots of *niños*, he insisted, especially an Englishman. He kept returning to the subject and casting his eye among the girls, picking out any that he thought I should impregnate.

"How's life, Gareth?"

"*Fantástico! Siempre* fantastic!" he said. He still didn't have a job and his exams had become a Sisyphean endeavour; every time he neared the end of the course, a momentary lapse of effort or attendance would roll him back to the beginning. His mother supported him and he had a smelly flat near the port.

"Do you live alone?"

He made a half-hearted noise that was supposed to indicate that a trail of lovers came and went. Otherwise, yes, he lived alone.

"I am sure you have a dog," I tried.

"No, mice," he said. "I hunt mice."

22

Lino Oviedo was arrested in Brazil.

When the police burst into his sensuous apartment in Foz do Iguaçu, they found him holed up with a revolver and a magnificent ladies' wig of auburn hair. He'd been using ten mobile telephones. "We have over ninety hours of recorded telephone conversations," said a weary spokesman from the Shock Police. "The man just couldn't stop talking . . ."

His arrest triggered a whole new range of problems. Whether he was a terrorist, a transsexual or just a trumped-up little cavalier, he would have been the Paraguayan choice in a straight election. The government asked the Brazilians to return him, but it was the last thing they wanted.

Gareth had become an *Oviedista*.

"He is the only one. *Solamente* Lino. *Todos los otros son mafiosi*. He is *fuerte*—really *fuerte*. He can take those bastards. *Puede, puede* . . . he can stop *mafiosi*." He bailed some sugar into his coffee whilst I tried to disentangle his languages. He never touched beer nowadays, he said.

I was surprised at Gareth. "I heard that Lino is a homosexual."

"Who cares who you fuck? *No me importa.*"

It occurred to me that Gareth might also have a *Stronista* tendency. I wondered how to broach the subject.

"Do you think Stroessner fucked children?"

Gareth looked surprised. "Children?"

"You know—*niños*. The fourteen-year-old . . ."

Gareth laughed. The sound was crackled and dry.

"Listen, John. If she's got thirty-two kilos, she's ready."

23

The Gran Hotel had once been out in the countryside and it had captured a last little bit of jungle within its walls before Asunción swarmed up the hill and surrounded it with mansions.

The jungle was held in small courtyards of red and white cloisters. The ferns and palms were flecked with parakeets and were so dense that, after dark, they hissed and rattled with eerie and vaguely disconcerting noises. All the rooms, which were cool and shuttered, smelt faintly of forest.

Surprisingly, there were clearings in these miniature forests. One contained a brilliant blue scoop of swimming pool. In another, there was a tennis court with a crimson surface that glued itself to everything. Tennis shoes turned pink and players were drenched in vermilion. By "one set to love," they'd be lobbing clods of fluffy red clay back and forth across the net.

At the far end of the gardens was a dire warning in several languages. "Don't go in there," said the English effort, "in where an he animals may hit you very badly." A tiny deer with a nose of shiny toffee was pressed up against the wire. Beyond the harmless menagerie, there was only the hit-you-very-badly city.

There were woodlands of a different nature in the ballroom.

Here, the creepers and vines weren't of muscular, fertile Paraguayan stock but were neatly dabbed on walls with sable brushes and tiny mops of gold. Here were *faux* trellises of pretty, pale fruits—grapes, peaches and juiceless apples—and *trompes* of plump game and loping fawns. The patron of this art had been homesick for Les Tuileries of 1850, for Paris in the autumn and for the delicate shades of the Bois de Boulogne. She'd brought with her strange imaginings: weird creatures—grouse, pheasants and lobsters—and the peculiar trimmings of imperial power—swords, drums and coronets. Then she'd put her astonished Guaraní artists to work, recreating the *salons* of St. Germain here in the stifling, tropical folds of central South America.

The only peculiar thing about this was that she wasn't French at all. She was Irish, born in Cork in 1835 and weaned in poverty just a few, skinny years before the Great Potato Famine.

Her name was Eliza Alicia Lynch. She was about to become the most enduring and undeserving heroine in the history of Paraguay. In her own lifetime she was both loved and loathed, a pattern which has continued more or less unchanged ever since. But if it were possible to clamber into the Paraguayan psyche, one would still find her there, in brilliant white ball-dress—armed, bloodied and erotic—rising above the wreckage of the nation as Delacroix's Greece had risen above the ruins of Missolonghi.

The truth was more prosaic, but no less startling.

24

Some years before Don Carlos Antonio López drowned in his own bodily fluids, he sent his heir, Francisco Solano, to Europe. The young Francisco had begun to make a nuisance of himself by violating the daughters of the gentry, and so, in September 1853, Don Carlos sent him off to purchase the tools of imperial grandeur.

The trip was a success. Francisco arrived in Paris with a cast of forty and found himself delighted. He planted a willow at the tomb of the heroic poet Alfred de Musset, and when he saw Les Invalides, he decided that Paraguay should have a copy. He got a tailor to fit him out like his champion, Napoleon Bonaparte, and had the magnificent uniform topped off with a few flourishes of his own—some lace, some ostrich feathers and a huge pair of silver spurs.

Now gloriously attired, he strutted the Paraguayan national purse among the merchants, scattering cash around a coterie of sycophants and opportunists. He bought himself seventy pairs of patent leather boots and several trunks of outlandish military costumes.

Francisco Solano even had an audience with Bonaparte's nephew, the deflated Napoleon III. Here accounts of López's Parisian adventures—particularly among Mr. Washburn's American disciples—become a little overheated. They have López squeaking before the Emperor in clothes so obscenely tight that he could hardly walk. Their Empress Eugénie vomits when López plants a kiss on her. Whilst it is true that López's teeth would one day become so putrid that his agonies could only be soothed with schooners of brandy, for the moment he had the ability to raise a little charm. There would be plenty of opportunities for the monster in him later.

That is not to say that the French appreciated his charms. They found him frankly distasteful, and behind his fatty back, they called him the "half-civilised monkey in the mountebank attire." The Paraguayan retinue was blissfully unaware of the ridicule and set off on holiday.

They went to Spain and then on to Rome, where they bought a presidential dinner service. Then they set off again, cruising down to the Crimea to watch the Europeans tear each other limb from limb with exciting new weapons. Francisco was deeply impressed by the grandiosity of annihilation—and by the technology that could deliver it. He had to have some.

He set off for England, but its government was unimpressed by "the man from Paraguay." López was disappointed that Queen Victoria was unable to see him.

"I am," she instructed her staff, "quite too busy to see the little savage."

There was only one other setback: Francisco had hoped to visit the armourers of Manchester, but when he heard a rumour of cholera, he decided that a trip to the north wasn't worth the risk to his health. He found what he wanted in Limehouse in the East End of London. Alfred Blyth & Co. sold him several thousand muskets and a gunboat which he called *Tacuarí*. They also provided him with a body of engineers, who would, it was hoped, haul Paraguay into the nineteenth century.

Francisco had not been neglecting his ravenous sexual urges, and back on St. Germain, he was hauling himself on and off selected courtesans. Then one of them stopped him in his sweaty tracks.

She was a young woman of slender and translucent beauty. All through her life she'd have a devastating effect on men, stripping them of their better judgement and fomenting dangerous urges and unruly bravado. The effect on López—and ultimately Paraguay—was disastrous, but he was by no means the only man bewitched. Even that sniggering Argentine hack Varela was left gibbering. His prose simply jellified:

> She was tall and of supple and delicate figure with exquisite and seductive curves. Her skin was alabaster. Her eyes were of a blue that seems borrowed from the very hues of heaven and had an expression of ineffable sweetness in whose depth the light of cupid was enthroned. Her beautiful lips were indescribably expressive of the voluptuous, moistened by the ethereal dew that God must have provided to lull the fires within her, a mouth that was like a cup of delight at the banquet table of ardent passion . . .

This heaven-sent vision was of course Eliza Alicia Lynch, or—as she was known professionally—"Madame Lynch, Instructress of Languages." Although López would never restrict his ardency to Eliza, she'd be his soul-mate, the mother of seven of his children and the survivor of his madness. It was she alone who was with him at his agonising death.

She was his most dazzling acquisition so far.

Eliza would have said that it was she who acquired López. She'd been considering how to secure her future for some time. She was now eighteen and couldn't rely on her looks to keep her in truffles indefinitely. For some years she'd been living dangerously close to penury, surviving on a series of connections negotiated between expensive sheets.

On reflection, she'd been keeping only one step ahead of poverty ever since the Lynches fled the Irish famine in 1845. She'd found brief respite in a marriage when she was fifteen. A French army vet called Xavier Quatrefages had whisked Eliza over the Channel to take advantage of both her and the indulgent Common Law. The couple were married at landfall, Folkestone, in the parish church. It was a short-lived match spent in blistering army camps in Algeria and it all ended when Eliza caught her eye on a Russian. That too had proved an insecure tenure, and she was now begging—to borrow Varela's words—with her cup of delight at the banquet table of ardent passion.

When this slightly exotic, explosively potent sultan dandled her on his fleshy knee and murmured of his empire in South America, the future began to map itself out in front of her. When she discovered that she was pregnant with his baby, the way offered became the only way out. There would be little future for her in Paris with a hungry runt, half-Irish, a bit Spanish, a bit Guaraní, a tad negro and goodness knows what else. She agreed to accompany him home on the *Tacuarí*.

25

On 11 November 1854, the *Tacuarí* set sail. Paraguay was 13,000 miles away.

Eliza Lynch had no idea if she'd ever see Europe again and was determined to take as much of it with her as the *Tacuarí* would carry. In the hold was the hardware and the flummery of the new Paraguay. There were the boxes of guns and bayonets and sabres. Then there were the seventy pairs of boots, each with raised heels and silver garnishes, and the presidential dinner service. Best of all were the things that she and Francisco had thrown in after a delirious flurry round Paris: crates of Tokay and French brandy, bolts of muslin, satin and lace, gauzy parasols, matching sewing-machines and several jewelled coiffures, perfumes, perfumed gloves, vials of essences and sandalwood fans, make-up pomades, a Venetian mirror, a chiffonier, heaps of exquisite porcelains, two more dinner services (one Sèvres, one Limoges), a Pleyel grand piano, a presidential landau and an American buggy.

It took nearly three months to heave this cargo and its spooning owners across the ocean and up the Plate, the Paraná and the doleful Paraguay, to Asunción.

The *Asunceños* were on the quayside to watch them dock. Here was Paraguay's first-ever metal gunboat delivering her first-ever blonde.

As eager as they were to see her, Eliza Lynch was keen to review her new subjects. She'd already sailed through the territory of the Guaycurús, who would have happily ripped her pretty scalp off if she'd put so much as a satin toe on the eastern bank of the river.

The sight that greeted her on the quayside was not encouraging; her admiring citizens were roughly dressed in a sort of toga called a *tipoi*, that left one breast exposed. They were puffing on foul cigars and had some of the most extravagant hookworm in the world. An English traveller, arriving three years earlier, had reported that, of the ladies he saw, "only one is good-looking (and many of them have goitre) but she is very handsome . . ."

Don Carlos was also on the quayside. He didn't look encouraging either. He was furious. His spies had warned him that Francisco was returning with a fancy lady who was neither diplomatically useful, nor rich, nor *virgo intacta.*

"What," he sloshed, through angry folds of oedema, "is my son doing with this *ramera irlandesa?*"

It became all too clear what Francisco had been doing with "the Irish Strumpet" when she stepped on to the gangway, blooming in lilac gown and matching bonnet. Don Carlos blubbered with rage and ordered his buggy away. He managed not to address a civilised word to Miss Lynch for the next—and last—seven years of his pusillanimous life.

There was hardly a more civilised reaction from the so-called Asunción gentry. They'd never held their rutting, greasy-pawed *Infante* in great affection, and when he returned with this hoity-toity little filly, they were green with admiration.

The diplomats articulated their contempt. The British Minister declared Eliza Lynch to be "an Irish Pompadour." The French Minister, Monsieur Cochelet, was less oblique.

"I would," he announced, "as soon break bread with a nigger as accept a morsel from that devious Irish slut."

Eliza could expect even less charity from the patricians themselves. They went to great lengths to ignore her. But she knew—because she'd hired her own *pyragüés*—what they called her. It was the same old slings and arrows; the Whore, the Irish Hussy, *La Concubina Irlandesa* . . .

In hindsight, Eliza wasn't helped by the fact that her old professional name had survived the voyage. She'd seldom been "Miss Lynch," occasionally "Mrs. Lynch" and never "Madame Quatrefages." For now—and for ever—she'd be known among her uncertain minions, the Paraguayans, as Madame Lynch.

López's own family were hardly any warmer in their reception. Don Carlos was, of course, maintaining his wall of watery silence. His wife, Doña Juana, joined him in his determined spat, rocking backwards and forwards in her crib, babbling, "I will not accept that woman! I will not accept that woman!"

Their other children—Francisco's siblings—were as repulsive as their parents and equally as determined to be vile to the girl from Cork. There were two sisters, Inocencia and Rafaela, who—according to the waspish Varela (he'd regained his grip)—occasionally appeared in public "decked out like Bavarian eggs." Then there were two brothers, Venancio and Benigno—both lush, elephantine and probably syphilitic. Venancio had grossly underdeveloped sexual organs and busied himself trying to stuff them into unwilling young virgins. He continued to make a pest of himself in this way until Francisco found him a more profitable position, as the admiral of the nonexistent Paraguayan Fleet.

They all refused to speak to *La Concubina Irlandesa.*

Madame Lynch would in due course have her revenge.

The Argentines watched the developments upriver with a sense of helpless, breathless hilarity. "Big chief Francisco," ran the Buenos Aires press, "now has a ridiculous Indian squaw." Asunción had become "a dismal collection of wigwams."

It wouldn't be long now before they too found their smirks spattered across their faces.

26

There were only a handful of other guests at my hotel and they were all very ancient. In fact, they were all so old that, every other day, an American doctor came up to The Gran to see how much longer they'd be. The doctor had a stoop and an old-fashioned instrument bag and a silver pocket-watch, as if he'd just popped out of a nursery rhyme. He left his patients with small brown envelopes of pills which, at breakfast time, they obediently poured in their tea.

I was intrigued by these elderly gentlemen, but they stubbornly refused to register my presence. Their obduracy was admirable. I tried saying good morning to them in a range of languages. Each morning, at breakfast, I tried a different one—Spanish, German, English, French— and I even looked up the Guaraní *("mba' eichapa ne ko'e, karai").* There was not a flicker of response.

I'd pinned all my hopes on the German breakfast. The hotel was, after all, owned by the Weiler family. Old Bobby Weiler had been an energetic Nazi in the thirties, and the hotel dining room had been a rallying point for Germans and Austrians who saw the future in Prussian field-grey. Their numbers—it was said—were swelled by the crew of the *Graf Spee*, who'd wandered up the River Plate after their battleship was scuttled.

"Guten Morgen!" I trilled. Not an eyelid moved.

That left only two options: dementia and disapproval. When I saw one of them give another a bottle of chocolate brandy, I was forced to the conclusion that it had to be disapproval.

My fellow guests, I decided, were the noble heirs to Asunción's old patricians. Or perhaps even their ghosts.

27

Madame Lynch set about establishing her court.

First, she and her paramour took separate houses to maintain a semblance of decency (though no one can have thought the storks were bringing all those babies). To maintain an aura of sophistication, they addressed each other only in French—even though Madame Lynch was soon proficient in Spanish and Guaraní.

Then she installed a French hairdresser, Monsieur Henry, and ordered a massive marble bath from Italy to freshen up the malodorous López. She even managed to work a few gastronomic refinements upon her snuffling admirer. She weaned him off "meats and stuffings"—at least in company—and he and his coarse friends learnt to sup up sauces and custards from the best Sèvres.

Her attempts to refine the gentry were less successful. The "French Academy," set up to produce a Paraguayan Delacroix or Liszt, flopped for lack of attendance. When Mesdames Balet et Dupart—two old poodles from Paris—arrived to start a finishing school, the *Asunceñas* were defiant; they weren't leaving their daughters with that pair of powdered French sluts. The two *cocottes* took to their heels and howled their way home.

Francisco had been delighted by the arrival of an heir, Juan Francisco, and had ordered an artillery salute. In the American accounts, there were

101 guns blasting off from the roof of the palace, destroying eleven
houses and wiping out an artillery troop. In reality, there probably
weren't that many cannon in the entire Plate region, and the Government Palace didn't yet have a roof. Anyway, Francisco was undoubtedly
delighted and it is highly probable that something, somebody's
property, was blown up in celebration.

These were heady days. López ignited his Napoleonic ambitions and
Madame Lynch fanned the little flames. López now looked for an
opportunity to win his spurs. When a row broke out in Argentine
Corrientes, he marched down to add his considerable bulk—and that of
his piffling army—to an imbalance of power. Although not a shot was
fired, the matter resolved itself triumphantly and López returned to
Asunción as "the Hero of Corrientes." He was compared favourably
with Alexander the Great by the hookwormed rabble—and by some of
his own, bleating pamphleteers.

The imperial build-up began.

Packed in among the powder-puffs and sewing machines on the
Tacuarí were the Blyth & Co. contractors. They were faced with the
awesome task of building a railway system, an armoury, an army, a shipyard, waterworks, roads and even an iron foundry. Remarkably, they
would have achieved all of this if the imperial goulash hadn't over-
boiled.

Chief among the engineers was William Keld Whytehead, a rather
desiccated Scot who'd lived in Whitechapel on the Mile End Road.
There was always a niff of tragedy about Whytehead, and in Paraguay he
was a lonely, bookish character, appalled by women and, in any event,
emotionally uninhabitable. He had an invalid mother and a sister who'd
been forced by her circumstances into the service of a widow in
Eccleston Square. He sent them money and they returned his kindness
with packets of seeds, to plant on his little *quinta*.

Whytehead's smallholding was on a hill some way out of Asunción.
The track that ran past the *quinta* was—to his disgust—a lovers' lane
known as *Tapé yaú nde yurú*—"the path where my kisses eat your
mouth." He lived at the farm with a large collection of books, an English
servant called Amos Eaton, two pet capybaras and an ostrich that kept

him in eggs. His only other luxuries were sent to him from England: some hams, a telescope and bottles of his favourite sauces.

Frugally installed, he applied his energies to the construction of Paraguay, destroying—as he did so—his own brittle sanity.

Madame Lynch had not been idle. Her mansion was now a picture. Schooners had been ploughing busily backwards and forwards across the Atlantic with her delightful manifests of bronzes, porcelain, French tapestries and oriental carpets. The ensemble was now lavishly complete.

Varela, purring with pleasure, was asked to visit Madame Lynch in her *salon*. With one eye to the decor, he reported back to his readers. "Everything," he panted, "was laid out with the most excellent taste, making it a delight to look at."

Several times a week, Madame Lynch held soirées of poetry and music. The invitations became an important barometer of regal favour. Initially, Whytehead was asked, but he tended to mop up any gaiety and so Madame Lynch later restricted their intercourse to exchanging packets of seed.

Rather more lively—too lively as it turned out—was the American Minister, Mr. Charles Ames Washburn. He was a strange appointment to the diplomatic post, as he was exuberant, volatile and peculiarly lacking in tact. At his core were dangerous magmas that would erupt whenever there was a crisis demanding good sense and calm. He was volcanically unsuitable. Before Asunción, he'd been a novelist, a Wisconsin attorney, a newspaper editor and a gold-prospector, skills which equipped him for dealing with most things—but not López.

Initially, however, relations were effusive and Washburn was often to be found at the *salon* throwing back Tokay and singing away on the Pleyel.

At his elbow was another drifter, Baron Franz Wisner von Morgenstern. This incongruous fop had been hounded from the Court of Vienna for offences against nature and had wandered off to South America to offer his services as a military adviser. Like President Wasmosy—120 years his junior—he was a Hungarian aristocrat, and to prove the point, he wore fancy hussar uniforms, embroidered with green frogs and topped off with astrakhan collars. He was the only trophy that Francisco had brought back from the Corrientes campaign.

Unfortunately, whenever war broke out, Wisner was indisposed through illness. This—and the fact that he could be relied upon not to meddle with Madame Lynch—not only placed him very close to the Lópezes but ensured his survival; his dandy presence on the Paraguayan scene would continue long after the other players were dead or in exile.

Meanwhile, Madame Lynch was delighted to have his company; here was an utter bitch with whom she could share her scorn for the gentry.

After the death of Don Carlos in 1862, an opportunity arose for Madame Lynch to address her tormentors. It was not revenge exactly, but it enabled her to make her point.

She organised a ball.

It was to be a fancy dress ball—but with a difference: she got to choose what each guest wore. Now that she and Don Francisco were in charge, no one could possibly decline her invitation.

She herself was to come "in the gorgeous style of Queen Elizabeth I of England," complete with a diadem of brilliants, a ruffed collar and a golden gown steeped in seed pearls. Naturally, she allowed Don Francisco to come as his hero, Napoleon, Emperor of the French.

Her friend, Baron von Morgenstern, was to be Lorenzo de Medici.

The Bishop of Asunción was tactfully given "the Apostle Paul," but the first ladies of the city were required to appear as Swiss shepherdesses, Italian fruit-sellers and other manifestations of the peasantry.

Washburn refused to dress up and fell from grace.

For Don Francisco's mother, who was by now a viperous old crone with a fluffy moustache, she chose Diana the Huntress. When she got her invitation, Mother López wept acid tears and swore that she'd shoot an arrow into the little strumpet's heart.

Her corpulent daughters were to come as "two emaciated Guaraní Indians."

But for the woman Madame Lynch loathed most of all—the French Minister's wife, Madame Cochelet—she ordered "Queen Victoria." In that lot, even this old trollop wouldn't be tempted to steal the glitz.

The evening was a triumph, and President Francisco Solano López ordered Congress to grant to Madame Lynch all those privileges usually accorded to a head of state.

28

Apart from the half-dead gerontocrats, there were other, more occasional guests at The Gran Hotel. Twice a week there was a small *té-canasta* party in the lobby. I suspected that the ladies were the delicate rump of what had been a larger card circle. They arrived with silvery perms and kidskin gloves and drank tea from china cups and saucers. They conversed in Spanish and played their cards in French, and when the games were over, they slipped their gloves back on and swarthy drivers took them home.

Things were more lively on the weekends. There were the tennis-players, of course, and every Saturday, the ballroom was tinselled up for a ball. It was usually a fifteenth birthday party for a debutante. These weren't like the office girls, but were winsome little slips—tutored in Miami, pastured in Uruguay and heeled in Buenos Aires. They had long cataracts of courtly Spanish names—Caballero, Ibarra, Yegros, Elizeche, Espinoza—which had often been hitched together as evidence of unimpeachable pedigree. They'd be photographed with their parents—bundles of startling tuxedos and organza—and then, as the whisky flowed, they'd all polka and sing in Guaraní. It was now chic to be an Indian.

All visitors were monitored by a smouldering reptile in reception. Because her lair was faced—in the Teutonic style—with lumps of rock, she was often difficult to see in the gloom. However, whenever a stranger stepped into the lobby, she was quickly on the scent and her loose-skinned neck craned out of its cave. This being Asunción, most people knew exactly who she was.

"She's a terrible snob," one friend told me.

"Her father was a minister in the *Stronato*," said another.

"She's not there working for the salary, she just wants to know what's going on and who everybody is."

Meanwhile, she devoured their details, mentally weighing up their carats and boring into bank accounts, clambering into their family trees and sniffing their blood for its blueness. She was a sort of social *pyragüé*, mounted with crimson talons.

She called me "Monsieur D'Juim au Lait," and I didn't care to correct her.

29

The relics of the golden López years were scattered around Asunción. I found bone-white statues and several baubles of Eliza's jewellery, dispersed among factious museums. It was even said that the enormous Italian marble bath was somewhere, turning green in someone's garden.

The palaces of the sensual brothers, Venancio and Benigno, had survived, as slightly raffish hotels. Sadly, the glorious staircases that had carried the lechers to their seamy cots had long ago been plundered.

Whytehead's home-foundered cannons now lolled in the turf on Plaza Mariscal López, aiming their empty blasts at the Sodom that he'd engineered.

There should have been an opera house.

An Italian architect, Alessandro Revizza, had been commissioned to design one as swagged and as tailed as Milan's La Scala. It had never been finished. "The only singers," wrote Washburn, "were the parrots that trilled their arias in the empty cavern."

What remained of the enormous, flamboyant shell had been colonised by tax officials. One day, I joined a line of debtors and clambered up into the resplendent gloom. Revizza's lavish swoops were all bedded in concrete and his auditorium was cluttered with bureaucracy. The place should have been tingling with airs and intermezzos, but instead there was only the sinister, leafy murmur of paper. The debtors went to their forms. Barefoot children swarmed down on them, crawling amongst their feet, polishing shoes and sifting litter. One of the waifs had an intriguing pump. "Blood pressures taken," said his sign. "Live happily."

The day after my visit, the operatic tax office was raided. The thieves turned up with a lorry and hauled off a day's precious tax: £53,428.

The frippery and cruets of Napoleonic Paraguay were kept at the Ministry of Defence, guarded by young conscripts with gruesome antique guns. I went up there on a day as hot as any that spring, and—once again—I found myself before soldiers, dripping and pleading to be let in. They parted like toys; the Ministry of Defence was a shrine.

It was also thickly peopled by officials. They followed me as I threaded through the basement, through meticulous displays of despair and failure. We passed wooden cannon that had exploded on their third ignition, wiping out their crews, paintings of naked troops and bayonets thrust so hard that they'd shattered. At the far end, we came to the inner sanctum and there they left me.

I wasn't alone, however. There were two well-jawed females sitting at a desk, rasping at each other in what they imagined to be whispers. They were so strikingly similar to the creature that terrorised my hotel that I wondered if she hadn't somehow replicated and sent two of herself down to the Ministry to oversee my visit. I instinctively apologised but they waved me forward into the room.

I found myself standing next to President López's underwear. They had "FSL" embroidered on them and had been partially devoured by unthinking weevils. There were other remnants of his wardrobe in the same mildewed case: lacy dinner shirts, linen drawers, his pyjamas, silver-buttoned waistcoats as elegant as tea-cosies, a brass breastplate and the bicorne hat with a spray of egret feathers. Nuzzled in at the side were his little indulgences—a mint silver tea-service, some well-licked forks, three swollen wine-pitchers and the medals that he'd awarded himself for outstanding vanity and for discretion (placed well before valour).

Madame Lynch's bric-a-brac also fell under the watchful eye of the clawed guards. For all the shiploads of fancy ballast, she'd left her subjects with very little—a few bustles and velvet shawls, some baby-pink porcelain, a surviving piece of Sèvres and a book signed by 87,000 people who still adored her when the fight was done. That was impressive—87,000 was rather more than the number of literates that had survived the carnage.

Such niceties wouldn't have troubled Madame Lynch and her consort. In their portraits they looked supercilious and indestructible. Francisco's daguerreotype had been taken when he was younger and—whilst hardly lissom—still capable of getting his legs around a horse. In his own mind he was already a man of destiny.

Madame Lynch, on the other hand, looked middle-aged. Her pearled skin had yielded its delicate features and her bosom was now luxuriously pillowed. Her gaze, however, still gave nothing away. She could have been happy or bitterly angry, she could have been exhilarated or chronically weary. She was the consummate courtesan, deeply, fascinatingly impenetrable.

The photographer had clearly found her picture uncomfortably chilly and had tried to warm it up with pinks and oranges and ridiculous yellows. The effect was not only tawdry, it was something else; it made his subject seem strangely fictional.

Madame Lynch's town house had been designed by Revizza around a courtyard on Estigarribia.

It was now stripped bare. Gone was the silk and gone the gilt. The housekeeper took me through the rooms, throwing open the shutters, allowing sunlight to seep in among the clammy shadows. It's a law faculty now, she explained, but everyone's away.

She let me wander around. The doors had stiff, wincing hinges and the ceilings were furred with dust. All the rooms were empty—except for a curious stack of cooking oil in a chamber upstairs. It was no longer a house of possessions.

Stripped of its lavish purpose, this great yellowing carcass stood hollow and ugly, like a stage-set at the end of a very poor run.

Thinking back on it, I'd wanted to find ghosts in the Asunción of Eliza Lynch. But there was nothing, just a few artefacts, a few props. It was as if she'd never existed. Rather, it was as if her life had been merely a role in a cruel burlesque or—less charitably—a dreadful penny-opera.

30

"What do you think Madame Lynch gave to the Paraguayans? Anything?"

I was having tea again with the lady who believed in theatrical *coups d'etat*. Her name was Cinthia and her family made wine that had the reputation for being virtually undrinkable. She was very sweet and never encouraged me to try it.

Having friends to tea at The Gran was a useful way of tackling the vagaries of a Paraguayan social life. Often, if I tried to meet people in the evening, they would try and shuffle the appointment towards midnight. They thought the idea of meeting at eight was ludicrous. It was a sort of reaction to the passing of the *Stronato*; nobody went out until the time when—previously—they should have been in. If I suggested eight, they'd protest: "But there are still people walking around out there!"

I didn't mind waiting around until ten, but there was no guarantee that they'd show up. No one ever wanted to organise anything more than three days in advance and there still had to be an elaborate system of confirmations. Even if our arrangement survived that, there was a good chance of cancellation on the final day. The disappointment of cancellation was, however, always softened by the lavishness of the excuses.

"I can't come. I've been standing in the wind too long."

"Sorry, John, I can't make dinner. I've got to be sterilised."

"Can we make dinner another night? I've just bought a sack of oranges and I want to clean my stomach out. Did you know that you've got eight metres of intestines?"

It was polite to be half an hour late, customary to be an hour and not unusual to be two.

Somehow, I didn't mind all this if it was teatime rather than in the small hours of the morning. Besides, the Paraguayans liked tea at The Gran. The teatime menu was long and inspiring. One day a girl from a conservation group came up to talk about birds. She studied the menu.

"I'll have a plate of biscuits, a litre of strawberry milkshake and a large steak. I'm lactating."

Cinthia thought about my question.

"Madame Lynch," she said, "made a great contribution to our lives."

She paused to dab some cake away from her mouth.

"She brought us nice shoes. Before she came, we were barefoot."

I made an impressed noise.

"And she introduced hairdressing."

I found that harder to react to.

"And she taught us to dance indoors. Before she came to Paraguay, we only danced outside."

31

Before returning to Paraguay, I'd gathered together some advice as to how I should conduct my social life. The best—or perhaps the most enjoyable—source of advice was a pamphlet published by "The American Ladies" in Asunción. Your problems, they explained, may well begin before you've even entered the house of your host; there may not be a doorbell. "Do not be disheartened," soothed the matrons. "It is customary to clap your hands together several times, as loudly as possible, and in no time a maid will appear to announce your visit."

Once inside, there were other traps for the unwary. It was necessary to sit on the correct part of the sofa; the right-hand side was reserved for the guest of honour. Then, in relation to conversation, The Ladies had even more alarming news: "After a particularly congenial talk a Paraguayan man or woman may embrace you lightly, touching cheeks and kissing into the air."

As to what we might talk about, my Paraguayan friends in London issued a stern warning: "You must be careful what you say. The Paraguayans will express their views forcefully. There have been many years of repression . . ."

As if the threat of being besieged with kisses or pounded with strong opinions wasn't enough, the news about the women was equally disconcerting. I was taken aside and given another strong warning.

"They know," said the London Paraguayans, "exactly what they want."

I assumed this meant that they were predatory. In a country where men had attained a certain scarcity value through two devastating wars, it hardly surprised me that women had developed a tendency to take the initiative. On the other hand, Paraguayan women were among the most disempowered in South America: they were the last to get the vote, in 1961; until recently, husbands who killed their wives on the grounds of adultery were spared prison. Paraguay called itself "The Land of Women" (mostly at times when all the men were dead), but who were these powerless, predatory beings?

I turned to the work of earlier travellers to see what they'd gleaned. Ruiz Díaz de Guzmán provided the conquistador analysis: the women were "virtuous, gentle and of a gentle disposition." By the 1880s, a Scottish traveller thought that their "virtue is so largely a matter of convention that it is generally wisest to leave such matters uncommented on." An English lawyer, writing at about the same time, was more forthright; he was delighted by the ladies, with their "soft, supple, panther-like tread" and tunics that revealed "the statuesque shoulders and breasts rather more than would be considered delicate in Europe." Thirty years later, another Scotsman reported back that the ladies were:

Just a little bit unconventional—as all unspoilt daughters of Eve might be expected to be in a land where the bread and butter question does not exist; fond of pretty things, and loving to flit about in the sunshine like humming-birds, rarely taking life seriously . . . If not frequently blessed with classic features, they have always smiling faces, splendid dark eyes and a wealth of glossy raven tresses, which might grace the head of a Queen in Fairyland.

So—fairy queens, humming-birds and ample-breasted panthers—the women of Paraguay seemed to have satisfactorily defied rational generalisation. As to whether they were predatory, it was hard to tell.

One evening, a sugary blonde who called herself "Fluff" came up to The Gran to cart me off into town in her white jeep. She was the fluffy end of my little network of contacts and had a husband who'd vanished in Central America (or had fled there). Fluff wasn't really fluffy at all. She tossed back two gins and then hurled us into the traffic on España. One minute she was solicitous and insisting that I wear a safety belt and the next we were taking a roundabout on two wheels or throwing the jeep down Mariscal López—in reverse. In slightly less than three minutes, we were in a rather velveteen Italian restaurant where the pasta managed to be both gooey and raw. When I told her that my mobile phone wasn't working, she offered to smash it there and then, and I was only able to restore order by splashing our glasses with fierce draughts of Argentine wine.

"English men," she announced, "are so contracted, so unemotional."

I was perplexed by this; Fluff didn't speak any English and had never been to England. As for me, she'd only seen me drink two gins and then bury myself in her dashboard during three minutes of terror. I realised, however, that it was merely a vehicle for what was coming next.

"Except you." She was purring.

Was it predatory? Perhaps, but I preferred to think that she was merely marking out her territory. Escape was easy.

"We get terribly badly bitten by your mosquitoes," I said, and showed her a thing like a glacé cherry that was erupting from my wrist.

She took the point and with one bound I was free.

Dinner parties presented slightly less of a challenge than I'd feared. Most houses now had door chimes, so getting in was obviously easier than it had been. Only outside Asunción did I find myself out in the street, clapping and howling for the domestics. The sofas weren't the social encumbrances that the American Ladies had suggested and I soon got the hang of the kissing.

I was taken to some of these occasions by Margarita Kent. She knew everybody and was happy to bring me along as a sort of English curiosity.

Margarita's own family were notionally English but none of them had seriously ventured outside Paraguay for three generations. Margarita's grandfather had been Charley Kent, who arrived in Paraguay in 1904 to trap furs and trade egret feathers with the Chaco Indians. Charley was a hard-boiled, rust-haired man who believed that men should be men and that a little suffering did no one any harm. He'd been at Harrow with Winston Churchill, and in 1889, they'd carved their names next to each other on a school desk, which is still there today. Charley had despised Churchill, who he'd considered to be "a sissy," and after collecting some wounds at the siege of Ladysmith, he set off for Paraguay. For the next thirty-seven years he'd hacked his way to and fro across the thorny seas of the Chaco, in slouch-hat and waxed moustache. The Kents were now a Paraguayan institution.

Margarita had inherited something of her grandfather's flair for the uncomfortable. She was mid-forties and painfully punctual at everything. She worked long days at the airport and then, in the evenings, she drove off to the gym to pound herself like a sprinter. For the dinner parties, she dressed in fine black silks that made her seem both sleek and angular. She was popular with hostesses and lavishly tolerated by other women. Men were powerlessly, palpably tempted by her jaunty, muscled body to speculate on the improbable prospect of holding her. But none had. And so Margarita remained athletically single.

Madame Lynch would have been proud to see that her Paraguayans had remembered everything that she'd taught them about entertaining. Dining rooms were decorated with gilt mirrors and colourful prints of fox-hunting scenes or erotic Rome. There would be canapés in the drawing room and then, at the tinkle of a little bell, a uniformed maid would lead us through to the table. In the best houses, the maids were so superior that they even had maids themselves.

The hosts and hostesses sat at either end of the table and pumped me for information about the London smog and "Lady Di," as they still called her. One host was so delighted that I was there, taking an interest in Madame Lynch, that he produced a little lilac teacup of hers from a glass cabinet.

"She was so beautiful," he sniffed, cradling the delicate porcelain in a meaty hand. Everybody cooed in agreement, as if—like Princess Diana—her death had been a recent event and her impress was still warm on society's sofas.

Usually, the food was not Paraguayan—Coronation chicken, glazed carrots, strawberries and cream—although occasionally *sopa paraguaya* made its heavy appearance. It was made with cornmeal and pig fat and was always greeted with murmurs of appreciation. Finally, the desserts would be trumpeted to the table, accompanied by an escort of tiny, delicate flutes of purple liqueur called *Parfait Amour*.

Madame Lynch herself could hardly have expected more exquisite taste.

On the weekends, the servants were often away, and those who could afford to went along to their clubs. Soon after my return, I'd caught up with Virginia Martin, and she and her husband often asked me to go along with them.

Virginia was even more gloriously red-haired than I'd remembered from eighteen years before. Her fantastic coppery tresses simply erupted—brilliant, glossy surges tumbling down her back. She was known in Asunción for her hair. To the Paraguayans, she was rather awesome, but when Virginia produced children with equally brilliant hair, they scooped up the shiny new curls in their fingertips. "Just look at this!" they squealed, turning it over cautiously, as if they expected the little orange filaments to be still red-hot from the furnace.

It occurred to me, as I got to know Virginia better, that her extravagant colouring was perhaps a cruel hand dealt by nature. Behind the magnificence, Virginia was wincingly private, a watcher not a performer. She shrank away from exuberance and bubbly groups at parties and seldom ventured an opinion. Despite this, she was curiously expressive, often communicating in tiny, subtle inflections, barely perceptible modulations of gesture. In a slightly voracious society like Asunción, it made her a survivor.

It hardly surprised me at all that since we'd last met, Virginia had become a painter. In her paintings she was a shrewd observer, but more than this, she was now demonstrative and passionate. I was surprised by the depth of feeling in her work. It was always Paraguay. Paraguay expressed in the gorgeous ochres of her soil. Paraguay through soft, rich muslins of dust. Paraguayan land rumbling with great red herds of cattle. I asked her why she didn't sell them. Her look told me that these paintings were how she felt.

"José wants me to keep them."

Virginia had married José Franco fifteen years ago. He was a lawyer and a big, bearded man who had a tendency to regard his life as a period of pasture after glorious years on the college sports-field. Although he spoke immaculate English, it often seemed deeply threaded with anguish. When I first met him, I found this a little disconcerting.

"I once went to England," he told me when we met. "To look for a girl."

"Your girlfriend?"

"No, not mine. She'd run away from her lover. Just as they were about to get married."

"Did she want to come back?"

"I don't know." He shrugged. "She was in a village in England, somewhere. We couldn't find it on our maps in Asunción. But we still set out."

"Where was she?"

"We travelled all over England. Eventually we found her near Leeds."

This intriguing little story didn't have an end, or if it did, it remained—like so much of José—unsaid. As with Virginia, José was a subtle individual and, like her, he was a survivor. His father had been a minister during the *Stronato*, and President Stroessner had given the testimonial at Virginia's wedding.

José was troubled by his proximity to the Stroessner regime. On the one hand, he felt a powerful tug of loyalty towards his dead father. He even made little stabs at trying to persuade me that the stability of the *Stronato* justified its means. But José was also a man of integrity, and I could sense that, not far down, beneath the clutter of loyalty, was a knot of revulsion. "You have to realise," he once told me, "Stroessner owned Paraguay. He owned us all."

As I got to know him, I became very fond of José. He was patient and thoughtful and always willing to indulge my rather skittish plans. Once, I even talked him into a trip to the *hipódromo*, to go betting on the horses. General Rodríguez had built the stern white concrete stands, but the whole place had a smack of Irishness and spontaneity about it; the betting was reckless and the horses had names like Cold Champagne and Libre Johnny. I think José enjoyed it, and when his horse won, he was briefly possessed by his instincts and cried out in triumph.

Much though I liked the Francos, I detested the clubs.

"In Paraguay," said a recently departed American ambassador, "the poor go to prison and the rich go to their clubs."

This was no exaggeration. There were two that the Asunción froth used: the Centennial and the Yacht Club. There wasn't much between them; both were ostentatious and brash, both twinkled with crystal and gold fittings and had doleful little bands or harpists tucked in alcoves for the amusement of the rich. Both had dining rooms for a thousand well-spread eaters and hot-plates dripping with roasted bullocks, sausages, slabs of *sopa paraguaya* and the massive, unfilleted fishy wrecks of poached *surubí*. All the Legolanders were there: men in Versace, nautical outfits and leather; bent contractors; molls trussed up in mink, boob-tubes and Dior; arms-dealers, drug-dealers, arbitrage manipulators and real-estate tycoons; girlfriends like ponies and mistresses like rocking-horses; a pimp, a hustler and the head of a dynasty eating an entire birth-day cake, watched by his ruminant wife.

I was slightly surprised that these Paraguayans didn't seem any happier than anyone else. For me, the only feelings that these flesh-pots stirred up were bleak, ancestral rumblings of Lutheranism. But what upset me more than the surfeit of indulgence was the nonchalance of consumption; this slender wafer of Paraguayan society—now in its third or fourth generation—had come to regard a life oozing with opulence as a birthright, as pedestrian. I wondered if another stratum of that society—a third of all Paraguayans, to be precise—now regarded life below the poverty line as similarly pedestrian.

The Yacht Club was, if anything, slightly more absurd than the Centennial because all the waiters wore sailor suits. On the next table was Tito Valiante, the restaurateur who shot his mother. He was typically drunk and swigging beer from a champagne bucket with a German-Paraguayan gun-dealer. Their women were sitting across the table look-ing rather weary.

"Would your English friend like to come back to Asunción with us?"

Valiante was now suspended between the tables, blowing gas up at José. "We've got the boat outside."

He waved his hand towards a trim white cruiser that was moored on the Río Paraguay. The German had just acquired it in Miami. A uniformed boatman was mopping the deck.

"$700,000," sloshed Tito, "and it still takes two fucking hours to get out here!"

"Well, John?" It was Virginia.

I blinked.

"I would rather," said this body language, "take my chances with *pirañas* than spend two hours floating along the Paraguay with this fatuous goon."

Virginia read it perfectly and wafted Valiante back to his table in a breeze of unlikely excuses. He soon forgot all about us.

32

In a city of eccentricity it was inevitable that I'd come across someone like Carlos Yegros. Our meeting was not, however, coincidental; I was channelled in his direction by his network of relatives and friends. I don't think they ever thought that Carlos would enlighten me as to the workings of his peculiar city, but they knew that I'd like him all the same.

They were right, of course, on both counts. Carlos was seamlessly charming, untidily handsome and just a little disconnected from reality. I think he must have had some sort of aura, because whenever he took up machinery, it simply stopped working; telephones broke down and cars ground to a halt. But the effect on people was quite different; they seemed oddly transformed. Disappointments turned to amusement and confrontations to banter. Even the dragon in my hotel melted, and the street vendors loved him; he never said "no" to them, just *"Otro día!"*— "Another day!"—as if every relationship was too precious to fracture and should merely be deferred.

I arranged to meet him one morning in the lobby. He strode in wearing wraparound sunglasses and a tweed jacket bulging with broken telephones and oranges. I don't know whether Carlos ever contrived to be comical or whether being comical was just an accident—like being forty-seven, divorced, broke and blind in one eye. These, Carlos' attributes, were probably the equal and opposite elements of tragedy that all comedians are supposed to be possessed of. Like everybody else, I soon found myself laughing and I couldn't think why.

There was only one car that worked for Carlos, and fortunately he owned it. It was a hideous, gnarly Japanese thing which he locked up with a giant brass padlock. It had been broken into so many times that the only way in was through the driver's door. Beyond the driver's seat, I couldn't see where the path went.

"What's all this newspaper for?" I asked. It wasn't just newspaper. The car was packed with rubbish. There were shoes and boxes and pieces of fruit, another tweed jacket, some roller skates and lots of socks. Perhaps it was all propellant and any minute Carlos was going to ignite it and we would hurtle through Asunción like a firework, trailing sparks and rust.

"Just throw it in the back," he said.

As there was no room in the back, I simply burrowed my way into the heap.

"Is there a safety belt?"

"You won't need it here," he said airily. "In Paraguay it is the law to put on safety belts but it is only to make sure that the driver stays near the wheel."

There was no danger of either of us straying far and so we sat there, held in place only by the debris of Carlos' chaotic life.

Eventually we set off into the Asunción traffic. It wasn't really a tour, more a series of incidents that began and ended at my hotel. Carlos couldn't see anything on his left—his blind side—and so we lurched from near-miss to near-miss. The orange-sellers scattered before us and a man carrying a *manguruyú*—a sort of river monster with a beard—dived for the bushes with his gigantic fish.

It was probably a good thing that Carlos didn't see these things, because he was easily distracted. We stopped to buy two sacks of oranges, to visit a Canadian girl (who was out), to surf the Internet in McDonald's (and reduce it to whimpers and dandruff) and to visit three supermarkets. Carlos seemed strongly attracted to supermarkets, and whenever he saw one, he swerved off the road.

"You'll like this one."

The first thing that struck me about the supermarkets was the fact that the glass doors were thickly sheathed in leaflets for lost dogs: lost show-dogs, missing mastiffs, retrievers that failed to return, whelps gone for ever, poodles left in the park, lurchers left in the lurch, hounds, tykes, absent friends and Alsatians. How could the *Asunceños* lose so many dogs? And hadn't I seen them walking themselves round the parks? Now that I came to think about it, I couldn't remember having ever seen a dog and its *Asunceño* together. Perhaps the dogs had had some sort of premonition about the city and had co-ordinated a mass breakout, to take their chances in the wild?

For the dogless, premonition-less citizens, the supermarkets and *"shoppings"* were a sort of consolation. They were invested with the same extravagance of hope as medieval man had lavished on his cathedrals. Whilst they didn't offer access to the afterlife, they lit the path to a place that was—in a way—even more desirable: the Americalife. These places may not necessarily have been recognisable to Bostonians and New Yorkers as home, but they were not of Paraguay either.

Here, bathed in cool, machined air, lit by a million pins of artificial light, the *Asunceños* could communicate with another world. The shopping centres of Babel. It was a world of white skin, yellow hair, lip-gloss, Hellenistic promises ("Aphrodite Boutique") and Anglo-Saxon wizardry. Here, everything was creamy and sterile in a city that was hot and green. There were perfumeries, Swiss coffee shops, computer pods and bouncy castles for children who'd never seen a real one. One shop sold nothing but Barbie dolls and was run—apparently—by Barbie herself, in a stiff pink tutu. It was like a nightmare that felt good to be lost in. I half expected to come across a boutique full of inflatable pigs, but the Paraguayans were now both more and less obscure. One glassy floor up, there was the New America household store, where they could equip themselves as New Americans with ninety-four-piece Sheffield-steel cutlery sets, assault rifles and Louis XV electric hostess trolleys. Nobody was buying anything of course—just touching, stroking, genuflecting.

"Who paid for all of this?" I'd shout after Carlos. The floor was so marbled and polished that I had to skate to keep up.

"Nobody!" he replied.

So it really was a heavenly gift? Or an intergalactic trading post?

"Yes," I insisted, "but somebody must have built it."

"It's a dollar-wash," said Carlos. His good eye was wrinkled up in amusement. The other one looked stonily unimpressed. I imagined that he felt rather as he looked.

I'd heard the expression "dollar-wash" many times before. Every time something twinkly and new went up in Asunción, it was greeted with sneers of "dollar-wash." As to who was laundering what kind of money, people were rather unspecific. This was hardly surprising; despite—or perhaps because of—the most gluttonous corruption in the world, no one has ever been successfully prosecuted. Most people, on the other hand, saw the trail leading back to General Rodríguez—now tucked up in his mini-cathedral—and ex-President Wasmosy—now confined to his luxury bunker. The democracy that they'd so assiduously nurtured had served them well, putting a pleasing veneer on a social structure so unequal and imbalanced. Sultanism had been replaced by neo-sultanism, and the palaces of the new regime were its shopping centres and lustrous malls.

The supermarkets only differed from the *shoppings* in that they spread out like fields of eager landfill rather than climbing glassily upwards. Carlos and I wandered up and down the aisles, looking—he said—for the Canadian girl. She wasn't with the champagne or the garlic sausage, nor did we find her among the hundreds-and-thousands and the chocolate milk. When I came upon a rack of copies of the Marquis de Sade's *Filosofía en el Tocador*, I suffered a temporary loss of reality. Where exactly was I? I was revived by the sight of an Indian child, mottled with dirt, pedalling through the aisles in a plastic play-jeep, trailing price tags and high-pitched store assistants. I felt an unsaintly urge to encourage him but all I could think of was winking. He looked at me blankly and then reversed away as fast as his little eighteen-inch legs would pump him. When I saw that all the Pokémon packets had been eviscerated and their cards scattered around like a fox-raid, I credited the tiny driver with leadership skills. He gave me hope that not all *Asunceños* were held spell-bound by the shopping malls.

Carlos was wriggling free of the spell and had forgotten about the Canadian girl.

"I'll take you to the Botanical Gardens," he said.

I was impressed; our little adventures were beginning to show signs of turning into a tour. Actually, Carlos was toying with a rather different idea; her name was Angela and she was a goddess of science.

I would have been quite happy if we had never reached the Botanical Gardens. I was enjoying spluttering around Asunción in Carlos' self-propelled garbage bin. He kept me constantly drip-fed with intriguing gobbets of information that he'd gleaned, mostly from Paraguayan newspapers.

"Did you know, John, that in your country McDonald's are trying to burn people by serving the coffee very, very hot?"

Whenever he told me any local political gossip, he made a little beak with his finger and thumb and his hand chattered in time to his words. It was a sort of disclaimer; it's only what he'd heard from a funny little bird called "the Gossips."

I asked him about his family. It seems that Carlos was born to a family rich in vicissitudes. His father was a conscientious objector during the Chaco War but had earned extraordinary respect for his courage in carrying water to the front lines. Carlos' brother, on the other hand, was a general in the Paraguayan Marines, an entity which is in itself amazing for a country that doesn't have a drop of seawater. The brother had died from unhealthy overindulgence, and so Carlos' life was dedicated to healthy self-restraint; he was a trader of herbs and minerals.

"That's Freddie Stroessner's house."

Carlos' car was scraping along a kerb on his blind side. Beyond the grinding and gnashing of hub-caps was an area of wasteland, thickly forested with tall, crackling grass. I could just make out the outline of the White House, Washington. It looked dejectedly different from the original; there was no glass in the windows and it appeared entirely hollow. A group of boys were playing football on the terrace.

"It was never finished."

I noticed that this was the Gossips talking, telling tales from its perch on the steering wheel.

"When Stroessner heard that Freddie had stolen all the money from the bank," the beaks paused and jabbed in the direction of another concrete blob, the National Bank, nestling in equally long and rank grass some distance away, "he put a stop to the building."

"How long ago was that?"

"Stroessner left in '89." Carlos whistled though his teeth. "It must have been in about the early eighties. It's been abandoned for nearly twenty years."

"Why is it just left like this?"

The Gossips were on their perch again, twittering. "Freddie's dead—drugs. No one knows who owns the land. It was all fake companies. Now no one will touch it."

It was the last and most enduring monument to the *Stronato*—a wretched eyesore, built with plunder, abandoned in haste and recriminations, ensnared in a tangle of law and weeds.

When we got to the Botanical Gardens, we didn't go straight to see Angela. Instead, we walked through the grounds and the little zoo. This had, until 1862, been the summer estate of Carlos Antonio López, and—however sweaty and ballooned-up on his own fluids he may have been—I had to admire him for the park he chose to rest in when the mercury lurched into the upper nineties. I'd been here before, in summer, but now—in spring—the grounds were feathered in pink *lapacho* blossoms and cool, sweet clumps of frangipani and jacaranda. It was all achingly attractive and I would have been happy to sprawl out on the grass all day, admiring a cocktail party of ostriches and parakeets. But Carlos tugged me away—on through the zoo, to cast an eye over a giant anteater, six jaguars and, of course, Angela.

In terms of their excitement value, Carlos would have put them in that, ascending order. I would have put them the other way round. The giant anteater was exorbitantly exciting. It had a tail that fanned out like a great cloud of ash and its tiny (but brilliant) brain was encased in a strangely conical velvet head, like a Womble from Wimbledon. But this was no Uncle Bulgaria; any dog that ventured to attack it would have found itself admitted into the arc of the beast's paws, and then two sets of claws—each like tailor's scissors—would scythe into the dog's back, take a purchase on the attacker's flesh and pull it apart. Dogs, it was said, simply opened up and spilled themselves like ripe fruits.

By comparison, the jaguars looked rather plump and tranquil—or was it tranquillised?

Angela was already clamped within the arc of Carlos' paws by the time I got up to the curator's building. She was looking neither plump nor tranquil but bore an expression which said that, though she was very fond of Carlos, she wished he was a little less demonstrative. A slender, vigilant hand was already slapping away the Gossips that were nibbling their way across her thigh.

"You like her, John?"

Angela was very pretty and I had to admit as much, in a way which I hoped didn't sound even fleetingly demonstrative. She offered up her lovely face to be kissed. She had cool, creamy skin, deep black tresses and deep black spectacle-frames that ought to have been unappealing but which made her seem inquisitive and paradoxically desirable. It was only when I found out what she did with her days that she plummeted in my league-table of tingles.

I'd felt slightly awkward, standing in front of Angela and Carlos, she rather formal and zoological and he uncomfortably natural, and so I slid imperceptibly into the next room. It was Angela's laboratory.

I was horrified at what I found. Hundreds of dead, chemical eyes were staring at me from their bell jars and tanks, creatures swimming in poison, frozen at the moment that they'd yielded up their lives to science. There was a sickening reek of formaldehyde, and the walls prickled with butterflies and scurvy moths speared on to cemeteries of cork. Here were stuffed monsters too: monkeys leaking straw and stockings from their fatal wounds, the gangly *aguara guasú*—the maned wolf—now grotesquely deformed by taxidermy, and a capybara that had been so plumped up with enthusiastic stuffing that it looked like a clawed cushion. I wiped a little scurf from one of Angela's pickling jars. The eyeball of a whale, the size of a croquet ball but veiled in lacy white tissues of meat. His brain in the next jar. Above them, armadillo foetuses, curled up like armoured roll-mops.

In the remaining jars were Angela's prize specimens—the freaks in a collection of horrors: a calf foetus with two heads, each regarding the other with bleached, unbridled loathing; finally, a pickled puppy with a horn like a unicorn.

I returned to the others. It was now impossible to regard pale Angela without gagging on a tiny, phantom hiccough of formaldehyde. I unhooked Carlos from his specimen and towed him back out into the sunlight.

I'd surprised myself with the volatility of my perceptions. Perhaps I shouldn't have been all that surprised; pickling freaks all day puts even a pretty girl deep into the territory of the weird. It can't do anybody any good to direct their life's energies solely to the preservation of pain, deformity and death. Anyway, my perceptions were going to be nothing compared to those of Asunción's children; their entire appreciation of the animal kingdom was based on an anteater, six dopey jaguars, the runaway dogs, a unicorn and half a dozen other marinated curiosities.

33

"See that?" Carlos had said, on the way back. "That's our railway station."

I knew it well. It took me back to the days of Eddy and Kevin, now nearly two decades ago. We had called in at the station every night for bowls of beef and manioc. In those days, it had been full of grumbling steam trains.

"We've just finished paying for it. After a hundred and fifty years!"

The San Roque railway station was the quirky, mechanical sister to Government Palace. It was both functional and whimsical, a whole series of ideas that had set off as one thing and arrived as another. Partly *hôtel de ville*, partly gothic cathedral, it played on arches, frets, pinnacles and Paraguayan cloisters. There was even a latticed cantilever roof somewhere among all the garnish. The whole ensemble had then been lavished in creams and pavilion yellows and floated off on fancy Roman columns.

The railway station was Whytehead at his most exuberant. Everything that he felt unable to share among the *salon* sophisticates, he now expressed in architectural fantasy. This building made him indulgent and ethereal, qualities that were repulsive to him in the flesh. If San Roque seemed at all ecclesiastical, this was no coincidence. To Whytehead, the completion of the project had become a spiritual quest and it would whip him to the limits of his endurance. In his curly mind, he now saw in these benighted, infested tropics an industrial Jerusalem.

Whytehead zealously urged the works on. Blyth & Co. shipped out the railway parts and dispatched more engineers. A tiny locomotive arrived and was called *Sapuchai*—Guaraní for "The Scream." Benson's of Ludgate Hill sent station clocks and whistles and badges for the porters. Convicts were put to work, digging footings and embankments. A railway company was formed—the first in South America—for "The Paraguay Central Railway." Within six years, sixteen engineers and foot-platemen had constructed an extraordinary forty-five miles of line, snaking off into the Paraguayan jungle.

The first stretch of line was ready and inaugurated on 23 June 1861.

Sapuchai was to haul carriages of spectators to Trinidad, just outside Asunción. She was a pretty little engine with a cigar-shaped funnel and cow-throwers front and back. Tickets were immediately sold out.

The day arrived, and *Sapuchai* was packed. On her first run, she reached the phenomenal speed of fifteen leagues per hour. No one had ever seen anything like it. The Paraguayans were ecstatic. In the excitement, the drivers overlooked the end of the line at Trinidad. *Sapuchai* left her rails and ploughed across the fields. Although she lost two wheels, she was hauled back on to the track and trundled back to Asunción. She managed another eight trips before sundown.

The day was a triumph for Whytehead. He was promoted to Chief State Engineer and his contractors were clapped and fêted. Paraguayans even became curious about their British visitors and began to copy their novel ways. They already had chimneys and now they wanted fireplaces. They started having dinner parties and inviting their friends to supper. They filled their homes with pictures (fox-hunting and erotic Rome) and statues and hung the curtains—English-style—across the windows instead of round the bed. It was the beginning of the age of English sauces and puddings. There was even a new dance—called the London *Carapé*. Paraguay was becoming eccentrically modern.

The station-master was delighted that I wanted to see his station. He was a pleasant man who said good morning to the prostitutes that worked the station steps and shook their hands politely. You're free to wander, he said. And so, I suspected, was he.

The truth was that he had nothing to do. The trains no longer ran. San Roque was now all quiet, only pigeons ruffling the silence. It was as if the nineteenth century had simply ground to a halt. Beautiful old trains stood dumb, feathery and awkward—steam locomotives, First Class, dining-cars with gold letters down the side and carriage-handles cast in Leeds. I even found *Sapuchai,* looking dusty but as coltish as the day when—140 years ago—she'd taken to the fields.

The Morse-code machines no longer chattered down the line and the station clock had stopped. The whistles and the porters' badges from Ludgate Hill had been gathered up for curious visitors and sat in musty cases. I rubbed away the foxing on the glass; an ink-blotter, an engine plate from Newcastle and *Molesworth's Pocket Book of Engineering Formulae.*

Out in the marshalling yard, the weeds grew waist-high and were menaced by sly, green-eyed dogs. The water tower had burst and was weeping on to the tracks. I saw that the station-master was watching me.

"Go on," he shouted, and waved his arms in encouragement. "They won't bite!"

I pushed into the long grass. The people from the *viviendas* had already started to dig up the sleepers to burn them in their shacks. A little way down was a carriage that had been smothered in white paint, even the windows. A small sign was nailed to the door: "Orthodontic Clinic."

At the far end of the yard were three more locomotives. One I recognised as having somehow barged its way on to the front cover of *The Old Patagonian Express*. I didn't think Theroux had ridden the Paraguayan trains. But this mighty iron beast might just have gone anywhere—even now it was loaded up with logs, only waiting for a match to its boilers.

The other two trains were occupied, one by cats and the other by electricians, fast asleep on their toolboxes.

Even after San Roque, Whytehead wasn't finished. There was more to be done. He renewed his contracts with the Paraguayans even though his letters home ached with the pain of separation. He worked on through the nights, through bouts of amoebic dysentery and through the bitterness of his staff, who now regarded him as arrogant and detached.

Whytehead drove them all on with work and scorn. The strain began to tell. Some went on strike. It was the first ever strike on Paraguayan soil. Whytehead had all the strikers fired.

Others turned to drink, consoling themselves with cheap draughts of *caña*. It was dangerously contaminated with acetate of copper and made them mysteriously ill. Several killed themselves and a certain Gibson threatened to cut his wife up. Drink became the greatest killer among the Britons.

Whytehead was ill-equipped to deal with such human failings. In 1863, one of his Paraguayans cracked and lashed out at him with a dagger. The man was taken off and put before a firing squad, but Whytehead was deeply scarred. He began to inject himself with morphine.

Most poisonous of all was his relationship with his manager, another Scotsman called Alexander Grant. Malicious and ill-tempered, Grant had a throat tumour that would only be settled with rum. Like cancer itself, his loathing grew. With San Roque completed, Grant cast around for ways to tip the balance of Whytehead's delicate state of mind.

Isolated by the other English and by Madame Lynch, Whytehead found friendship with the French Minister and his wife, the Cochelets. He professed great affection for their son. Any sort of affection for a Cochelet infuriated Madame Lynch, and she added Whytehead to her black book of undesirables.

Grant saw his chance. He and a feckless oaf called Newton went round to the *quinta* and bellowed under Whytehead's window all night: he was foul and unnatural, he'd seduced the Cochelet boy, he was a hypocrite, a fancy-man, a goat and a sodomite.

It was too much for Whytehead. On 12 July 1864, he tidied up his books and his bottles, fed his animals and left money out for Amos Eaton. Then he injected himself with a solution of pure nicotine, tied his neck to a rafter and jumped.

His body was conveyed to Recoleta on horses supplied by President López. His job went to Alexander Grant and all his property went to the Paraguayan state.

His mother and sister heard nothing for six months and then received word that he'd been replaced in his job. It would be some time before they were to discover that he was long dead.

I made my way back up the track to Whytehead's great lost tropical masterpiece. The station-master was sitting, drinking *maté* in his office. "When did the trains last run?"

I'd missed it by a month.

"Until then," he said, "we went once a week to Areguá. About ninety minutes away."

"Why did it all stop?"

"There was an accident. One of our engines came off the line. It was a great tragedy—a little girl was crushed." He shrugged. "So we're not running any trains."

"So that's the end of the railway?"

"No," he said. "The railway goes on."

He was right. The railway carried on. It carried on swallowing up eleven billion *guaranís* a year. Not a ticket was sold nor an ounce of freight moved. Once, these magnificent trains had rumbled all the way across the country and connected with others for Buenos Aires, for Brazil and the sea. They'd carried fruit and soldiers, girlfriends, sugar cane, Australian socialists to their Utopias and Polish peasants as far from feudalism as they could get. Then, line by line, the system had been overwhelmed by weeds and its sleepers pillaged for cooking. In the last few years it had run a wheezy service to the suburbs, but now even those trains had stopped.

But the railway carried on. It carried on employing nine hundred railway staff. Some, perhaps ten per cent, were *fantasmas*—ghosts—and were purely imaginary, the Mickey Mouses and Donald Ducks. Those that were real were often just *planilleros* or ticket-boys; moonlighting between their railway jobs and other distractions.

"The Paraguayan railways are just an example," an economist had once told me. "The public sector is plagued with nonexistent people doing nonexistent jobs. Who can change it? The World Bank plays zookeeper, trying to get the elephant back in its cage. Sure, there is some movement but it's only the zoo-keeper."

I raised it with Carlos. "Why don't they just shut it down?"

"It's an investment. There are lots of foreigners interested. Really. I heard that the Swedish government want to take it over. Or is it the Italians?" He grinned. "I forget. We get so many offers."

He became suddenly serious.

"We've got to keep it. We've only just finished paying for it."

34

On the Queen Mother's one hundredth birthday, the British Ambassador held a cocktail party in the square of jungle attached to his residence. He'd mustered the remnants of over a hundred and fifty years of British immigration to Paraguay and, each with a tumbler of Scotch in one hand and a fluffy pastry in the other, they just about filled the terrace. The numbers weren't great, but then the number of original immigrants had only been modest. They'd arrived in what could best be described as enthusiastic trickles—unlike the Germans, Russians and Poles, who'd arrived in their hungry tens of thousands.

If the British descendants now seemed rather sparse, it wasn't necessarily because the old engineers and ranchers had wilted under malaria and rum (although some had). Rather, most had flourished all too well and had become—through seepage and human osmosis—richly Paraguayan. As I picked my way across the Ambassador's garden, through bunches of descendants, I realised that these were only the ones who'd remained defiantly—and rather quaintly—British.

Some were very formal and wore old-fashioned clothes. Michael and Peter Burt (the uncles of Martin Burt, the beleaguered Mayor of Asunción) came in tweed suits and brogues, and others wore white tuxedos. Peter Beare Von Vietinghoft-Scheel ("My great-grandfather was a Northumberland man") sported a silvery three-piece suit and a brilliant set of bright red whiskers. He looked like Edward VII would have looked if he'd been coloured in by children.

"I am British," declared a dark, jowly figure, through thick tropical vowels. Rodrigo Wood was clutching his tumbler defensively to his chest as if it might suddenly be snatched away under some arcane nationality rules. "My father served with the British army in the First World War. He was a Royal Engineer!"

This was true, but it was only half the exotic truth; Rodrigo was the descendant of a doomed Australian socialist Utopia, established in Paraguay in 1893. "You must get out to the old colony," said Roddy, and I promised him I would.

Others brought their own tangled memories. There was a delightful little bird called Edna Green, who reminded me of the Gossips and who—feeling the chilly draught of mortality—wanted to share out eighty years of Paraguayan history and, in particular, the parts that impacted on her love life. She was surprised by how many men called Green had wanted to marry her. In the end, she'd settled for the one that was Chief of Stores on the Paraguay Central Railway. She chattered away about her life around Sapuchai Junction as if it were the Home Counties even though (a fact that even she found hard to believe) she'd never actually been to England.

Margarita Kent was there with her great-uncle, Robert Eaton. He'd arrived in Paraguay in 1929, an American farm boy in search of adventure. In his first week, his boss had had his head shot off in an ambush. After that, Don Roberto was always ready with his .38.

"It was all real," he said, in tones of genuine astonishment, as if his whole swashbuckling life had been merely the cowboy fantasy that he'd hoped for.

I merged back, in amongst the half-Britons. There were the Grahams and the Francos (of course) and the Federico Robinsons, who owned several farms each the size of Lincolnshire and just as flat; the Duncans, the Bishop of Paraguay and the Gibsons, who no longer spoke English at all. There was Don Roberto's daughter, Tuna, now in her sixties but still pungent and gingery, Rogelio Cadogan and a beautiful *surrealista* called Ysanne Gayet, who was born in Cheshire and took her name from *The Archers*. I also caught a MacLeod, but there were others whose names I either missed or didn't understand. Many of them now spoke Spanish, or perhaps some Guaraní, among themselves, and some—like Edna Green and Gareth Llewelyn (who was nowhere to be seen)—had never even been to Britain. The mother-country, if they had ever regarded it as such, was rapidly becoming abstract.

In fact, Britain itself was rather slipping from the Paraguayan consciousness. The islands had been marked on local versions of the world map as orange blobs almost denuded of civilisation. Paraguayan military cartographers had erased all but four of the cities and—rather mysteriously—had supplemented the survivors with Inverary and tiny, mealy Wick ("The meanest of man's towns," according to Robert Louis Stevenson, "situated on the baldest of God's bays"). Of course, the British were still vaguely remembered for their railways, but once the last sleeper had been grubbed up, this memory too would be overwhelmed by weeds and forgetfulness.

Interest in Britain had been temporarily reinvigorated by the death of Princess Diana. Her story was told in beach towels: "Princess Wales" and "The People's Princess." They'd even improved on her appearance slightly by giving her big, fruity pink lips and a crown. The papers reported her posthumous love life almost daily; she had far more boyfriends now than she'd ever had time for in her life. Paraguayans were inexhaustibly fascinated, but I soon realised that the fact that the Princess was British was merely incidental. For all it mattered, she could have been Tongan. She was revered for her whiteness, her blondeness and her unbelievable, unbelieved death.

The Ambassador's party compacted itself into a corner of the terrace, like a waggon-train under attack. For a while, all I could hear was breaking glass and splintering dishes as the waiters struggled to break out of the mêlée and then force their way back in again with fresh provisions. A large blood-red cloud of claret was spreading out across Roddy Wood's chest and his wife was dabbing at the ruined shirt with mineral water and wads of irritation. Roddy didn't seem to notice her and was busy summoning ancestral drinks.

"*Camarero! Camarero! Más Johnnie Walker!*"

Then the Ambassador made a speech in honour of HM Queen Mother, and everybody agreed that he'd delivered it with uncharacteristic warmth. Usually, everything about the Ambassador—his wife from Thailand, his silver elephants in the dining room, his sour Scottish accent and his raw complexion—said "I want to be anywhere but here." The Paraguayans were sensitive to his unhappiness and accused him of depression, socialism and frugality—all unpardonable imports. In fairness, it must have been a thankless task, representing a country known only for producing people and things that fell apart or died. The only British ambassador that the Paraguayans could remember with any great affection was the one who'd turned up with his ageing mother instead of a wife. At last the British were taking nepotism seriously.

Things were rather easier for the American Ambassador.

"You buy the job," an American friend told me. "You know, party donations. That kind of thing. We get some great ones here—we've even had a supermarket tycoon."

At least they wanted to be there. The State Department had them penned up in a place the size of a farm at the portentously named 1776 Mariscal López. It was rumoured to be the biggest U.S. Embassy in the world. It was also conspicuously close to the presidential palace; not much happened in Paraguay—people said—without it first going through Supermarket Man's star-spangled check-out.

Although their ambassadors may have found contentment doing a little diplomatic ranching, I never got the impression that Americans were very happy in Paraguay. This was partly because I couldn't erase from my mind the image of the young couple in The Gran, nerves jangling, screaming for airports, hair coming out in clumps. It may also have been because Paraguay—as it seemed to me—was everything that America tried not to be: tribal, crafty and institutionally opaque. The British may have been rather more at home with these attributes.

On the other hand, perhaps Americans were simply taking too seriously the advice offered by "The American Ladies" in their doughty pamphlet. Some of the advice made me clammy just reading it. They suggested examining the servants every eight months for parasitic infestations and venereal disease. Worse, they recommended coatimundis as domestic pets. Coatimundis are variants of the raccoon—sweet but perfectly homicidal. They make up for their absence of pity with fistfuls of dagger-like claws. I have seen them dismember a pile of Christmas presents—mine, to be precise—in three seconds and then, in the next two, fork up an entire Christmas pudding with their murderous cutlery. Only people who want to collapse their nervous systems should get coatis as domestic pets.

The Ambassador's party was coming to an end. Suddenly, to my horror, I found myself standing next to Langan of the old Strangers' Club.

I'm not sure why I hadn't seen him before. He was dressed in a white tuxedo with a rose on the lapel. He hadn't changed much in two decades; there were still the matching tussocks of whiskers and the look of well-earned misery.

"You're a new face around here."

Although I had a feeling that he was about to address me as "Young Man," I was pleased that he'd not recognised me. And why should he? Gareth and I had only sustained his revolting club for one evening, many years ago. "What are you here for?"

If I hadn't drunk so much Foreign Office whisky I might have managed a lie. Instead, I told him I was doing some writing.

"There's no bloody money in writing," he said viciously, and started to tell me all over again about his years of spooning muck for the *Daily News*. "I used to send them stuff from Spain, but no one's bloody well interested in Spain any more. If I want anything published, I have to publish it myself now. I get chicken shit for it."

He took a swig of whisky and captured a passing pastry in his livery hand. "And this lot," he was baring his whiskers at the whole of Asunción rather than just the Ambassador's stragglers, "don't bloody read at all."

Although Langan was now leaking bile profusely, he'd managed to absorb the fact that I was writing. Or at least he'd partially absorbed it; he'd convinced himself that I too was paparazzi. After that, I was never able to unravel this conviction, and whenever I bumped into him around Asunción, he'd palm me with mucky little titbits.

"See him? Covered in red wine? Never been the same since his kid blew his head off with a revolver. Just messing around with other kids." Langan's fishy eye was already swimming greedily among the party stragglers. "Terrible business . . . ," he murmured. "Terrible bloody business."

I tried to protest, too late.

"And that one? He once got so drunk that he fell out of his bedroom window." Langan was concentrating his malevolence on an elderly man in a charcoal suit. "If he hadn't got tangled up in his telephone wires, he'd be dead."

Tempted though I was by the sheer improbability of this one, I managed to change the subject. "I've got to go."

"Where are you staying, young man?"

I told him.

"The Gran Hotel!" He leered. "Full of Nazis! We could do something good on that."

I was troubled by the word "we." I now realised that merely by standing next to Langan, one could be sucked into his human form of quagmire. I heaved myself away.

"Get in touch." His vile invitations were swirling along after me. "I run a little discussion group. We get some good speakers. It's twenty dollars a go."

"How do I find you?" I said, nearly clear.

"We're called the Strangers' Club."

Apart from extracting paltry sums from dupes, Langan now survived by house-sitting for the absent rich. The little extras he charmed out of his lady-friend, a tragic woman who managed the car parks at the Shopping del Sol.

On the way out, I had to pass through the dining room full of silver elephants. I was making reasonable progress when I was ambushed by a night predator with a bulbous pink nose and a head of stiff white bristles. His glasses were so thick that they made his eyeballs huge and meaty, like Angela's unfortunate whale.

"It's like *The King and I*, non?" He waved a furry paw over the outlandish furniture.

"You're not British, surely?" I didn't mean it to sound rude. Generous draughts of whisky and surrealism had made me feel rather disorientated.

"No. I'm Breton, and don't ask me why I'm at the Mother of the Queen's party. I don't know!"

The Queen's Mother of Parties. The Mother's Party for Queens. I had to escape. But first I had to extricate myself from this French badger.

"What are you doing in Paraguay?" I tried.

"I have two adopted children." The eyeballs were gleaming with pride. "I wanted to live somewhere where they would not be called niggers."

35

This wasn't the first time that Frenchmen had sought heaven on Paraguayan earth. Weakened by López's flattery, Napoleon III had agreed, in 1854, to participate in the establishment of a French colony across the river from Asunción, in the Chaco. He dispatched a ship called the *Aquitaine*, a quantity of agricultural hardware and five hundred trusting settlers, mostly Basques and unanimously ignorant. Their corner of heaven was to be a hard-baked rectangle of desert, devoid of not only moisture but also nutrition. The only encouraging feature about the site was its name: New Bordeaux.

The antecedents for the French colony were even less encouraging.

Some years before, a grizzled Rhode Island entrepreneur called Charles Augustus Hopkins had sailed up into Paraguay, with the single aim of extracting as much for his own pocket as possible. He was a vindictive man with hooded eyes and mean, turkey-buzzard features half hidden in a dark thicket of beard. His determination to misinterpret the Paraguayans was admirable, and when his spiteful memoirs emerged many years later, his contemporaries were surprised to find that they contained "nothing remarkable except a seasoning of childish jealousy of everything English."

Hopkins bought himself the job of U.S. Consul in 1852. Using money raised in the United States and a loan from President Carlos López, he then set up a cigar factory and an ambitious industrial colony. But the Paraguayans had grossly overestimated Hopkins' abilities and he'd grossly underestimated the President's pride. Hostilities commenced when Hopkins refused to doff his hat at Don Carlos. At first, the two skirmished in the courts and all the *Yanquis* were expelled. Then things got out of hand. Hopkins persuaded the commander of an American gunboat, the *Water Witch*, that the pride of the United States had been insulted, and they steamed back up the Río Paraguay to demand from the savages a little respect. The Paraguayans responded by peppering the *Water Witch* with cannon-fire, crippling its steering gear and forcing it to float limply back to Buenos Aires. Unsurprisingly, the first industrial colony was closed down and the cigar factory abandoned.

That wasn't the end of Hopkins' war. In 1859, he was back, with a squadron of fifteen warships, to enforce the rights of his American shareholders. The whole adventure cost the U.S. Government $3,000,000 (which was a hundred times the value of Hopkins' investment). In the face of such overweening firepower, the Paraguayans sensibly compromised and agreed on a mixed commission to investigate Hopkins' claim. The commission found in Paraguay's favour. It appeared that the U.S. Navy's mighty manoeuvres had been in vain. Hopkins didn't think so and ungraciously resurrected his claims ten years later, against an economy emasculated by war. Even Paraguay's enemies, Brazil and Argentina, became weary of Hopkins, and in 1871, they sent him packing.

Madame Lynch was determined that the New Bordeaux venture should be a success, particularly because it was French. She had a vision of her noble Gallic peasants tilling a luscious Eden, transforming the dust into bountiful mulch. French society would blossom in the agricultural colony and the benefits would trickle down among the Paraguayans, bringing both culture and much-needed delicacies. Madame Lynch began to see the future in whipped creams and chicory, courgettes and *petit pois*. On matters of farming, she'd inherited all the elegance of Marie Antoinette—and unfortunately much of her insight.

She persuaded Don Francisco to allow her to host a reception on the day of inauguration in 1855. All the dignitaries and diplomats were invited, along with the surly gentry and an unsavoury complement of inflated relatives. She even invited the French Minister, Monsieur Cochelet, and his sniffy wife, and went so far as to make her the guest of honour.

The men were to ride and the women were to travel upstream in a small ship. A barque was found and decorated with streamers, bunting and lanterns. Madame Lynch had her cooks prepare a fine lunch of roasted game, hams, poached trout, pickled fruits, custards, Tokay,

French brandy and baked dainties. The State Military Adviser, Wisner von Morgenstern, offered the benefit of his *éclat* in the choosing of liquors and sweetmeats. Everything was then set out on deck, on trestles dressed in damask and trailed with fresh flowers.

It should have been perfect. Every spoon, every *burette* was in place. Madame Lynch had only overlooked one small detail: her guests still regarded her as an Irish whore.

Almost exactly one hundred and forty-five years after this vaguely promising start to the colony, I was setting out to join another battleship on a jaunt to New Bordeaux—or, as it was now called, Villa Hayes.

The excursion had been organised by a slightly overwound gallant called Oscar, who wore a suit of crushed peach and shoes of delicate ruby calf. He was extravagantly regal on these occasions and had managed to garner an impressive array of dignitaries to attend the opening of a museum. It was generally accepted that no one was interested in the culture that would be dolloped out in the Chaco, but it was otherwise a tempting day out. For the ambassadors, it offered a welcome respite from the ennui of a city that was, to put it delicately, diplomatically serene. For the Great and the Good, it was a chance to shake their feathers out and drink the Paraguayan Navy's whisky.

The *Itaipú* was not, I suspect, as pretty as the vessel that Madame Lynch had commandeered for her trip to New Bordeaux. The gunboat had taken up three hundred tons of Brazilian steel and was designed, it seemed, to appear conspicuous rather than daunting. When I first saw her belching up the river, she looked like a block of flats taking swimming lessons. But closer to, she had a certain appeal. Her crew obviously adored her, and she was lavished in glossy coats of battle-grey and all her brass bits gleamed like jewellery. The crew themselves were dressed in the uniforms of the Imperial German Navy circa 1910—dark-blue serge, black silk cravats and shiny patent boots. The whole glorious operetta was preceded by a launch that was so fat and so forested in heavy machine-guns that there was some concern that she'd capsize.

The midday sun had roasted the decks of the *Itaipú*, and her departure was delayed for an hour by the late arrival of the American Ambassador (as well as the Italian and the Ecuadorian—but she could easily have left without them). Even before they'd set off, the guests were mottled and sticky, but this didn't affect the frothiness of the occasion. The

had turned up in silk gowns and satin shoes and the ratings
d them, squealing and rattling with jewels, up the narrow
nways. I spotted Monsieur Cochelet's successor, the French
dor, among them, resplendent in a cream suit and a fruity tie.
y shadow on the dazzling grey ship was the British Ambassador,
and shrivelled with unhappiness.

e under steam, the courtiers, fops, diplomats and first ladies
away the whisky faster than the ratings could get it round. A
photographer, who was slicked with hair-oil, darted among them
a mouse, draining the paper cups of dregs. He never once got the
cap off his ancient Zenit.

s the *Itaipú* approached the iron-ore wharf at Villa Hayes, the
nch was dispatched, like a hornet, to disperse a little flotsam of row-
g boats. It buzzed around crapulously, rousing the floppy-hatted fish-
men from their fishy dreams and scattering them in the current. I
watched as the fishermen were hauled away by the muscular waters,
open-mouthed with astonishment.

They were entitled to their astonishment. The cultural party that
docked in Villa Hayes was a cargo of caricatures. The dames and fancy
ladies were carried off first and left on the wharf to wade through puddles of rust in their satin pumps. Oscar became even more energetically
thespian. At that point, the American Ambassador made good his
escape, clambering into a waiting limousine and disappearing in a puff
of iron ore.

A small party was on the quay to meet us. First, there was a line of
constables, whose main concern was to ensure that we didn't photograph them ("We're here to make sure you don't photograph us," was
how I interpreted their role). Behind them was the mayor, a gentle,
rather faded man with pale, sandy eyes and a scrub of brittle moustache.
He waved us to a bus and we juddered into his billowing, empty town of
dust and shacks. This is our museum, he said apologetically. More bayonets shattered in the vigour of combat. A stuffed armadillo and the
mothy flag of the Paraguayan Olympic Committee.

The mayor's name was Monsieur Rousillon. He was a descendant of
the survivors of New Bordeaux.

Madame Lynch was discovering that her sumptuous outing was not
bringing out the best in her ungrateful guests.

It hadn't been hard to get them there; curiosity, malice or just plain gluttony had driven them up the companionways. The problem now was to get them to acknowledge her. She greeted each of the ladies graciously as they tripped and trolloped aboard. Each of them ignored her. They simply skirted her formalities and made for their own lively, impermeable cliques on deck. Even Madame Cochelet returned her hostess' niceties with withering condescension. Madame Lynch, the most exquisite of them all, was neatly marooned, alone among her liveried footmen.

Although it was another fiery, tropical morning, the mockery and humidity didn't ruffle her. She ordered the barque to set sail and they moved off upstream. The recalcitrant ladies, meanwhile, bore down on the magnificent luncheon, twittering and grunting with satisfaction. They packed themselves so tightly around the tables that their hostess now found herself blockaded from her own brilliant reception. She responded decisively. Her orders cracked like whips among her footmen.

"Throw it all overboard! Everything!"

To splutters of collective amazement, the footmen heaved the feast into the Río Paraguay. Over the side went the bakes and the roasts, the glasses and glazed fruit tortes, and then went the trestles and the damasks and finally an entire dinner service of Limoges. But Madame Lynch gave her guests plenty of chance to reflect on the lunch that they might have had. She ordered the captain to moor the barque midstream. She then took her chair to a cooler spot in the shade, from where she could survey her lunch party's growing astonishment and thirst.

"By ignoring Madame Lynch from the moment they boarded the ship," one biographer observed, "the ladies had made their point. By the time the captain received permission to weigh anchor and return to Asunción—*ten hours later*—Madame Lynch had made hers."

For Eliza Lynch it was a moment of rare and bitter triumph. She and Wisner clacked with mirth for some days afterwards. But her laughter was hollow and lonely. As well as a triumph, the New Bordeaux picnic had also been a painful reminder of her isolation.

For New Bordeaux, the incident was merely a portent of the hunger and acrimony that would destroy the colony. Most of the settlers were back home within two years—destitute—and their ship, *Aquitaine*, was sold to pay off their debts. A few, however, remained, scratching food from this withered extremity of the Chaco.

There was only one beneficiary of this colonial fiasco. Ironically, it was Madame Lynch: she got a new French chef.

Our cultured group, now smudged and thirsty, was wafted back towards the bus. I asked the mayor if the Rousillons were the only surviving descendants of the French colony. He sounded surprised.

"No," he said, "there are a few of us."

He started to reel off their names. In his list, there seemed barely a hint or a shadow of the last hundred and forty-five years: the Mouchets, the Castagnets, the Cottets from Lyons and the Touchet-Cottets, the Bouviers, the Renauts and the Hellions from Bordeaux.

Old Bordeaux, that is.

36

After a prickly honeymoon, Madame Lynch's Paraguayan "marriage" began to turn to thorns.

She was no nearer securing a lawful union with Don Francisco, even if she'd wanted one. Her lawyers didn't seem able to extract her from the match that she'd entered as a child, even though—as a child—she'd always been told that the match was of doubtful validity.

But getting herself knotted up with the López dynasty can hardly have been an attractive option, even if there was no other. Although the death of his father, in 1862, had invested Francisco with power, it had not graced him with dignity. He was still greedily inserting himself into the daughters of the aristocracy, preferably the virgins, although he wasn't always fussy. Those that resisted him, like the gorgeous Pancha Garmendia, "the Jewel of Asunción," would pay a high price for their treasonous modesty. Garmendia's death—some years away yet—would be particularly agonising.

López was also still greedily inserting oily meats and stuffings into himself. The presidential corpus was now bloated and gargantuan, rather as the previous encumbent's had been. Washburn—still smarting from the fancy dress lampoonery—provided the world with this description of his old friend:

He had a gross animal look that was repulsive when his face was in repose. His forehead was narrow and his head small, with the rear organs largely developed . . . His face was rather flat, and his nose and hair indicated more of the Negro than the Indian. His cheeks had a fullness that extended to the jowl, giving him a sort of bulldog impression . . .

For Eliza, extracting herself was not an option. It was not just a question of losing a little wool on the way out of the brambles; she was deeply entangled. She'd had seven children by López and there was no prospect of support from any other quarter than the resources of their father.

Enigmatic as she was, it's hard to say what, if any, fulfilment Eliza found in her association with López. The crueller commentators of her time speculated that the children weren't born of any affection and that Eliza had even tried to stifle their existence. One account had her riding hell-for-leather round Asunción during her second pregnancy, trying to procure a miscarriage. But this wasn't the behaviour of a woman who was temperamentally cunning, physically Junoesque and—as a mother—exemplary. The truth is that she was delighted when Corinne was born on 6 August 1856, and was devastated when, six months later, the child died.

Corinne Adelaide Lynch was buried at La Recoleta, and I visited her tomb on the day of my visit. It was very white and prominent and obviously a spot much favoured by the grave-diggers. It was siesta time and they were sprawled out on her bed of marble. At the head of their cool couch was an obelisk mounted on four sets of thick claws, and a plinth decorated with scallops and a winged hour-glass. In its design, the spirit of Eliza was almost palpable; she'd added the misremembered words of an English poet, Samuel Taylor Coleridge:

> Ere sin could blithe or sorrow fade
> Death come with friendly care
> The lovely bud to Heaven conveyed
> And made in beossom there

I could almost hear her stumbling through the words, just as her Guaraní mason had stumbled on "blossom." It was, for me, the only time that Madame Lynch ever spoke up from her past. After that, she moved back into her half-world; powerful, controlling, conjuring and deeply elusive.

President Francisco López—bulldog, bully and glutton—still nurtured an ambition to be the resurrected Napoleon Bonaparte. "His solitary qualifications for the character," remarked another waspish contemporary, "were that, like his prototype, he was fat and liked women." These qualities were good enough for Don Francisco, but he was exasperated by the slow pace of imperial growth. Then he hit upon a scheme which, he envisaged, would see him crowned "Emperor Francisco Primero" within the year. It was a scheme of breathtaking cheek: he would conquer Brazil by marriage. He immediately started blasting off proposals to Isabella, daughter to Dom Pedro II, Emperor of the Brazilians.

Naturally, there was no place for Eliza Lynch in this design, and for the first time in her Paraguayan adventure, she had to contemplate the prospect of being marginalised. Francisco's wrestles with the gentry's daughters had never worried her; those pups were merely vessels for his excess of virility. Isabella was a rather different prospect.

Fortunately, her father didn't regard Isabella as a López prospect at all; the Emperor had absolutely no intention of coupling her to that ridiculous feathered savage in the interior. He pronounced Francisco to be "licentious, dissolute and cruel" and returned his lewd proposals with as little decorum and as much venom as possible. To add insult to injury, he had Isabella married into the French royalty, to a bloodthirsty dilettante called the Comte d'Eu.

Francisco erupted. He had never been so thoroughly and unmercifully insulted. Nor could he remember a time when he'd not been given exactly what he wanted. Something began to change inside him. He would never be quite the same again. From now on, the anger was always there, dangerously near to the surface. It was an alarming and precarious life for those around him.

"His eyes, when he was pleased, had a mild expression," noted one observer, "but when he was enraged the pupil seemed to dilate till it did not appear to be that of a human being, but rather a wild beast goaded to madness . . ."

For Madame Lynch, the path ahead was unclear. Her position as the presidential concubine was secure, and the President, in his scribbly moods, even became a little dependent on her. But what had she become queen of? The Argentines now regarded López as "a dangerous cacique heading a wild and alarming tribe of savages." Brazil had become a sworn enemy and Asunción's mob was inflamed on a diet of "bread and games." López ordered months of carnivals and flung open the hippodromes, the bullfights and the distilleries. There were endless patriotic balls and the President's grotesque masked clowns—the *camba rangas*—moved among the revellers extorting money for his war chest. Merchants were forced to subscribe their profits, and the terror began.

It is a measure of the intensity of that terror that, of López's original cabinet of ten, only two would be spared execution. Of his mistress' ladies-in-waiting—originally three—only one would survive. The accused usually danced to their deaths to the accompaniment of a fine polka called *La Palomita* (a charming tradition revived in the *Stronato*). Other potential opponents were incarcerated for life (which would be short) and then forced to pray for the happiness of the Chief Magistrate who'd condemned them. It was a period known as the Great Circus. The next stage would be the Grand War.

To Eliza Lynch there seemed no escape from the inevitable calamity. But just in case a pathway cleared, she'd opened a bank account in Edinburgh and had started feeding it with loot.

37

On its saint's day, the little town of San Lorenzo held a fair and a bullfight.

When I told friends in Asunción that I wanted to go, most were unimpressed. San Lorenzo was far enough outside Asunción to be regarded as the countryside, and although *Asunceños* were dependent on the interior, they preferred to ignore its existence. The countryside was coarse and backward. Every now and then they'd come across country people dancing in their restaurants, and although their bottle-dances and cooing, dovish waltzes were vaguely diverting, the idea of participating was rather distasteful. Cock-fighting and bull-fighting came within the same category.

"These bullfights," advised the American Ladies, with their usual delicacy, "are colourful but rather informal affairs. In fact, sometimes if a bull is made to fight too long, he may just lie down in the middle of the bull-ring for a rest . . ."

It took me some time to find anybody who was prepared to come with me to the San Lorenzo fair. It wasn't something that I felt I could enjoy by myself. Then, to my surprise, I found a volunteer: Carlos Yegros' student cousin, Silvia.

Silvia and her mother lived over on the other side of Asunción. Although I went to their house several times, I still have no idea exactly where it was. Silvia used to come to my hotel to collect me. It always seemed to be at night. Like Fluff, she had a jeep and, like Fluff, she launched it across Asunción like a torpedo. But this torpedo seemed to go on for hours, ducking and weaving down inky conduits and gutters, across great blackened ring-roads and junctions of snarling metal. Eventually we would stop somewhere very dark and I'd be hustled in through a back door. It was like being bundled into the hideaway of a secret organisation.

These early impressions turned out not to be so far removed from the reality. Silvia and her mother were the bohemian twiglets on a mighty family tree of politicians, the Caballeros. In fact, almost every new spasm of Paraguayan political thought had been initiated by a Caballero. The family was congenitally factious. Silvia's great-grandfather, General Bernardino Caballero, had been the founder of the Reds—the Colorado Party—and his son had then been president of the Blues, the *Liberales*. Silvia's father, splitting away from both parties, had formed the Greens—the *Febreristas*—who were originally fascists but who became revolutionary leftists and then expired. Finally, in an act of ancestral reunion, Silvia's brother, Guillermo Caballero Vargas, had formed the rainbow party, Encuentro Nacional.

"Encuentro," confided Silvia, "was a total disaster."

Her mother, Lucy Yegros, had nothing of her husband's political instincts and was rigidly *avant garde*. She had all the eccentricity that comes of being a Yegros. At first, she rather alarmed me, with her black velvet suits and skull-caps, cropped grey hair and brooches like car parts. She had an old Fiat that she'd painted red, white and blue, an awful parody of the Paraguayan tricolour, and at full throttle, she looked as if she was off on a bombing raid. She was, however, far less dangerous than she appeared. Only occasionally did she drop bombs into the conversation.

"I met Mengele several times," she'd say and then go on to sketch the Beast of Auschwitz as a dreary non-entity. "He was often around here." She waved a hand over her mysterious neighbourhood.

As I got to know her, it surprised me less and less that Lucy knew the Nazi war criminals; she knew everyone. I suspect everyone knew her. She was tirelessly conspicuous and conspicuously theatrical ("Nothing is chance!" she once roared at me across a restaurant). She'd travelled everywhere, soaking up languages and surrealism in Italy, France and Japan. Now she was back in Asunción, doyenne of the art scene and herself an exuberant painter. The two recurring themes of her paintings told the story of a strange life: a woman with unnaturally large breasts, each one a gramophone record, and cats wearing football strips.

Silvia and Lucy lived alone in the house. Silvia's father had died many years ago. I was right that the house was only a back door. The front end had been sold off at a low point in the family fortunes.

Silvia detonated her jeep, and with the engines exploding, we blasted off towards San Lorenzo. I was so proud to be sitting in the cockpit with my beautiful, angular, creamy-skinned pilot that it hardly troubled me that I was about to be wiped out in a catastrophic high-speed pile-up. As we flew along, she gave names to the lights that streaked past our windows. Near San José, there were some pink ones.

"The love motels! This is love city. People rent these places by the hour—or less."

Did she mean they were brothels?

"Not necessarily. Paraguayan boys can't take their girlfriends home and so they bring them here."

"But what happens if the girlfriend gets pregnant?"

"It doesn't really matter." She shrugged. "All the maids have babies. Ours does."

A truckload of Colorado supporters was thundering towards us, rockets and flares bursting out of the back. Silvia nipped to one side, ducked into the verge and then was back out on the road again.

"In fact," she said absently, "my great-grandfather never married my great-grandmother."

General Bernardino Caballero had had rather a reputation for irrepressibility. In war, he'd chopped his way deeply into the enemy's lines, and then, in captivity, he'd chopped his way back again. In peace-time, he was equally uncontainable. With dangerous good looks and a ready spark, he was soon the father of forty-five children by a dozen women.

"He is a fine-looking man," observed an English traveller in 1881, "with no Indian blood in his veins, indeed more like a fine specimen of an English squire than a Paraguayan. The expression on his face is kindly and no man in the country is more respected and loved."

The squire of love then bounded into the presidency of his own party, the Reds, and then on to the presidency of the Republic itself. It was not a position where his cut and thrust was at its most appreciated.

"He is not a great diplomatist," continued the traveller, "but is the very man for Paraguay in the present day—a plain, straightforward trooper."

What did Silvia's great-grandmother do with her straightforward trooper?

"She threw him out," said Silvia matter-of-factly.

More lights appeared. It was San Lorenzo. Who was he?

"Our saint. He got barbecued in the Inquisition."

Silvia had slowed down, and some barrack huts unblurred themselves from the darkness. It was Silvia's university. Did she stay in those huts?

She feigned a look of horror. "Those were the huts for the poor kids! I drove back into Asunción every night." She paused. "Do you know, I never knew they had poor kids until I got to university?"

We carried on into San Lorenzo. The outskirts were flattened out by truck parks and cement stores. Somewhere among them, we stopped and picked up Juan-José, who Silvia had known at university. He lived behind big iron gates in a pound of bickering, yellow-hackled dogs. Juan-José was cumbersome and droopy-lidded and desperately in love with Silvia. She pretended to ignore it. "He's a country boy," she'd explained. "He is not one of us."

The San Lorenzo fair was in its third and last day. It was like trudging into a giant hangover. The air was muzzy with roasted offal and disjointed songs and the farm-hands—the *peones*—were dreamy and broke. Ancient, battered fairground machines whirled emptily around our heads, animated scrap. Some of the *peones* were still colourfully drunk.

Others were already tucked up in their hats and leathers, snuggled into doorways and gutters. Around their feet nipped flurries of icy sand, brought in on a goose-pimpling southerly. Blunt with rum and poverty, they slept on.

Juan-José elbowed us into the crowds. He dropped a wad of notes on the poker table and, to murmurs of approval, lost the lot. He hardly noticed, he was so luminously happy. Silvia went with him on *La Rueda*, the Big Wheel. He could hardly believe his luck as they were harnessed together and *La Rueda* cranked them off the ground. It lingered deliciously at the midnight of its revolution and then jolted them back down to earth. Juan-José will remember those dangerous mechanical pleasures for ever. In his giddiness, he bought us presents of buttery beef. When they were gone, there were envelopes of cheese and manioc, all fried up in a glue of pig lard.

"Only *El Gordo* does them this good," he grinned, swollen with pride and pork grease. The eponymous Fat One was now heaving tongues and giblets into a pan of spitting oil.

"I think we'd better go," said Silvia sweetly. "Or we'll miss the bull-fight."

We needn't have hurried. The bullfight didn't start until two hours after its billing. "We don't start until the stadium is full," said the gatekeeper.

The stadium had been erected specially for the occasion on some wasteland. It was like a great basket, made of rough planks lashed together, and it creaked this way and that with the mood of the crowd. In the centre, in the bowl of the structure, was the arena, which was curtained with thick nets to keep its monsters in. The beasts were kept in a crate up one end, and every now and then it was stoked with a stick until its sides thundered with the reassuring sound of angry hooves. The audience shuddered with excitement.

The stands, however, remained only half full and the spectators packed themselves up one end, in the lee of the cruel Antarctic wind. This caused the stadium to be slewn, like a tipsy rhombus, to the north. When a fight broke out on the south side, everybody rushed over to watch and the stadium, momentarily upright, then scissored to the south. As the fight never reached a satisfactory conclusion, our seats pitched and yawed all evening on swells of curiosity.

Eventually, two clowns were released into the arena, to roars of meaty laughter. They sang songs that mocked love and played their guitars behind their backs and twanged them with their teeth. They made jokes in a strange language that made the stadium sway around with pleasure.

"It's a Jopará," panted Silvia, clenched with laughter. "A mixture of Spanish and Guaraní. Everybody loves it in the country."

"What are they saying?"

Silvia cocked her head. The clowns were poking tongues and arses at a woman in the front row. "Hear my salty words!" came the translation. "Your mother is dead!"

The crowd, the stadium, lurched with delight.

Then the first bull was released—an anxious-looking zebu. Loudspeakers thrilled with polkas, the trumpets and drums urging the bull to fight. The clowns did headstands on him and wove themselves between his legs, but he still refused to move. Even the sight of a toreador in a suit of lights didn't impress him. The toreador was not armed. Not a drop of blood would mar the evening.

"Espectacular!" roared the speakers.

The bull was taken back to his crate, looking bemused. Between each contest, the clowns were back at their prattle. They leered and pouted and pumped and wriggled. They clambered up and down the nets and brought a boy on and hauled three foot of ribbon from his backside. There were whoops of approval.

"Magnífico!"

A little girl came on in a miniskirt and danced in time to "Sex Bomb." Her mimicry of an adult world was compellingly hideous. The stadium seethed and wobbled with appreciation.

"Sexy! Sensacional!"

The last bull was a little more like the steaming, snorting monsters that the conquistadors had brought from Castille. He had thick, glossy black flanks, strong horns and a weighty pair of velvet balls.

"Superman toro!"

The clowns fled up into the netting and sat up there whimpering like monkeys. A lone toreador ducked around the arena, trying to snatch the furious animal's tail. Eventually, the bull tossed him lightly into the crowd.

"Maravilloso!"

But it was soon over. The toreador recovered his dignity and the bull ran out of steam. As the American Ladies had predicted, he lay down and refused to get up. A clown came down from the netting, sat on the bull's nose and dispatched him with a loud fart.

I thought the stadium was going to collapse.

38

"If you want to eff your life up, that's cool," said Silvia Caballero, "but if you want to eff your country up, that's not."

We were trying to extract ourselves from the wreckage of the San Lorenzo fair. Silvia was furrowed with gravity. Even though Juan-José—who'd worshipped President López all his life—trotted at her side, she dug deeper.

"López was mad. He effed up Paraguay. But you know what? My great-grandfather did the dirty on López, and—to me—that's cool."

I couldn't think what was coming next. In Paraguayan history, General Caballero was López's loyal lieutenant, the national hero and the survivor of all the conspiracy charges that had devoured the court of López.

"My grandmother told me everything." We were nearly back at the jeep, crunching over little drifts of sand and icy bones.

"Caballero was having an affair with Madame Lynch." Silvia smiled mischievously. "Why else do you think she stayed around?"

39

The murder of Vice-President Argaña had left a gap in the hierarchy. With President Cubas fled, González Macchi had furtively slipped into the presidency but that still left the vice-presidency to be filled. There had to be an election.

"The tragedy of Paraguayan politics," one of the half-Britons had told me, "is that the Paraguayans have never had the leader they actually wanted."

It was a curious thought. The *Stronato* could hardly be described as a period of free will. Since then, there had been four presidents: in the first election, Rodríguez had ambushed the electorate with the suddenness of his democracy (he'd also got an impressive number of votes from dead people and Donald Ducks); in the second, Wasmosy had cheated Argaña out of the primaries; in the third, Cubas had taken the votes for Oviedo (who was under disqualification for involvement in a coup that may never have happened); the fourth president, Macchi, hadn't been elected at all but was filling dead men's shoes.

Even more disturbing was the thought that, of the last two presidencies, if the choice had been put fairly and squarely to the Paraguayan people, they'd have chosen Lino Oviedo on both occasions. Why was he so popular? Everybody had different explanations.

He was brilliant in Guaraní and this triggered deeply patriotic obsessions among the Paraguayans of the interior.

He was strong and offered stability in a country where stability was dangerously overvalued by those traumatised by the 1947 civil war.

"He is," said many, "the only one who can beat the criminals."

"He *is* a criminal," said another. "He's the only one with enough money to do the job."

One man—a lawyer—thought it had something to do with Lino's sex life. "He's homosexual. I can't see how else he gets his support."

It was all academic; Lino was in prison in Brasília. But it did give rise to a difficult question: what would Lino's supporters, the *Oviedistas,* do?

There was only one party dominating Paraguayan politics, and that was General Caballero's old Red party, the Colorados. They had now ruled the country for the last fifty years. Graham Greene, working on *Travels with My Aunt* in 1969, had found Asunción completely dipped in Colorado:

> There were red flags everywhere: you would have thought that the town had been taken over by the Communists, but red here was the colour of conservatism. I was held up continually at street crossings by processions of women in red scarves carrying portraits of the General and slogans about the great Colorado party. Groups of gauchos came riding into town with scarlet reins . . . Decorated cars carrying pretty girls with scarlet camelia blossoms in their hair went by. Even the sun looked red through the morning mist.

Greene's anti-hero, Henry Pulling, is at one stage beaten up by party thugs for blowing his nose on a red handkerchief. This sort of goonery was uncomfortably close to the reality; Colorado authority permeated deep into Paraguayan life.

Quite apart from repression—the *pyragüés* and *La Técnica*—the Colorados had made the Paraguayans dependent on them. The army, which—during the Civil War—had been nine-tenths *Liberal* and rebel, was purged and replaced with Colorado men. They then took over the civil service—without a party card, there was no job. By the end of the *Stronato,* at least an eighth of the working population had to be Colorados before they could begin to work.

Things were no better after the *Stronato.*

"There are now a hundred and sixty thousand civil servants," one despairing *Liberal* told me. "Let's say ninety per cent of them are dependent on the Colorados for their jobs and that each job determines say four family votes. That's six hundred thousand votes—the government only needs nine hundred thousand to win. This way, the Liberals may never win."

But the death of Argaña changed all that. The Colorado Party was now deeply split; the *Argañistas* wanted the dead man's son, Félix, in the presidential palace and they wanted Oviedo's head on a platter. They offered a $100,000 reward for his capture. It was hardly a partnership. The *Oviedistas,* meanwhile, threatened to take their share of Colorado votes to the Liberals.

Suddenly, the chessboard started looking rather different.

Old Colorados acted with panic. "If the Liberals win," announced the chairman of the party, Bader Rachid Lichi, "there will be a civil war."

Félix Argaña tried to reassure the country that that would not be the case but when a middle-aged man threw a Molotov cocktail at him on a visit to the prickly north of the country, he must have had his doubts. Colorados armed themselves. In Hernandarias, the party boss and his canvassing staff—all armed with sub-machine-guns—were arrested for assaulting the chief of police. With no differences in policies, the parties had had to find other ways to make an impression.

Once again, Asunción erupted into political colours.

This time, however, there was as much blue as red. The street of my hotel might start the day in blue and then be red by lunchtime. Soon every surface was covered in a thick crust of fly-posters. Sometimes, the glue-teams worked so intensely that it was possible to watch them following each other up the street, the leading team gluing and the one behind peeling their posters away and replacing them with their own. When they ran out of posters, they took to their rivals' work with pens and paint, adding red noses, whiskers and horns. Argaña was an easy target; his face was so hairless and empty.

The Liberal candidate was more difficult to defile because he was already covered in hair and his huge bulk filled every spare inch of his posters. He looked like a bear stuck in a box. It was also rather harder to defile his reputation; allegations of impropriety wouldn't stick. In this candidate, there was a real danger of probity. Even his name was growly and severe: Julio César Franco. To soften the effect a little, he campaigned as "Yoyito"—or Little Joe.

But would the *Oviedistas* vote for him? A long, bleeding splash of words along Independencia spelt out the consequences for baby-face Félix: *LIBERALES* + *OVIEDISTAS* = *KILLER TEAM.*

The police and army put all their men on the streets. Some of them looked as if they'd marched back from the thirties to save Asunción from civil war; there were rain capes and tin hats, rifles from the Chaco War, webbing and Mannlicher bayonets. Others put on plastic armour and crow-stepped up and down in front of the *Congresso*. It was a determined show of force, but only the peanut seller and I were watching.

The city had become seized with lethargy. *Asunceños* were weary of politics, of its *pó-caré*, its twistedness, its glue and its awful leaflets. Years of deceit had left them unable to relate to politics rationally; to criticise, to analyse, to question. They just wanted it all over. "Don't vote," urged the bumper stickers.

"I'm certainly not going to vote," the lactating mother had told me, through mouthfuls of steak and strawberry milkshake. "What's the point?"

I shouldn't have been surprised that when election day came, the city centre was deserted. Even the police had abandoned it. It felt as though democracy had overslept. But, somehow, I suppose people did vote— they had to by law—and by the evening, the results started to seep out.

I decided to await the outcome in The Lido bar. I still had an idea that it was the centre of Paraguay, and as a practical matter, it was one of the few places open. There was also something satisfyingly obstinate about it: it had been at the rim of several revolutions, had seen the *Stronato* come and go—and then the neo-sultans—and had refused to change. It had barely had a new coat of paint. There were the same tangerine ladies and the same dishes of steaks and *pirañas*. Even the customers didn't seem to have changed much, still blank, intense and watchful. I couldn't think of anybody more appropriate to bring me the news of Paraguay's future than The Lido's duckling waitresses.

The *Oviedistas*, they told me, had teamed up with Little Joe's liberals.

Then they brought me a steak the size of a paving slab. By the time I'd chewed my way from one end to the other, the liberals were in the lead. By one per cent.

A faint ditty of fireworks crackled over the city and then all was quiet again. It was a beautiful, torrid night; vintage Asunción, treacly and whispering with surprises. But few had ventured down to the Plaza—or into The Lido—and the waitresses were bored and chattery. There was nothing to do but wait and study the diners. The one next to me was a prostitute. Her short, plump fingers were tipped in lacerating crimson and her belly lolled into her lap. She ordered a fish and a cake of pig fat and maize and scooped it all up in her nails. Her chrome-plated phone never rang.

The Reds never regained the advantage. At midnight, I walked home through a city hot and furtive and stunned into silence; the Colorados had suffered their first election defeat for over half a century.

There was no civil war. For a while, the Reds contested the election in the courts—more from a sense of disbelief than grievance. It was a sign of the times that the Supreme Court decided against them on every charge. The *Argañistas* abandoned conflict and reverted to conspiracy. They wound up their persecution of the *Oviedistas* and called off the *pyragüés* and their surveillance. The two factions then bedded down together, in a sleazy, reproachful truce. They now had to wrest back control.

A week after the election, Asunción's schoolchildren were ordered into the streets and made to clean up. They scraped the city clean of politics. Down came Félix and Little Joe and all their cheeky derivatives: Dracula, Hitler and the red-nosed reindeers. The walls were scrubbed of controversy and the paper battle-cries were bundled up and burnt. When it was done, all that remained of the fight were the shadowy rectangles of glue.

40

The day after the election, I left The Gran Hotel and moved back downtown. When I told people that I wanted to be nearer the old heart of the city, they shrivelled with horror.

"You'll be robbed," they said with disconcerting harmony.

Virginia advised me to hide all my money in my socks. Others advised me not to go out at all. "It's like the Bronx in London," said Fluff.

"We don't have a Bronx," I protested.

She wasn't interested. Asunción had one. For those old enough to remember the sinister tranquillity of the police state, it now seemed that the city was in the grip of chaos. A crime rate had arrived and the fear of crime had seeped out into the suburbs like cholera. The police hustled the fear along by sending up clouds of statistics into the air waves every morning. In their broadcasts, crime was visited upon the city in awesome columns and rows.

"Motorbikes stolen in Zone 3, two. Cars stolen, four. Property recovered, nil. Motorbikes stolen in Zone 4 . . ."

Who was listening to this fretful mantra? Everyone, it seems. People talked of emigrating and gun sales tripled. The banks snapped up nearly all the police to guard their money (the rest busied themselves defending police stations). Homes were patrolled by liveried private soldiers. Even the kindergartens had armed guards, usually little fat ladies with revolvers and plenty of malice.

Most people fed their fears on bloodthirsty newsprint. The worst was *Crónica*. Its photographers had a nose for mutilation. Every day, half the nation terrified itself on three scarlet pages of suicides, murders, drunks burst apart by lorries and torsos slashed with knives. There was little respite in the next three pages—spreads of teenage girls apparently gagging to be violated—and then *Crónica* plunged its readers back into the afterworld. "Taxi Driver Mutilated. Left Arm and Ear Amputated." There was no other news from around the world (except for Princess

Diana's persistent, ghostly love affairs). Life was just a brief bloodbath. Small wonder that the Paraguayans were now—like their ancestors—frightened of the dark and of their eerie forested city.

Despite the concerns of my friends, I moved into the centre.

I took a room in an ugly house on Fulcrencio R. Moreno called Residential Itapúa. It had been built by an aviator called Ríos whose days of wartime glory were remembered in a propeller of black pebbles, embedded in the garden wall. After the Chaco conflict, Dr. Ríos had made a tidy fortune as a dermatologist. There was a portrait of him in the hallway of the house, taken at Niagara Falls in 1949, wearing a thick coat of fox pelts. As his practice had expanded, so had his house, creeping in lumps and growths first into the garden and then up the back. Inside, everything was painted cheese and pale green in deference to the unhealthy skin on which he'd prospered. His fortune made, he'd then put a brave face on the whole thing—with an enormous pair of Ionic columns.

On his death in 1998, Dr. Ríos had left the house to his daughter, Miriam, and her husband, Víctor Giosa. Víctor described himself as Sicilian, but as to the details, he was hazy; he wasn't even certain where Sicily was and had no idea which generation of his threaded ancestors had finally abandoned it and wandered off to South America. Although—with his family—Víctor was affectionate, he was not the provider that the doctor had been. He had a fry-up in Tacuary Street and a look of deeply ingrained penury. When the Ionic columns had erupted in a mange of neglect, he and Miriam had decided to take in lodgers.

Dr. Ríos' house had made an easy transition from cheesy home to cheesy *pensión*. Every little nook and graft of the doctor's labyrinth was colonised with beds. There were tiny cells for salesmen and dormitories for the Peace Corps "kids." On the second floor lived two old ladies and a terrier that hated me with clockwork yaps. I usually had the room above them, an architectural afterthought on the roof. Although by day it was too hot to sustain life, at night it was a thoughtful place from which to survey the neighbourhood. It looked out over a sierra of corrugated rust, and some nights, power-cuts swept over this landscape like sciroccos, enveloping it in silence and fiery darkness.

At breakfast, the hallway became a dining room. The only decoration

Madame Lynch, the Irish courtesan who would be Empress of Paraguay.
The Guaranís remember her in her ball-gown, armed, bloodied and erotic.

LEFT: Dr. Gaspar Francia, "The Supreme One" (1766–1840), whose brand of absolute power was much admired in Europe. He ruled with savagery, genius, madness and extreme probity (even returning his unused salary to the Treasury).

ABOVE: Carlos Antonio López (1790–1862), who scared off all opposition by the sheer monstrosity of his appearance. Despite personal engorgement, his presidency brought wealth and European sophistication to the isolated republic.

LEFT: Francisco Solano López. Obesity and toothache brought out his less attractive side but diplomacy and warfare would reveal "The Monster."

ABOVE: The grave of Madame Lynch's daughter, Corinne, today. She is buried in Recoleta cemetery, among those who—in life—had spurned her mother.

LEFT: Captain Richard Burton, whose best-seller brought the world news of the "Sebastopol of South America."

LEFT: Robert Cunninghame Graham (1862–1936), explorer, rebel, gaucho and co-founder of the Scottish Labour Party.

ABOVE: Wilfrid Barbrooke Grubb (1864–1929), the "Livingstone of South America."
He rode deep into the Chaco, introducing the Indians to God and vicarage teas, and was almost butchered for his efforts.

From the left: the naturalist Graham Kerr with his rescuer, Chimaki,
and another great survivor, the wily Dr. William Stewart.

ABOVE: Paraguayan soldiers with a jaguar in the Chaco, at around the time of the war of 1932–35.

INSET RIGHT: Present-day Chilupí Indians of the Chaco, wearing European clothes but living in another world.

BELOW: The Braun family, skinning a pig, the Menno colony, circa 1930.

ABOVE: Support for Hitler in the German *Kolonies* of the 1930s. The Reich sent schoolbooks and flags and, after 1945, some three hundred Nazis sought refuge in Paraguay.

BELOW LEFT: Dr. Josef Mengele in about 1948. Never happy in Paraguay, "The Angel of Death" was soon on the run again.

BELOW RIGHT: Martin Bormann, Hitler's Reichsminister. According to the Paraguayan secret police, Paraguay was his last stop—at least in life.

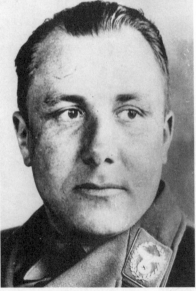

LEFT: General Andrés Rodríguez (1924–1997), smuggler-in-chief and usurper of the throne, he lived in a miniature of Versailles, and became unnervingly saintly.

RIGHT: Pastor Coronel, Chief of the Secret Police and Chief Torturer. He re-introduced music to the art of interrogation.

General Alfredo Stroessner, described by Graham Greene as looking like "the amiable well-fed host of a Bavarian *Bierstube*." His dictatorship lasted thirty-four years, outlasted only by Kim Il Sung. Stroessner took a fifteen-year-old mistress and called himself "The Lighthouse."

was a brass frieze of The Last Supper and a Houses of Parliament ashtray from London. Miriam wasn't interested in breakfast and left it to her daughters. She left most things to her daughters. The two heavy teenagers—like a pair of book-ends—padded around noiselessly, keeping everything upright and orderly. Most of the time they actually ran the place and Miriam disappeared on long, mysterious shopping trips that sometimes ranged as far as Buenos Aires. After her longer absences, Víctor would decorate the hall with balloons and a banner saying *"Bienvenidos."* As the family awaited her return, the balloons exploded around them, pricked by vicious insects that Víctor called the *bichos*—the little beasties. Just enough gaiety would survive until Miriam's well-parcelled return and then, once she'd distributed gifts of talc and cigarettes (and a statue of Aphrodite for Víctor's mother), the debris of her welcome would be swept away and life would return to normality.

Fulcrencio R. Moreno was a quiet, tree-lined street that rolled gently over several hills. Once, other professionals had practised in the street— doctors, psychoanalysts and a good number of quacks and mountebanks. A few doors down was the old dental surgery of Dr. Heikel, who'd polished up teeth for Mengele and other Nazis. But it was all gone now. The only traffic was the Number 11 bus. For its drivers, the street was the roller-coaster in their otherwise tedious rounds of the city. For us, the Number 11s were like passing meteorites. But they too were soon gone, and when the dust had settled, Fulcrencio R. Moreno settled back down to its genteel long afternoon of snoozes.

From Moreno, the streets tumbled down towards the river in increasingly sleazy layers. A few blocks on was The Britannia pub, the latest attempt at English seediness. There were beer mats and pumps and pictures of Stonehenge and guardsmen. But I only ever went there once; somehow it made me feel lonely because its Englishness was just a trick. *"Servimos tu Guinness en manija de 355cc"* said a sign, and the waitresses wore Union Jack aprons and fake-ocelot boots. Even the owner was part of the illusion; I'm German, he shrugged. I preferred to press on to The Lido bar.

Further down were the prostitutes and transvestites and the watchmen, grilling little sticks of meat on dirty fires. The girls, up to their heels in litter and reproach, clustered in tight knots, muttering in Guaraní. Beyond them were the transvestites, long-legged and boldly denying the dinginess and smoke with their extravagance. One night, a particularly spectacular creature pitched out of the sickly shadows. Heels, suspenders, glossy thong and choking bodice. Long, pale legs sheared into the road; a BMW bundled to a halt, threw open its door and the apparition was gone.

Plaza Uruguaya was for the older prostitutes.

I often came down to the plaza during the day. Like Plaza Independencia, it still affected a raffishly Parisian air. Instead of statues of whippets and frogs, however, it was graced with goddesses and Greek muses. Perhaps that was why the prostitutes had originally liked it, feeling that the sight of all that white flesh was good for business. Strangely, the plaza also had the best bookshops in Asunción, housed in great glass tents. I often wondered if Langan was right that no one read in Paraguay. Anyway, literature and old prostitutes now shared the square. The bookshops stayed open late into the night, to mop up any loose intellectual urges.

Mostly, people came down to the plaza—as I did—just to feast on the colour of the blossom. At the beginning of the spring, the whole canopy of trees blushed the deep pink of *lapacho rosado*. Then as the air lost its brittleness, there was a second seething of colour: the hot, ripe yellows of *lapacho amarillo*. People just sat and let the winter drain out of them. Many spent the whole day like that, simply lying back and thinking in oceans of colour. Others played chess or sat at tiny stalls selling iced tea—*tereré*—or sugar-cane *mosto*. Occasionally, one of the old ladies might heave her way over and probe around for business.

"Would you like to buy me a *tereré*?" one asked me. She was wearing green culottes and a red tunic, well filled with leathery flesh. Despite her life and the loss of all her teeth, she was oddly ceremonious.

It was easier to pretend I didn't speak Spanish. But she wouldn't have it.

"Buy me a *tereré* and then you can take me to bed." She sat down next to me and laid a dry, clawed fist on my knee.

I kept up my charade but there was something that I simply had to know. I decided to find some Spanish. "How much?"

A zig-zag of gratitude and gums broke across her face. "Fifteen thousand."

Fifteen thousand Guaraní, the price of her remaining dignity. It wasn't much, even in Asunción; it bought seven cans of Coke or fifteen little buns of maize, thirteen short bus rides, fifteen copies of *Crónica*, supper at The Lido or an aluminium cooking pot. It might just be enough for two mobile phone calls, as long as they were quick.

I now had to pay for my curiosity with the task of extracting myself from the little claws. I made excuses; I'm waiting for a friend. But she wasn't persistent.

"Maybe later," she said, and went back to join the other ladies, clustered in the shade of Diana the Huntress.

The fact that I survived and thrived downtown puzzled me. How had I survived Fluff's criminal anarchy?

I began to get the feeling that perhaps the crime question was more subtle than it first appeared (and certainly more subtle than it appeared to readers of *Crónica*).

It was obvious that crime in Paraguay terrified—but it also empowered. The threat of criminal chaos had aroused magnificent gusts of rhetoric throughout the election. It was the new menace. I'd read that, during the *Stronato*, Don Alfredo had enjoyed a partnership with another, equally appalling bogeyman: communism. Communism justified everything he did. It even justified crime; *"El Contrabando es el precio de la paz,"* as he'd say. The fight against communism provided useful justification for his *caudillo* power; for authoritarianism, for 33,000 men under arms, for gunboats and states of emergency. Now, Stroessner may have gone, but Colorado power had survived and so had the hardware of the *Stronato*. Once communism had evaporated, what other justification could there be for *caudillaje*? No one was rushing to dispel the perception that Paraguay was slipping back to primordial chaos.

That's not to say that crime wasn't worse. Everything I read about crime in Paraguay was discouraging. One would hardly expect it any other way in a country where half the workforce was without work and where the economy was unbolting itself nut by nut. When—just after I arrived—a gang of thieves stole $11,000,000 of foreign exchange on its way out of the country, the whole structure visibly tottered.

Crime was thriving. The most spectacular example of this was in cars; over half the cars in the country were now *mau*, or "dodgy." Newspaper advertisements could barely be bothered to disguise their curliness; sale by *contrato privado* was a sure indicator that there wouldn't be a shred of documentation. The Paraguayan market was now so saturated in stolen

Brazilian cars that many were now just rushed straight through to Bolivia.

Paraguay's crime incensed her near-neighbours. The Chileans accused the Paraguayans of flooding them with marijuana and the Brazilians accused them of importing seventy per cent of all its cocaine. The Argentines continued to accuse Paraguay of polluting them with everything: drugs, cars, toasters, immigrants and even foot and mouth disease. None of this was particularly new; Paraguay had always been a merry roundabout of contraband. It was now just better at it.

This was all still a very long way from criminal anarchy. Could it be that the perception of crime was out of proportion to the reality?

"I come from a normal American city on the West Coast," said one of the aid workers at my *pensión*. "Compared to that, these guys don't know what crime is."

My feeling was that he was right. But meanwhile the politicians watched for chaos with greedy interest. As to the citizens of uptown and Legoland, they thought their city was unravelling itself and could only look on with a growing sense of horror and fascination.

Crime was no more horrible and fascinating than at the Police Museum.

It occupied the top floor of a police station called *"Identificaciones."* The whole building was full of surprises: Indians camped out on the ground floors, pleading for an identity; kitchens and banks of typewriters on the first and dormitories on the second. Some small boys were selling bottles of shampoo up here, and when one of them saw me clambering up through their dreary concrete sandwich, he peeled off and followed. I eventually arrived on the third—the museum—with the waif at my heels and two litres of conditioner pressed in my back.

The police had made a determined effort to horrify. Death was seized upon pointlessly and blankly. Each of the exhibits brought to mind not the detection of crime or the prevention of evil, but the moment of agony, the violent extinction of life. Here were the hands of a strangler, his cold grip cast in plaster. Or a little bowl of skull, hacked from the head of Gastón Gadín, who'd sliced up his parents in 1915. One whole wall had death glossily preserved in snapshots: wives dangling on ropes, blue-lipped and sleepy, throats cut; drivers sloshed around their cars; bodies pulled from fires and a decapitated baby. Perhaps worst of all was the pickling jar: six aborted foetuses clutching at each other blindly, furious at a life wasted in formaldehyde. "The most abominable crime against humanity," said their little cardboard tombstone.

An elderly policeman appeared at my side. The shampoo boy melted away. "If you have any questions," said the policeman, stiff with pride, "just ask."

I was so numb with horror that I couldn't think of a sensible question. Everything was so appallingly vivid that I wasn't sure I wanted him to clarify it further. But I could see he was hovering, waiting to furnish me with ghastly details.

"Tell me about this one." I aimed a finger at a photograph of a man, cold on the slab. "What happened here?"

The policeman peered into the photograph. "That's Cáceres, a drug runner. He was shot as he was driving round the back of The Gran Hotel."

"Who shot him?"

"Well, it must have been one of his own men. There were three of them with him in the car at the time. We arrested them all but none of them could remember which one had pulled the trigger." He was still gazing deep into the picture. "Anyway, *they* didn't kill him."

"Well, who did?"

"After he was shot, he got out of the car and escaped down the road. He flagged down another car and the driver picked him up."

"To take him to hospital?"

"Maybe," shrugged the old constable. "But he never made it. The driver shot him."

That, I supposed, was about as much clarification as I could expect. I edged away, towards the guns. There were muskets and shotguns and reptile little pieces that had once chattered with bullets. Among them, I spotted the *Montoneros'* machine-gun and the rocket-launcher used to kill Somoza. Even the dud projectile was there. Its sides were scuffed with trembling abrasions where the rocket-man had torn it from the launcher, before stuffing a fresh one in and blasting the old voluptuary to pieces.

Spread across the far wall was a shoal of knives, swimming along like deadly, silvery herrings. Each had been used in a murder. There were bayonets and kitchen knives, stilettos, daggers from Brazil and hunting knives from Spain, flick knives, butterfly knives, survival knives, machetes, cowboys' *facones* and scalpels. There were even knives cut from pieces of cars, and cutlery sharpened up to kill.

Above the blades was a declaration painted in loud gold letters. *"82% of homicides in Paraguay are committed with knives."*

I thought of something else to ask the policeman: why, with so many guns, didn't people just shoot each other? He considered this very carefully.

"I think people like to sneak up on their victims," he said. "It is the Paraguayan way. Like the Indians."

41

The moment when Spanish and native Indian blood first became commingled can be pinpointed—with almost indecent accuracy—to 17 August 1537. It followed a short but unnecessarily vicious struggle on Lambaré Hill.

The first European to enter Paraguay was not, however, a Spaniard but a Portuguese. He was a swaggering thug called Aleixo García, motivated a little by piety but mostly by greed. The greed was the catalyst; stories of a fabled city of gold, El Dorado or the City of the Caesars, had set his imagination ablaze and fuelled his recklessness. But the piety was useful too; García was a conquistador setting out in the name of God to bring the heathen lands within the fold of the Church. If the savage inhabitants of these lands—the "hidden Jews"—were foolish enough to oppose him, he felt himself charged with putting them to the blessed sword. The enthusiasm of his type for skewering the natives (and raping their women) was soon to reach such alarming proportions that even the Church felt constrained to act; in 1537, Pope Paul III decreed that the savage was capable of redemption. This gave him the status of a human being. Unfortunately, this news came too late for those visited by the early conquistadors.

Meanwhile Aleixo García—and his son—were ideal material for these adventures. In 1515, they found themselves on an expedition led by the Pilot-Major of Spain, Diego de Solís. The expedition was fated from the start. The first disaster came as the party of ships attempted to enter the River Plate in their search for an inland passage to the sierras of gold. Diego de Solís was surprised to find himself beckoned on to the beach by a group of charming Charrúa Indians. He paddled ashore, but his pleasure was short-lived as the natives broke him apart with axes and ate him.

This was not how it was supposed to work. Without their navigator the expedition leaders decided to turn for home. They headed north, and then disaster struck again as one of the ships was separated from the others and shipwrecked off Santa Catarina, Brazil. Only eighteen men of its complement survived, among them being Aleixo García and his son. They clambered ashore, thanking God for their deliverance. They then contemplated their next move.

The Garcías had been marooned among the Tupí, the coastal Guaraní. They were a handsome race, who had lustrous, coppery skin and strong, thick hair and who kept their teeth well into old age. Their name—the Guaraní—came about through their custom of painting their bodies with paint (*gua* means "paint" and *ní* is the indicator of the plural—"the painted ones"). However, as the Garcías would discover to their cost, there was—even in their name—dangerous ambiguity. "Guaraní" also meant "hornet," a mark of their warlike propensities.

For the castaways, their own warlike tendencies were held in check. In their straitened circumstances, the prospects of plundering seemed suddenly remote. There was no choice but to settle down among the Guaraní. Their hosts were forest dwellers who lived off the land, growing only simple crops of manioc and maize. They didn't know the wheel, the plough or draught animals. Their lives were intertwined with the cycles of forest life. They had names for some 1,100 plants, and their paradise—*Yvaga*—meant simply "the place of abundant fruit trees." They even mimicked the sounds all around them in their strange, onomatopoeic language. With little else to do, Aleixo García set about learning it, the first European to master Guaraní.

Despite their simple existence, the Guaraní were unsettled people. In the seven hundred years prior to the arrival of the castaways, they'd swarmed—like hornets—across an area from the coast of Brazil in the east to the River Paraguay in the west and extending south well into what is now Uruguay. They were restless partly because they were too many for their original territories. But they also had a deep conviction that there existed—within their finding—an earthly paradise—the Land without Evil. Their failure ever to find it was a constant source of melancholy.

But in their wanderings, the Guaraní were energetic conquerors. Their warriors, the *kyreymba*, literally engulfed the tribes in their path, taking their wives, adopting their children and eating whoever remained. Cannibalism afforded them rare pleasure in their restlessness.

It was not, however, a pleasure that they kept to themselves. As far as possible, those who were about to be eaten were expected to share the enjoyment of the occasion. In being prepared for the cooking fires, the victim was accorded the best of Guaraní hospitality. He was soothed with music and dancing and plumped up on the best food. That wasn't all.

They give him their wives and daughters [wrote one Spanish chronicler, Hernández, some years later] in order that he may have every pleasure. It is those wives who take the trouble to fatten him. Those held in the greatest honour among them admit him to their couches, adorn him in various ways according to their custom, and bedeck him with feathers and necklaces of white beads and stones, which are much prized among them. When he grows fat they redouble their efforts; the dancing, singing and pleasures of all kinds increase.

At this point in their crescendo of pleasure they were hacked up with axes and roasted. The task of dispatching them was an honour usually granted to small boys of six or seven. They were given tiny hatchets to work with. The victim's captivity which had, until that point, been flying by, must suddenly have seemed hideously—agonisingly—protracted.

It wasn't only the men that were eaten. Women and children were jointed and roasted if there was no other requirement for them. Like their menfolk, they were fattened up—according to a Flemish adventurer, Hulderilke Schnirdel—"no otherwise than wee doe Hogges."

"They keep a woman some years if she be yong, and of commendable beautie," slavered Schnirdel, twenty years on, "but if in the meane time, she apply not herselfe to all their desires, they kill and eate her, making a solemne banquet as marriages are wont to be celebrated with us."

Aleixo García was impressed by the warrior Guaraní—and intrigued by their weapons and armour; although they were almost naked, they carried copper machetes and wore breastplates of beaten silver. Where did they get them from? he asked.

They came from the mountains, said the warriors, and indicated to the west, far away. They said it was the empire of the White King.

García decided that he'd found El Dorado. The expedition, which had now been stalled for several years in the camps of the Tupí, was back on. He would march west and capture the city. He had no conception of how far away the mountains—the Andes—were. He had no conception either of the dangers that he'd encounter on the way: the most powerful rivers in the world, the carnivorous cats, the thorns that would tear and poison his flesh—to say nothing of the savages. He would be the first European to cross the continent—one way, as events turned out.

Not all his companions were so enthusiastic, and only a handful—including his son—agreed to go with him. Undeterred, he recruited the Guaranís.

A lesser man might have been troubled by the idea of heading a cannibal army off in pursuit of gold. Cannibalism held special terrors for the early explorers of South America; the word itself was a reminder of the horrors they'd first encountered among the *caribs* of the Caribbean, and the name had stuck, albeit slightly deformed. To men who'd supposedly sailed under the banner of the Church, cannibalism was a crime as unnatural as *pecatus nefandus*, homosexuality. In the minds of many, the two were inextricably linked. Even today, Indians in Brazil are often still referred to as *Bugres*—or *Bougres* in French—the Bulgarians (the unfortunate Bulgarians having, at some stage in history, acquired an extravagant reputation for sodomy).

Aleixo was untroubled by his conscience. He had no difficulty putting business above piety when the situation demanded it.

His ill-assorted party set out in 1524, and after covering nearly two thousand miles on foot, they reached the River Paraguay. There, he enlarged his militia by recruiting a further two thousand Guaraní warriors; they were delighted at an opportunity to carry out another raid on the Vultures, as they called the Incas. Some of them already knew the territory that they were bound for, having raided it before.

They set off, followed the river north, skirted the Chaco and after some months found themselves in Peru. They began to harvest the silver in vast quantities. Only when the Incas—under their leader Huayna Capac—mustered for a counterattack did García pause in his looting. He and his savages were forced to retire with their gains. The booty was hauled back to Paraguay, and García sent a message to those that had remained on the Brazilian coast, inviting them to join him. With it, he sent tempting samples of the treasures that he'd stolen. They weren't moved and refused to join the party in Paraguay.

The Guaraní, meanwhile, had tired of the Garcías. They fell on them and ate them.

Their fate was to remain a mystery to the outside world for several years. There had, however, been some encouragement in the fact that they appeared to have reached El Dorado, and so, in 1526, a party was sent to investigate. The new expedition, under Charles V of Spain's new Pilot-Major, Sebastian Cabot, consisted of four ships and six hundred men, including old cronies of Cabot's from the English West Country. One of them, Roger Barlow, was particularly impressed by Paraguay and wrote in glowing terms to King Henry VIII of what he'd seen. Fortunately for the Spanish, Henry wasn't at all impressed, and from then on, the only interest in the territory came from Madrid.

Even then, Cabot's expedition gave a misleading impression as to the natural resources of the region. They'd found a little of the booty remaining from García's raid, and believing it to have come from local sources, they named the river the Río del Plata, the River of Silver. It was a cruel error; the name stuck even though it was soon realised that the area was totally without mineral wealth of any kind. The Cabot expedition was in all other respects a failure; Cabot had failed to find the City of the Caesars and his attempts at colonisation had failed. On his return to Spain, he was hauled off to the slammer and then banished to Africa.

Although it was ten years before the next expedition up as far as Paraguay, the dream of El Dorado continued to nag at the avarice of young Spanish wolves. In 1536, Madrid sent a massive expedition to conquer the lands adjacent to the Plate—and what is now Paraguay—and drive a route through to Peru. There were eleven vessels and 2,500 men. Three of the ships were sent up to Paraguay, each under a separate commander: Ayolas, Salazar and Irala. The first of them was short-lived. Ayolas had a rush of blood to the head and dived into the Chaco in search of El Dorado, only to be ambushed and diced up by Indians.

When there was no news from him, the others gingerly followed. They were only two ships and about a hundred men, and they found themselves under constant attack from the Indians on the west, the Chaco side. The Abipones had mustered 10,000 *bravos*—or wild men—to oppose them. At one stage, the braves launched 500 war canoes but they were no match for the Spanish muskets, which cut them up in the water.

"We slew a goodly number of them," recalled Schnirdel, "they having never in their lives before seen a gun or a Christian."

The conquistadors anchored their ships for repairs some 1,300 miles from the mouth of the River Plate, in the lee of a strange conical hill. It was 15 August 1537, the feast of the Assumption of María, and so they called the place Asunción.

The hill was occupied by a local Guaraní chieftain who would, as his final service to his people, give it his name: Lambaré.

I travelled out to Lambaré on the bus.

I always enjoyed bus journeys around Asunción. It wasn't that the views were particularly good or that the buses were even comfortable—they tended to be raw-boned hulks that whined and belched their way across the city; it was the *mercantes*.

There was an understanding among drivers and vendors that—for a few stops at least—the vendors could ride along for nothing. At each bus stop there would be new *mercantes* and we were always eager to see who'd climb on next. They were like little dramas punctuating our journeys. Some of their efforts to raise money were ingenious and others were just plain desperate. Some got on and made speeches ("Only Christ can save us from drugs") and then passed hats around for our coins. Others sold things—stickers, fizzy drinks, *chipa*, cigarettes one-by-one, hair-clips—anything worth a coin. There was one man who had a string of balloons, each dangling a tiny polystyrene aeroplane. When he moved up and down the bus with his flock of bombers fluttering along behind him, the coins jangled into his pockets. The only *mercantes* that the drivers wouldn't let aboard were the fishermen, with their yokes of slimy *pacú*. They lay in ambush for us at the lights.

On the day I got the bus to Lambaré, two small boys got on, barefoot and shadowy with grime. They stood at the front of the bus and sang in Guaraní. Their strange, ululating words carried high above the engine, and when she heard them, the woman next to me started to cry. I looked around. The other passengers were choked and grey with silence. What was it that had unearthed such deep, grainy emotions? Poverty? Maybe. Or perhaps it was the sound of Guaraní, surviving—miraculously—in the mouths of another generation?

After an hour, the bus dropped me at the bottom of the conical hill. But the road was fringed with a tangle of shacks, wrecks and wire and I couldn't see a way through. Two men were sitting at the side of the road, smoking. One had no teeth, and the other had too many and they filled his mouth like broken china. Neither man looked up. I stopped at their knobbly feet.

"Excuse me, how do I get to the hill?"

"Follow the road along," they said, "until you get to the San Marino girl. Then you'll see the way through."

The San Marino girl? I went back along the main road until I came to a large billboard: the San Marino girl. It was an advertisement that I'd seen before, an absurd image that—until then—I'd hardly bothered to look at. A young slick was sitting in a sports car offering a girl his cigarettes, two of them erupting temptingly from his packet. The girl was swooned against the bodywork—voluptuous, milky-skinned, thick tresses of satin-gold hair rippling over her back. She wore only a thin silk slip which barely covered her buttocks and which was slashed up to her waist. Her rump was tilted up to the camera—a nice touch this—so that fevered smokers could see she wore no knickers. She was seconds away from sex, possibly even orgasm.

What I liked best about this image was the expression on the boy's face—a look of doggy glee. Even he seemed surprised at the effect that his foul, cheap cigarettes were having on this gorgeously available creature. Who was she anyway, this kerbside goddess? Too classy—too foreign—for a hooker, she must have been recruited from a dream. I looked back towards the two men sprawled out by the road; a life of San Marino hadn't brought them such kerbside fortune. They looked as if they were asleep and so I turned up the road to the hill.

A little further on, the road was joined by another one, broader and asphalted. It seemed that, as the road climbed upwards, corkscrewing around the hill, it got wider and wider still. Near the top, three lanes of tarmac were sweeping up through the jungle, enraging the parrots and scattering the trees. It was Stroessner who'd unleashed this road. He was obsessed with asphalt and trying to spread as much of it as possible over Paraguay. When Isabel Hilton, a journalist, interviewed him in exile, in September 1989, it was about all that he could remember of his achievements (700 kilometres of asphalt! Or was it 1,500? He'd lost count). This coil of grit and bitumen was his most fatuous project, curling up into the sky and ending in a car park and a great concrete pylon. It was supposed to commemorate Lambaré's Indians, though why Stroessner felt moved to make such a gesture is a mystery; elsewhere, his army trucks were carrying Indians into slavery and Christian fundamentalists were picking others off with rifles. Don Alfredo had little patience for the Indians.

It was quiet at the top. Only one car appeared but the occupants didn't get out. For a while, I saw some feet pressed up against the window and then the car drove away. As it was early spring, most of the kiosks were shut. There was one open and a man and woman and a dog were watching television. They lived up here all year and didn't welcome my unseasonal intrusion into their altitude.

Spread out, way below, was the glitter of a rubbish tip. Minuscule figures, like hot insects, scoured it for nutrients—for cans, buttery papers, dead cats, anything. Beyond them was the city of Asunción. I was surprised by how forested it looked from up here. When in it, only the people reminded me of the forest.

I crossed to the statue of Chief Lambaré. He looked like a great brass socialist, bare-chested and bulky with muscles and balls and a chin like a plough. He was a ludicrous sight and someone had shot him. Where the bullet had entered his pectoral there was a perfect, shiny puncture, and on the other side, a brilliant tussock of yellow metal sprouted from his back. Bang, bang. The Indians are dead.

When Lambaré's Guaraní saw the approaching Spaniards, they came down from the conical hill to greet them. They tried to offer them food. The Spaniards were wary of such friendly overtures. They'd only just chopped and blasted their way up the river, through a dense tangle of crazed savages. They chose instead to fight. The Guaraní fled back to the hill and put up the best resistance they could against squalls of lacerating ball and shot. For three days, forty of their warriors held out at the summit. Chief Lambaré was killed, and when his warriors could stand the stench of their dead no longer, they made a second attempt to sue for peace. They sent their enemy a party of young women as a gesture of their submission.

It was a well-aimed gesture. The girls were bare-breasted and biddable, and at the sight of them, the Spaniards—and Irala in particular—were devoured by their urges. After months at sea and weeks in the ecstasy of slaughter, the opportunity to plant themselves on these pretty creatures was too great a temptation. Irala, a powerful, thick-limbed hooligan with a taste for splitting savages limb from limb now found that he had a taste for their women. Happily unencumbered with scruples, he greedily took them to his bed, several at a time.

A truce was established, on the rather unpromising principles of lust.

42

For their part, the Asunción Guaraní were more than satisfied with their truce with the white men—the *karai*. It was what they'd wanted from the outset. They were living, at that time, right at the margins of the Guaraní area of influence, and those margins were being worn ragged by the merciless tribes of the Chaco. The river pirates of the Abipones and the Payaguás constantly harassed them, sating themselves on their women and filling their canoes with Guaraní booty and scalps. Now, here were the *karai*. They had horses and weapons, and an alliance with them offered the prospect of a swift victory over their old enemies. The provision of harems for the Christian warriors was but a small price to pay.

They might have felt differently had they anticipated the enthusiasm with which the *karai* would gather up their sisters and daughters. Having long abandoned their own sets of values, the invaders saw no reason to adopt the savages'; family ties were waved aside. Irala took seventy women to his name—and to his bed—and didn't stint at reminding his colleagues in Buenos Aires of this fact (they, at the time, were being rigorously mauled by the Indians and were on the brink of starvation). This lewd, rutting warrior would soon be able to claim as many offspring to his name as there had been soldiers in his expedition. Even today, the name Irala fills several pages of the Asunción phone directory.

Other Spaniards took on dozens of women each. "One is poor who has only five or six," wrote Francisco Paniagua to the King, "most having fifteen, twenty, thirty, forty . . ."

Over the next twenty years the Spanish residents of Asunción would produce six thousand *mestizo* children. At the time, it was conservatively reckoned that, on average, each conquistador must have heaved himself on to at least three different Guaraní women.

Even the doughty Fleming, Hulderilke Schnirdel, relished the pleasures of this flesh-pot, dipping more than a finger in the sauce; he procured himself a household of over fifty Guaraní, including children.

"Amongst these Indians," he thrilled, "the Father sels the Daughter, the husbande the wife. Sometimes the Brother doth either sell or change the Sister. They value a Woman at a Shirt, a knife, a Hatchet or some other thing of this Kinde."

The missionaries that accompanied the warriors were appalled by the scale of the concubinage and licentiousness (to say nothing of the cannibalism of the brothers-in-law). But they also saw the establishment of a Christian colony, and in the end, their concerns were mostly for the savages' cultural flabbiness. "They are," wrote François-Xavier de Charlevoix, "of extraordinary small intelligence, more or less stupidity and ferocity, an indolence and distaste for work, and absence of provision for the future that has no bounds."

There was only a brief moment when this stew of debauchery was threatened with a chilly dose of moral rectitude. It came with the appointment of a new governor from Spain, Alvar Núñez Cabeza de Vaca, in 1543. Núñez was a man of starry naiveté who attempted to bring a little humanity to the treatment of the Indians.

His early experience of American Indians was impressive. Like Aleixo García, he had a fine tradition of being shipwrecked. On his very first expedition to the Indies in 1529, his ship was caught in a storm off what is now Florida and wrecked. The sea swallowed up the wreckage and then regurgitated Núñez—completely naked—on the beach. The natives thought he was a god because of his two beards—one on his face and the other in his groin. This didn't dissuade them from enslaving him, and for five years he remained their captive. He made productive use of his time, working his way up from slave to pedlar and then on to doctor and chieftain. Finally, at the head of an army of Indians, he set off for New Spain. After some months, he encountered a roving Spanish mercenary and was eventually reunited with his countrymen. He urged them not to harm his loyal Indian followers but they thought this a curious instruction and had the whole lot put to death. The intransigence of his compatriots in their treatment of the Indians was to become a recurring theme in Núñez's unhappy life.

He set off for South America again in 1537, to take up the appointment of Governor of the River Plate. His first task, however, was to assist in the relief of Buenos Aires, which was still being dismembered by Indians. He never made it, and once again arrived on the continent in a wreck. By an unhappy coincidence, he and his men were washed up in exactly the same place as Aleixo García—at Santa Catarina in Brazil. Hearing that Buenos Aires had been all but abandoned, they decided to head for Asunción. Their walk took them four months. All the way, Núñez infuriated his men by insisting they pay the natives for everything they bought. They arrived in Asunción in March 1542, in disagreeable shape.

Asunción too was hardly agreeable at that moment. The city was under attack from the Guaycurú, who came from the other side of the river. These savages were a group especially to be feared; they existed purely for the torment of white men. It was known that they particularly valued the scalps of the *karai*. They even plucked their eyelashes out so as to better enable them to see the Christians and slay them. Worse, they were adept horsemen, "more truly of one flesh with their horses than with their wives," as one disgusted onlooker put it.

Governor Núñez was concerned about the legality of going after the Guaycurús, and sought the opinion of the clerics. To Irala, who was all ready to go and swipe some heads off, this was the action of a nincompoop. A rift developed. For the time being, however, it was plastered over; the opinion of the clergy was that not only was a counter-attack legal, "it was also expedient."

The expedition was a disaster. It had got off to a bad start when Núñez discovered that his soldiers had imprisoned Guaraní girls in the ships' lockers—to pleasure them on the campaign. He ordered the maidens to be released, and in doing so secured the loathing of his men. Meanwhile, the Guaycurús had evaporated into the heat and mockery of the Chaco. After several months upriver, the conquistadors encountered nothing but a few straggling Payaguá pirates. They sliced their ears off, of course, but it wasn't the bounty they'd hoped for.

On his return to Asunción, Irala raised a revolt and had the over-fond and dabbling governor dumped in prison whilst he contrived a case against him. Although Núñez was not to see anyone except the Indian girl who prepared his food, he still managed to get word to his allies. This infuriated Irala, who ordered that the girl be stripped naked and her hair cut down to a prickly stubble. Still Núñez managed to smuggle the messages out—on pieces of paper hidden between the girl's toes. Irala was intrigued. He procured an Indian boy to seduce the girl and find out her secret.

"This he failed to do," noted a nineteenth-century historian, "owing, perhaps, to his love-making being wanting in conviction on account of her shaved head."

Núñez was eventually sent for trial in Spain, with his defence documents secretly bolted to the ship's keel. He spent an agonising journey home. He was convinced he'd be murdered and he trailed his piece of unicorn (probably rhinoceros horn) through his food to protect him from poison. Back in Spain, he was acquitted—after an eight-year battle—but he was never reinstated to his post, nor was he ever paid for his well-intentioned services to date.

With Núñez out of the way, the field was clear for Irala. He ruled Paraguay until 1557, when stupor finally overwrought him. There had only been one small disappointment in all his delightful years of slaughter and debauchery: his expedition to Peru had been too late. His fellow-countryman, Pizarro, had already picked the carcass clean. The conquest of Paraguay had—to some extent—been in vain.

With the death of Irala came the end of conquistador rule in Paraguay. Apart from a few powdered buffoons that Madrid would send out to lord it over them, the country would now be in the hands of its half-breeds; the new Paraguayans.

The Guaraní, in saving themselves, had inadvertently secured their own extinction. Within three decades of the Spanish arrival, there were almost no pure-bred Guaraní left. The degradation of their people wasn't confined to Asunción either; the genetic colonisation of Paraguay fanned out, deep into the interior.

"There were now a number of half-breeds," wrote the French anthropologist Pierre Clastres, "the offspring of hidalgos and beautiful Indian women. Their features and rather coppery skin clearly show that there is Indian blood in their veins, although they might not want to admit it."

Why should they not want to admit it?

Clastres, who lived in Paraguay for several years in the early 1960s, had a simple answer: half-breeds often treat their "purer-bred" cousins with the contempt that the white men show for them. Paraguay was no exception; even the poorest *mestizo*—only one notch above the undiluted tribesmen—was apt to treat them with scorn. His attitude would vary between amusement at the antics of the *indigenas*—as they're now called—and loathing.

He would be very surprised [wrote Clastres] to learn that he and the Indian share common ancestors—in fact he would refuse to believe anything so absurd. He instinctively puts a high value on what he does not have; not material wealth, to which he attaches little importance, but white skin and light-coloured eyes. This preoccupation is evident in the popular aesthetic's ideal woman, expressed bluntly in Guaraní; the most desirable woman is *kyra, moroti ha haguepa*—fat, white and with thick hair.

That, it occurred to me, broadly described the San Marino cigarette girl.

43

The Guaraní had, however, survived in their language, as I was often reminded. The strange, bird-like noises chirruped from the radio and jingled on the buses. Politicians made speeches in tweets and growls and commercials went on air in forest sounds. Newspapers ran off long, peculiar rafts of vowels, and menus made themselves giddy with Guaraní. The dishes' names, it seemed to me, had simply been shredded, whisked around and then sprinkled freely across the page, delicious acrostics and anagrams.

One of the early English visitors to Paraguay, in 1852, had reported back that the natives spoke "a very queer gibberish, but not devoid of elegance." But for the Paraguayans, this "gibberish" is what they hear in their thoughts. Almost the entire country speaks Guaraní—ninety per cent at the last count—and many speak no Spanish. Paraguay is the only truly bilingual country in South America. Spanish may be the official language but Guaraní is the language of love, of the hearth and of friendship.

"The Paraguayans are the happiest people I have ever met," wrote an Argentine journalist, enviously, in 1888. "They only become grave and serious when they speak Spanish. Even the educated Paraguayan abandons restraint when he speaks Guaraní."

Guaraní is also the language of patriotism, and in the Chaco War it had flourished as a secret language on the battlefield. Some war veterans still preferred to speak Guaraní to Spanish, Stroessner being one. Those who followed him, like Lino Oviedo, also used Guaraní—to inflame the populace. But as well as being passionate and superficially unifying, Guaraní is also divisive: it creates a whole class of people excluded from higher opportunities by their ignorance of Spanish. The line between the haves and the have-nots follows a disconcertingly similar course to that between those who can get by in Spanish and those who gibber.

As a language of the forest, Guaraní has retained its vast diversity of names for animals and plants. Some Guaraní words have been swallowed whole by English—examples being "capybara" and "coatimundi." A few have got a little mauled on the way; *jagua* should have meant "dog" (in Paraguayan Spanish, the confusion is avoided by calling the big cats *tigres*). As to thousands of other Guaraní names, taxonomists have simply absorbed them into their science.

"After Latin," an Asunción scientist told me, "it is the most prevalent—of all the world's languages—in the scientific naming of organisms."

Guaraní is rather less elegant, but no less charming, in adapting to the world outside the forest. A watch is literally "the gold that counts," a tape recorder "a retainer of words" and—best of all—a television is "a machine that imagines." Counting too presents problems; there was little need for numeracy in Guaraní culture. Numbers therefore tend to lurch up in handfuls of five or ten (for example, 25 is "two of ten and five"). Most people prefer to drop back into Spanish once they get beyond five (*po* or "hand"), or even blend the two. This way, 25 might be *cinco po*—or five hands.

There was only ever one man who was upset by my failure to master Guaraní, and he was magnificently drunk. He spotted me typing an e-mail to my wife at the Shopping del Sol and swooped across the mall, nose-diving on to the keyboard. My first thoughts were in English.

"What the fuck," I asked, "are you doing?"

He glared at me. His first words were in Spanish. They were carried into my face on hot, wet gusts of whisky. "Say it in Guaraní!"

With that, he paddled a scaly hand across the keys: *sesgmta-e-4386f.*

It could have been Guaraní for all I knew. I tried to learn a little and even bought a skinny phrasebook. It had only eighty phrases. As I sat riding the bus out into the Interior, I wondered—grimly—how many of them I'd need.

Ne tú hetapiko nde? Do you have many sandflies?

Some of the phrases might lead me into intriguing and dangerous conversations from which I might never safely extricate myself: *Ha oñe'ë, okaurö guáicha.* He speaks like he is drunk.

But at least I would know when my position was irretrievable: *Pa'i ko hína pe oúva.* The priest is on his way.

EASTERN PARAGUAY

It is stated and indeed proved that the Garden of Eden was in this place, in the centre of the new World, the heart of the Indian continent, a real, physical actual place, and that here man was created. Any of these trees might have been the Tree of Life.

—Augusto Roa Bastos, *Son of Man*

Another type of slave is the working-class foreigner who rather than live in wretched poverty at home, volunteers for slavery in Utopia.

—Thomas More, *Utopia*

Some day Paraguay will become the garden of South America.

—A. K. MacDonald, *Picturesque Paraguay*, 1911

44

When it came to finding a map, I was hardly any better prepared for the Interior. The only one I could find in London was an air chart, produced by the U.S. Air Defense Administration. It might have been useful to someone organising an air strike, but not for me. Water featured prominently, but not roads. In some parts it simply blanked out altogether with the words "Maximum elevation figures are believed not to exceed 3800 feet." Worse still, it was the size of a Persian carpet. I decided to leave it at home with Jayne, chicken-pocked with stickers that gave her clues as to where she might find me—among 407,000 square miles of white space and water. That's the size of California, or thirteen Belgiums.

"If you find a better map in Paraguay," they said to me at Stanfords the map-sellers, "bring us back a dozen copies."

I didn't find a better one. The only one I did find had been produced by the Paraguayan military. But their printing machines had been possessed by resentment or forest spirits and the resulting map showed the country in a state of detailed chaos: roads ploughed into rivers and railways shrank away from civilisation; towns were stranded without communications or dumped in swamps; there was often no water in the rivers at all and it was to be found a few millimetres away, wandering around the countryside; worst of all, international borders had leaked into foreign territory, dangerously tempting yet more war. With a little imagination, I hauled Areguá out of Lake Ypacarai and that's where I went first.

Although Areguá was only twenty-eight kilometres away, it took the bus an hour to unravel itself from Asunción. I studied the pandemonium with guilty fascination. Rubbish bins here were on stalks, to keep their bounty from the dogs. The fickle, runaway packs, meanwhile, grazed the fruit stalls, licking up peel and pools of sticky juice. *Chipa* sellers, with mountainous baskets of fresh cornbread, urged themselves in among the crocodiles of lorries. We passed a circus—the *Circo Latino*—with pie-bald horses and grey dollops of marquee. Then the bus ducked under a crashed aeroplane—an obscure advertisement suspended over the road—and suddenly we were free.

The bus bounded away into the countryside. It was easy to see why the conquistadors had so happily embedded themselves in this landscape. Like their Guaraní girls, it was alluring and blushed, curvaceous and drenchingly fecund. I could never tire of it. It reminded me of so many places—Ireland with the heat turned up, Umbria only bursting with reds and tropical succulents, Brazil expressed in miniature—but in the end the comparisons were absurd; they all needed such radical refinement. I would try, as we bounced along, to linger on the details: farms painted like toys, cattle tethered on the verge, miniature *panteóns*—monuments to motoring catastrophes—exquisitely coloured and candled, like tiny theatres. Then the bus would be rolled up in a dark weft of forest, held for a moment and then unrolled again in a different world; on grassland perhaps, swashed and billowing all the way to the horizon, or—like now—before the improbable blueness of Lake Ypacarai.

Lucy Yegros had lent me her cottage in Areguá. I don't think she used it often; it was merely a place of exile for her sculptures, which, she said, her husband hadn't understood. They made uneasy companions— leering elves, tree spirits and women with fantastically exaggerated genitalia. When the trees creaked at night and rubbed themselves raw on my tin roof, I half-imagined these freaks unlocking themselves and sawing each other up with joyless lust. But when I looked out, there was nothing in the courtyard but the swinging lantern and the shadows of the caricatures, swaying in the wind.

I also suspected these spirits of having an evil effect on the plumbing. Although the cottage was small, there was a Gordian knot of pipework and I could never get the water where I wanted it. There were twenty stopcocks and I tried them in every combination I could think of. Most of the time there was no water at all. Then—occasionally—it would erupt from a water tower and I would have to rush around flinging stopcocks into reverse to bring the deluge under control. Once, I elicited a dribble from the courtyard tap but the pleasure didn't last; when I went back inside, I found that the main body of water was now gushing through the rafters.

In the end I gave up, turned everything off and went out to eat. There was one restaurant in the town, called Old Vienna. My problems were nothing compared to those of the Austrians who ran it: they'd come to Paraguay twenty-six years before—for reasons they couldn't remember—and were now too poor to go home. They hadn't, however, forgotten the art of making food taste Germanic, and every night, I had to work my way through a hummock of gravied meat, nestled in a soggy marsh of cabbage. I was their only customer.

Despite the goblins and the haunted waterworks, I was very fond of the cottage. It stood at the top of Lake Avenue, a steep, cobbled street that ran down to the shore. All the houses, including the cottage, dated from the seventeenth century and had been the homes of gentry, cattle breeders and cigar-makers. They were single-storey buildings with deep verandas and rattan chairs and gardens that could barely restrain their great bouquets of ferns.

The house opposite had once been the Bar San Carlos. The owner, Carlos, had been a resplendent host, according to Lucy, and was famous for his scrambled eggs and for dying of AIDS. In better days, Graham Greene had stayed there and I tried to imagine him sitting on the terrace opposite me, ploughing through the meaning of evil and love and drawing Areguá into his troubled Greeneland. "I came to Paraguay by a writer's instinct," he once wrote. Had he found what he was looking for? In *Travels with My Aunt*, it may be that all the disparate threads of his anxieties met at a single point: a land that was comical and shamelessly immoral, a place of "sweet orange blossom" and goose-stepping soldiers ("Very peaceful," my Aunt said. "Only an occasional gunshot after dark") and where the Chief of Customs was also the worst of the smugglers. Had he been happy in Paraguay? Greene would probably have had difficulty in identifying any single moment in his life as properly happy, but I like to think that in the heady, crumbling charm of Areguá, he found a little solace.

Further on, down next to the railway station, were the later villas of the Italians who'd settled here in the 1890s. Some had prospered and built themselves scaled-down castles and palaces that reminded them of the landlords they'd fled—and wanted to be—in Piedmont and Liguria. Many were now abandoned or, like the Castillo Carlota Palmerola, which had once been white, were sleepy with heavy green mould. The orchids and Lady of the Forest, once trained to delight, now rose up as conquerors. Swimming pools had long ago stopped struggling and had become exotic lagoons of emerald lilies and deep green neglect. The little bridge that led to the villas had collapsed, and so now the only visitors down here were the curious and the furtive. I clambered back, along the overgrown street, to the railway station.

The last train had ground out of here only two months ago and the station cat still sat on the platform, gazing up the track. The last goods waggon was now snuggled deeply into its siding. Its axles had been rapidly colonised with weeds. The inside too had been eagerly colonised—by an Indian and her noisy family. She looked like the Old Woman that lived in the Shoe, children sprouting from every chink in her home.

"Is it a good home?" I asked her.

"Of course, it is high and very dry up here. And I have electricity!" She pointed at a wire that was nailed to her roof and which dog-legged its way off into the jungle.

At the top end of Lake Avenue was the church of Areguá. Like many Paraguayan churches, it was solid and squat and surrounded on each side by deep, cool arcades that shaded its walls from the summer sun. There was a halo of lightbulbs round the altar and—all day long—a rasping sound as a gnarly brush and a gnarly devotee scraped away at the flags. Behind the church was the Town Square, walled in on three sides by low buildings with heavy pantiled roofs and deep colonnades of stores and snuggeries. This square was once the site of an extraordinary ball, held in August 1881 by an Englishman called Edward Frederick Knight.

The story of how he ended up in Areguá is one of courage and eccentricity.

Edward Knight was a barrister with a head full of adventures and little appetite for the law. Like me, he practised at the Inns of Court in London, and like me, an unseen hand plucked him from his sensible work and sent him off to Paraguay. Our adventures, however, unfolded in very different ways.

To get to South America, Knight needed a boat and a crew. His Cornish fishing lugger was hardly ideal for the southern oceans—or the great Paraná and Paraguay rivers—but Knight adored it and renamed it *The Falcon*. He knew nothing about sailing but persuaded Arthur Jerdein—who was an officer on a packet—to join him on the adventure. As to the remainder of the crew, there were two more barristers— Messrs. Andrews and Arnaud—both of whom were as feckless as their captain when it came to matters of the sea. Various cooks were also supposed to accompany them, but when they saw the crew, they reneged on their contracts and fled. At the last minute, a homeless waif called Arthur Cotton, who'd been wandering the docks at Southampton, was recruited as a cabin boy.

Knight was unsure what to expect when he got to Paraguay. He took his copy of *Westward Ho!* and read it on the voyage. It didn't seem to trouble him that Charles Kingsley had never actually been there, but he was mindful of the need for care. A brass swivel-gun was mounted on the prow of *The Falcon,* capable of delivering devastating fusillades of grape and canister if the excursion ran into difficulty. As an extra precaution, the barristers also armed themselves with cutlasses and the latest in Martini-Henry rifles. Finally, they recruited a kitten, but it got no further than Cape Finisterre before it abandoned all hope. As Europe slipped away, it jumped overboard.

The kitten's pessimism proved misplaced, and after two months' sailing, *The Falcon* made it to Brazil in October 1880. There, Mr. Andrews, who the others now considered to be a milksop and a dandy, deserted them and returned to his sensible life. The others carried on, and by early 1881, they were in Buenos Aires.

They had to wait two months before the river was high enough to sail upstream. To pass the time, the crew rode around Argentina dressed in ponchos and cartridge belts. Knight delighted in everything he found: the bullfight which left fourteen horses disembowelled, the stocks where criminals were held upside down, and the railways run by Irishmen who'd run away. On the way back to Buenos Aires, he bought a puma to amuse them on the voyage, but—when they set sail—it became unruly and had to be shot.

It took them ninety-one days to sail up to Asunción, and they survived on the game that they caught on the way. Knight relished his new diet.

"A dish of young monkeys," he wrote, "is not to be despised by anyone."

The Falcon arrived in Paraguay in the aftermath of its great war. Despite the destruction, the crew were deeply impressed by "the country of women." It was, said Edward Knight, "a very fairyland of romance." Naturally, the Englishmen were delighted by the attentions of the "statuesque beauties" who now outnumbered men by ten to one. The Argentines had warned them of the *paraguayas'* enthusiasm for dances, and so Knight's crew had arrived with a hurdy-gurdy. Everywhere they went they threw balls, but the greatest of these was to be in Areguá. In mid-

August 1881, they took the dawn train out to the lake town, loaded with their music, beer and several demijohns of wine.

Every hour or so, a thin metallic carillon was tapped from the church belfry. In Knight's time, the carillon had been rung by two naked boys who scrambled up there "to ring the bells in most energetic style." Now their work was done by a computer, the unwelcome innovation of the last priest—Lucy's cousin. The machine was loathed—a constant intrusion in the town's sleep—and had eventually cost the priest his living. The people of Areguá disliked being reminded that time was moving on.

Many of those who lived up here, near the square, were potters. They lived in little cottages next to their *alfarerías*—or kilns. There was a cup-tree at each door and a smaller clay oven for baking *chipa* and roasting slabs of beef. The smoke from the kilns was sweet and woody and seeped downhill through the trees. Each morning, ox-carts laden with firewood heaved themselves up Lake Avenue, past my door, to restock the fires, as they'd done for the last four hundred years.

Sadly, tradition had not survived in the work of the potters. There were a few pots and wood spirits—with astonished vaginas and stumpy penises—but the rest was kitsch. The roadsides were four-deep in Father Christmases and Winnie the Poohs. There were hundreds of thousands of cold, ceramic Dalmatians and whole piggeries of money-boxes, all pink and vaguely obscene.

When the *Falcon* crew arrived, they were greeted off the train by a dozen portresses who carried their liquor up Lake Avenue to the square. A spare house was found among the colonnades and hung with clean hammocks.

In honour of the foreigners' arrival, the local priest got extravagantly drunk and publicly announced that he'd be unable to open the church for the duration of their stay. He was a fat old Indian who wore a dog-collar with a broad-brimmed hat and no boots. He lent the church collections out at an extortionate sixty per cent and delivered his sermons in slurred Guaraní. The only Spanish that he could ever remember were the names of beers, but his parrot had a repertoire of indecencies and blasphemies which were screeched across the square. He'd also taught it to imitate the wailing of women at funerals and the mumblings of the

Latin mass. Whenever his high spirits overwhelmed him, the priest was heaved into his hammock and rocked into a crapulous slumber by his squall of grimy children.

The ladies cleared the largest room on the square for the ball. They covered the mud floor with Areguá's most luxurious piece of carpet and hung the walls with petroleum lamps and Chinese lanterns. When everything was ready, fireworks were blasted over the town, "for this," observed Knight, "is the Paraguayan way of issuing invitations."

All night, the Englishmen danced. But they were not enough for the women, who mostly had to dance among themselves. "It was curious," said Knight, "to see a girl and her partner puffing away at their long cigars across each other's shoulders while waltzing vigorously." Knight found himself with the belle of the ball, a lady "who gloried in the possession of boots and a golden comb."

The next day, the priest refused to let his Englishmen leave without attending the feast of Santa Rosa, a picnic held outside the town. Knight agreed, sharing a horse with the lady with the boots. A cart of beer led the procession, followed by Santa Rosa, decked out in parrot feathers and humming-birds. They didn't go far and the day was spent at cock-fighting and *sortija*, a sport still popular in Paraguay today; a hoop the size of a wedding ring is planted in the ground and lancers scoop it up on their *lanzas*, riding at full tilt. Paraguayans excel at it—even, apparently, after a day of rum and cock-fighting.

At midday, the party had lunch. "Our meal was a luxurious one," recalled Knight, "*chipa*, roast parrots and stewed iguana or lizard being a few of the many delicacies that were spread before us."

The ladies did not eat with the English guests but stood behind their chairs, feeding them delicate morsels on their forks. The priest was also unable to eat with them as he'd drunk himself into a state of imbecility.

The women of the place [noted Knight] had tucked his fat carcase into a hammock and were engaged in fanning his apoplectic-looking visage. Women in all lands show affection for the ministers of the Church but the devotion of the Paraguayan women towards their pastors out-does anything in the way of curate worship at home. It was very sad to observe what a lot these kindly girls made of that horrid old man.

As he lay in his cups, a boy crawled into the shed. "Father," he said, "may I have a blessing?"

The priest swore at him. "Not today!" he slushed. "Not today, those farces! Tomorrow; today is Santa Rosa and I am drunk—very drunk!"

That evening, the lovely ladies came down to the station to see the Englishmen off, on a train bound for Asunción. There were flowers and plenty of tears and then the train was gone. Within a fortnight, *The Falcon* had sailed, leaving for ever the Land of Women. But for two of the Argonauts, it was also to be their Land of Sirens—they were unable to tear themselves away; Jerdein abandoned his dreary life on the packets, and Arnaud threw in his practice at the bar, to live in Paraguay.

Of the original crew, only Knight and Arthur Cotton set sail for home. After its journey of 22,000 miles, *The Falcon* had to be abandoned in Barbados, when Knight was called back on urgent business. He completed his journey by steamer, rounding Hartland Point exactly eighteen months after he'd left. He'd always intended to return to Barbados to collect *The Falcon* and sail her home, but four years later, she was smashed to pieces in a hurricane.

It was not the end of Knight's adventures. He never went back to the bar. He became a war correspondent and galloped off to wherever there was trouble: the Hunza-Nagar campaign, Matabeleland, Madagascar, Sudan, Cuba and many others. His right arm was shot off at Belmont, in the Boer War, but it didn't stop him. Two years later, he sailed round the world in the *Ophir*. Next, he served with the Russians in the Japanese war of 1904, and later rushed home for the Great War, throwing himself into the Royal Navy. His adventures only ended in July 1925 when death finally caught up with him.

He was buried in Putney, London, a mile from where he'd been born, seventy-three turbulent years before.

45

On the other side of Lake Ypacarai was San Bernardino. One day—an icy day when the wind sliced in from the south—I took a bus around the shoreline to pay it a visit. There were only two other passengers: a woman with hundreds of empty yellow plastic bottles tied up in a sausage of netting, and a soldier in ceremonial dress. He had a dagger with an eagle-head handle swinging at his hip and a blue stripe speeding down his uniform. As the bus wheeled and banked around the lake, the yellow sausage burst and we arrived in San Bernardino with the cold and the bottles swirling round our feet.

Everything was still shut for winter. It was a summer resort for rich *Asunceños,* and now the sailing boats were pulled up on the beach and the pier was shut. There were villas along the shore and tennis clubs and camping sites for Baptists. Stroessner had had a lake-house here and so had Somoza, guarded by his apes in speedboats. But all was clammed up now and nothing moved except the gardeners, brushing winter into their smoky fires.

Towards the centre of the town were alpine chalets and stern, stony flanks of Bavarian architecture. There were *Bierstubes* and a miniaturised *rathaus* made of softwood and corrugated iron. Hugo Bottner's factory had long since ceased to be a place of "Carpentry and Steam," but other businesses had survived, defiantly German: the Schulz Mercedes dealership and the place where I had breakfast, all *Kaffee* and Viennese cakes. San Bernardino was established by German colonists in 1881.

"We called it New Bavaria for a while," a man had told me at the café, in his lugubrious Spanish. "But later it was renamed, after the Paraguayan president, General Bernardino Caballero."

"Do you know why?"

He thought about it for a moment. "I think he put the road in," he smiled. "Without it, we were just a few German hicks stuck up here in the hills."

Silvia's great-grandfather would have been delighted; his name carried into posterity by twelve mistresses, forty children and now a little German city. But the pioneers, too, were delighted with their home from home. They built their chalets and a German club—the *Deutsche Verein*—and gave the streets their throaty, guttural names. Others came out to join them, and after the Great War there were more, from Tanganyika and Sudetenland. The rate of immigration was torrential and San Bernardino took its share. Even today, over 100,000 Paraguayans can claim German ancestry—or one in every fifty-five of the population.

Although the Club had long ago burnt down, much of the paraphernalia of colonial lives had survived elsewhere: ugly oak chairs at the sailing club and—in a museum—their china and their photographs. Most of the pictures were of wasp-waisted ladies with hunting rifles and of young Germans marching off to fight Bolivia, in 1932. One—my favourite—had Nurse Hilda Ingenohl in Red Cross uniform, deep in the Chaco War, a young ocelot cradled in her arms. There was all the civic livery too; of the town's thirty-two presidents, only five, I noticed, hadn't had German names.

I wasn't sure that I liked San Bernardino. Perhaps I ought to have done; it was prim and scrubbed and stiff with pride. Perhaps I'd just come on the wrong sort of day. The damp and the smoke held the place in a grizzled embrace and the turgid architecture and the bolted doors left me anchored in deep disappointment. Surely the colonists had wanted more than this, an *ersatz* alpine resort seeping nostalgia? They'd have loathed the flashy riff-raff that came down here in the summer to churn up the lake with their wet-bikes. And what would they have made of "Crazy Pizza"? Or the casino—a "dollar-wash"—now steeped in cob-webs and debt? When a pretty ginger spaniel was run over in front of me, I think I must have caught a little of its outrage. It lay in the road, astonished at a life snuffed out on such a promising walk, barked twice and died.

I walked back towards the lake, along Weiler Street. Bobby Weiler had been the town president from 1931 to 1934, and at the end of his street was his father's rambling creation, the Lake Hotel. It was built on a bluff slightly above the lake and surrounded by lawns of long wet grass and heavy, dripping trees. It had white walls and dark green shutters, two floors of verandas, Romanesque columns and gothic windows. There was a brick terrace at the back, overlooking the lake and a swim-ming pool that was now a soup of leaves and old chairs.

Although it was shut and workmen were shovelling dust out of a win-dow, I went in and crunched across the front hall. All the old Weiler furniture was draped in dust sheets and an electrician was crumbling the ceiling with a crowbar. I crossed into the dining room. The chairs that had come out with settlers were heaped in the middle of the room, bearded in dust. I thought I smelt cooking and picked my way along cavernous corridors, hung with servants' bells to the kitchens. It took me a moment to get used to the dark, but then gradually, intriguingly, the details of the late nineteenth century unblacked themselves in front of me: zinc game cupboards, a stone scullery, marble pastry tops and an "Alexanderwerk" mincer, now spotted with age. A fire was glowing in the range and, very softly, a figure stepped into its orange halo. I saw a pair of feet in slippers and then a glint of gold teeth.

"I'm the housekeeper," she said. "Are you looking for something?"

I was. The Lake Hotel had been the scene of a strange and sordid incident on 3 June 1889. In fact, it could justly claim to have played a small but decisive role in the disastrous pre-history of German fascism. It came about when the hotel provided rooms to a remarkable—and unequivocally repellent—individual, a white supremacist who'd come to South America with the single intention of breeding his type. His name was Dr. Bernhard Förster.

Förster's attempt to establish a master race in Paraguay is brilliantly autopsied in Ben MacIntyre's *Forgotten Fatherland*. The story is hardly edifying and is certainly not the obituary that Förster would have wanted.

Bernhard Förster was born in Berlin on 31 March 1843. From an early age, he busied himself with the torment of others until, in his mid-thirties, he found a vessel for his inexplicable loathings: the Jews. He was a doctor of philosophy, but by ranting dangerously on the Jewish Threat, he'd thrown away his teaching post. With time on his hands, he cooked up his hatred. Sometimes it over-boiled; on at least one occasion he simply flung himself at people whose Jewishness upset him. The worst occasion was in 1880, when he was arrested and fined for mauling a Jew on a tram.

Within a few years he'd got his most violent impulses under control and had organised his prejudices into an ugly political movement. Anti-Semitism was leavened with anti-vivisection, anti-inoculation and passionate vegetarianism. To complete the picture, he squashed himself into an undersized frock-coat, in the belief that it made him loom a little larger, and grew his beard like a biblical prophet. With a German Iron Cross pinned on his lapel, he set out to raise the rabble, booming hatred all over Berlin. He called his party *Deutscher Volksverein*—the German People's Party. It and its unlovely successors were to prove themselves persistently troublesome over the next sixty-five years of German politics.

Förster had also become deeply impressed with Richard Wagner, who, in 1880, had published *Art and Religion*, which snorted at the emancipation of the Jews. Förster edged his way closer into Wagner's circle at Bayreuth and often made the mistake of taking the composer too literally. Whenever Wagner released another half-baked idea into the hot air that surrounded him, Förster was often there to seize on it and convert it into blunders.

"What," Wagner asked one day, "is to prevent our carrying out a rationally conducted migration of the Teutonic races to those quarters of the globe whose enormous fertility is sufficient to maintain the entire present population of the earth, as is claimed for the South American peninsula itself?"

Förster snapped up the idea. The economy of Germany was, at the time, near collapse, and more importantly, he had no work and nothing better to do. When reports filtered through of San Bernardino's prosperity, Förster set out to investigate the prospects for his own new colony in Paraguay. In London, *The Times* reported his departure under a tittering headline: "The comedy of the modern Pilgrim Fathers," and had Förster billed as "the most-representative Jew-baiter in all Germany." But they had no idea of the scale of Förster's ambition; he envisaged more than just a settlement of gentiles confined to Paraguay—it was to be "a nucleus for a glorious new Fatherland that would one day cover the entire continent."

After eighteen months, he returned with a site in mind. His fiancée, Elizabeth Nietzsche—sister to the philosopher, Friedrich—was equally enthusiastic about the project. She was a waspish woman, three years his junior, but as distorted with racial fanaticism as Förster was. She might have been attractive, with neat and delicate features, but her hair was screwed back in a matronly bun and she had a disconcerting squint. This defect gave people the impression that she had her eyes on every opportunity at once, an impression which turned out to be uncannily prophetic.

"The mission has a name," Förster had told Elizabeth, "the purification and rebirth of the human race and the preservation of human culture."

Her brother meanwhile thought the whole enterprise was ludicrous. He disapproved of his sister as an anti-Semite and disapproved of Förster in any form. He refused to invest any money in the scheme, telling his sister that "our wishes and interest do not coincide as your project is an anti-Semitic one. If Doctor Förster's project succeeds, then I will be happy on your behalf and as far as I can, I will ignore the fact that it is a movement that I reject. If it fails, I will rejoice in the death of an anti-Semitic project." As to Wagner, Friedrich thought him pompous and a hazard to humankind and said as much in his writing. Wagner responded by writing to Friedrich's doctor telling him that he thought Nietzsche was making himself ill with excessive masturbation.

Recriminations continued until 1896, when Förster and his followers set off aboard the *Uruguay*, bound for Buenos Aires. Things started to go wrong for the colony from the start. There were forty families with the Försters, all facing grim financial futures in Germany (and blissfully ignorant of what the future held in Paraguay). One of the settlers' children died two days before they arrived in Asunción, having spent several days vomiting blood. Then, from Asunción, an advance party set off upriver, to prepare the site—Nueva Germania, as it was to be called. The rest followed some months later, another 150-mile journey to the colony. They lost a second settler on the way when he became drunk, slipped in the river and drowned. There was little encouragement when they arrived. The advance party had barely made an impression on their sweltering, tangled plot. All they'd done was to build the Försters a commodious log mansion, called the Försterhof. As for the rank and file, they'd have to make do with grass huts.

Elizabeth never saw the blow coming. She was thrilled with her new home. "Just think how grand it would sound," she wrote, "Förster of Försterhof." She even spoke of her "Princedom" and enjoyed the title of the "Little Queen of Nueva Germania." Even though her subjects were now barely better off than the poorest Saxon peasants, she had no sympathy. She chided them to work and even ordered them to carry her piano up from the river, to her splendid Försterhof.

Förster was hardly any better. He made the settlers dismount from their horses whenever he passed, as a sign of respect. So inflated was he with the grace of his own leadership that he even considered offering his services as the President of Paraguay.

It was all pride before the fall. The settlers were deeply resentful; their German seeds simply rotted in the warm, torrid soil, and such savings as they had evaporated in Elizabeth's overpriced colony shop. Within two years, a quarter of the settlers had headed home. Worse, Förster realised there was no prospect of his being able to pay for the 40,000 acres he'd bought in the name of the colony. He sent desperate appeals to Germany, but when an ex-settler, a voraciously spiteful creature called

Klingbeil, published an exposé on the colony, support collapsed. Klingbeil had reported that whilst the colonists were picking lice off themselves for sustenance, the Försters were making themselves fat on luxuries, wine and—worse—meat. Funds simply dried up. As a last, desperate measure, the sole remaining benefactor—Mr. Julius Cyriax of London—suggested that the colonists could raise some money by selling native handicrafts to the South Kensington Museum. Förster's by now ragged state of mind began to unravel.

He set off for San Bernardino and booked himself into the Lake Hotel.

"Yes," I said to the housekeeper. "There is something I'd like to see. Dr. Förster's room."

She tutted knowingly, gathered up her hoops of keys and led the way out into the hall.

"We open again in two months," she said. "Once the work is done."

The electrician was still raking the nineteenth century out of the ceiling. Soon it would be all buried again under drifts of fresh plaster and emulsion.

"Everything came from Germany," she said, casting a fleshy arm over the ghostly outlines in their dust sheets. She was enjoying having a visitor, and as she shuffled along, little merry puffs of plaster danced around her slippers.

"All original wiring," she glowed. Untidy nests of perished wires were strewn up the walls and stretched across the ceilings. Our tour munched its way though the grit, towards the stairs.

Förster had stayed here for six weeks, trying to drink away the spectre of failure. His reasoning—always brittle—now crumbled. He developed uncontrollable shakes and was only able to bring the tremors under control with more and greater draughts of spirits. Sleep was gone and so too was any hope. "I am in a bad way," he wrote to Elizabeth. "When will things ever end?"

It was almost over already. The same night he locked himself in his room.

"This was the room," said the housekeeper, and stood aside to let me in. There were two rooms, joined by a set of double doors. The walls were white and the woodwork painted the same dark green as outside. There was a fussy bed of *faux*-bamboo and a cabinet and chiffonier of fruitwood. The housekeeper was still behind me, tattling off her inventories ("There were seventy sets of everything, made for us in Germany and then shipped all the way out here!").

Dr. Förster ended it all that night, 3 June 1889. First he took morphine to soften the pain, and then a fatal dose of strychnine. At forty-six, he was dead, and with him died his dreams of a master race. His body was found the next morning by the maid and Elizabeth was summoned. She tore down on the steamer and arrived just in time to persuade the Paraguayan doctor to certify death as having resulted from "a nervous attack." There was then six weeks of Förster's deranged drinking to be paid for. Elizabeth had no money, and so instead, she offered the hotel a plot of land at Nueva Germania. They had no choice but to accept.

I wondered if the housekeeper knew what had happened to Elizabeth Förster. She didn't.

"What about the colony, Nueva Germania?"

She shook her head. "I know that there is still a place of that name, somewhere in the north, but I don't know what happens there. Are you going to go there?"

Yes, I said, I might do that.

Did she know what had happened to Förster's body?

"Of course. They buried him up here, on the hill."

That afternoon, I climbed up to the San Bernardino cemetery. It was high above the lake, lurking in the shadow of thick, murmuring woods. Förster would have been disappointed to find that he was not its most distinguished tenant; that honour went to the singer Luis Alberto del Paraná. He'd toured the world with his band, Los Paraguayos, according Paraguay a rare moment of recognition if not exactly fame. In England, he'd played to an appreciative London Palladium and promptly dropped dead. He was brought home to a nation in deep mourning. Throughout his travels, he'd been inconsolably homesick and had carried with him a bag of Paraguayan soil. At least he was now peacefully mingled in with it.

Förster was buried a short distance away, under a headstone of granite, resting, I suspected, a little less peacefully. *"Hier ruhet in Gott Dr. Bernhard Förster,"* read the inscription, *"begrunder der colonie Neu Germania."* It gave his dates and then—with every ounce of Elizabeth's breathtaking insouciance—an epitaph: *"Die Liebe horet nimmer auf"* ("The love never ceases").

She'd worked hard to bury her husband with honour. She then set about resurrecting him with glorious distortion. The memoirs of his life that she unloosed six months later left Dr. Förster quite unrecognisable. He'd become "a battling hero worthy of Valhalla, in the image of whose face the true Christ is re-united with the real German race, who has fallen on a foreign field for his belief in the German spirit."

She preferred not to reveal that he had actually fallen flat on his face with drink and rat poison. Surprisingly, her freshened-up version of events survived. Forty-five years later, in 1934, the Nazis gave it another fetid breath of life. Adolf Hitler—keen to commemorate any ancestral bigots—ordered a ceremony at Förster's tombside. Once again, soil was on the move. A bag of the real German stuff was brought from the Fatherland and local *Kolonie* schoolchildren were paraded into the cemetery. As the children sang, the soil was solemnly scattered over the grave.

It was inevitable that, once Nazism starting trumping and hooting over in the Fatherland, the Paraguayan Germans would dance to the same jig. There were now 30,000 of them, German-speaking, German-thinking and conveniently poor. Hitler went to some trouble to court their affection: the Third Reich supported thirty-one schools in Paraguay and educated 1,161 children; it sent books and brown uniforms and bales of swastika flags; a pastor called Carlos Richert toured the country emulating the *Führer* with his own piping version of the Nuremberg rally. The *Abwehr* even sent out agents to sniff out support and stifle resistance. Typically, they were goons like Herr Studt, an officer of the Great War cruiser *Emden*. He thought he was inconspicuous but he travelled the country in yellow cotton breeches, soft riding boots, a shantung jacket and a pair of pebble glasses. Allied secret agents watched his every move with weary amusement before reaching the conclusion that their energies were better spent elsewhere.

As one of the larger German communities, San Bernardino became a centre for these shrill idealists. Bobby Weiler raced between the Lake Hotel and his other hotel, The Gran in Asunción, organising Nazi Bund-fights. A large portrait of Hitler was hung in the dining room of the Lake Hotel, and on the weekends, the German farmers and their ample, petticoated wives gathered on the terrace. They danced polkas to a gramophone and drank tankards of frothy *chopp*. Then, as the evenings turned to nights, there were beery Horst Wessel songs and Nazi salutes.

"Heil Hitler!" they sloshed, as they fell into their carts. Whips cracked and off they went, hauled back to their lonely farms in the hills above Altos.

The Paraguayans didn't discourage this spread of Nazism among the Germans, partly because they had, for a number of years, been toying with fascism themselves. Paraguay had the doubtful distinction of having the first Nazi party in South America, in 1929—four years before Hitler came to power. It also proved to be the most enduring and wasn't disbanded until 1946, the last to go. Even mainstream politics began to drift towards the right in the mid-thirties. From 1936 there were a succession of strongmen who dabbled in corporatism, professing to admire Mussolini and the Brazilian *Estado Novo*. In 1937, Jews were prohibited from entering the country, and in due course, trade unions found themselves rudely disbanded.

Then, when the Germans went to war with the world in 1939, Paraguay gave serious consideration to throwing its bantamweight behind them. The debate continued until 1943, when President Roosevelt managed to persuade his Paraguayan opposite, President Morinigo, that such a move would be unwise. When Morinigo saw the way the war was going, he edged towards the Allies. Eventually, on 2 February 1945—three months before Germany surrendered—Paraguay declared war on the Axis.

In the end, it probably came down to cash. The United States offered generous rewards for those coming into the fold. The entire Paraguayan cabinet was invited up to the White House for red-carpet treatment. Washington even sent them a small package of military treats (some of this hardware—like the Sherman tanks—was still in service forty-five years later, in 1990). Curiously, having vacillated for so long as to which side to join, Paraguay was one of the first South American countries to sign up for the Allies, after Brazil and Ecuador. It was followed—each a few days apart—by Peru, Chile, Venezuela, Turkey, Uruguay, Egypt, Syria, Lebanon, Saudi Arabia, Finland and then—finally, at the end of March—the Argentines.

The decision to join the Allies was hardly an ideological matter. One minister moved to reassure the Paraguayan Germans that "the Axis powers will know full well what Paraguay's real sentiments are and will take them into account when they finally triumph." But whatever the "real sentiments" might have been, Morinigo was keen to show solidarity with the Allies. When, on Roosevelt's death, a group of Paraguayans were imprudent enough to throw a celebration, they suddenly found themselves—to their surprise—hauled off to prison.

Nazism had become dangerously unfashionable.

46

The road to the San Bernardino cemetery carried on, up to Altos.

I'd often been told, by people in Asunción, that this was where Dr. Mengele—the "Angel of Death," the Butcher of Auschwitz—had lived. Lucy Yegros, who'd said she'd seen him several times, told me that he had lived at the top of the hill, "near the aerials." Another, who'd lived in San Bernardino in the 1950s, said the same—"at the top of the hill, where the drain ends." Others added their own embellishments, which, as they gathered momentum, became increasingly colourful: Gareth said he'd been at school with all of Mengele's bastard children; Mengele had been Stroessner's doctor; Mengele had taught Pastor Coronel all there was to know about torture (in 1982, he'd been a popular suspect as the blow-torch killer). One man even thought Altos was still a smouldering bed of Nazis. They all urged me to go and have a look.

Strangely, however, the Paraguayans' own interest in Mengele was usually little more than idle curiosity about where he'd lived. No one seemed unduly concerned about what he'd done.

"I don't know what he did and I don't really care," Lucy had said. "It was all a long time ago and a long way from here."

Her weariness with the detail was repeated everywhere. Robert Eaton, the old American rancher, had put his finger on it.

"The Paraguayans are not interested in Mengele," he'd said. "They have too many Mengeles of their own."

I often wondered whether, if they'd known quite how much of a mengele Mengele was, they might have felt differently about him.

Captain Josef Mengele was thirty-one when he volunteered to be a *Lagerartz* or camp doctor at Auschwitz. He was handsome—almost pretty—and an impassioned Nazi. He liked freshly laundered clothes and well-scrubbed hands, and although he was a nimble ballroom dancer, he regarded deeper human attachments as frivolous and contemptible.

It troubled no one that he had no experience as a doctor. He'd spent the previous four years with the SS, latterly on the Eastern Front. He'd served with the Viking Division, bitterly intertwined with the Red Army in the wreckage of Rostov. The Russians had fought the Vikings with paving slabs and petrol bombs, and after they were thought beaten, they rose from the rubble and slashed the throats of the German wounded. Mengele absorbed the hatred. He won the Iron Cross for his calculated brutality and then—to his shame—was invalided out. The job at Auschwitz was a sick man's posting.

For Mengele, however, the work at the concentration camp was deeply satisfying. Before his service with the Vikings he'd been a medical researcher at the Institute of Heredity and Eugenics in Frankfurt. His new job allowed him to indulge his enthusiasm for this work without any of the squeamishness of peacetime. He could also indulge his other passions—for music, of which, surprisingly, there was plenty at Auschwitz, and for the extermination of Jews. He had found a form of happiness.

In all I'd read about Mengele's work at Auschwitz, it was his clinical detachment that disturbed me most of all. He couldn't claim to have been deranged. For most of the time, he was calm and even gentle with the inmates (although on one occasion he lost his temper and pulped a woman's head in with a log). He was not a particularly intelligent man but he was admirably thorough in his research and chillingly objective in his conclusions. His first task in Poland was to implement the *Sonderaktion* (the shooting and burning of large numbers of prisoners). It was familiar territory—from his Russian experiences—but the absence of science in this slaughter irritated him. It was wasteful and cumbersome. He became interested in ways of radically realigning entire races using medical science; of sterilising, purifying and—if the race was worth it—reconstructing.

He affected a professorial air in the conduct of his experiments, even though many of them were pointless or were the product of his wilful curiosity. He bound up breasts, to observe the effect on strangled milk, and removed healthy kidneys, to watch the body slowly poison itself. Women were de-sexed in dozens and their wombs invaded with instruments, X-rays and excoriating drugs. Healthy teeth were pulled and inmates' blood-streams flushed with unmatched blood and fascinating doses of detergents. He looked for faster means of castrating young men—dispensing first with anaesthetic. Some he sentenced to scientific deaths in icy water. Others were grilled with electricity or seeded with poison bullets. Mengele then gathered up the data—the blood loss, the saliva flows, the rectal cramps—and sent it all off to the Institute in Frankfurt. He made collections of racial curios—skulls and different-coloured eyeballs—and sent them off too, in parcels marked "Urgent." The Nazi medical establishment marvelled at his industry.

His humdrum work at the camp was in the selection of those new inmates who should die and those who should work. He'd never regret the slaughter that was perpetrated to his order, although in later years he'd prefer to emphasise the numbers of those he "saved." The numbers weren't indulgent; of the last 509 arrivals, in November 1944, only forty-eight were spared. The rest were gassed. For these, his freshly laundered powers of life and death, he would always be known to Auschwitz survivors as the "Angel of Death."

In January 1945 Auschwitz was liberated, but Mengele had fled ten days before. He was seen departing in a chauffeur-driven car. It was just the beginning of his life of cat-and-mouse. Over the next four years, there are few clues as to where he went. Then, in 1949, he resurfaced in Buenos Aires; a chemical salesman. He'd joined a fashionable bridge club and had listed himself in the telephone directory as "Mengele, Dr., Jose." It was as if nothing had happened, not the eyeballs, not the ice, not the agony nor the grief. He became ever more confident. He took a holiday in Switzerland. For ten years he lived like this, and then, in 1959, the Nazi-hunters found him; his address had been arrogantly scattered among his wife's divorce papers. An arrest warrant was issued by the West Germans, but as the Argentines dithered, Mengele made good his escape. He took off for Paraguay.

By this time, the Paraguayan presidency had recovered from the bad case of self-righteousness that it had suffered in February 1945. Stroessner was now in power and he expressed his distaste for the accusations that were being levelled at the Nazis. He scoffed at the figure of six million Jews perished in the Holocaust, but even if it was true, it didn't bother him.

"That is a European problem," he said, "not one of ours."

Paraguay, for Nazi war criminals, became an attractive alternative to Argentina and Brazil. There was the large German population who, regardless of its shortcomings, had seen Nazism as the force needed to throttle communism. Among them was plenty of support for the Spider's Web—*Die Spinne*—the Nazi escape organisation. Of the 5,000 ex-Nazis who made their way to South America, around 300 were thought to have been in Paraguay at one time or another. Among the least charming was Eduard Roschmann, an SS captain who'd been responsible for 33,000 Jewish deaths in Riga, Latvia. Although he died in the pauper's hospital in Asunción, he was richly immortalised in *The Odessa File* (the second of Frederick Forsyth's villains to find himself in Paraguay).

There were also plenty of Nazis who had the ear of the President. One of them was Hans Rudel, a former Luftwaffe ace and an accomplished weaver with *Die Spinne.* He gladly took up Mengele's case. Another was Alejandro Von Eckstein, a White Russian who'd fought under Stroessner's command in the Chaco War. Von Eckstein had arrived in Paraguay in the twenties, a feeble-minded snob on the run from the Bolsheviks. He was still prickling with indignation and alarming prejudices.

"Most of the Jews were communists in the Red Army," he squeaked. "Who killed the Russian imperial family? Commissar Sverdlov, another Jew!"

Although he professed to be an ardent Nazi, he wasn't averse to a little racial intertwining. Soon after his arrival in Paraguay, he'd joined an expedition into the Chaco with the Russian anthropologist, Ivan Belaieff. It proved an excellent opportunity for combining a little science with pleasure; whilst Belaieff was busy studying the Stone Age Chamacocos, Von Eckstein was busy thrusting himself into their daughters. Years later, he was forced to admit his carnality but with admirable dexterity—and churns of sentimentality—he managed to recast the affair as "a romance in the Garden of Eden."

With friends like this, Mengele's application for a Paraguayan passport was assured. As a Paraguayan citizen, Mengele was now immune from extradition. The passport wasn't revoked until twenty years later, in 1979, by which time all records of how it was obtained had been destroyed. For the time being, Mengele had found himself a useful bolt-hole.

"And when he got here," my friends insisted, "he went to live in Altos."

The bus passed the aerials and the end of the drain but I decided to carry on into Altos, the hotbed—perhaps—of Nazism.

Further on was a sign for "The German School for Dogs" and soon afterwards the bus pulled up on a common fringed with low, colonnaded buildings and a church. There was no sign of life. Perhaps Altos was in the seventh day of a siesta. The first person I found was a cowboy, asleep on a plinth. His hat was pulled down low over his whiskers and it didn't seem right to wake him and ask him about Nazis. I studied the monument above his head. It was dedicated to Estigarribia, war hero and head of state. In 1939, the propeller had sheared off his aeroplane somewhere over Altos, bringing to an end his life and the most promising presidency of the century.

The debris of a fairground was scattered across the grass, arthritic chair-o-planes and flakes of eggshell. Rum bottles were heaped in little cairns, monuments to a forgettable evening. The village dogs came sniffing across the common and it occurred to me that I must have looked like they did: scavenging, hopeful and aimless. What did I expect to find in Altos? What should a hotbed look like? I knew that there was another *Deutsche Verein* somewhere in the village and so I detached myself from the dogs and went off to look for it.

The clubhouse was on the other side of the common, a buttery blockhouse with yellow shutters and a tiled roof.

"If you want the keys to get inside, ask Julia at the shop."

I'd been caught scavenging. I turned to find a man with pale hair and raw pink skin. Although he was young, his eyes were goggled with misfortune. He introduced himself: Guillermo Copens Büttner, tractor driver and grandson of Baron Copens, an early colonist. I gave him my notebook and he wrote his name in it, in great looping copperplate.

Julia appeared with the keys. Julia de Weiberlen was copper-jowled but with hair dyed a shade of German. Her husband, she explained, was from Germany (though what she meant was that his grandparents were). She unlocked the doors and turned on the lights in the club room. It was almost bare. The buttery paint had surged over everything except one wall and the red-chequered tile floor. On the unbuttered wall was a mural: half of it depicted Paraguayan countryside, a thatched farm, a *peón* sucking on a cup of *maté* and a mortar for grinding manioc; the other half was Germany, an exotic Silesian farm and a stickman in a Homburg hat, smoking a curly pipe.

"Have either of you been to Germany?"

They shook their heads. "That," said Guillermo, jutting his chin at the throbbing colours of Silesia, "is as near as we'll get."

I don't think Julia saw any point in going to Germany. It was all here. "We have two balls a year," she said, "and an *Oktoberfest.*"

"There used to be other dances too," added Guillermo, sadly, "but no one has the money any more."

We exchanged *auf Wiedersehens* and I retraced my path back across the eggshells towards the aerials. On the way, I stopped at the German cemetery. I found Baron Copens, bedded down under his Iron Cross, alongside all those who'd lived and struggled with him on these hills. For some, the struggle had been short—infants carried off by outlandish diseases—and for others it had been a battle with homesickness. One settler was buried under an anchor, a thousand miles from the nearest sea. Another had words of Goethe dangling over his head.

For some reason, I found the colonists' names strangely pleasing and I wrote them down. Even as I read them back, I can picture the settlers, feel a crackling handshake or hear their dry, mirthless laughter: the Dohmens and the Ottos, Stelmacher from Berlin, the Baumans and Hasses, the Spindlers and the weedy Kunzles.

Mengele lived some distance away from the settlers, up on a hog's-back of orange earth and bitter scrub. Way below, the lake looked grey and inert. I walked back, almost to the aerials, and came upon a sculptor. He was working in a hide made of branches and leaves and had six children. They were all rubbing down elves and wood spirits with tiny stamps of sandpaper.

"You want Men-gelly's house?" he echoed. He'd cut his thumb and the blood was pooling in his uninjured hand. He looked at it blankly and then thought about the question. "That's the big estate opposite. It's owned by some people in the town."

"Do you remember him?"

"Not really. I was only a kid at the time." He licked up some blood. "I wouldn't advise you to go in there. It's private."

I didn't intend to. Trespass in Paraguay is often greeted with gunfire. Besides, what was there to see? Mengele was assiduous in covering his tracks, and when he moved, he took with him every crumb of proof that he'd ever lived. It was enough to peer through the barbed wire at the bottom of his driveway, at the drive that looped through the termite mounds before vanishing into cactus. It was enough to sit with the view that he'd had and to try—in vain—to untangle his thoughts.

"On the one hand," he wrote to his son, back in Germany, "I can never hope from you for understanding and sympathy for the course of my life. I, on the other hand, have not the slightest inner cause to 'justify' or to make apologies for any decision, any actions or any relationships in my life . . ."

Mengele's time in Altos was not a happy one. His new wife (who also happened to be his brother's widow) detested the emptiness of their lives up on the hill, and after a miserable year of marriage, she headed for home.

Mengele himself was uneasy. Although at the start he'd often driven himself into Asunción, he became increasingly concerned about the interest in his whereabouts. He'd been spotted by two survivors of Auschwitz in a jeweller's in Asunción and they alerted the world to his presence. Sympathisers in the capital then warned him of Jewish Nazi-hunters—in the city and asking awkward questions. When, in May 1960, Adolf Eichmann was abducted by Mossad agents in Buenos Aires, Mengele was terrified and a virulent rash blossomed across his body.

Soon afterwards he abandoned his hideout among the termite hills of Altos. Seized with panic, he bolted for the other end of the country, to the German colonies in the south.

For the time being, he was lost again.

47

The bus to Itá took longer than I expected. It was only twenty miles south, across low foothills of fruit orchards and *lapachos*. But the road was busy with country cars, surviving on luck and body-filler. Some of them had no doors or had windows cut from shopping bags. One had no bonnet-cover and its engine thrashed around in the driver's face, like a bucket of eels. Down the road, there were ox-carts heaving monstrous, useless machinery back to the city, and a cattle truck crammed with mourners in straw hats and weeviled suits. A few miles before Itá, the procession wheeled to one side and we rolled clear, into the town.

It was a pretty town of cobbled streets and rare excitement. There was a parrot loose in the draper's, and bird and assistants were flapping round the shop, fouling the air and fouling the bolts of cloth. It was lunchtime, and the only sound in the market was of an old seamstress sucking marrow out of a bone. A cowboy rode into town on his horse, stopped outside the hardware store and called for a bag of cement. It was brought and heaved into the saddle and he turned and rode thoughtfully home. It occurred to me that if I was to come back here in fifty years, I would still find the people of Itá chasing parrots and chewing ox-bones. After all, it had hardly changed in the last three hundred years; its cathedral was finished in 1598, only sixty years after Irala's first mewling litter of *mestizos*.

One of the first Englishmen ever to settle in Paraguay had lived in Itá. He was Luke Crosser, a soldier and a veteran of the Battle of Waterloo. In 1825, he set out with an expedition to find a river route through to Peru. He got to Paraguay but no further. After a short spell in prison, he found himself a native wife and settled in Itá. He only left it again in 1865 when he realised he was about to die. For such an important occasion, he travelled up to Asunción, like Moses off to meet God.

I asked everybody I met if there were still Crossers in Itá.

"We've got Crotas," they told me.

But others thought the Crotas were from Argentina. Luke's progeny, it appeared, had simply soaked into the gene pool.

The town is said to have received another strange foreign visitor on 17 February 1959. He was a short, stubby oaf who throughout his life had bubbled with aggression and whose face was gravelled with scars. The son of a bricklayer, he'd enjoyed modest success as a petty criminal, but his adventures had too often ended in police cells. Then, in his mid-thirties, he discovered he had a flair for bullying and he tumbled into fascism. He hacked his way to the top, dispatching friends and foes with firing squads and gossip. In the end, he was the Robespierre of Hitler's bunker: Martin Bormann.

On that, his first visit to Itá, he arrived in a truck in the middle of the night. With him were Von Eckstein (now almost incapable of doing anything decent) and another scaly ex-Nazi called Werner Jung. Jung's greatest moments had been in shorts—with the Hitler Youth—and he'd come to Paraguay in 1933 to prepare it for its glorious immersion in fascism. He was now an ironmonger in Asunción.

The only strange thing about the *Reichsminister*'s visit to Itá is that he was already dead.

For most people, Bormann committed suicide on 1 May 1945. Convention has it that he was with the *Führer* until the very end, in the Berlin bunker. During a break-out, he and Hitler's surgeon, Dr. Stumpfegger, had killed themselves by swallowing poison. Their bodies were supposed to have been found near the Lehrter Bridge, taken to the Ulap Fairground and buried. The exact circumstances of the deaths were, however, uncomfortably vague, and certainly vague enough for the War Crimes Tribunal to try Bormann in his absence, at Nuremberg in 1946. Whilst his past may have been obscure, they removed any doubts about his future: he was sentenced to death.

The search for his body continued. The Americans interviewed his dentist, Dr. Blaschke, who'd last seen Bormann in early 1945. They took detailed notes of the teeth they expected to find. The Ulap Fairground was dug over in July 1965 but nothing turned up. Then, in 1972, the digging was extended and—to everyone's surprise—the corpses of Bormann and Stumpfegger were heaved out of the sand. Both corpses were positively identified from dental records—Bormann's from Dr. Blaschke's recollections. For many, it was the end of the Bormann mystery.

For others, there was something not quite right about the discovery.

No one doubted that the skulls were those of Bormann and Stumpfegger, but there were odd features about them. Part of Stumpfegger's skull had been sheared off but the missing piece was never found (it had been smashed off by the mechanical shovel, concluded the police). More troubling was Bormann's skull. Although the teeth matched Dr. Blaschke's descriptions from 1945, he seemed to have forgotten several fillings and a lower jaw incisor bridge, a two-millimeter drift of the upper jaw bridge and a number of extractions. Perhaps he'd been thinking of an earlier time in Bormann's dental history? But there was something else too: Bormann's skull—only his skull—was covered in a thick red muck.

For many, it was a great disappointment when Bormann turned up on the Ulap Fairground. They'd wanted him alive. It seemed so unsatisfactory that he should have died in the ruins of Berlin selfishly and secretly, leaving—until then—no trace of himself. People had learnt to enjoy the idea of him sweltering in a hideout in South America, brewing up nerve-gas or cloning little dolly Nazis. They'd feasted on newspaper titbits: "Eichmann's Son tells Argentine Police Bormann is Alive"; "Letters in Eichmann's Home are Bormann's"; "Asunción Physician Dr. Otto Biss Treated Bormann for Cancer, 1959." It wasn't much to go on, and when the corpse turned up on Ulap Fairground, these stories began to look rather tall.

For the time being, people abandoned the idea that Bormann had lived in Paraguay. Then, in 1992, three years after Stroessner's downfall, the secret files of *La Técnica*—the brain of his clowning *pyragüés*—were released for public inspection. The first people to take any interest in them were the old *pyragüés,* who cleaned up the carcass and looted the files of their guilt. One of those to survive was a curious document—on Bormann in Paraguay.

The file suggested that he'd arrived in 1956 and had lived in Hohenhau. For some reason, the secret police had noted that he'd seen a dentist on Fulcrencio R. Moreno (the one next to my *pensión*). Then, in 1958, he'd complained of stomach pains and—according to the *pyragüés*—Dr. Mengele had called to visit him. Unable to find out what was wrong, he'd referred Bormann to a physician (none other than Dr. Biss), but the position was hopeless; the man was packed with cancer. He died—after some well-earned agony—on 15 February 1959.

Two days later, says the file, he was on his first—and last—trip to Itá.

The cemetery at Itá was built at the top of a small rise. As at La Recoleta, people here liked to stay within a few feet of the surface, in touch with those they'd left behind. I could now recognise all their different graves: the landlords in *panteones* with windows and lacy curtains; the Germans laid out in iron bedsteads—as if a good night's sleep had been suddenly engulfed in turf; the *peón* with his wooden cross and a crocheted shawl.

I asked at the gate if anybody knew the graves. A man with a look of practised sloth peeled himself off his seat and came to help.

"Have you got Martin Bormann here?" My words suddenly seemed so ridiculous.

The man had brilliant new red training shoes, too clean for work.

"I've heard he was here," he said, "but I don't know where. We'll have to ask Ramón Sosa. He used to be the grave-digger—but he's retired now."

Señor Sosa was summoned and arrived surprisingly quickly. Perhaps he lived somewhere among the tombs? He appeared as if from a sleep, everything curled up: his straw hat, his shirt and his well-creased grin. He was told what I wanted.

"We get four journalists a month coming here looking for Bormann," he said, wrinkled in amusement. "I'll show you the grave they dug up."

We threaded through the tightly packed tombs until we came to a clearing of red soil. Bright red, sticky muck.

"One of the journalists," went on Señor Sosa extravagantly, "came with a head in a suitcase and asked us to bury it . . ."

"There are lots of stories . . .," said the other man.

I pulled my dictaphone out, but when they saw it, the men looked at it sceptically. Now, when I play the tapes back, all I can hear is them scrambling to be noncommittal.

"I don't know any of the stories, of course . . ."

"I wasn't working here at the time. I only started here in eighty-three."

"I wish my mother was alive. She knew everybody. She even knew the clothes they were buried in."

Three heads popped up among the tombs. "What does he want?" called the ladies. They were overalled in nylon flowers and twitching with curiosity.

"He's another one looking for Martin Bormann."

"Ah!" they chorused knowingly. "Martin!"

So did "Martin" ever live in Paraguay? There seemed to have been plenty of people who thought he did. What about the body on the Ulap Fairground? It's his all right, they'd say, but it got there by fraud. This was no twiddling fraud either, but villainy of Jacobean complexity and—without being uncharitable—somewhat Jacobean absurdity. The champion of the theory is an English writer, Hugh Thomas, who sets it out with all its loops and whispers in *Doppelgängers, The Truth about the Bodies in the Berlin Bunker*. The nub of it is as follows.

Bormann did not die in Berlin in 1945. Instead, he made his way via Denmark, Italy and Buenos Aires to Paraguay. There he settled down, just as *La Técnica*'s file had said. Stumpfegger, on the other hand, did perish in Berlin: he was shot in the head. His body was buried secretly at a military cemetery by Nazi sympathisers and remained there for over twenty years. Meanwhile, in 1959, Bormann died and was buried secretly in Itá.

That ought to have been the end of it except that, in the late sixties, the Nazi sympathisers—*Die Spinne* possibly—felt that the Nazi-hunters, in their search for the dead Bormann (who was still considered to be alive), were coming uncomfortably close to other fugitives. They therefore decided to give them Bormann's body—or at least enough of it to make them think they had it. They dug up his skull from the cemetery at Itá, took it to Berlin and planted it in the Ulap Fairground, still caked in Paraguayan soil. The teeth would confirm it was Bormann. They would also show, say the theorists, that Dr. Blaschke was right as to the teeth in 1945. Bormann had simply lived a further fourteen years and, in that time, he had lost some teeth and had had work done on others.

To make the Ulap Fairground find more convincing, the Nazis retrieved Stumpfegger's body, sawed the bullet hole out of his skull (both men were supposed to have been poisoned) and dropped him in beside Bormann. Once everything was ready, in 1972, the West German prosecutors were encouraged to do a little more digging on the fairground and the bodies were found. For the second time, Bormann was shovelled out of his grave.

"Do you think he was here?" I asked Señor Sosa. Could bits of him still be here?

"Who knows?" he said, and we stood around staring at the ground as if we had X-ray powers and could see Indians and Nazis curled up in the soil. For a moment, I thought he'd spotted something.

"There are so many people in there," he whistled. Then he shook his head. "Who knows if Martin was ever there?"

For me, the theory wasn't without its drawbacks. For a start, the whole plan failed; it did not create a diversion. Nazi-hunting has remained good sport in South America to this day. Did anybody really think they could throw the Nazi-hunters off the trail? If the plan went wrong, it would merely have provided confirmation that there was indeed a Spider's Web in South America.

The only reason that it didn't go wrong—if the theorists have their facts right—is that the Berlin police conducted the investigation like clowns and failed to notice the obvious: that Bormann's head was covered in red clay and not Berlin sand; that it didn't belong to that body; that both bodies had only been in the ground a short while and not twenty-seven years. Could the Nazis have predicted such buffoonery, which was essential to the success of the plan?

And who had buried Dr. Stumpfegger secretly in 1945? And more to the point, why? Had someone foreseen that his corpse might prove useful later?

Perhaps the weakest link in the theory—and it is supposed to be its strongest—is that it relies on documents found in the litter of the *pyragüés'* nest. Their information tended to come from people who were either venal or spiteful or drowning in baths of sewage. The *pyragüés* were not famous for getting it right.

On the other hand, there is still a £20,000 reward outstanding for anyone who can prove that Bormann did *not* live and die in Paraguay. It was advertised in *The Times* and the *Independent* in October 1996 and has never been claimed. It is obviously not enough to cite the Ulap Fairground findings.

The mysteries of Bormann—and Itá—seem likely to trouble us for many years to come.

48

The Great Lunch that had overwhelmed Itá followed me up the road and subdued the town of Big Dog, or Yaguarón.

I had the church to myself, the greatest church in Paraguay. It was started in 1640 and took sixty years and 4,000 Indians to complete. The walls were nine feet thick and carried a swoop of roofing—a hundred feet wide by two hundred long—over the edges to form deep, shaded arcades. The front door was twenty feet high and thick enough to withstand a determined siege. I went inside, into the darkness.

The air was fizzling with bats.

"I'll put the lights on for you."

I suddenly noticed the sacristan. He crabbed his way off to the vestry, and as he crunched and ground the electric levers into place, light seeped across the ceiling. As it fanned out, it released arc after arc of paintings— scrolls, lianas, lotus leaves and colossal feathers.

"The Indians painted them," he whispered. "The gold is from Bolivia and the green is extracted from the leaf of the *yerba*."

The bats squeaked miserably as their cavern became a brilliant baroque jungle. The sacristan looked at me apologetically.

"I don't mind them," I said.

"I do. Every now and then I smoke the *bichos* out."

It was exactly this sort of casually violent authority that had made another inhabitant of Big Dog briefly famous throughout Europe. His name would become synonymous with absolute power, a torch for autocracy and a champion for those shrugging off the liberalism of the enlightenment. He ruled Paraguay for nearly thirty years, from 1814 to 1840, sealing it off from the world and meeting every whimper of opposition with unhesitating savagery. He was Dr. Gaspar Rodríguez Francia, "the Supreme One."

Francia was born in 1766 and raised on the main street of Yaguarón, which was now a gentle scree of sand and cobbles. His house had become a national treasure, a long, squat manor on a rectangle of clipped grass. There was a deep veranda of *quebracho* pillars and four heavily fortified doors. Beating on the middle door roused a ferocious curator.

"It's lunchtime," he snarled. "When am I supposed to eat?"

He never got over his resentment, but he agreed to show me the house.

"This is Dr. Francia," he said, introducing me to a portrait, horribly life-sized. The doctor was skinny-framed and bloodless, his hair scraped back from a bleak expanse of forehead. His mouth was thin but pinching and viperous and the eyebrows were furled up with bristly malice. The limbs were crabbed and spindly and yet oddly effeminate. He was hardly the superman I'd read about.

He wore black, as he always had, and next to him was a small tobacco case, a candlestick and a pewter sweet-box. These same objects now lay next to the portrait and were his only possessions. His meanness was congenital. His contempt for his fellow man took a little longer to develop.

Dr. Francia had seized power by telling Congress that Paraguayans had been "humiliated, oppressed, degraded," but that "these times of oppression and tyranny have ended at last." He offered them a choice: anarchy and Argentine hegemony, or himself. Congress was bewitched. They agreed that not only should he rule them but that he should rule alone and with absolute power, *El Supremo*.

But far from being the end of oppression and tyranny, Dr. Francia's accession was merely a beginning. He was deeply impressed by Rousseau's *Social Contract* and believed that people—had they the intelligence to realise it—would be happy to forsake personal liberty for the sake of order. Autocracy was the only safeguard against chaos. There were few heroes in his world—just Robespierre and Napoleon—and no place for education. All the colleges were closed. Then the post office was shut down and all the newspapers. Fiestas were banned.

At first, opponents of his philosophy found themselves merely stifled with heavy fines or confiscation of land. Then Dr. Francia established the Paraguayan secret service—the *pyragüés*—and sent them out, sniffing for dissension. Those accused could expect to end their lives in Francia's prison on Independencia. The ceilings were so low that a man would never again know what it was to straighten his back. Loaded with chains, he could do nothing but await putrefaction. Dr. Francia, who was rather previous with totalitarian doublethink, called the prison his "Chamber of Truth." The luckier prisoners were dragged beneath his windows and bayoneted.

Eventually, the entire country was shackled. The borders were closed. Control of trade was so tight that when an English merchantman arrived in Asunción, Francia had the ship impounded until he'd learnt enough English to determine exactly what was on board. The Church's property was seized and monasteries converted into barracks. Although Francia had once trained for the priesthood, he was more attracted to Voltaire and Diderot and abandoned his vocation. He humiliated the bishop and had himself appointed head of the Paraguayan Church. Then he invited the Pope to come to Paraguay—to take up a position as an altar boy. To his delight, he was excommunicated.

Next, he set about rebuilding the gene stock of his terrified people. He decreed that the Spanish could not marry amongst themselves. The mingling of the races which had started under the conquistadors as a matter of lust now became a matter of law. Spanish bloodlines came to an end. He toyed with the idea of outlawing marriage altogether, but this was overambitious. Instead every marriage was subject to his consent and heavy taxation. These laws were strictly enforced. When his sister married without consent, he had her seized, together with her husband and the priest who'd married them. All three were shot.

The curator pointed to two claws in the wall. "These are the hooks where he hung his hammock."

It had been an ascetic life, just whitewash and stone flags. Francia avoided relationships with any smack of friendship. He kept a ledger of the women he slept with and saw no offence in consorting with prostitutes. He had at least one child, a daughter, by an Indian woman. The child grew up to become a prostitute herself and worked a patch near his residence in Asunción. Though Dr. Francia never recognised her as his own, he demonstrated his own peculiar affection by declaring prostitution an honourable profession. From then on, Asunción's whores were to wear gold combs in their hair; the *peinetes de oro*. The name has stuck.

As if reading my thoughts, the curator took me to another portrait, in gouache. "This is his daughter," he said. "Ubalde García de Cañete."

Ubalde was as gaunt and loveless as her father. The curator licked his tooth, "Her family still own a lot of property."

Eventually, the rivets of cast-iron power began to pop. Absolute authority, having enfeebled his people, now began to enfeeble *El Supremo*'s mind. He ordered all dogs to be shot. Large areas of Asunción were pulled down on the grounds that they were pestilent. Everybody was ordered to doff their hats as the President passed (those naked Indians who had no hats were made to carry little brims, which they were to raise in salute). He developed paranoia and had all his food tested for poison. He became obsessed with security, trusted no one with his keys and locked himself in at the end of every day. When he ventured into the streets, troopers went ahead of him hustling people indoors and beating those who lingered with the flats of their swords.

Eventually, on Christmas Day 1840, he throttled himself in a massive attack of apoplexy, refusing medical treatment for fear of assassination. He died during an extravagant thunderstorm at the age of seventy-four. No Paraguayan priest was prepared to officiate at the funeral and so one had to be brought from Argentina. Most people hardly dared to believe that he'd died at all. They couldn't even bear to mention his name, and from then on he was referred to only as *El Difunto*, the Defunct One.

On his death, Ubalde burnt her father's furniture to drive out his spirit. Others, who'd worked up twenty-six years of resentment, got hold of *El Supremo*'s corpse and had it dismembered. They then tossed the pieces to the alligators in the Río Paraguay.

Elsewhere, there was no shortage of admiration for *El Supremo*. He'd presided over an unprecedented quarter of a century of peace, ruling with energy and vicious impartiality. His "National-Revolutionary" regime had relieved the Church of its cumbersome land holdings, and in the National Farms, food was churned out with almost sickly abundance. There was no debt, no crime, no frivolity. It was almost as if Dr. Francia had regarded the country as the personification of himself.

In Europe, there was admiration too. Men like Thomas Carlyle, who were always on the look-out for paradigms of autocracy, literally overflowed. Francia's death coincided with the most astronomical phase in Carlyle's thinking, and he lavishly accommodated *El Supremo* in his thunderings on heroes and hero-worship. Power was delivered by means of fear, he thrilled, to ignorant savages who knew no other form of governance. In the cult of heroes then prevailing, the eccentric Paraguayan dictator became—strange as it now seems—a champion. Insomuch as Carlyle ever influenced British political thinking, it's a curious thought that this influence derived in part from the spindly doctor who kept a sweet-box and had people whipped for looking at him.

Carlyle and the caretaker who'd not had his lunch were among *El Supremo*'s greatest admirers.

"These were good times for Paraguay," rumbled the old man.

49

Carlyle's type weren't the only people beginning to look admiringly in Paraguay's direction. A handful of other writers had started to take an interest in this strange, forbidden Paradise perched high in the headwaters of the Paraná. Voltaire was intrigued by what he'd heard, and sent Candide to a land of gold plates and caged humming-birds and natives that were pleasured by the monkeys. Robert Southey, the English poet laureate, had little more to go on when—in 1813—he named his longest poem *A Tale of Paraguay* and dreamed up an Arcadia:

> For in history's mournful map, the eye
> On Paraguay as on a sunny spot,
> May rest complacent; to humanity,
> There, and there only, hath a peaceful lot
> Been granted, by Ambition troubled not,
> By Avarice undebased, exempt from care . . .

Southey was to be better known for "The Three Bears."

With the death of Dr. Francia and the opening-up of Paraguay, the literary world had an opportunity to think again about this, its lost Elysium. Among the first to go was one C. B. Mansfield of the Philological Society, in 1852. Although, until then, his only published work was *The Constitution of Salts,* he considered himself the right man to rekindle public imagination. He reviewed the travel literature: the English marooned adventurers, The Robertsons, had been "amusing" but their book was got up to sell; the account of Rengger, the Swiss physician, was "dreary"; Hopkins, the American, was unspeakably boring. Mansfield would better them all. With hindsight, he was over-laden with preconceptions. "I went to Paraguay," he wrote, "to gratify a whim . . . to see the country I believed to be an unspoilt Arcadia . . ."

His more pressing problem was that he was profoundly deaf. This, he admitted, was "a Great Drawback." He couldn't understand anybody at all. His hopes that Queen Victoria would make him the first British consul in Paraguay were always rather over optimistic, but at least when she appointed someone else it gave him the excuse to go home. His travels (which never got beyond Asunción) were to be seamlessly disappointing. This was a shame, because everything had started well enough.

"Paraguay," he wrote on arrival, "is the most interesting, loveliest, pleasantest country in the world."

After a month, he was bored. "I have lived a very monotonous life, without any incidents to make it worthwhile to keep a journal."

Wearily, he wrote down anything that vaguely intrigued him: the priests smoked big cigars; the only amusement was in making housecalls; there was lots of red hair; the cathedral choristers spat at each other across the aisle; the Payaguá women were distinguishable from the Paraguayan women by their "extreme hideousness"; there were only four Englishmen in Asunción. Poor Mansfield drank away his last few weeks aboard a British warship, the first in Paraguay, and then went home. The task of editing his lovable ramblings fell to his friend, the writer Charles Kingsley.

Although Kingsley was never able to make much of Mansfield's jottings, he nursed them through to publication. More importantly, Mansfield's wanderings provided inspiration for Kingsley's own work; three years later he produced *Westward Ho!* Although, strictly, it was a swashbuckling adventure on the Spanish Main, Kingsley strained the plot a little with a short, freshly painted glimpse of Paraguay. The effect on

Victorian readers was startling. The image of a "fair land," a lost Eden, was back, embedded in the public perception. Even G. K. Chesterton, writing at the end of this period, identified Paraguay with the earthly Utopia:

> Ye bade the Red Man rise like the Red Clay
> Of God's great Adam in his human right,
> Till trailed the snake of our trade, our own time's blight,
> And man lost Paradise in Paraguay.

For some, it was not enough to see Kingsley's prose swinging around the page. They had to be there. Edward Knight was not the first traveller to arrive in Paraguay with a well-thumbed *Westward Ho!* When a group of Australian socialists arrived in the country in 1893, searching for Utopia, Kingsley's book was one of the few that accompanied them. It was not only their inspiration, it was their guide; they had little clue as to what else to expect.

But perhaps the greatest work of English literature to be set in this region was yet to come. It would be inspired by the dreadful catastrophes that befell Paraguay in the second half of the nineteenth century. This time, the perception would shift the other way; whilst still the land of the Improbable, Paraguay would no longer be Paradise but Purgatory—torrid, amoral and despairing. The book would be Joseph Conrad's *Nostromo*.

The curator told me that Dr. Francia's house was acquired by Stroessner. It was no surprise that Stroessner compared himself with *El Supremo*—nor was it any surprise that he hated others to make this comparison. When Roa Bastos published his Francia burlesque, *I the Supreme*, in 1974, Stroessner felt a stab of mockery and had it banned. Roa Bastos was exiled for life.

I asked the curator when the government had acquired the house.

"We didn't buy it," he said, and embarked on a story about the previous owner, Velásquez, who'd dithered over the sale and then lost his papers. "Without his papers," he crowed, triumphantly, "we were able to say to him 'On your way, Velásquez! Hop it!'—and that's how we got it."

It was, I suppose, brute power wittily applied. Francia's entire regime had been about demanding surrender. That, by 1840, is what he got.

Things might have worked out well but for the fact that—when he died—Francia delivered his cowed and dangerously obedient nation straight into the hands of those who were bound to abuse it.

The López dynasty.

50

The war came—as it inevitably would—but rather earlier than Francisco López had hoped for.

The immediate causes of the conflict were obscure, but once the four newly fledged nations had committed several hundred thousand men to the meat-grinder, they didn't seem to matter much anyway. Some say that Francisco, still smarting at the Emperor's refusal to hand over his daughter, was champing to blast away at Brazil, and that any excuse would do. Some saw it as part of a wider demand by López for "respect and attention," the twin peaks of his majestic folly. Others weren't prepared to blame Paraguay at all.

Even now, Paraguayans often see the causes as foreign, and trawl the improbable for explanations. "It was all started by the British," one man told me (on a bus). "Paraguay refused to sell them cotton cheaply. They took revenge by destroying the country. That's how it happened."

Others accuse Paraguay's neighbours of plotting to carve her up amongst themselves. The difficulty with this is that the Allies—Brazil, Uruguay and Argentina—were traditionally enemies and were caught wholly unprepared in their war against Paraguay.

Besides, it was always Paraguay that made the first move. In December 1864, López grabbed the remote Brazilian province of Matto Grosso (it was so remote that news of its capture took a month to reach Rio de Janeiro). When Buenos Aires objected to his trespassing, López simply captured Corrientes and two Argentine gunboats. His declaration of war (conveniently lost in the post) followed a week later, in February 1865. Within the space of a few months, López had made enemies of his three old friends and had united three enemies as The Triple Alliance. In diplomacy, he'd shown himself to be little more than the sweaty, ham-fisted oaf that he was. He now had the next five pitiful years to demonstrate his imbecility in warfare.

Whatever the cause, the mouse had roared. There were barely 1,300,000 Paraguayans compared to ten million Brazilians. Brazil was the second largest empire in the world, and—in theory—her National Guard outnumbered the entire population of Paraguay.

But the contest was not as unequal as it first appeared; in the previous six months, López had drilled 65,000 men and (if he counted all old men and boys) he could raise 100,000 troops. The Argentine regular army was only 6,000 strong and was scattered through its untamed provinces. Had López faced them alone, his loopy fantasies might just have prevailed. Instead, he was already committed to tussling with the mighty Brazilians, who were now steaming up the Paraná in their impressive fleet of ironclads.

Another problem for López was that events had unfolded sooner than he'd expected. Although his men were ready, quivering with obedience and desperate to die for their republic, the arms were not. López had ordered massive consignments of modern weapons from London, but they hadn't arrived and the Allies now had the country under siege. Paraguay would have to cook up its own weapons, and by the end her troopers would find themselves facing the latest technology—Krupps' rifled artillery and Whitworth shells—with wooden cannon, spears and pieces of glass.

Initially, López was buoyed by his successes—even though his enemies hadn't even been on a war footing. Paraguay had captured enough gunpowder to sustain it throughout the war and was ecstatic. López announced two months of victory balls and circuses. He appointed himself *Mariscal* and Congress meekly conferred upon him a diamond-encrusted baton, at a cost of $30,000. Madame Lynch was to be honoured with a coronet in the style of the Empress Josephine. She then further enraged the First Ladies by inviting whores to the victory balls and by relieving every lady of her jewellery—in the name of patriotism. It wasn't entirely clear how she intended to turn the jewels to her besieged country's advantage, but her supporters generously assumed that Paraguayan cannon were nine parts iron and one part gold.

Then the fantasy began to crumble.

López's Argentine campaign quickly fell apart due to his curly strategies. His invasion of Río Grande was totally unsupported, and when his army was split by a river, the two disembodied flanks were picked off piecemeal and 12,000 men were lost. At Riachuelo, he threw his precious wooden gunboats against the ironclads, and although the Paraguayans and their English engineers fought with wincing courage, they were mashed. It didn't help that they'd not been supplied with grappling hooks and were therefore never able to exploit the Paraguayan gift of bravery. Five ships and ten barges were lost. Modest though the losses may seem, the battle is still regarded as the greatest-ever riverine engagement in the history of naval warfare.

It is an honour that López's commander, Robles, could have done without. He ordered a retreat, and for his cowardice was hauled against a wall and shot. From now on, everything that López did was tainted with desperation.

In April 1866, a year into the war, the Allies—in sluggish pursuit—crossed the Paraná into Paraguay. But the country was like a great inverted bottle, naturally impenetrable on all sides except upwards, through the neck. To get to the interior, the Allies would have to force their way up the Río Paraguay, but there—in the bottleneck—stood Humaitá, "the Sebastopol of South America."

All the armies converged on Humaitá, and that's where I went next.

51

It took me eight hours to get from the central highlands down to Humaitá.

At first the bus was full, so I took the only seat left, by the lavatory. The lock kept jamming, and as I released people, I got to know nearly everyone on the bus. At the very first wail I was up tugging at the door, and then, with a loud pop, imprisonment would be over and a hundred and fifty pounds of panic would bowl me backwards into my seat. The reaction of the detainees was puzzling. Where I come from, people in this situation would extract themselves from each other with paddling apologies and plenty of pinkish giggling. Not here. People gathered themselves up with yellowing suspicion. Perhaps they thought I was playing some nasty foreign joke on them? One lady, who was magnificently bosomed in turquoise satin, stabbed a short brown finger at me.

"It's not safe," she snorted. "I could have been in there for hours."

Looking back on it, this was the first and last time that I ever saw anger in Paraguay. Every other indignity had been borne without words, without faces, without any expression at all. That always surprised me in a country where people were—apparently—so eloquent with their knives.

I was able to forgive the angry lady. Her indignity and panic must have been unbearable; as she lurched back to her seat, I noticed that parts of her magnificent underwear were still trying to escape, over the waistband of her skirt. A little girl two rows ahead of her was unable to stomach the prospect of incarceration in the privy. In fact she was unable to stomach anything at all. She was colourfully sick in the aisle. As we dipped and looped through the *cordillera,* an orange swell lapped backwards and forwards like the tide.

At some point an artilleryman got on board. He was very young, cropped and athletic and wore olive-green breeches tucked into jack-boots. There was something about him that was oddly heroic and beck-oned an early tragedy. He might have been a nineteenth-century statue to Patriotism except it wasn't carnage swirling around his heels but unstomached orangeade. He fixed his gaze on the road ahead, and then, when an artillery base appeared, he swaggered off. His comrades were posted around the camp perimeter with gas-capes and rifles. It was as if an attack was imminent. The army, it seemed, was unable to shrug off its conviction that an old-fashioned war was about to re-erupt.

Once again I settled into a rhythm. I decided I liked what I'd seen of the rural Paraguayans, despite their determined suspicion. Perhaps it was this that attracted me most of all. Their intense privacy, their quaint military costumes, their inexplicable emotions—it all made them so amenable to make-believe. Deep down, I was appalled by my reaction— it seemed so superficial—but I couldn't help inventing lives for my fellow-passengers. There was of course the heroic bombardier and the lady with the migrating knickers. Then behind me were two cowboys in *sombreros* and whiskers and gun-belts bobbled with shiny bullets. I placed them on the outer limits of lawfulness. Right at the back was an old woman with brilliant blue slavic eyes. She wore a head-scarf and had a large home-made cigar clamped in her gums. I decided that every male in her ancestry had met an early and unjust death wherever their migra-tions had ended.

Make-believe scenery tickled these fantasies along. At first we rolled through woodlands of feathery grey-green trees and pink *lapacho.* Then, at the edge of the *cordillera*, the bus tumbled through an outlandish rock-garden of brilliant red fissures and finger-like projections, all nuz-zled in luxurious clumps of tropical greenery. There were mountain streams glittering among the rocks, and bathing spots and paddocks of crimson ant-hills and ragwort. Then suddenly the garden was gone and we double-jolted across the disused railway into the flatlands of the south. There was Paraguarí, with its cobbled plaza and its market of plastic footballs and straw hats, and then we were in the swamps.

It took nearly all day to cross the swamps, or *esteros*. At first, in the north, the horizon was toothed with pale volcanic cones, but as we moved south, there was nothing but the curve of the planet. The road, no more than a ridge of banked sand mounted with asphalt, launched itself directly south into the submerged grass and the emptiness. Where the land was at its lowest, tiny lines of cattle nosed their way through the water, whipped along by leathery horsemen. Where it was raised a few inches above the surroundings, trees seeded the drier soil and packed themselves together in dark, cramped tufts. They looked like islands, but the swamp-dwellers, who had no concept of altitude, had long ago named them the *montes*, literally "the mountains." Apart from telegraph wire which looped from one crooked stump to another, there was no other sign of human life. Oddly, however, death was often bleakly present: tidy clusters of pink and yellow tombs, set back from the road. After a life spent waist-deep in mud, the *estancieros* would at last find themselves blissfully submerged in it.

By the time the bus reached Pilar, there were few other passengers left. One by one they'd asked to be let off in the *esteros*. I imagined that they'd seen the colour of the grass subtly change or had recognised a particular post and had then known that they were home. I turned and watched them shrink to a shadow, then a speck, then vanish. Everything I'd dreamed up about them now seemed rather inadequate.

No one was going beyond Pilar to Humaitá. There were no buses until the next day. I was slightly surprised. Humaitá was the scene of the greatest siege in Latin American history. It was the seat of perhaps the bloodiest conflict that modern man has known; eighty per cent of all Paraguayans perished, dwarfing even Poland's Second World War losses (twenty-two per cent of population). For Paraguayans, Humaitá was the crucible of their heroism and everybody had an ancestor buried in its sand. I was surprised that no one ever seemed to go there any more.

An awkward thought occurred to me.

"Is there a hotel in Humaitá?" I asked one of the *mercantes*. He had a tray of daggers and plastic robots in front of him.

"No," he said after some elaborate thinking, "there isn't."

"What about here?"

He peered down Pilar's main street as if for the first time in his life. I followed his gaze along a scrape of grey, furrowed sand, past grey, caked cars to a slab of grey lodgings. The only colour I could see was a poster: TOGETHER WE CAN BEAT MALARIA AND DENGUE. I hardly felt equal to the challenge. My optimism had evaporated. I decided to get a taxi the remaining thirty miles to Humaitá.

The taxi had all its windows darkened with blue plastic. It was like climbing into a small, self-contained twilight. The little box of captured nightfall was even well attended by mosquitoes. As I offered my juicy limbs to the darkness, they rose in a joyous cloud, each gnashing and thrumming with greed.

"Are these dengue mosquitoes?"

"Dengue mosquitoes," began a lugubrious voice somewhere out to the front, "are big and black and very stupid."

Although I could only see the mosquitoes in silhouette, I was sure that they were big and black. "Are these the stupid ones?"

I saw an eye leering into the mirror. "No," he said, "I don't think they are."

It was, I suppose, the commercial answer. Thrashing myself wildly, I urged the driver on to Humaitá. Then I opened all the windows and dawn spread throughout the Toyota. The mosquitoes vanished and the grey, sandy road turned white again.

My contentment was restored. Again, the track followed a thin ridge through the lagoons and the *montes*. Cattle egrets were skimming over the *esteros* and a stork took off with a tiny snake in its mouth. The sand was deeper here, and we slewed and yawed along the track like a drunk. We passed some Indians washing their clothes in the swamp and a cyclist grinding up the sand in his cogs. He had a rifle slung across the handlebars and a spoonbill slung over his back. Absently, I waved at him, but the look he returned was one of assessment, as if I were a portent of murky weather.

The Paraguayan army had marched down this same track 136 years before me. They too must have made a curious sight. Each soldier wore white with a scarlet *camiseta* faced in blue. They were all barefoot— except the cavalry—and some shouldered old English "Brown Besses," stamped "Tower of London." Others had only knives or *lanzas*. Every

man wore a leather *kepi* in which he kept his comb, cigars, matches and a needle for stitching up his wounds.

Behind came Mariscal López's personal escort in dandy Parisian uniforms. They were known as the *Ácá-carayá*—"the monkey-heads"—because their leather helmets were topped with brass and trimmed with black monkey tails. López usually rode among them—until he became too fat to ride—in a spiffy royal-blue cloak embroidered with gold oak leaves. His men called him *Taitá Guasú* ("Big Daddy") but he of course preferred to think of himself as Napoleon Bonaparte.

Although much imagination had gone into the soldiers' uniforms, little thought had been given to their diet. Most men were unused to meat but were expected to survive on *chaqui*—strips of blackened, dry beef—and for many this simply brought on long, candid bouts of diarrhoea. Others tried to freshen up their diet by shooting whatever moved on the swamps—egrets, alligators, ducks and frogs. They devised a means of loading their weapons with nails and pieces of scrap, so that by the time the fighting started, there was hardly a gun left with any rifling.

The problem of food was partially solved by the cavalry, whose horses were so honey-combed with bone disease that—after the first pitiful lance charges—they were diced up and fed to the troopers.

52

After an hour, the taxi lurched over the long ripple of sand that was all that remained of the outer trenches. "Welcome to the Heroic City of Humaitá" said a sign, but there was nothing there. The track simply curled away into the grass and cactus. Then, after more slewing and retching of sand, the track uncurled itself and bolted straight for the Río Paraguay. In the verges were the shacks and cottages of the Humaitá that had survived—all that remained of a fortress that had been a mile long, three miles wide and home to 24,000 skinny troops.

Although I was to become fond of this relic of nineteenth-century warfare, it is almost easier to think of Humaitá in terms of what it wasn't rather than what it was. There were no cars, no trucks, no children and no sounds but for the river and the birds. There was no glass in the windows and no stone on the paths. The horses grazed without boundaries on great scrapes of spiky emerald grass, on the football pitch and on the Square of the Heroes. There was no rubbish, no advertisements, no writing, no frivolity. Boisterous gardens of sunflowers and dahlias were restrained by neat, white picket-fences. No one looked up as we passed, no one knew if the village had a hotel and no one had shoes.

"I'll leave you at the shop," said the taxi-driver. I could tell that he resented the sand and the strain on his engine.

We churned on, down the last half-mile towards the river. There were other shops along the way: a sewing machine clacking busily in a dark doorway; a cave of unguents and potions; a bicycle-man with a tray of parts but nothing to ride.

The river widened in our strange blue windscreen. It would not be long before the Río Paraguay lost itself for ever at its confluence with the Río Paraná. After its magnificent south-bound roll, 1,700 kilometres down from Brazil, it seemed to have made one last effort to save itself and to loop north again. On the outer curve of its hopeless U-turn stood Humaitá. Half a mile away across the water was the fearsome Chaco Desert. There was still nothing there—just a tangle of reeds and thorn. The Chaco had played little part in the siege; it'd still been dangerously infested with Guaycurú tribesmen. For a while, the Brazilians tried to recruit them, but the Guaycurú would not be owned; they sold their new weapons to the Paraguayans and then returned to the Brazilians for their scalps.

"This is the shop," said the driver.

The taxi slumped into the sand, a short distance from the waterfront. The sun was scattered across the water and brilliant shivers of light escaped into the trees and played among the dark silhouettes of cattle on the shoreline. Long-tailed swallows scribbled their whirling crescents in the blue, all gone before the ink was dry. I paid the driver, and in a glorious cumulo-nimbus of dust, he flogged his taxi back to Pilar.

The shop was one of several buildings on the waterfront, all rebuilt some thirty years after the siege. Each was single storey with a pantile roof, lolloping plaster scrolls and curly neurotic ironwork. The shop was beginning to crumble away. The split-palm rafters were unscabbing themselves from the ceiling and the termites had undermined the floor so industriously that it now lunged dangerously towards its customers. Although it was a barn of a place, it was cluttered with the wreckage of the last hundred years: three bony bicycles, an antique motorbike, two billiard tables stacked with cement and a Christmas tree trimmed with steel wool and cobwebs. The cabinets around the walls had once been glass-fronted, but much of the glass had gone now and the shelves were silted up with dust and sand. I would often have to wait some time for the old shopkeepers to emerge from their slit in the shelving, but I didn't mind. It gave my eyes a chance to forage among the shelves, enjoying all the unwanted stock of the shopkeepers' blunt, unprosperous lives: grimy bottles of "Golden Drops" rum, holsters, whips, rodent traps, cakes with crusts of dark fur and bread rolls heaped up like cobbles.

She was grey with pain and he was purple with drink.

"I'm not well," she'd creak whenever I came in. I soon realised that her only hope was that one day a stranger would walk in with a diagnosis. Until then, she—like nine-tenths of Paraguayans—couldn't expect to benefit from any healthcare at all. It was small wonder that, in such a place, symptoms were allowed to develop from merely life-threatening to spectacular. *Crónica* had recently run a horrid front page about a woman in Guairá who'd just been detached from a seven-kilogram tumour.

There was no help to be had from the husband. He only appeared at the slit when his wife rasped for him to fetch something down or to open the money drawer. His flesh was as plush and liquid as sausage, and a little medallion winked among the cushions of his chest as he barrelled around the shop. There was something unpleasantly comical about him. In his rotting shop, ravaged by termites and drink, he was a source of Micawberish, quite unjustified optimism: the motorbike would run again and the billiard tables would soon be busy with sport; he invented buses back to Asunción and dreamed up delicious breakfasts which, on the table, turned to mould and cups of gluey grey milk. As I never knew their real names, I came to think of the shopkeepers as the Micawbers.

"Is there a hotel here?" I asked them.

Another brittle mosaic of pain spread across the old lady's face. She unclenched some fingers from her abdomen and crooked one at the other building on the waterfront.

The Hotel Municipal had also, at some stage, suffered an attack of optimism. In 1896, a grand building had been planned with a cloistered courtyard, heavily ornamented doors and brilliant French tiles fading into the distance. But only one corner had been completed, an abandoned "L" with its ends whittled away by misfortune. Recently it had been given a fresh coat of lime green on the outside and whitewash on the inside, but it was otherwise determinedly abandoned. There was no sign that it was a hotel. I peered into all the unlocked rooms calling—rather absurdly—for service. Eventually a woman appeared from the cottage opposite, heaped with sheets and pillowcases. She put me in a room with five beds and showed me the shower room. Its walls were patterned with tiny green tree-frogs which, at the smell of soapy water, detached themselves from their patterns and slithered into the foam. There was only one other guest and he kept his lights on all night and snored like a band-saw. In the mornings, he started up his motorbike in his room, revved it into the cloister and then hurled himself through the front doors and disappeared.

These were not easy nights. My bed was only yards from the river. After dark, thousands of operatic frogs slipped from the ooze and launched their plaintive arias at the crackly, tropical night. Whilst their songs were glorious in the evening, at night they intruded on my dreams, begging, pleading thousands of times over. I piled all of the spare beds against the door and burrowed under my mosquito net. But the attack came from below, from the carnivores that inhabited the mattress. By the morning, my back and buttocks were lumpy with rude, cherry-coloured blobs and drunken trails of blood.

After the hot, noisy struggles of the night, the day dawned fresh and serene. My room was angled partly at the river and partly at a curious brick stack, a sort of giant, toppling ginger cake that had—like me—been gruesomely nibbled. It was the ruins of an eighteenth-century Jesuit church. During the siege, its ginger towers were all that protruded above Humaitá's earthworks, and for the Brazilian ironclads, they offered an easy if rather unsatisfying target. At the height of the conflict, the allies poured 4,000 shells a day into the fortress. Had it been the age of high explosive, the church would have been powdered instead of merely chewed.

Among the crumbs of ginger brickwork, I found a cannon of the Paraguayan defence. It was a honey-combed Portuguese relic, already 200 years obsolete by the start of the siege. There had been 195 such guns, mounted in earthworks with names like "Madame Lynch" and "The London Battery." The defenders had even produced a new cannon, weighing over twelve tons; it was cast from church bells and was called the "Cristiano."

"It's now in the museum of Rio de Janeiro," Micawber later told me, his voice slushy with pride.

The Brazilians had lumped all their confidence in the ironclads. These fearsome, unwieldy vessels had already proved their fury in the American Civil War. The military world had gaped in wonder as the *Monitor* and the *Merrimac* had slogged it out at Hampton Roads. Now the Brazilians had fifteen of their own, each covered in four-inch plate and armed with 70lb Whitworths in revolving turrets. As marching across the *esteros* was out of the question, the ironclads would punch through Humaitá and up into the underbelly of Paraguay with laughable ease.

But the Brazilians were soon choking on their mirth. Quite apart from the Paraguayans' refusal to present them with a target, the ironclads weren't as formidable as expected. The river could rise or fall by up to fourteen feet, and treacherous sandbanks would swell up and leave the monsters helplessly grounded. When they weren't floundering, they were guzzling coal, and no sooner had they reached Humaitá than they had to retreat. The enemy's pipsqueak artillery couldn't sink them, but it could batter them enough to disable their gear. This wasn't their only trickery. For a while the Paraguayans launched home-made torpedoes at the ironclads until their engineer, an American called Cruger—blew himself to kingdom come. Simpler and more effective was the iron chain strung across the river. Until a freak high water eventually carried the ironclads over, this simple device kept them from Paraguay for what seemed a political eternity. The Brazilians now threw 40,000 men into the conflict, joined by 18,000 Argentines and 4,000 Uruguayans.

When the Allies first established a toe-hold in southern Paraguay, López responded with flamboyant stupidity. Although the advantages of defence were obvious, he launched 23,000 thin, dysenteric troops across the swamps to meet the Allies at Tuyutí in May 1866. They were shredded. The worst to suffer was the 40th Regiment, comprised of the Asunción gentry. Vindictively, López had them placed in the spearhead. To ensure their colourful destiny, he tossed them into the maelstrom without any training or shoes or even weapons. If nothing else, Tuyutí tidied up the opposition.

"That battle," wrote an Englishman on López's staff, "can be said to have annihilated the Spanish race in Paraguay."

But the rank and file fought with blurring ferocity. They were Guaraní warriors again, relishing the *mano-a-mano* fighting. Such was their tenacity that the Allies took only 350 prisoners. They only managed to capture the Paraguayan standard by chopping it from the hands of a sergeant (another dying standard-bearer prevented his flag falling into "monkey" hands by tearing it apart with his teeth). In the end, however, it was hopeless. The Paraguayans were forced back by hot, sticky mud and the lacerating technology of their enemies. They left 6,000 dead on the field. Often, the corpses of fighters were found locked together, transfixed on each other's bayonets. López had lost the pick of his garrison.

"The Allies," noted one stupefied report, "heaped up the Paraguayan corpses in alternate layers, with wood, in piles of 50 to 100, and burnt them. They complained that the Paraguayans were so lean that they would not burn."

Both sides fell back to lick their wounds. López ordered the bands to play victory marches to make his men think he'd gained the day. Stalemate ensued. The Allies in the southern heel of the country became so established that they built themselves brothels and a theatre. In Humaitá, 7,000 wounded soldiers were committed to hospital. The doctors, who were mostly British contractors, were endlessly astonished at the brawn of their Paraguayan patients; whilst the Brazilian and Argentine prisoners allowed their wounds to overwhelm them, the Paraguayans simply heaved themselves from their straw and stumbled back into battle.

Paraguayan women began to arrive at the front. At first, they simply followed their menfolk down to Humaitá, but later, all women of age sixteen to forty were conscripted as labourers. Most prominent among them was of course Madame Lynch (who wasn't going to be penned up in Asunción when issues of power were being resolved 250 miles to the south). In the Paraguayan imagination, she is to be found leading a cavalry charge of Amazons against a barbarous foe. It's a preposterous image; in reality, the Irish adventuress turned up in Humaitá with a train of ball-gowns, the Pleyel piano and some geranium seeds to prettify the presidential bunker. She only briefly toyed with the idea of military activity, dressing up a small troupe of ladies in sashes and Irish tam o'shanters. Their main task seems to have been to extract jewellery from other women.

In the months that followed, Humaitá achieved its own Paraguayan version of normality. A Prussian telegraph engineer called Baron Heinrich von Fischer Truenfeld produced paper from *caraguatá* pulp, and the army printed two newspapers. One was in Spanish and the other in Guaraní—both plum-full of jokes that the English found "wretched and sometimes scandalous." The ink was made from black beans. There were even experiments with orange wine and trousers made from raw hides (the wine was nauseously sweet and the trousers ripped the wearer's skin). Then, to the fury of Madame Lynch, her tropical Paris was cannibalised for the war effort: the carpets from the ballrooms were cut up into ponchos "so stiff that they stood up like advertising boards"; the books of the National Library met a similar fate, chopped up into cartridge and squib cases.

Discipline was enthusiastically violent. Every third man was detailed to shoot deserters, and the floggings were lavish. Those who finally made it back from the previous year's defeats in Argentina were whipped without hesitation. Two men who returned with smallpox were whipped to death. A Correntino girl who tried to slip away was whipped before the eyes of the Englishmen in López's service. "She received 60 lashes on her bare flesh," one reported, "which was considered a very good joke."

The Allies seemed unable to enjoy the war in quite the same way. The Paraguayans' behaviour unnerved them; first their ferocity and then, worse, their domesticity. The Allies again resorted to technology to find out what was going on. At a cost of $15,000 they bought a hot-air balloon, but on its inaugural flight, it blew up. The French pilot was sentenced to death for sabotage. Later efforts, employing the American Allen brothers, were more successful and the spies managed to float over the batteries at Humaitá. The Paraguayans' response—one of the first-ever responses to aviation warfare—was to loosen their breeches and show the Americans their grubby backsides. They then set fire to the grass and forced the balloonists—hacking their lungs out—into retreat.

Strange as the war in the air may have seemed, it was nothing compared to the bizarre naval battles that were taking place on the river.

I returned to the river several times a day during my stay in Humaitá. It was constantly changing colour: gorgeous magenta mornings bled themselves white by midday, and then—none too soon—this wincing light dissolved itself in the subtle infusions of the afternoon. But in the evenings came the real rewards—the rewards for so much heat and fine-blown dust. I sat on the rump of the earthworks and watched this great inland sea slide crimsonly towards the ocean. Most of the fishing skiffs now lay rotting in the lilies on the water line, but some evenings the last of them was out, a fragile arc of green, hunting the great golden fish— the *dorado*. The locals said it weighed thirteen kilos and fought like a *tigre*.

At the end of the soft turf beach was a large white villa called the Paraguayan Navy Southern Prefecture. It always smelt deliciously of oxtail and was manned by two bristly, blistered marines armed with assault rifles. They never put their guns down—even when crunching up ox-bones in their powerful teeth. I had to go up there one day to get the keys to Mariscal López's house, which the navy guarded against termites and sacrilege. The captain tossed me the keys without looking up from his bowl of gravy and ribs.

López's house was the third building on the waterfront, a squat ranch house, whitewashed on the outside and vaguely catty on the inside. I didn't believe that López had ever lived there (his contemporaries had him as far too much of a coward to be on the front line), but it was just possible that he'd visited to watch his little ships tearing themselves apart in front of him.

One of the steamers that the Paraguayans had captured from the Argentines was the *Gualguay*. Although it was barely more than a pea-pod, nothing delighted López and his mistress more than to watch it bob around among the ironclads. They watched it through opera glasses as it pinged its pathetic 12lb cannon against the impenetrable Brazilian armour. The Allies responded with balls of 70 and 150lbs, and every day, the plucky *Gualguay* ran its pointless gauntlet through the giant waterspouts and blizzards of red-hot metal. Once, she ran aground and was abandoned, but when the Brazilians came to reclaim her, her crew rose from the slime and butchered them with knives. The *Gualguay* was free again. The hilarity lasted a full three weeks before her funnel was blown away and His Excellency was forced to find alternative entertainment.

He was determined to capture an ironclad.

An opportunity came some time later, when the *Rio Grande do Sul* anchored sleepily offshore. López made a plan of hare-brained audacity: a raid by twenty-four canoes lashed together and disguised as *camelotes*—or clumps of water hyacinths. Madame Lynch saw the raiders off with cigars and girlish encouragement and they floated alongside the ironclad and drove its terrified crew below. The naked warriors then scrambled on to the armour, looking for holes for their grenades. It was too late. Another ironclad steamed alongside and raked the decks with canister and shot. A few jumped clear and swam off to uncertain adventures in the Chaco. The rest were fish bait.

It was now the Allies' turn to make a blunder. Unable to reach the Pilar road at Humaitá, they went for Curupayty, fifteen kilometres downstream.

They launched a full-scale attack. Across the swamps.

I decided to go there.

53

The defence of Curupayty owed everything to a young English railway engineer called George Thompson. He was only eighteen when he arrived in Paraguay in the late 1850s, to work with Whytehead. He was ambitious and eager to learn, and when the war started, he, like the other fifty-odd English contractors, chose to stay: "My personal motive for taking part in the War was not however so much political as physical. I wanted a change of air . . ."

Even before the war began, Thompson had earned the trust of López, and as the storm clouds gathered, he was given the task of fortifying Humaitá. Work had already begun under that purpled fop, Baron von Morgenstern, but at the first crack of powder the old Hungarian had succumbed to one of his mysterious wartime illnesses. He was indisposed for the duration of the conflict, and so Thompson took over.

It didn't seem to matter that he knew nothing about military engineering. He bought the best textbook on the subject, Macaulay's *Field Fortifications*, and sprawled its exotic jargon all over the swamps of Humaitá: enfilades, epaulments, embrasures, berms, breachings and the jangly-named re-entering angles. Even the chain across the river had been his idea.

I'd heard of Thompson before leaving London, and sought him out at the Royal Geographical Society, where he'd been a fellow. There, on the shelves, was a copy of his book, *The War in Paraguay*. It had been donated to the Society by the author himself, and under his name was his full title: "Lieutenant Colonel of the Engineers in the Paraguayan

Army, ADC to President López, Knight of the Order of Merit of Paraguay et C." The author was barely thirty.

Although the book was dashed off before the war was over and after Thompson had been branded a traitor by his paymaster, it was written with luminous candour. The characters are fresh and the events still steamy and grotesque and Thompson's own decisive role is trotted out with airy nonchalance. In places, the strategies of López simply fall apart under thoughtful analysis (and even those of the Allies are steeped in disunity and torpor). Elsewhere, Thompson is a boy again, regarding the war with refreshing detachment as if it was indeed just "a change of air." "During the bombardment," he wrote at Curupayty, "the Brazilian fleet threw about 5,000 bombs. They fired some very beautiful one-pounder Whitworth rifled balls and percussion shells. These were so pretty that it would be almost a consolation to be killed by one."

But for all his wonder, Thompson kept his head down. His brilliant fortress was elaborately reproduced in the maps in his book. Every star-fort and jungle, every redan and every lagoon is exquisitely recalled in skipping curlicues and copperplate. I photocopied the lot and stuffed them in my pack.

In Humaitá, I showed the maps to the Chief of Police, who was weeding the path of the *comisaria*. It was Sunday and his hair stood up like silver pins and his check trousers were worn at the knees. When he saw the maps, the air rushed out of him in astonishment. He flip-flopped back through the weeds and retrieved his own notes of the events of 1866. A thick brown finger followed Thompson's dotted track into Humaitá, past the church and then on—south—stopping abruptly just before the curly words "Thick jungle."

"This is Curupayty," he said, consulting his notes. "Forty thousand men died here."

On the map there was a dense weft of revetments and banquettes. I asked him if I could go there. He whistled.

"Maybe. It's about fifteen kilometres away." He then drew me a little map of thick, ugly gates and ponds. "Perhaps someone will lend you a bicycle."

"Does it get many visitors?"

"Hardly any now. It's got overgrown and people don't like the snakes."

Then he remembered something else. "A lad turned up with one of those metal detectors last year. That was interesting."

"What did he find? Lots of musket-balls, I imagine."

"Yes, those," said the Chief. "And three bottles of champagne."

Micawber was less than enthusiastic about lending me one of his fossilised bicycles. "These are good bikes," he blubbered. After a cold pail of scepticism, he tried again. "I'm keeping them safe for my grandchildren."

The man in the bicycle shop shrugged helplessly over his disembodied stock.

I asked an old lady digging manioc if she had a bicycle. To my surprise she had a mountain bike and I paid her a day's wages to let me ride it out to Curupayty. It had flabby tyres and no brakes and along the main strut were the words "Real Wild Stuff Buddy."

I didn't go straight to Curupayty. With Thompson's maps over the handlebars, I set off down the track that led to the eastern revetments of the village. I was soon alone with the sand gushing through the spokes. After a few kilometres I stopped. The swamps were softly globulating with life; there were grebes and crakes and a family of pigletty capybaras, all slicked with ooze. I don't know how long I stood there, fascinated. A vermilion fly-catcher zig-zagged past like a brilliant spark. Then, suddenly—out of nowhere—a sad, shrivelled cowboy was at my shoulder astride a very small chestnut mare. He wore a wide straw hat that made a ludicrous grin above his head.

"Do you know where the *trincheras* are?" I asked him.

He hardly spoke Spanish. But, he knew what I meant: the trenches.

"Here," he said, pointing ahead at a little fold in the road. "And there! In the *montes*."

On each side of the fold were shallow creases leading off into the distance, each densely colonised with thorn trees and palms. The miniature horseman clicked his tongue and was gone.

These were Thompson's trenches all right. Over a century of tropical rain had merely blunted their angles. I scuffed my boot in the sand. Thick shards of green glass broke the surface, and then a brass button. It was grey and crusty and had sheared violently from its mounting. I now keep it on my desk, a reminder of the suddenness of momentous events.

I returned to Humaitá and took the track that led out to Curupayty. I passed the spot where the villagers dumped their dead dogs. They lay in the dust, stiff-legged and barrelled, like furniture knocked over. A giant kingfisher eyed them thoughtfully, and then gathered his wits and flopped away across the lagoon.

I furrowed on, along the thin ridge that led through the swamps. Twice I passed pairs of cowboys, floppy-hatted and nestled in sheepskin saddles. They regarded me with unadorned curiosity—a strange pink man booting an iron skeleton through the sand. I wanted their horses. The "road-kill eagle" wanted us all, conveniently dead. I was alone again, with the enervating heat and the endless barbed wire and the breath roaring in my chest. Then I wasn't alone. There were waiters in the swamps in white tuxedos. Not waiters. Jabiru storks, ankle deep in mire and jolly tragedy. This was the third most massive bird in the world and all it could do was mimic the servants. I was tired already, and almost out of water.

After ten kilometres, there was a small rise to the left, a *monte* crowned with a rosy clump of *lapacho* blossom. It had the only view for miles around. Thompson had marked it on the map as "Head Quarters." I got off my bicycle and wheeled it up into the orange grove. I'd arrived at Paso Pucú, the presidential bunker.

President López's psychological state was becoming ever more scribbly. Even Thompson, who had—until then—naively admired his bloated commander, began to sense that López was unthreading. But it was Washburn, the American Minister—now dizzy with contempt—who provides us with the most animated description of the President:

> His teeth, were very much decayed, and so many of the front ones were gone as to render articulation somewhat difficult and indistinct. He apparently took no pains to keep them clean and those which remained were unwholesome in appearance, and nearly as dark as the cigar that he had almost constantly clamped between them.

Whilst López could steady the pain from his rotting gums with hefty draughts of port, his paranoia was harder to soothe. He was terrified of his subjects and terrified of the war he'd started. He passed a law that prevented him from "exposing his own precious life in times of war," and tried to make himself less conspicuous. His "Monkey-heads" lost their fancy brass hats and the sentries were forbidden from presenting arms. The President even abandoned his natty uniforms near the action, wearing his golden saddle cloth inside out and shoving his fat head into a straw hat. At all times, his carriages were to be harnessed up, ready to bolt at a sniff of trouble.

"He possessed a peculiar kind of courage," recalled Thompson drily. "When out of range of fire, even though completely surrounded by the enemy, he was always in high spirits but he could not endure the whistle of a ball."

This was not an impressive quality on a battlefield that was now permanently raining metal. Thompson built the bunker at Paso Pucú to insulate the President from the sounds and splinters of war. It was covered with nine feet of earth and protected on each side by embankments eighteen feet thick. López lived in there like a mole.

But it was still not enough to calm him. Even when Thompson visited him, he demanded that his visitor write out exactly what the sentries had asked him. Thompson obliged and solemnly set out the sergeant's questions:

Does Queen Victoria always wear her crown when she goes out for a walk? Would Sir still wear his Paraguayan uniform when he returned to England?

López had the sergeant shot anyway, and gave the rest of the guard a hundred lashes each.

Apart from the cackle of firing squads, life at Paso Pucú was surprisingly humdrum. The President spent much of the day in his hole, walloping down port and playing draughts with the bishop.

He entertains friendly feelings for no one [said Thompson], as he has shot all those who have been most favoured by himself, and who have for years been his only companions. He is a great smoker and lover of table; he eats enormously; after dinner, when in good humour, he occasionally sings a short song. He has a very large stock of good claret, of which he is very fond, and which no one at his table used to drink but himself—not even Mrs. Lynch or the Bishop . . .

Whilst her brave knight sloshed his way through songs and claret, Mrs. Lynch made herself at home. She planted the geraniums on the casements and unpacked some gilt furniture. When the British Minister called by, she baked him a fine plum pudding and provided frothy English ale for his escort. She gave bomb-proof dinner parties which were described by one guest as "capital" affairs. Another marvelled at her capacity: "She could drink more Champagne without being affected by it than any other woman I have ever met."

If it hadn't been for the little matter of the war, Paso Pucú might have been a breezy little break before the storms that lay ahead.

I left my bicycle at the gate of Paso Pucú. As I clambered up into the orange grove, a squall of parrots rose from the fruit and crashed away across the grasslands. There was a *quinta* in the clearing with a yard of rammed earth and cow-skin hammocks hanging from the eaves. The old farmer rose to greet me with watery eyes and a glint of gold tooth. A flotsam of chickens and puppies bobbed along in his lurching wake.

Of course I could see the casements. He ordered his son to take me, and a younger man emerged from the carcass of a car, wiping his hands.

"There's not much to see now," he said apologetically.

Under the banana trees the ground was lumpy and uneven. It was deliciously cool and the grass swayed with blue flowers. After its evacuation, López had ordered Paso Pucú to be levelled, wiping out every trace of his architectural cowardice. There was nothing left but an ugly white bust of López, gloriously erected on the orders of another bloater, His Excellency President Stroessner.

We picked our way back to the farm yard.

There was a 70lb Whitworth shell lying in the earth. I tried to imagine its strange journey from the foundries of the English Midlands, across the Atlantic to Brazil, transhipped by ironclad up the Paraná and then lobbed 7,000 yards through the air at Paso Pucú. Perhaps, on its last journey, it had killed. Perhaps it had simply cuddled itself into the soft Paraguayan soil.

"We get lots of this," said the father. He poured a little handful of musket-balls and buttons into my palm. "Keep them. Take them back to your country."

His daughter-in-law was grinding up *chipa* with a knotty wooden stump. Here, the intervention of the modern world had been brief and inconceivably violent.

And then it was gone again.

On 12 September 1866, the warring parties squandered their last opportunity of peace. Mariscal López agreed to meet the Argentine commander, Mitre, in the swamps of no-man's-land. His American carriage hauled him out of Paso Pucú and back to the track I'd cycled down. It turned left and through a huge breach in the earthworks, and then descended into the *estero*. López had dressed himself in a new uniform frock-coat and *kepi*, grenadier boots and a scarlet poncho lined with vicuña and trimmed with gold. As he neared the enemy, he steadied himself with a powerful draught of brandy and clambered on to a white charger.

Mitre was waiting for López down in the swamps, dressed in an old hat. The two men greeted each other and toasted the health of their nations with further draughts of brandy. Mitre set out the Allied terms of withdrawal: López must go into exile. López stoutly refused. The men argued for five hours and then parted, exchanging riding-whips in remembrance of the day.

For López, it had been a day in which he'd showed his mettle. For Mitre, it had been a wasted morning with a fat old drunk in fancy dress.

Ten days later, the Allies threw themselves across the swamps at the earthworks of Curupayty.

It was cooler now, and I got back on the bicycle and passed through the breach in the escarpment. I turned right and followed the police chief's smudgy scrawls through the gates and ponds along the edge of the drop. On Thompson's map, I was skirting the southern limits of the Paraguayan defences and heading for Curupayty. Around the gates there were a few shacks with their meat ovens and ox-carts and then the track hooked over the top of the escarpment and on to great whispering grasslands. I looked back, over the green slime of the *estero* Bellaco— where Mitre and López had met—and then set my course five kilometres north through the dry, sandy grass.

Despite the emptiness of the horizon, the grass was busy. It seethed in the wind, and owls and oven-birds flapped and bickered among the tussocks. As I cranked along, billowing sand, two rheas—or South American ostriches—rose from the straws in panic. In their walnut-sized confusion, they high-kicked along beside my bicycle for several hundred yards. I found the energy to keep pace with them: two ballerinas tiptoeing over hot bricks, whipped along by a cyclist riding silvery bones. There was then a spark of self-preservation and the birds burst away at a tangent, whirring themselves off into nothing. For all her feathery frivolity, the rhea is said to have a glimmer of insight. The locals said that in grass fires, *ñandu-guazú* dunks herself in water and then sprinkles her soggy feathers over her eggs to protect them from the heat. Before hatching, every tenth egg—*el décimo*—is smashed and the yolk is farmed for maggots, to feed the new chicks.

The track passed through several desiccated copses. The oven-birds had their fortresses here, red concrete nests plastered on to tree stumps—a labyrinth to intruders. This little chatelaine, a russet creature like a thrush, is held in much affection by the Paraguayans, who call him *Alonzo García*; he mates for life and sings like an angel; he works all day and every day except, they say, Sunday—for he is a bird of deep convictions. Unafraid of man, the oven-birds often flew close to my bicycle before the appalling, grinding sight became too much and they fluted away. I heaved myself onwards, towards the battlefield.

I now had no more water and my mouth was cloyed with dust. Sensible voices were urging me to turn back, and I was about to give in when I spotted something arising from the grass: a thick, crumbling obelisk with the date of the battle, 22 September 1866. Beyond it was a massive rampart of earth—Thompson's greatest work—split by a narrow breach. I cycled through this channel and paused at the edge of the swamps which stretched out towards Argentina.

The Argentine troops had been so confident of success that they'd even brought their saucepans with them across the *estero*. They expected to sup that night in Humaitá.

They hadn't counted on Thompson's preparations. He'd moved some two hundred cannon from Humaitá and concentrated them at Curupayty. The angle of the berms was calculated down to minutes of a degree. He'd even adjusted the standard formulae to take account of his firepower's impotence. There were chain cables to emasculate the enemy cavalry and interlocking enfilades to send a stiff shower of missiles into the enemy's unprotected infantry.

As the Argentines closed in, the ramshackle artillery pieces opened fire.

The sky was filled with earth and the grasslands turned to thick grey cloud. The air was bent and stretched by the boom of powder and ears filled with blood. Parrots rained into the river and the water boiled with ashy foam. Horses were caught by whirling scimitars of metal and frankly chunked and charred. The Paraguayan artillery blasted on. They fired 7,000 rounds that midnighted morning. Their commander, a carnivorous maniac called General Díaz, went wacko in the heat and noise and ordered his musicians to play huge, drowning reveilles. He urged his men to redouble the bloodshed and then double it again.

The Argentines never even got near the trenches. They were mown down like partridges and their bodies thrown quivering into the bog. When the barrage stopped, Díaz ordered his men out into the swamps to bayonet the wounded. They did so with unembellished pleasure (the previous year, the Argentines had maltreated their captives—a dreadful mistake—and they now paid for this in agony). Only six Argentines were taken prisoner; 9,000 perished. The Paraguayans lost a mere fifty-four men. It was one of the most unequal slaughters in modern military history, and for the Paraguayans, their greatest victory—and almost their last.

They then harvested the dead. The Allied soldiers were stripped of their sovereigns, watches and uniforms and their corpses rolled into the ditches. When the swamp was full, the mangled bits were dragged to the river and fed to the *caimanes*, the greedy alligators who now had a taste for war.

Díaz now thought he was invincible and took a canoe out fishing among the Brazilian ironclads. They got him in the end, of course, ragging his leg with a 13lb shell. His officers swam him to the shore and Dr. Skinner, the English doctor, amputated the tattered limb. Madame Lynch drove the general back to Paso Pucú in her buggy. Díaz, now chronically unhinged, had his amputated leg soldered into its own little coffin so he could haul it round with him. The insanity didn't last: a few days later the old cuckoo was eaten up by gangrene.

*

There was a bust of General Díaz shoulder deep in the grass, like a petrified sniper. I didn't hazard a closer look, partly because my imagination was haunted by the police chief's warnings about the snakes. There were rattlesnakes, he'd said, and corals and the deadly *yarará*—the Brazilian fer-de-lance. Of these, there was little encouragement from my Lonely Planet. The rattlesnake, it said, "transmits a highly potent neurotoxin that can cause paralysis so severe that the neck muscles cannot hold up the head and the neck appears broken."

"Worst still," thrilled the chief, "is the *cinco minuto*. One bite and five minutes is all you've got."

My more immediate concern was that I was already under attack. A fuzz of oily black mosquitoes had settled fatly on my clothes. My jeans were mottled with their glossy limbs and I could feel them probing the cloth for weakness and sniffing at my blood. I swatted them off with Thompson's map, and although they rose in a lazy blurr, they soon fell on me again. I saw the rest of Thompson's trenches and the banks of the River Paraguay in a state of excited flapping and thrashing. I only managed to regain my dignity very briefly, when a barge washed past, hauling BMWs and whisky up to Asunción. As soon as it had rounded the bend I was off again, slapping and dancing and twisting like a puppet. Eventually, the haze of insects lifted and floated away.

Unmolested, I suddenly felt the isolation of the place. I was alone with the extravagantly crazy General Díaz. The grass hissed, and beyond the thorn trees of the earthworks, a strangled roar was lifting eerily from the forest. It was Thompson's "thick jungle" to the south. The roar was the howler monkeys, bidding the day to end. I climbed back on my bicycle and left this bloodied place, churning up its terrible sand in my retreat.

The rheas were back, to watch me go and to reclaim the place for their own.

The Allies took Curupayty as a terrible blow. Argentina lost any remaining enthusiasm for the war, and the greater share of the fighting now fell to the Brazilians. Allied strength was built up to 80,000, but even the Brazilians struggled to find the numbers. Brazilian rural life was fractured by violent recruiting gangs, and eventually the plantation slaves of Bahía were drummed into the ranks on the promise of freedom and land. The cost was debilitating at £14,500,000 a year, of which

£2,000,000 went on maintaining the horses of the imperial cavalry. All sides were now desperate for a conclusion.

Curupayty held out for another year. At first the Allies were paralysed with shock, and then the ranks of both armies were liquefied by cholera. López was so terrified of the disease that he forbade anyone to mention it by name, and it was known simply as "the Chain." It claimed fifty men a day for six months. Then the bombardments began again and Thompson pulled the artillery back from Curupayty. The Paraguayan bombardiers hauled them back so fast that they were able to blast the ironclads as they passed Curupayty and then blast them again as they arrived at Humaitá, fifteen kilometres upstream.

When Curupayty was finally abandoned, Thompson mounted the earthworks with one last, sullen garrison. The wary Allies shelled them for three days before mustering the courage to advance. They were in for a bitter surprise.

The last defenders of Curupayty were merely scarecrows, stuffed with straw.

I turned back, for Humaitá.

A few kilometres from the battlefield, the track in front of me suddenly exploded and a *caimán* blasted itself from the dust and into the lagoon. It landed on the surface like one of Cruger's unfortunate torpedoes, belly-flopped towards the deep water and sank. I got off my bicycle and sat on the bank to watch. A pair of cold reptile eyes broke the surface, and then the nostrils. It lay like that for some time, wondering, I fancied, whether I was a predator or another juicy war.

"The *jacaré* won't harm you," the police chief had told me. "They're too small. And they're stupid. The brain is just jelly. They're just little killing machines."

The *caimán*'s brainless, villainous, armour-plated face emerged—almost imperceptibly—from its soup.

"They'll play dead for hours," said the chief, "even when you shoot their feet off."

54

Although Mrs. Micawber said she'd once run a restaurant—before her pains overwhelmed her—there was now nothing to eat at the shop except the green rocks of bread. Go to the restaurant, said the Micawbers, at the end of the village.

The restaurant was the last shack before the swamps. It had three rooms: one for eating, one for pool and one for the family. There was a counter in the pool room, and as the place became a home from home, I could soon list every item under its gritty glass: pastries, biscuits, lighters, spaghetti, bullet-rolls and rum. Clumps of brown damp bloomed across the walls and a sausage hung from the ceiling, absorbing the smells and smoke of the cowboys. There were six splintery chairs and two pictures; one depicted The Last Supper and the other a delicious naked blonde who was about to be eaten—or ravished—by a giant black cat.

It was run by a woman whose face was scrunched with sand and work. Her husband came in from the fields at sundown and changed into a stiff, flowery shirt and matching shorts. Their daughter lay on the pool table all day, dreaming up poems. "America is the continent of love . . ." she wrote.

"What would you like?" said the mother. It was a ritual. There was no choice but the day's dish would be deconstructed and reassembled with ponderous relish. "There is minced beef. And butter. And peppers and some tomatoes. There's bread. And fresh chopped onions. Would you like mayonnaise on that? And salt? And pepper?"

I would say "yes" to it all, and moments later a succulent hash would be borne to the table, latticed in mayonnaise. On the night I returned from Curupayty, they had *dorado*. I have never tasted such luxurious fish meat. Its creamy flesh flopped from a flank of thick, hard bones. I polished my plate.

When I'd finished, a crew of *peones* called in at the restaurant. Their spurs scraped across the stone floor, the sound of exhausted men. They had hands of alligator-skin and heavy gun-belts, whips and woven *fajas*—their cummerbunds. Word had reached them of the *dorado* and they wanted to buy what remained. The great golden carcass was hauled from the eating room and thrown across a horse. I listened for a while as the scuff of hooves retreated into the darkness.

Then Humaitá was swirled again in silence.

By the anniversary of Curupayty, the Allies had cut the road to Humaitá and it was surrounded. Five months later, in March 1868, López broke out of the encirclement, crossing the river and marching up through the

Chaco. Of his original army of 100,000, only 20,000 remained, and—elsewhere—widows and orphans were beginning to starve. Even Madame Lynch was forced to abandon much of her sumptuous plumage in Humaitá, but the wine, the silver and the piano all made good their escape on the presidential ox-train.

Three thousand men were left behind to defend the fortress, under the command of Colonel Alen. He was unhealthily besotted with Madame Lynch and determined to put up a fight commensurate with his ardour. In the end it wasn't to be, and he blew his eye out with a pistol (later, López had him finished off with a ball in the back of the head).

Meanwhile, the Allies poured fire down on to the defenders. The Paraguayans responded with all they had left, often just blowing their *túrútútús*—or trumpets—and infuriating the Allies with their stoicism. They dug themselves fox-holes with names like the Hotel Français, de Bordeaux and Garibaldi and fed their gallows humour.

"If a Paraguayan in the midst of his comrades was blown to pieces by a shell," wrote Thompson, "they would yell with delight, thinking it a capital joke, in which they would have been joined by the victim himself had he been capable."

The allied commander, the Brazilian Marqués de Caxias, was less inclined to see the funny side. He still holds the world record for being the youngest soldier ever (he entered his infantry regiment at the age of five in 1808). After sixty years of soldiering, he wasn't amused by an enemy that blew *túrútútús* at him and that thought his bombardments "a capital joke." At first he tried bribery and offered Colonel Alen 2,500,000 gold francs to surrender. Alen replied by return.

"I am sorry, General," he wrote, "not to be able to follow your example by offering money but if you will consent to deliver your squadron, I will give you instead the Imperial Crown of Brazil." He signed off the letter, "May God Preserve you and the peoples of your great and noble nation."

Caxias was incandescent. He had seldom been so insulted in his life—let alone by these howling, painted savages, the Guaraní. The killing was placed on a higher plane; from now on, the annihilation of the Paraguayans was to be industrial. Thompson—who wasn't shocked by very much—was appalled at Caxias' ruthlessness and suspected him of prolonging the war for his own profit. His anxiety was shared throughout Europe and the United States. *The New York Times* railed against the futility of it all. "The Allies," ran one editorial, "must see the impossibility of achieving their object without simply destroying the Paraguayan race from the face of the earth."

Caxias could see it all too well; the bloodshed escalated.

Even some of the Argentines began to chafe at the relentless slaughter of the Paraguayans. One group—the *Montoneros*—rekindled old anxieties and came out in armed revolt. They would be a thorn in the side of Argentine authority for the next one hundred years.

After López's departure, the defenders held out for another five months. When the jerked beef ran out, they survived on robbery. They ran improbably bold raids deep into the allied lines, stealing horses and occasionally whole herds of cattle. Thompson was constantly surprised at what the raiders came back with; it was the only time that he'd enjoyed fresh artichokes in Paraguay. On other occasions they came back with Mitre's letters from his wife (with a piece of cheese enclosed), tea, boots and—more bizarrely—parasols and crinolines.

Caxias launched another full-frontal assault with 12,000 men. Hero though he may have been to Brazilians, to Thompson he was an inexcusable buffoon, always throwing his men against the strongest sections of the fortress. Two thousand Brazilians were minced up in the Paraguayan response. The battle is said to have lasted only an hour. The Guaraní lost just forty-seven men.

But food and powder were now perilously short. It was time for the Paraguayans to bluff their way out of the trap. Under the cover of a vast birthday celebration, the 2,500 survivors of the garrison crossed the river in canoes. The military band was the last to leave, thumping and tooting their outrageous deception until the very end.

Suddenly, after two and a half years, Humaitá was silent.

Realising they'd been cheated, ten thousand Brazilians rushed round to cut the fugitives off. For several days the two sides fought miniature naval battles in canoes on the lagoons. A thousand Paraguayans got away, including Alen (stretcher-bound, an eye hanging out and dreading his fate) and Thompson. The rest, under the new garrison commander, Colonel Martínez, fought on until they were too weak to hold their guns. On 5 August 1868, they surrendered.

On hearing the news, López declared Martínez to be a traitor. His wife, who was Madame Lynch's lady-in-waiting, was seized and bound. She was flogged by a common trooper and then, more thoughtfully, tortured for a week. When López realised that she was no longer really appreciating any pain, he had her hauled away and blown apart.

It was harder to get out of Humaitá than I'd imagined.

At first, I tried to find a lift, but nothing moved all morning except some horses. I was forced back to Micawber, who was the agent for the daily bus. It was a five-hour wait. Sugary with rum, he showed me the junk he'd grubbed up in his yard: bayonets sheared at the hilt, shards of cavalry swords and the skeleton of a revolver. I asked him if he sold these things. His face rolled itself up in horror.

"Never!" he sloshed, clutching the rusty pieces to his chest. "One day this lot will be worth a fortune!"

All afternoon I sat on Micawber's porch with his friend, another drunk in bare feet and a pin-stripe suit. The suit was far too big and it so overwhelmed him that his head completely disappeared. This headless, snoring rag was draped across a cradle of massive four-inch iron links.

It was all that remained of Thompson's brilliant river chain.

55

After the fall of Humaitá, the fort received a visit from a group of tourists, probably the first Paraguay had ever seen. They'd chartered a motor-yacht called the *Yi*, a floating hotel of white panelling, freshly starched napkins and silver plate. It was a sort of plumply upholstered Turf Club, eased into the war zone to offer the rich comfortable views of the carnage. Modern military technology has made this sort of holiday rather unfashionable, but at the time, it was capital sport. Naturally, eating was an essential component of the pleasure and the first feast was served daily at ten a.m. It consisted of sausages, ham, olives, cabbage, meat stew and puddings, and was chased down with table wines, port and cowslip tea. If this wasn't enough to permanently anchor the guests in velvet plush, the whole collation was repeated again four hours later. This gluttony continued upstream at a very satisfactory twelve knots until the cook, fearing enlistment, jumped ship, followed one by one by the stewards.

The passenger list was a microcosm of the Triple Alliance. There were a few Argentines and a handful of Uruguayans—who flipped their noses up at the Brazilians and called them "the monkeys." The Brazilians didn't mind; they were stupendously wealthy, on holiday and in the majority. They got up in the middle of the morning (missing a few tureens of cabbage and sausage) and argued about the order in which the sherry was served. Their gambling was imperial and tended to cause the splendid saloon to overheat. It would have been enough to make a splendid economy overheat; one of the guests lost £2,000 on the leg from Buenos Aires to Humaitá. This was an admirable extra on the already lavish cost of the trip: £14.

Some guests were there to blend a little business with their pleasure. Segundo Flores, son of the assassinated Brazilian president, had an idea to sell uniforms to the armies. Another passenger was an old friend, that snivelling weasel of a journalist Héctor Varela, as eager as ever to delight in the discomfort of the Paraguayans.

Among the Argentines was a military man called General Gelly. He was variously rumoured to be Irish, romantic and even Paraguayan. On one of his walks through the abandoned fort, he found Madame Lynch's imposing collection of shoes. He selected some black satin pumps and sent them to his wife in Buenos Aires. She wrote back, "I have received the booty of Madame Lynch. After three years' blockade, Madame Lynch leaves her elegant latest fashion shoes lying about . . . it's a pity that woman is not López's wife. Her heroism would be worthy of every eulogy for following the destiny of her husband."

Whilst the idea of abandoning a promising shoe collection (for the sake of a man) might have seemed exorbitantly heroic to a fine lady like Mrs. Gelly, she was obviously not in command of all the facts. Little did she know that, at that very moment, Eliza Lynch was having eight boxes of jewels and coin smuggled on to an Italian gunboat for a European retirement. It was just a precautionary measure.

Scowling amongst this strange assortment of passengers was a hard-drinking and slightly mothy Englishman. His thinning hair was brushed forward like a Roman and he wore a forked beard like the devil. This comparison would have pleased him very much because he loathed Christians—as well as liberals, English riff-raff, women and Americans (he shared something with the yacht's captain here, who thought all *yanquis* were "rascals"). He'd already made himself vaguely unpopular with his fellow-passengers by repeatedly throwing open all the windows and introducing blasts of cold air to their gambling. There was little they could do; the man was breathtakingly famous and something of a Victorian super-hero. He was Captain Richard Burton.

Burton's little excursion to Humaitá came at the end of a lull in his boisterous wanderings. It was now fifteen years since his bowel-churning, face-painted adventures in Arabia. The Nile Survey of 1857–9 and a well-publicised spat with his fellow-explorer, Speke, had left him depressed, broke and more querulous than ever. He even managed to infect his fiancée, Isabel Arundell, with some of his misery, fomenting a colourful nervous breakdown. Whilst Isabel sweated it out, Burton took himself off to America for nine months. Although the presence of so many Americans was obviously an irritation, Burton found America satisfactory in almost every other respect. He was particularly fascinated by the Sioux and delighted in the details of their lives—trial marriages, scalping, abundant sodomy and an imaginative punishment for female adulterers (the tips of their noses were bitten off). He also visited the Mormons in Utah, and on his return expended much energy in singing the virtues of polygamy. Adoring though his readers were, they weren't ready for this.

By now, however, he could do no wrong. The public recognised him as a man of towering intellectual and sporting ability. He was a scholar, poet, diplomat, botanist, anthropologist and a powerful boxer. He could speak twenty-five languages and brought some of the world's greatest poetry—like *The Arabian Nights*—to an English readership. He wrote forty-three travel books of his own, each dashed off so quickly between adventures that he had neither the time—nor the patience—to proof-read them. Those who knew him well might have added to his list of talents a flair for spending money quickly and a well-founded appreciation of prostitutes (women did have their uses). These talents were more obvious at some times than at others; always near the surface was a tendency for Burton to plummet into deep, alcoholic melancholia.

His return from America coincided with Isabel's recovery. For unfathomable reasons—and against doctor's orders—she agreed to hitch her fortunes to his. They were married in 1861.

Burton also managed to extract quite unwarranted loyalty from the Foreign Office, which appointed him to a post as HM Consul, Santos, Brazil. It was a decision that Lord Russell would live to regret. He'd spend four years demanding that Burton explain what he was doing with Her Majesty's funds, and more to the point, what he was doing at all. The answer was simple: he was out exploring the Brazilian hinterlands. Officially, these expeditions were described as "sick leave," but as covers go, this wasn't even a fig-leaf. Enthusiastic illness wasn't the only source of rancour; Burton refused to implement the suppression of the Brazilian slave trade. To him, the money would have been better spent shipping a million British paupers to Brazil (as well as 60,000 defeated Confederates) and letting cheap labour and market forces take their course. Slavery—a "peculiar institution"—would be quietly smothered. Lord Russell was unimpressed.

Isabel too was less than impressed by her husband's adventures, but she put a brave face on it all. Santos was sheer hell ("The Wapping of the Far West"), and as all the men were off fighting the Paraguayans, the women had become dangerously lustful. When Isabel tried to improve her lot by taking on Chico, a midget slave, he roasted Burton's favourite cat and ate it. After that, Chico emulated his master in every detail, even in a miniaturised version of his clothing. Burton sought—and got—extended sick leave.

He learnt Guaraní and booked a passage on the *Yi*, return fare to Humaitá.

Never at his best in matters of the human spirit, Burton was positively waspish after 676 miles cooped up with his prattling fellow-passengers. As for the crew, or what remained of them, they weren't even worthy of his contempt.

"The three stewards," he swiped, "are expected to do the work of one man; they are exceedingly civil, and they do nothing. Of course, this is the fault of the *comisario*, or purser, a small Spanish bantam, or rather 'hen-harrier,' who spends all his time in trifling with the feminine heart."

After three weeks of cabbage and enervating human frailty (fancy trying to trifle with the feminine heart, or anything feminine), Burton was in a foul state when he arrived in Humaitá. He'd missed the fighting by two months. The fortress itself was a bitter disappointment. He'd read the French geographer Elisée Reclus' description of Humaitá in *Revue des Deux Mondes* and had conjured up an image of the fortress as hyperbolic as Sebastopol, Vicksburg or Gibraltar. What he found instead he described as "absurd," and Reclus, he decided, was "the Prince of Humbugs." But he was also mystified at how the Paraguayans had managed to keep the Allies at bay so long, and when he saw what remained of their antique artillery, he was forced to admit to the inconceivable power of human emotion.

"I felt something of the hysterical passion," he wrote, "at the thought of so much wasted heroism. And this personal inspection of the site where the last struggle had so lately ended impressed me highly with Paraguayan strength of purpose, and with the probability of such men fighting to the last."

Just as I had, Burton toured the twenty miles of fortification in a day. However, unlike my tour, on a fretful bicycle, he had an obliging horse. I was pleased to read that, though war had only just passed through, Burton was able to enjoy much the same fauna as I had; peewits, spoonbills, *jacuanas*, lily-trotters, *urubús*, snipe and snippet. His mood lightened.

I was also gratified to see that the carnivores had spared him no more than they had me. His skin was barnacled by sandflies and mosquitoes. I like to think that the fact we were both insect-food in the swamps of Humaitá is all that Burton and I have in common. Admire him as I might, I was finding it hard to like him and was glad that when the Brazilians refused him permission to follow the fighting, he turned round and went back to Argentina.

He wasn't away for long.

56

The rump of López's army headed north—back across the swamps—and after some delay, I followed.

As the land rose from the sticky green bogs, the grasses browned and then erupted in flames. The slough of winter was being burnt away by the cowboys, thousands of hectares disappearing under great orange banners of fire. The horsemen stood at the scorched margins of this catharsis, staring thoughtfully into the brilliant, gassy plumes. They looked as though they were tending animals and not destruction on such a geographical and—some say—pointless scale. Sometimes their fire sparkled along a charred horizon like a fuse, and at other times it rushed at the bus as an outrageous coloured storm. The swirling, crackling vapours were then so close that I imagined that I could feel their heat through the glass. It was merely my anxiety. I am sure that if there had been any other passengers on the bus this anxiety would have blossomed into a group activity, like panic. As it was, I had the possibility of being roasted in an old bus all to myself.

I was reminded that López had set fire to the landscape as he retreated north. His scorching of the earth was as pointless as the present one. The idea that the Allies would be foraging off the land was fanciful. They moved their massive armies northwards—complete with its brothels and theatres—under steam and phenomenal horse-power. They even had a little railway built to chase López out of the Chaco. Whereas previously the Allies had moved only haltingly forward, they now began a menacing, unstoppable conga. It would be a merry dance indeed. For the next nineteen months López led them backwards and forwards through the bogs and forests of eastern Paraguay.

As to what López hoped to achieve in his baroque, jungly ramblings, one can only guess. He kept with him all his wine and the National Treasury, several cartloads of swanky uniforms and the Pleyel piano. Perhaps he hoped that the Allies would tire of their pursuit and he'd be able to set himself up as a well-looped despot in the extremities of civilisation. Perhaps he hoped that his "faithful agents" in the United States would swing opinion in his favour and a spanking-new relief force would smash its way through and save him. It was pure fantasy.

Salvaging anything from the wreckage of the Marshal-President's thinking was now an increasingly delicate task. The first truly alarming signs surfaced when he had all the stragglers in his vaudevillian entourage dragged into the grass and bayoneted. Then, in the spring of 1868, his homicidal tendencies became rather more grandiose. Deep in his brandy-pickled synapses he'd stumbled upon the Grand Conspiracy. He saw treachery wherever his eye settled. The first to enjoy his retribution were his brothers, Venancio and Benigno. As they were now well-established sex-pests, no one was unduly concerned by the sight of their fat buttocks getting the flogging that they should have had years ago. Encouraged by their squeals, López turned his attention to his sisters—those two gigantic Bavarian eggs, Inocencia and Rafaela. He'd already had their husbands shot, and now he had the women nailed into crates. They were let out only on special occasions, to be whipped.

López then applied considerable imagination to winkling out the other conspirators. Generals were flogged and ladies-in-waiting rudely sliced open. The Marshal-President appointed his priest, Father Fidel Maiz, as the Chief Torturer, a task the warted cleric took up with surprising enthusiasm. His methods were inspirational; 110 years later, Pastor Coronel was still setting torture to music—*La Palomita*—and thinking of ways to make the nervous system burn. At first, "conspirators" had their fingers smashed with mallets or were strapped across anthills to be devoured by the sun and the ants. This was later refined; victims had their eyelids torn off so that they could better appreciate the glare. But the greatest refinement of all was the *Cepo Uruguayo*, where the victim was bound into a parcel with a weight of muskets on his neck. The effects are described in a deposition made by Alan Taylor, the builder:

First the feet went to sleep, and then a tingling commenced in the toes, gradually extending to the knees, and the same in the hands and arms till the agony was unbearable. My tongue swelled up and I thought my jaws would have been displaced. I lost all feeling on one side of my face, for a fortnight afterwards. The suffering was dreadful. I should certainly have confessed, if I had anything to confess.

Taylor wasn't the only foreigner to face such neurological challenges—or worse. Of the fifty-nine British contractors caught in the war's blockade, twenty-five perished. Several were protractedly tortured, including Taylor and a gentle apothecary called Masterman. Had it not been for the ominous presence of two British gunboats on the river, these two might also have "died in prison."

With the administration of justice proceeding colourfully, the war in the swamplands now lurched into fresh disasters. The remaining 12,000 Paraguayans faced the Allies for their last set-piece of the war, at Lomas Valentinas. As 25,000 Brazilians bore down on him, López loaded the carts and fled, leaving his men to cover his retreat. He managed to get clear with all his liqueurs, his treasures and his caged sisters (he'd got tired of flogging Benigno and had had him shot—along with the bishop, blind Colonel Alen and several others).

"He went away in a great hurry," said Thompson, "leaving to her fate Mrs. Lynch, who went among the bullets, looking for him."

Eliza Lynch made her own escape just in time. By 27 December 1868, it was all over. The "Waterloo" of South America had annihilated López's forces.

Oblivious of the catastrophe, Colonel Thompson held out for a further two days in his impenetrable redoubt at Angostura Narrows. He had with him 800 soldiers ("the greater part being small boys . . . most having lost their arms") and ammunition for two hours' fighting. He dispatched a raiding party for supplies and was encouraged when it returned with twenty-seven mules, a Brazilian colonel and 120 cases of claret. But the Brazilians sent him an English messenger to assure him the situation was hopeless; he was surrounded by 20,000 allied troops. The Marqués de Caxias and General Gelly were present to accept his surrender personally, with all the honours of war.

Thompson's captivity was a rather informal matter. He gave Caxias a stern lecture about the treatment of Paraguayan prisoners and refused the duke's offer of a lift to Buenos Aires. He said he wanted to pay his own way. In truth, he despised Caxias. Not only did he think he was a warmonger but, worse, he thought Caxias was an "imbecile." After a frank and distinctly frosty exchange of views, the two men went their separate ways.

Despite Caxias, Thompson was full of admiration for the Allies. On his return to England, he stopped by in Rio de Janeiro to pay his respects to Dom Pedro II. The Brazilian Emperor was far more his man, a scholarly individual, disinterested in the affairs of state and unfashionably concerned for the well-being of the common negro and the Indian. Emperor and mercenary bade each other well and parted.

Thompson wasn't back in England for long. His bold, battle-smoked account of the war was complete by the end of the year. He gave the Royal Geographical Society its copy and there I found it—much as he'd left it—with its spidery maps and "with the Author's compliments" looping over the title page in coppery ink. I read it again on my return, with both fascination and a sense of emptiness which I couldn't decide was his or mine. Thompson's yellow-paged war—the bloodiest mankind can remember—had become an adventure, a brilliant technical exercise. Was it really just a "change of air"?

Thompson had fooled himself if no one else. He'd lived among the Paraguayans for eleven years and he now found it hard to live anywhere else. *The War in Paraguay* had wholly failed to exorcise the affection he felt for those he called his "Guaraní." When it was completed, he returned to his troops, his beloved Paraguayans, for ever. He married a *paraguaya* and produced a generation of Paraguayan Thompsons, whose descendants are still found in Asunción today. He lived just long enough to take a role in the rebuilding of his adopted country and to get the railway running again. He died six years later, in 1876, and was conveyed to the cemetery at Recoleta by the President's horses, plumed in black. He was thirty-seven.

Stricken with grief, the Paraguayans repaid his affection with a small town, west of Asunción, renamed in his honour: Thompson.

57

A week after Thompson's defeat, Asunción fell to the Allies. There was no resistance; it had been evacuated a year before on one of the Marshal-President's less than rational orders. *Asunceños* had spent a freezing winter in the forest and were secretly grateful for defeat. As the Allies headed for the city, López's scabby remnants veered west into the central highlands. Caxias was so confident the war was over that he went home.

His celebrations were premature. López had yet to be extracted from the jungles of the central highlands, and whilst the Allies hesitated, he built himself another army—from children, the old and the maimed. Dom Pedro sent another champion out to extirpate the monster. It was his son-in-law, the Comte d'Eu. Doubtless the Emperor was enjoying a little symmetry: López had once presumed the Comte to be his rival for Isabella; now he could regard him as his nemesis. In reality, the Comte was hardly a champion at all. He was only twenty-seven, and although he was extravagantly cruel, he cut a mincing figure in magenta and gold. Repeatedly shrilling disgust at the muckiness of war endeared him to no one. To make matters worse, he conducted an uncomfortably public and torrid affair with one of his generals (who got his head blown off) and then, when the war moved back to the jungle, he declared that the whole business was beneath his dignity and flounced back home.

In the same week that the Comte was taking up his appointment in Asunción, Burton returned—in typically foul humour. He'd spent the last five months avoiding Isabel and scowling around Argentina, Chile and Peru. He was now drinking his way back home, to take up a diplomatic post in Damascus. If the Foreign Office had known half of what his friends knew, they might once again have paused to reflect on the wisdom of the appointment.

His dress and appearance [reported the poet and fellow-Arabist, Wilfred Blunt, from Argentina] were those suggesting a released convict rather than anything of more repute. He wore habitually, a rusty black coat with a crumpled silk stock, his throat destitute of a collar, a costume which his muscular frame and immense chest made singularly and incongruously hideous, above it a countenance the most sinister I have ever seen, dark, cruel, treacherous, with eyes like a wild beast's . . .

Asunción perfectly reflected his mood. Just as the amoral Asunción of 1969 had, to Graham Greene, been the embodiment of Greeneland, so the Asunción of 1869 was pure and vicious Burtonia. The men were all gone and the Brazilian slave-soldiers were lavishing their syphilis on the women. The buildings had been punched about by ironclads and the streets were broken and fissured like tumbling mountain rivers. The port was cluttered with sunken ships and the ruins seethed with López spies. Into this smouldering nest of misfits and thieves, Burton's steamer discharged more of the same; his fellow-passengers were, he said, "the veriest ruffians, riffraff, ragamuffins that I had ever seen in South America, even at Montevideo." Burton was briefly happy.

One surprising discovery on this ravaged Boschian landscape was that of an old friend, Baron Wisner von Morgenstern. The Minister of War had been utterly successful in avoiding any contact with the war he'd started. Burton now found him running a downtown *pulpería*, dishing out rum to the Brazilian officers. There's no telling whether the little Hungarian *volupté* still wore his waistcoats embroidered with green frogs, but Burton noted (with ill-disguised relish) that he now kept a pretty "daughter" who—in return for important intelligence—offered most favourable rewards.

A sad thought occurred to me: perhaps—as publican and pimp—this might be the last we'd see of Wisner. Happily, I was to be proved wrong.

Meanwhile Burton's own happiness was beginning to sour. The Brazilians still wouldn't let him near the slaughter. There was only a brief moment of satisfaction when the Paraguayans brought the fighting to him—by train. López threw South America's first armoured train into the heart of Asunción. Burton loved it. "The Paraguayans, after doing some damage, leisurely retired, and stopped the train to pick up two of their wounded who had fallen out of it."

With an uneasy calm restored to the city, Burton vented his frustrations by uncorking his most vintage spleen. He set himself the formidable intellectual task of rehabilitating López (who was still lumbering around in the jungle, thrashing his relatives). He reasoned—against reason—that López was the victim in all of this, that the Allies were the protagonists and that Madame Lynch was the heroine of the piece. As to the complaints of the British employees, these were essentially contractual grumbles enlivened by "fancies, theories and fictions." Masterman's accounts of being tortured were all lies. Washburn's version could not be relied upon because he was a hopeless neurotic (and American), and Thompson's reports were all hearsay (he didn't wait for the book). After three weeks cooped up in Asunción, he had the measure of the situation and bundled his theory up for publication. A month later, he was back home and Paraguay was well in his past.

To his apologists, *Letters from the Battlefields of Paraguay* is a work of genius pre-empting the revisionists' view of the war by sixty years. Genius he may have been, but the conclusion bolted on to his report is hardly inspired. If he's right and the Paraguayans found themselves in this predicament without so much as a pinch of duress, they emerge as fondly helpless and faintly absurd. As to the revisionists, their work is hardly admirable, coinciding as it did with the demands of Paraguayan fascism.

Some claim that *Battlefields* provided the inspiration for *Nostromo*, but I doubt it. Whilst Conrad may have admired the Arabian adventures, Burton's treatment of the dictator seemed rather generous as a template for Conrad's "Perpetual President" ("who ruled the country with the sombre imbecility of political fanaticism"). Far more likely, Conrad borrowed his characters from the work of a friend, a fellow socialist and another explorer of the southern cone. He was yet to arrive in Paraguay.

As to *Battlefields,* I prefer to regard it as six bad weeks in the life of a brilliant but fractious old cynic.

58

On the plain of great blue vents that marks the beginning of the central highlands, I stopped at Ybycuí.

It was an unmemorable town of tool stores and tyre shops. I booked into the only hotel and a small child showed me up to a room wedged (somewhat disconcertingly) full of bunk beds. The floors were so glossy with disinfectant that I could see myself walking around upside-down, looking rather alarmed at all this sudden hygiene. It was then that I discovered that the building doubled as the district pathology laboratory and that its constant stream of visitors weren't guests but supplicants, each with an offering of bodily fluids. I had a sudden and horrible image of a cholera epidemic sweeping the town and my dormitory being swamped with tyre-fitters sludging themselves into a stupor and being swabbed down with boric acid. My enthusiasm for the hotel rapidly dispersed and with it went any residual fondness for Ybycuí. I decided to be gone by nightfall.

There was one place I had to see, the oldest iron foundry in South America. I asked people in the street how I might get to La Rosada, with mixed response.

"That's in Asunción, isn't it?"

"I'm sorry I can't understand a word you're saying."

"No idea. Are you from Germany? How is Lady Diana?"

Eventually, a bleak picture began to emerge. The foundry was fifteen kilometres away. The last bus had gone. There was nowhere to stay out there. It was in the forest.

"Ask the builder if he'll take you."

The builder looked at his pick-up doubtfully. "I don't think it will go that far."

He was right. There were too many essential structures missing. It would have been like driving around in a diagram.

I started reinforcing my pleas with offers of cash. I worked my way up the street, making more and more outrageous proposals at each tyre shop. My bidding reached its critical momentum in the grocer's. I was now offering the equivalent of fifty newspapers, three old prostitutes or a night-and-a-half in the Hotel Dysentery. It was good enough for Lino the grocer. He was soon packing me into his fancy new pick-up, with his wife out on the back. I was pleased that she was coming because it took the hard commercial edge off our transaction, turning it into more of a family outing. Mrs. Berera brought her swimming costume, a beach towel, a garden chair and a bottle of frozen cherryade. It was obviously an excursion they'd enjoyed many times before and Mrs. Berera wasn't the least perturbed when her chair slid backwards and forwards across the truck as Lino whirled along in a tornado of red volcanic gravel. We tried to keep an eye on her in the mirror but sometimes Mrs. Berera slid completely out of view and it wasn't until the next fold in the earth's crust—and the reversal of centrifugal forces—that she made her stately reappearance.

"This is the most beautiful place in Paraguay," said Lino with unre-strained happiness.

He may well have been right. The red road curled across the rolls of greenery between flawless young, volcanic cones. The forests of the lower slopes were swooping down to meet us, and there, at the head of a shallow valley, the Mbuyapey gushed greenly and deliciously out of the rocks. It all seemed such a beautifully improbable site for an English ironworks. But it was true: in 1849, at a time when England was perfecting the darkness of its own satanic mills, Henry Godwin was putting in the foundations of an exquisite red-rocked foundry here in the heart of Arcadia. His work was enlarged by the tireless Whytehead, and as if to prove the point, a crew of local engineers now had photocopies of Whytehead's plans spread out in front of them and were rebuilding the foundry exactly as he'd ordered. The plans were signed, and dated 1854.

Lino waved his hand over the things he thought I ought to see—the great brick furnace, the water-wheel and the charcoal shutes—and then waddled off down to the river with his wife. I crossed the spiky grass, past a statue of an Indian with head-feathers and a shovel, and peered inside. There were more engineers clambering over the wheel, barefoot and thickly greased with soot and oil. They worked without pause, chirruping to each other in Guaraní. Their bedrolls, I noticed, were spread out below them, among the hoisting gears and the massive iron teeth of a crusher. In Whytehead's day there was a labour force of convicts, supplemented by foreign technicians: Englishmen, Italians, Americans, Frenchmen, Swiss, a German and two Spaniards.

Perhaps the most endearing of these technicians was Charley Twite, the mineralogist. He was brought out to survey for coal, and whilst he didn't find any, he found plenty of iron ore. He and Cruger also developed the Paraguayan torpedo, and although the American was blown to bits by an early prototype, the final model was no laughing matter. The ironclad *Rio de Janeiro* took one smack on the waterline and sank with all hands. But it is not for this that Twite is best remembered. "He turned out to be a prospector in more senses than one," wrote one historian. "The sight of a Paraguayan Venus would exalt his investigating powers to their fullest stretch and his prospecting enthusiasm in this direction led him into more than one scrape . . ."

Despite Twite's uncontrollable prospecting, production was staggering. Ybycuí produced several hundred artillery pieces, boilers for ships, parts for the railway and even the railings that run around Recoleta cemetery. Whytehead galloped between the Ybycuí and Asunción in a day and perhaps the strain contributed to his downfall and final interment among his railings. My only regret about Ybycuí is that the museum hardly credited Whytehead at all. He would be mortified to discover that all the honour goes to that foul-mouthed drunkard Alexander Grant, who took not only his job but also his life.

In the end it perhaps matters little. Four months after the capture of Asunción, in May 1869, the Brazilian cavalry poured into La Rosada. The foundry commandant, Insfran, greeted them, unsurprisingly, with chilly detachment and so they beheaded him. They then dismantled the machinery, pulled down the walls and jammed the water-channel to flood the valley.

"La Rosada," says the memorial, "is still a symbol of pain. Its destruction was the destruction of an era."

I left Ybycuí that night and went north, to Piribebuy.

59

The weather changed again and I found Piribebuy damped down in highland drizzle. The hammock-makers' doors were clumped in soggy purples and pinks and the elderly were snuggled together in ponchos beneath the jacarandas. A small figure was hopping with surprising dexterity through the cloisters, selling jams and honey from a basket on her head. She got to the tavern and they shrugged her away. Three soldiers were seated at the back, as gaunt and silent as watchers in a triptych. This was the town where they still made the best ox-carts in Paraguay (as they had since 1636).

In the middle of the square, mounted on a mat of neatly nibbled grass, was the church, a great creamy afterthought from 1737. In some places, the loggias had been chewed by gunfire and large divots scooped from the woodwork. It was a reminder that for a few months after the fall of Asunción Piribebuy was the capital of Paraguay. It had known happier days; the population swelled from 800 to 10,000, and with the newcomers came bouts of malaria and outrageous starvation. Her new citizens ate saddles and rats and built their new capital in branches and strips of rawhide. The cloisters were requisitioned as official residences. President López made himself a palace of the squire's house, and Madame Lynch took a place over on the south side. Hers has long gone, home now to a crumbling lorry and a tethered heifer.

The American Embassy—or Mission—was much as it had been on the day it was abandoned in 1869. It was the only house still determinedly empty. I climbed on to the veranda and wandered among its blunted scrolls and columns. The windows were boxed up in powdery shutters. I pressed my eye against a crack in the panelling. There was nothing; it was empty and dark.

That, I supposed, might well have been the epitaph for the American efforts at diplomacy. Mr. Washburn had long gone. He'd never recovered from the unfortunate fancy dress incident, and his stabs at peace-making had had a peculiarly inflammatory effect. Proposing to the Allies that Emperor Dom Pedro should abdicate rather suggested that he didn't have a grip on the issues. When, after a period on leave, he tried to smash his way back through the blockade on a U.S. gunboat, it was agreed that he didn't have a grip on his senses either. He was recalled. The USS *Wasp* hauled him back down to Buenos Aires and that is where Burton found him, gibbering incontinently and trying to untangle himself from a nervous breakdown.

He was replaced by General Martin T. MacMahon. With his impressive moustaches and a pedigree of Civil War bravado, he ought to have been just the man for the job. Instead, MacMahon found himself hopelessly disorientated by his desires for Madame Lynch. "She was," he later blubbed to a Senate committee, "one of the most bewitching and gallant ladies it has ever been my privilege to meet."

Whilst the loyal soldiery munched their way through their vermin and tack, MacMahon was being comprehensively bewitched. Eliza had resurrected her soirées. "Even in this backwater," conceded her physician, a half-thawed Scottish kipper called Dr. Stewart, "Madame Lynch's house exuded an air of Europe." As to her gallantry, the starving British contractors doubtless wouldn't forget the mouthfuls of tea and sugar that she'd given them. MacMahon meanwhile was moved to excruciating poetry, now safely encased in the town museum:

Bella y nubil república de la zona
Incantada, Reina de mil arroyos,
Tu nombre solo ayer disconocía . . .

Were it not for the fact that this doggerel was written in Spanish, I would have eagerly assumed the relationship between the two Celts had become furtive. Instead, I had to accept that it probably remained a rather public, puppy love. Besides, if Silvia Caballero was right, her great-grandfather was still bounding around, well within Eliza's sensual orbit. He'd just chopped his way in and out of the Allied lines and was as irrepressible as ever.

MacMahon's residence was still there, on the plaza. It was now a ladies' boutique, selling leopard-print boots and jeans under the unpromising label, "Botch." The Minister himself had proved less enduring than his house. Washington had heard all about Piribebuy's "Air of Europe" and recalled the minister to the rather less comfortable Air of the Committee Room. MacMahon was due for a carpeting and it wouldn't be a red one. In his last service to Madame Lynch, he smuggled several boxes of coin out of Paraguay aboard the *Wasp*—to be deposited in Dr. Stewart's account at the Bank of England. Some of the booty got stuck to his fingers on the way.

To the south of the square was a steep, wooded slope leading down to the river. The bathing pools were empty that day and the fields beyond were smudged with mist. At dawn on 12 August 1869, the Allies had rumbled across the flats and up into the Paraguayan trenches. López had long fled, leaving 1,500 waifs to defend his rear. The Guaraní fought with what they could. When they were out of shot, they loaded their cannon with slivers of glass, broken swords and finally coconuts. When the men were spent, the women rose from the trenches and fought the Brazilian slave-soldiers with clods of earth, their nails and their teeth.

In the filth and smoke, the Comte d'Eu's boyfriend was separated from his head. The Prince of Orleans' grief was genocidal. He had the Paraguayan commander strapped between two cannon and his head sawn off with a bayonet. He then hunted down the wounded in the church and cut their throats. Among those who choked on their own blood was Master Fermín López, a schoolmaster who'd led his pupils in the final defence of the town. The Comte's men then rode out to the hospital, stopped the doors and set it on fire. Only one child escaped. She would walk almost the length of Paraguay to be reunited with the remnants of her family. Her granddaughter would be my brilliantly zigzagged friend, the artist Lucy Yegros.

Apart from MacMahon's solid verses and his solid front door, everything else at the museum was in an advanced state of destruction. It was really a sort of anti-museum, a display of things that no longer enjoyed a recognisable existence. There were splinters of metal and pieces of ugly, misshapen shot, charred beams and fractured puddles of molten glass. To my horror, there was even a tussock of human ponytail—sheared, matted and brutally disowned.

It had been no better for the Brazilians. The booty from Piribebuy was lamentable. Even López's wine cellar was a source of disappointment. It was liberated by a young cavalry officer called Alfredo d'Escragnolle Taunay, who would become one of Brazil's greatest writers.

"Unfortunately," he later recalled, "the quantity of champagne was quite small."

Two days later, the Allies fell on Caacupé.

60

I stayed in Caacupé for several days before I realised with a pang of disappointment that I'd seen everything three times over. People were beginning to recognise me and I'd subconsciously established diversions around the town, to carry me clear of the most voluble beggars, the Makás with their bows and arrows and the most insistent of the cathedral guides. Now, every time I paused at the San Blast Chicken shop, they automatically thrust a few limbs of San Blast Chicken at me, never giving me the chance to see if they did San Blast Anything Else. As it turned out, San Blast was not the industrial process that gave my chicken its richly gritty texture but was the patron saint of Paraguay. Caacupé was the spiritual capital of the country and most things in the town were adoringly San Blasted.

It didn't surprise me that spirituality here was as opaque as anything else in Paraguay. Two hundred years of sultans and despots—none of whom were spiritually enthusiastic—had given the Roman Catholic Church a rather fugitive character, and local doctrines had a decidedly foresty flavour. To its eternal credit, the Church had been Stroessner's most obstinate thorn and many priests had lost their eardrums, their wits and their lives in the *pileta*. In spiritual matters, however, the Church was rather less obstinate. My friends in Asunción insisted that once you got to the countryside the priests were healers and sorcerers and that religious devotion was largely a matter for women. Less charitably, they suggested that the holy fathers were a little overattentive to the needs of these, their devotees. It was an observation that hadn't escaped the barrister-captain of *The Falcon*, at the end of the *Grande Guerra:*

> The Paraguayans are reported to excuse the errors of their clergy by stating that the Pope has, in compassion for the now unpopulated condition of poor Paraguay, been pleased to grant to the priests there,

dispensation from their vows of chastity. This excuse is a very good one, but from all accounts this people were not famed for their morality even in the days before the war.

At the heart of this flowering, generous love-child of Catholicism was Caacupé. The Virgin of Caacupé was a distant relative of the Virgin Mary and lived in a star-burst of light bulbs and sequins at the Basilica of Miracles. She was the product of advanced miscegenation; Indians carved her, Indians found her bobbing around in a seventeenth-century flood, Indians worshipped her, and yet she looked like portraits of Madame Lynch at her most plushly upholstered. The effect, however, of that blank, *Gioconda* smile was both spiritually and electrically startling. Nuns threw themselves headlong at her tiny feet. Pilgrims came from all over the country to seek a little of her magic. The President came by helicopter, hoping for a lot of it. Conscripts came barefoot from the Chaco to have their national service blessed. Others brought their pets and their cancer. On her special day, 8 December, it was said that all these people came, with rocks on their heads and thrashing themselves with leather whips. There was room for 300,000 of them in the cathedral square.

Even now, with the square empty, it was somehow crowded. All the frills and riff-raffery of religious devotion were there. I counted fifteen types of pottery Virgin and navigated my way through a great glittering cardiological stew of bleeding hearts. Some of the pink pigs had made it from Areguá and so had the Teletubbies, the Virgin Laa-Laa and the Immaculate Tinky Winky. Even more surprising were the stuffed calves' heads and the racks of plastic machine-guns. Sensing a little theological weariness, an Indian offered me his stool. It was for rent, by the half-hour.

I took a room on the edge of the square. It was a pilgrims' hotel and the sheets were printed with rabbits wearing children's clothes. Each morning I was woken by the sound of Guaraní carried in dreamy ululations across the square from the basilica. Swaddled in cheeky bunnies and the now-persistent aromas of San Blast Chicken, I decided that this was the nearest that I would ever get to spiritual overload.

On the Sunday morning, a television crew arrived in the plaza and bottled up these effervescent sources of enchantment, uncorking them across the nation.

*

There was only one vaguely troubling aspect to all of this: the face of Madame Lynch (as I was now sure it was) replicated fifty thousand times throughout the town. Sometimes the lipstick missed her lips or her little pottery pupils were up on her forehead but she was consistently, icily demanding. Even if the Virgin hadn't borrowed her face, she had— according to Eliza's detractors—come nose to nose with her chilly demands. In those days the statue stood in a "sea of jewels" and her gown was festooned in the pearls and diadems of her supplicants. On a fleeting visit to Caacupé, Madame Lynch had reaped the lot, substituting them with paste. She even stripped the Virgin of her gemencrusted gown, replacing it with an old fancy dress outfit.

That, they say, is the reason the Virgin of Caacupé is now to be found attired in the sumptuous manner of Elizabeth I of England, on the day of her Coronation.

When the Allies arrived in Caacupé, they found that López and his twinkling doxy were, once again, a step ahead of them and had fled. López had sent an officer back to Caacupé with an order that the British contractors were to follow him. Happily, the officer was far too drunk to give any intelligible commands. One of those who gratefully surrendered to the Brazilians was the apothecary Masterman.

"Bacchus," he wrote, with uncharacteristic religiosity, "to whom so many of the English had sacrificed so devoutly, laying even their own lives upon the shrine, now came to their help."

61

The Presidential cortège lurched northwards, scattering the last odds and ends of Napoleonic Paraguay in the forest. Madame Lynch rode in the American buggy and López in the landau. The Pleyel had long been abandoned in a village that is still known to this day as Piano. Then, one of the last brigades of the Presidential Guard made its final stand at Acostá-Nú. I passed their pitiful monument on the road out to Caraguatay. Here—at long last—General Caballero had surrendered. His little soldiers were not so lucky. All of them were slaughtered, most barely more than children. They'd painted moustaches on their faces.

But the most impressive abandonment of all was out in the marshes, at Vapor Cué, the Place of Steam.

From the gentle, colonnaded plaza of Caraguatay, I walked the last five kilometres out into the swamps. My pursuit of the presidential rabble had taken me right through the central *cordillera* and out the other side, into the flatlands. As the village bedded itself into the horizon, my world became—once again—a great green soup of well-frogged ooze. As the sun rose higher, it all began to suck and bubble.

Eventually, the track came to a sticky halt on the banks of a rivulet, the Río Yhagüy. It was just one of a number of thin red capillaries that wriggled out of the swamps into the Manduvirá, an artery of the Paraguay, fifty miles to the west. The Yhagüy must have been wider in August 1869 when López heckled the last of his imperial navy into this vast, glutinous wilderness. Six groaning steamers were flogged along the creek. Vapor Cué was as far as they got before the reptile riverbanks clamped around them. They gave the place its name and settled into the grit, now and for ever a fossilised shipyard.

Four days after the bloodbath at Piribebuy, the Paraguayans set fire to their beloved fleet. The wooden ships had been consumed, and all that now remained were their boilers and paddle-wheels, some axe-heads and rivets and the coal and timbers that had been below the waterline. Three of them—*Río Apa*, *Ypora* and *Salto del Guairá*—had been built by Whytehead at the Asunción shipyard in the happier 1850s. The fourth was the carcass of the *Aquitaine*, which had brought the hapless French to New Bordeaux. The courage—or rather cheek—of these little ships was so brazen that at the skirmish of Riachuelo, they'd completely over-whelmed the fifth steamer, a handsome Brazilian warship called the *Anhambay*. She was captured along with her English engineer, John Foster (who simply changed sides and served his Paraguayan masters until the end). Being made of iron, the *Anhambay* had fared rather better in the conflagration.

But for me, the most exuberant of these peeling hulks was the *Piravevé*. Forked from the slime, it seemed as though the flames had barely touched her. She'd once served the Royal Navy—as HMS *Ranger*—and when she arrived in Paraguay, in 1865, she was to be the fastest in the Guaraní fleet. Her graceful, parabolic lines had now been hauled upright again and her mast and rigging restored. She was thirty-one metres long and I had to slop down to the riverbanks to take her all in: a powerful nineteenth-century war machine now harmlessly pickled in the sludge of central South America.

A snake slithered over to investigate my astonishment. We regarded each other with momentary panic before fleeing in opposite directions. My head suddenly emptied of courage and I was pelting back through the slick, to the safety of the warships. It was only when I'd recovered my breath and a little dignity that I remembered the *Tacuarí*. The little ship that had started it all, that had set out from Limehouse with López and Eliza and all their baubles and guns, was nowhere to be seen.

She had, I later learned, suffered no lapse of courage. A few miles upstream of Humaitá, she'd taken on the ironclads and, after a particularly vicious little flurry, she'd scuttled herself and gone to the bottom.

As the Allies watched the fires burning at Vapor Cué, they must have wondered how long the Marshal-President would go on. The next day, the provisional Paraguayan government, installed by the Allies, declared that Francisco Solano López was a "monster of impiety, a denaturalised Paraguayan, the assassin of his country and an enemy of the human race." He was outlawed. The Comte d'Eu had had enough and went home. It was left to the Argentine president, Sarmiento, to express the frustration of them all: "The war is finished although that brute still has twenty pieces of artillery and two thousand dogs which will have to die beneath the hooves of our horses. These people do not even move one to compassion. A pack of wolves."

But for now, López and his two thousand dogs had no intention of getting themselves ground up in allied hooves.

They simply vanished into the jungles of the north.

62

The sudden disappearance of the monster spawned an obsession that has tormented the Paraguayan character ever since: the fixation with hidden treasure.

Perhaps the Paraguayan character had always been vulnerable to an overenthusiasm for buried gold. In a land where food flops effortlessly from cassava and orange trees, the idea of sustenance without effort had always been appealing. The idea of wealth without effort was irresistible. Paraguayans were, after all, descended from treasure-hunters. It was only natural that when the Allies discovered Asunción stripped of every carat of gold, the *Asunceños* assumed that their inheritance was out there, buried in the dirt. There was a certain logic in this; after all, in five years of asphyxiating siege, not much had left the country (except the loose change of Madame Lynch's retirement). Rumours began to flourish.

The survivors of the fighting provided the bare bones of the plot. Even Thompson believed in caches of treasures scattered through the forests. Another settler, an Australian called Alexander MacDonald, got the story from his carter, Miguel Faria. The old trooper had followed the presidential cortège north, living on cats and vermin. They had with them seven carts of "specie" from the National Treasury, "amounting to £1,000,000 sterling." In the agony of hot pursuit, the Treasurymen buried the gold in a swamp. To preserve the secrecy of the location, López had them all shot and their bodies heaped on the bullion to protect it from thieves. Even in 1911, wrote MacDonald, "Paraguayan woodmen are terrified by their imaginary ghosts."

Unfortunately, these deliciously crenellated stories had already made their appearance in European fiction some fifteen years before. An Italian writer, Emilio Salgari, had kept his fans momentarily breathless with a cowboys-and-Indians classic called *The President of Paraguay's Treasure*, and in its Spanish translation, the yarn had leaked back into Paraguay. Another equally curly version had appeared in London in 1887, *A Paraguayan Treasure*. When I discovered that its hero was a barrister-explorer called Arthur Penistone and that the author, Alexander Baillie, was an equity draftsman up in Gray's Inn, I began to hear imaginary ghosts of my own. It was the crew of *The Falcon* having the last, the lawyer's laugh.

It was far too late to stop the Paraguayans. MacDonald reported that they were digging up the countryside. In the 1950s even Paraguay's whelping-new dictator—Stroessner himself—joined the search and sent "treasure-hunting machines" off to the Interior, in pursuit of Marshal López. The hunt, the obsession, has proved an incurable itch. It flared again in January 2000 when the magazine *Reportaje al País* published a list of another 150 possible treasure sites. Credulity erupted all over town.

"We go every weekend," a rancher told me over his well-stacked lunch, "treasure-hunting in Vapor Cué."

And what did the gold-diggers think about the *espíritus*?

Ah yes, they'd say, the ghosts that guard *los tesoros escondidos del Mariscal López y su Concubina*. They are out there too.

63

I travelled back into the swooning farmlands of the southern central *cordillera*.

Although I sometimes had to pinch myself at the unreasonable charm of it all—at the meadows deeply splashed with flowers, the streams, the ox-carts and the villages with their palisade fences and whitewashed tree-trunks—this land had proved grimly resistant to colonisation. Nearly every attempt to resettle it after the great war had ended in disaster. This may have been due—at least partly—to the involvement of the inexplicably durable Baron von Morgenstern. The old fop had been plucked from his bawdy house, polished up a little and installed as Minister of Immigration. It was a calling that he carried off with his own distinctive sloth.

The most pitiful of these fiascos occurred at Itapé, where my bus stopped briefly, to disgorge three sleepy cowhands. The new arrivals in 1873, Lincolnshire farmers sponsored at $5 a head by the Paraguayan government, were about to discover that they hadn't arrived in Arcadia. The Paraguayan government was about to discover that it hadn't acquired "Lincolnshire Farmers."

Instead, the conman who'd packaged them up had sent the Paraguayans 1,400 London scruffs, scoured from the East End. There were matchmakers, costers, Polish Jews, blind men, acrobats, cripples, minstrels and general dupes. The insects weren't fussy and spared the government its litigation. Warble-fly laid their eggs in subtle London flesh. The jiggers burrowed upwards from their feet. At dusk, the *polvorinos* settled on their skin and in their hair and clothes, as fine and maddening as pepper. There was no refuge but rum, and when that was done, the colony was swept with typhoid. A few escaped, fleeing south to merge with the rot of Buenos Aires.

Ten years later, Edward Knight met one of them, a former jockey and a melancholic wreck, digging the railways, way out in Tucumán, Argentina.

"Here I am," said the shadow, "less of a Lincoln Farmer than ever, I guess."

I stayed that night at one of the more enduring colonies. It was established by Japanese peasants and was called La Colmena: The Beehive.

64

I was the only guest at the Hotel Fujimi. It was tucked into a garden of trumpet flowers, bonsai and orchids. There was a pool of carp, neatly defined by an ornamental bridge and neatly tick-tocked by a chorus of water-pipes. Behind the bar were silk flowers and bottles of Chivas Regal, nipped and drained at different rates and busily scored with pencil marks. The landlady, Mrs. Matsui, ate her breakfast of beef and eggs with chopsticks and a gulp of green tea. A large poster of Mount Fuji reminded her of a homeland that she'd never known.

At sundown, Mr. Matsui came in from his orchards, kicked off his boots and billowed himself in fresh cotton. His daughter approached, with cold beer and slippers. He began the story of the Matsuis in Paraguay:

My grandfather had a small farm in the highlands of Honshu. For three months a year it was buried in snow. In 1935, a government department—the *Yika*—offered him the chance to come and grow his fruit in Paraguay. The *Yika* would support them, they said. My grandparents accepted and arrived here in 1936. There was no road through the jungle but the *Yika* bought them a good truck. After the conquest of Manchuria there was no more money from Japan and the *Yika* abandoned us. The first years were the worst, before the land was cleared. Many died of malaria and several were attacked in the forest by *tigres*. Then, when everything was planted, there was a plague of locusts that lasted seven months. They left us nothing. Perhaps one in ten abandoned the colony and went home.

My grandfather and my father worked all the time. There wasn't even time to teach us Japanese. I learnt *jopará* with the cowboys. We even became Catholics (although Grandfather was always a Buddhist). Then in the seventies I went to study in Japan. Although I looked Japanese, they couldn't understand me. At first I felt ashamed but then I told them I was Paraguayan. Of course, they didn't understand this but it made me feel very proud. I am Paraguayan. I feel Paraguayan.

Nowadays, we get some help from Japan. They built us the road to get our fruit to Asunción. A few years ago, we had a visit from His Highness Prince Hitache. There are only seventy families here. It was a big moment for us.

The air became fizzy with insects and Mrs. Matsui laid out a supper of beef, potatoes and noodles. Some more Japanese fruit-farmers arrived, muscly men with spiky hair and gargantuan thirsts. They sprawled out in chairs below *The Last Supper* and the daughter relayed backwards and forwards with beer. All evening, Mr. Matsui and the farmers joshed and snapped at each other in *jopará* and Guaraní and everybody ripened like peaches. Understanding nothing, I slipped away, but Mr. Matsui caught up with me in Spanish.

"The young have it easy now," he said. "My grandfather was three months under snow. You always had to be ready. Now they stick *mandioca* in the ground and have three years' food! They go to Japan and they have money!" There was a spark of indignation. "And they won't even buy me a tractor."

Back in my little magnolia room, I leafed through the writings of one Reginald Thompson. It was the best and the worst of travel writing. It was the best because—if travel writing is merely the soul-baring of the traveller—Reginald was often startlingly naked. In this state of exposure, I caught glimpses of the traveller that I'd become myself—bewitched, confused, nearly always lonely, at once enchanted and then candidly homesick. For the time being, Reggie was a soul-mate, even though we'd missed each other in La Colmena by over sixty years. He'd stumbled through here at about the time that the Matsuis were being stripped down by locusts, in 1937.

He was the worst of writers because these, his best bits, weren't intended at all. They simply slipped out. What Reggie had intended, at least originally, was a book to encourage the great British working classes to emigrate to Paraguay (ideally before the Germans had the same brilliant idea). What he ended up with was a warning to the world that the Germans were already there and that they were about to march out and overwhelm the continent. As the thrust of his manifesto veered off in this new direction, the "terrifics" and "tremendouses" fell like plums from his prose.

Things hadn't gone well from the start. His research brought him nothing but hangovers and saddle-sores (which had to be lanced by an old Indian). He had a punch-up with a leading French settler called Naville and then—quite understandably—his wife (who he'd left in Asunción) had a nervous breakdown. Reggie was forced to cut short his trip and haul Patricia back to England, where he promptly divorced her before settling down to pen his excruciating memoirs.

Even that didn't go well. Although he was the first English writer to address Paraguay for perhaps thirty years, he was unable to make his jottings nutritious. Worse, the only aspect of Paraguay that he'd really admired was the Japanese at La Colmena ("silk dressing gowns . . . cigarettes in long holders . . . terrific *caña*." He doesn't seem to have noticed their suffering or the plague of locusts). An admiration for the Japanese was hardly a selling-point at a time when Britain and Japan were squaring up for a fight—and so Reggie stitched a few new bits in, saying how beastly they were. By the time this Frankenstein script was laid before the publishers, the two countries were doggedly at war. Reggie's book emerged as *Germans and Japs in South America* and immediately flopped.

"I never made any money from my books," he wrote in 1963 on what he assumed would be his death-bed. It was his twenty-third book and the failure of each of them had been a life-long source of surprise.

Reginald did, however, express an abiding hope for Paraguay. Perhaps, he said, it will prove "a kind of ark, into which the bewildered, harassed and oppressed peoples will march to seek shelter; maybe to establish the nucleus of a new civilisation and a new race . . ." It rather sounded as if he was blundering down a familiar path, the path of Dr. Förster, the Lincolnshire Farmers and the Australian Utopians. Poor Reggie, he'd had a nose for dead-ends.

But had the Japanese of La Colmena found the nucleus of anything?

I thought about this as I walked through the colony in the morning. The police station looked Paraguayan enough, with its typewriter, its rack of carbines and a shrine to the Virgin. So did the stores, with their pioneer stocks of barbed wire, shovels, tinned milk and axes. It was only when I saw a barefoot *peón* ride into the plaza, floppy-hatted and gun-belted, and saw that he was Japanese that I realised that this great green country had simply absorbed these, its most exotic colonists. Far from nucleating, the Japanese had been roundly engulfed.

65

Curiosity for the Australian Utopia landed me by the side of the great east–west road, *Ruta Dos,* at the dead of night. The bus dropped me at the sign for Nueva Londres.

"It's up there," said the driver. "Eleven kilometres."

Up where? The road leached away into the darkness. There was a *mercanta* hurriedly packing up her stall.

"No," she said, "there are no hotels, no taxis, no buses. At this time, the only people out on *Ruta Dos* are bad ones."

Faced with conspicuously bleak options, I shouldered my pack and groped my way towards the junction. I stepped into the black. I could just feel the camber of a road beneath my feet—so at least I could distinguish forward from ditchwards. These were grasslands. I could tell by the seething of the straw. There were frogs, too, chuckling and sucking and (I soon decided) groaning in horror. Nightjars added their own texture to my burgeoning apprehension. The locals described the noise (aptly I now realised) as the dying screams of the Old Lady of the forest. Then, the last streaks of light from *Ruta Dos* flickered out, depriving me of every sense except hearing and, of course, terror.

Robbers, snakes, rabid dogs and wounded jaguars contributed the outlines of my anxiety. Paraguayan mythology contributed some unnecessary embellishments. This was not the time to be thinking of the *mboya-jagwa,* the huge dog-snake that eats travellers, ravishes women and yelps like a puppy. Or the *carbúnculo,* a revolting carnivorous hog that disguises itself as a trough to engulf the unwary drinker. To the Australian settlers of 1893, these creatures all seemed real enough. MacDonald added to the list with a bird that shone in the dark, a giant bisexual ant-bear and a sabre-toothed sheep of uncommon ferocity named—a little ineptly perhaps—the *ow-ow.*

There was heavy breathing in my face. The thought of ending my days savaged by a sheep or violated by a giant ant-bear was more than dignity could bear. I untangled a flashlight from the soppy dishcloth of my shirt and shone it in the monster's face. In confronting my fears, I'd confronted a cow, which now regarded me with undisguised contempt.

I had two hours to go, on an invisible, croaking road now obstacled with steers. Only one car passed. I caught the look on the driver's face as he accelerated to safety. It suggested that he'd just seen an awful, soggy, hunch-backed creature picking out the cattle with a pen-torch. I was uncertain of the reception I'd receive in Nueva Londres, now famous for not having any hotel.

At last, a speck of white on the skyline turned into a light, several lights, a street. Disconcerting rasping noises turned into enormous slavering guard dogs, all making little secret of a desire to eat me. Nothing, of course, turned into a hotel.

"You can sleep here if you want," said a boy at the police station. "Or ask the priest."

I opted for the priest, who had a cottage on the square. I shouted through his letter-box, causing a small crowd to gather at my shoulder. Soon they were all shouting through the hole. Nothing.

"I know someone who has a room," said a boy with a horse.

Five minutes later, I was bedded down in the dog-house of a large villa. Everything, including my bed, was richly gravelled in rabbit-flavoured biscuits. I was embarrassingly grateful. What, I asked the horse-boy, was his name.

"Kennedy," he said. "Welcome to New Australia."

The story of the foundation of New Australia is the tail-end of a brutal struggle: the Queensland shearers' strike of 1891. When the government turned a 9-pounder on the strikers and threatened them with extinction and copious hard labour, many decided that enough was enough. They were through with Australia and with parliamentary democracy. They sought a socialist Utopia, and a bushy-tailed English hack called William Lane persuaded them he'd found it, in South America. There was no limit to his ambition, nor his imagination.

"A disciplined army," he promised, "would emerge from the Paraguayan jungle to lead an inevitable world revolution."

But his lieutenants were a rag-tag of misfits. One was Dave Stevenson, a Scottish Highlander and a cousin to Robert Louis Stevenson (whose literary success funded much of the adventure); another was a Londoner called Arthur Tozer. He'd had his own experiences of revolution, in Buenos Aires (he'd spent many lazy afternoons popping off revolutionaries with a revolver, from the comfort of his flat). Another figurehead was Mary Gilmore, a woman of shrewish looks and temperament who had been variously a poet, a teacher and a terrorist. She said she'd been abducted as a baby and reared by Aborigines. Although the cause vaguely appealed to her, she came along because she had a passion for Stevenson. She even brought enough cloth for a wedding dress in case he ever returned her feelings. He never did, preferring to cast his net more widely among the young housewives.

Two hundred had set out in 1893, aboard *The Royal Tar*. In case any man had ideas of his own sexual adventures among the natives, Lane reminded them of the Colour Line: they were white and weren't to pollute themselves by contamination with the coloureds, Land of Women or not. There was no solace in grog either; the Utopians were on the wagon.

Initially, the Australians settled on what is now the *Ruta Dos* but soon the mosquitoes and the *polvorinos* drove them to the higher land of the present settlement. Within four months, the colony began to disintegrate: the food was unpalatable, as was Lane's socialism; Tozer strutted a revolver and behaved like the authority they'd all run away from. Within the year, Lane, Tozer, and Stevenson (closely followed by Mary) had broken away to start a rival colony at Cosme. That too floundered. After an allegation of sexual impropriety with a new recruit, Lane fled the continent in 1899 and rediscovered himself as a right-wing politician in New Zealand.

The others followed. Tozer abandoned politics, agreed he'd been "an ass" and went to work on the railways. Mary didn't give up politics altogether but concentrated on women, Aborigines and cats. She became an Australian institution, appeared on the ten-dollar note and died in her King's Cross cattery in 1962. Only Stevenson stayed on, at least for a while. He took a bullet in the lung at the Somme in 1915 and retired to a guest house in the Channel Islands. He died there during the Nazi occupation in 1942, succumbing to disappointment and malnutrition.

With the loss of all the colony's leaders by 1894, the Australian press crowed the demise of the "harum-scarum" New Australia. They were a little previous in doing so.

My host, the owner of the dog-shed, was Marcelino Godoy Vera. He was the local Colorado boss, a man of great physical and political mass. He was made of ham and leather and was best friends with Lino Oviedo.

"I only ever eat meat!" he declared.

"And what about Lino?"

"A man of military strength!" he thundered, so loud that his displaced dog began to bark. "Did you like the dog-house?"

"It was perfect."

Although Marcelino's superstructure swayed with laughter, he insisted that tonight I move inside. It was a curious lair, blushed in deep pink and decorated with cuddly toys, guns and a second and very tiny wife (the first had been killed in the same accident that left the ham unevenly distributed across his scalp). There was a Colorado Party clock, permanently stuck on mealtime.

"Ah, we must get breakfast."

We had three, in different parts of the old colony. At each farm they called it an "Australian breakfast," fried beef and coffee. Marcelino smacked it all down without knowing or caring who the Australians were.

"Ask the priest," he suggested.

This time I had more luck. To my surprise, he was Irish: Father Feehan.

"I came here thirty-three years ago from the Vatican," he mused, a note of satisfaction at the course his life had taken. "The Paraguayans have proved truly Irish."

We talked about the Utopians. "I knew some of them well. Of course, they weren't all Australian. Some were Irish, like Casey." A dry smile spread over his face. "He was a feckin' rascal."

Here is what happened after the departure of Lane.

For a while, they faced great hardship. Jaguars took their cattle and the men were eaten alive by jiggers. There was no money and *The Royal Tar* was seized to pay their debts. But they improvised, had cricket matches and balls with the natives and tied fireflies in their hair at Christmastime. Casey's father, Gilbert, took up with a *paraguaya* and the land was divided up. But it was still socialism and there were even fresh recruits: the Sheppersons from America, the Kennedys from Scotland (1900), and the Smiths from London (1909). The Smiths had a son, named after some impressive labour riots: Ricardo Lille.

The Kennedy boy and Ricardo became inseparable friends. They worked hard and every week they rode up to Asunción with their ox-carts full of surplus. By 1942, they had a cattle empire. It was time to dismantle the remains of socialism and establish a town. They were good men, and in deference to the original settlers, they asked the Australian government for permission to call it New Canberra. When no one answered, they called it New London instead.

"Ricardo only died in 1990," said Father Feehan. "We all miss him. He was ninety-three."

"Are there any Australians left?"

"You've obviously not met my neighbour, Bruce Murray."

*

Murray was lying in a chair, launching great flobs of tobacco juice on to his wife's clean patio. He had crumbling yellow nails and a head of wispy grey knots. He wasn't surprised to hear the sound of English and responded in crackling Australian. The good men in his stories (like himself) were "kangaroos" and the smart ones were "kangaroo-killers." He, of course, had never seen a kangaroo, or cricket, or a billabong, or Sydney Harbour Bridge. Nor had his father.

"Grandad just put a house down, caught a chicken and that was it."

His eyeballs suddenly seemed pink and angry.

"You don't mind me asking?"

"Ask what you like, mate." He rubbed his belly and spat. "As long as it's not who I sleep with!"

It was an unappealing thought. I brought us back to the language.

"I was brought up speaking Australian. My folks wouldn't have us mixing with no Paraguayans. Not until school anyways."

He talked of his forebears, a rattly collection of chancers and fiddlers, a Scottish nanny and an Englishman who drifted in with the railways. Little Bruce had himself wandered into the cattle trade. He'd merged his misfortune with a *paraguaya* and they'd produced a son who was everything Murray had dreamed of being: a corporal with the *policía*. Had it been a good life?

"That depends," he winked, "which way yer lies."

I thought it better to avoid this. "What about 1947? The Civil War?"

A wet, yellow grin. "It was a chance for people to have a good drink and kill one another . . . we all had the black cat."

My encounter with Murray should not have troubled me as much as it did. Father Feehan had warned me: "People here don't have the warmth of other Paraguayans. There is not that sense of belonging."

I thought about this as I made my way back through the square. It was planted with silky oaks, brought from Australia with the first settlers. There was a plaque to the villagers who'd perished in the war against Bolivia: Drakeford, Jones, King, Shepperson and Douglas Kennedy. Dying for Paraguay was, I supposed, only part of belonging to it.

The Australians had obviously proved rather harder to digest than the Japanese.

66

I caught Ricardo Lille's son on his way out to work. Although Harold Smith was nearly seventy, he was dressed for a day in the saddle; *faja*, gun-belt, *sombrero* and breeches. Unlike Murray, the sound of English left him shocked and floundering for words. He then did a very curious thing: he stood to attention and saluted.

"I'm sorry," he stuttered. "It has been such a long time."

We shook hands and he mounted his horse and rode off into the *campo*.

67

On my last day, Marcelino and I took a double breakfast at the Kennedys' ranch, which was called the House of Sarah.

Sarah had been a servant girl and the lover of James Craig Kennedy of Dalricket Mill, New Cumnock in Ayrshire. James was the eleventh of thirteen children, and already, by 1899, Kennedys were dispersing themselves across the globe: New York, Trinidad, Sydney and Kimberley. James left his wife with a broken heart and an empty house and was carried on a breeze of socialism and illicit passion to Paraguay. He brought his two children and his scullery girl to New Australia, where they settled. Sarah produced seven more little Kennedys, all boys, and the family grew rich on cattle. Their lives seemed charmed until 1935 when news came through that the favourite son, Douglas, had died of tuberculosis in a Bolivian prisoner-of-war camp. James buckled with grief and was dead by the following year. Sarah survived him a few years longer, before she too was carried away to the family plot beneath the *lapachos*. As the ranks of brothers thinned, the ranch passed to number six, Nigel.

Don Nigel was waiting for us outside, propped up by granddaughters and deeply cardiganed in Arran. "I'm eighty-five, aren't I, Ardyne? How old am I?"

The stately party moved into the House of Sarah, a low building of cement and *quebracho* logs. Nigel was lowered into an armchair, around him the artefacts of his adventures. There were horns and pelts, cattle certificates, furniture from the colony carpenter ("Mr. Martin"), mildewed books and crusts of photographs: Don Nigel with a Colt .45; with the Pope in 1988; with a prize zebu; with his son, killed in a car crash, the week of his graduation.

"I never went to school," he said absently. His English was brittle and old-fashioned. As he was deaf, the story of his life emerged unbidden, in fragments snatched from his memory, like the snapshots.

"Douglas shouldn't have died. He was stronger than me. I expected to die in that war. There was never enough water—or food. We advanced in ox-carts—there were no trucks until the end. I think we got all the way into Bolivia. I think so. We had dysentery."

The breakfasts arrived. Marcelino ate them and fell asleep.

"The Colorados renamed this place, you know. For thirty years, Nueva Londres was called 'Hugo Stroessner,' after the President's father." He snarled. "Colorados! The lick-bottoms!"

There were long silences. "My half-brother went to fight in the Great European war. He met a girl and never came back. They never came for us in the second war. I suppose I should have gone. How long did it go on for?"

I held up six fingers.

"That long! Good grief!"

Marcelino stirred. It was time to go.

"My father was always a socialist. He kept up with many of them in England. Show him the book, Ardyne."

The book was produced. On the fly-leaf were the words: "Dear

Kennedy, I was so sorry to hear of your fire. Please accept this as an addition to your new library. Yours &c, George Bernard Shaw."

68

In Don Nigel's youth, the round trip to Villarrica took seven days in an ox-cart. It took me fifty minutes, one-way, in the bus.

After the collapse of the original colony, many Utopians had drifted into Villarrica and it wasn't hard to see why. The settlement had been named by a conquistador called Captain Malgarejo in the fond belief that it straddled a stupendous cache of treasure (he wouldn't be the last to make this mistake). Although the *rica* never materialised and the *villa* fledged into a city, it has remained obstinately pretty. Everything about it was charming: the cobbled streets, the colonnades, the public dances and puppet shows, the horse-carts and the stalls of cattle-salts and powdery rifles. The policemen carried ornamental daggers and the Victorian sugar-cane factory still ran on steam. In the main square, there was even a replica of the Statue of Liberty, affectionately smothered in paint.

There have, however, been mixed fortunes for its inhabitants. A great classical writer, Manuel Ortiz Guerrero, settled here with his girlfriend, Dalmaccia. Although in the city's portraits she looks something of a herbivore, her loyalty was admirable; Guerrero was a rapidly deconstructing leper. Another transitory resident was ex-President Perón of Argentina. He was unimpressed by house-arrest in Villarrica and sought a fleshier pot for his retirement, eventually settling for Panama.

There were mixed fates too for the Australians. Laurence de Petrie, a one-armed anarchist who'd once tried to blow up a ship full of "double-breasted parasites," took a job at the railway station (now drifting in thistles). It ended badly when he tried to rescue the station-master's daughter from a train and was himself squashed flat. Things worked out better for Alexander MacDonald. He was so happy that he wrote a book, *Picturesque Paraguay*, encouraging other immigrants (though prudently omitting his involvement with the socialists). On reflection, Villarrica was a strange choice for such a rangy adventurer—who'd trekked through East Africa, ridden with the Egyptian cavalry and acted as adviser to the Emperor of Ethiopia—but something caught his eye.

"Men stand around discussing politics, race meetings and cock-fighting," he wrote, "the whole thing much after the style of an open-air fair in Europe in the Middle Ages."

This, broadly speaking, mirrored my sentiments. I stayed for a week.

69

One of my excursions from Villarrica was with an American who loathed me from the start. At first I found this a little disconcerting, but I soon realised that his hatred was not specific but was levelled at humankind in general. Our lives had been thrown together by mutual contacts in Asunción and a particular source of irritation was that I was British. As we drove along, he probed at this.

"Is it true you drink your beer warm, like piss? What you got a queen for?"

It was like discovering that *The Catcher in the Rye* wasn't just a nightmare, that Holden Caulfield had emerged from tortured adolescence and was now a tortured agronomist in central Paraguay. Just in case he can blush, I'll call him Garth (although his real name was Brian). In Garth's world, there were only two redeeming features: plants and insects.

"This is the fuckin' ant capital of the world. More species than anywhere else."

He particularly admired the insects that devoured mankind. It seemed there were plenty: *polvorinos*, ticks, jiggers (that bored their way in through the toes), widow-flies, mosquitoes, bott-flies and warble-flies (who implanted their larvae in living flesh). Even the taxonomy was excruciating, with names like *Hypoderma* and *Pulex penetrans*.

"The botts burrow deep into the muscle, about the size of maggots," said Garth fondly. "You just squeeze 'em out. I once had one on my asshole . . ."

He'd agreed to take me with him, camping in Ybytyruzú. It was a place that brilliantly combined his twin passions. "Ybytyruzú's a young range of primary forest. Once the trees came right down here, to the grasslands, but all that's gone. Just gallery forests and bamboo now. They've even started to clear the lower slopes, fuckin' pricks with chainsaws. The only wild bits left are up on the top." And then, absently, "The bugs are goin' to fuckin' love you."

Before the wild bits, however, was a strange, tropical outcrop of Bavaria. Suddenly, we were bounding up into meadows of Friesians, past alpine chalets and a little Saxon church steeped in oranges and sugar cane. There was a *Deutsche Schule* with a Prussian eagle and a *Bierstube* of yellowy Germans. It was Colonia Independencia, founded in 1919 with 12,000 peasants.

We stopped for *Schnitzel mit pommes frites*. Garth saw a man he knew and waved. The labourer waved a stump back at him.

"Hansee lost his arm in the sawmill," said Garth. "Some of the Germans have money, some have shit. Hansee has shit."

I was secretly rather impressed with Independencia. It was as pretty as a train layout.

"They still celebrate Hitler's birthday here," said Garth.

Was I supposed to find this endearing?

"Bunch of fuckin' pricks."

70

The Ybytyruzú range was everything Garth had promised (or threatened). We camped at Swiss Falls, where a gulch of green water crashed out of the forest and lost itself over a cliff. The isolated chalets up here had long been abandoned—in haste, it seemed, with the stoves still full of ash and the beds unmade. Everything was thickly matted in dust and bat-droppings and so we shrank away, to the open ground. As the pines and the *lapachos* threw their shadows into the clearing, the *polvorinos* clustered densely in my hair.

There was another treat too: the *mbaragui*. Each one was a chilli-grain of vengeance. They found my hands (everything else was parcelled up and drenched in deet), which for the next week looked like boxing gloves, studded with bright-red nail-heads. Garth meanwhile was cultivating serenity.

"I need to be alone," he said (superfluously). These were Garth moments, spent grubbing around in the forest, collecting leaves, dirt and bits of mould. I stayed behind on the lip of the falls, peering out over the grasslands way below.

These highlands, I'd read, were once the hunting grounds of a mysterious people. There were few of them; a hundred square miles of this forest will only support twenty hunters. They were naked and hunted with stone axes, like living fossils. If they'd ever farmed, they'd lost their skills in the great invasions of the Guaraní and had become fugitives in their own forests. They evolved to their life in the shadows; they turned white as their pigmentation faltered; they learnt to communicate in silence and birdsong; they became adept raiders of cattle and women. The Guaraní were terrified, believing these *guajakí*— or "rabid rats"—to be the scourged ones, punished by the Sun God for their nudity. In the seventeenth century, the Guaraní's allies and patrons, the Jesuit fathers, tried to understand these savages. A group of thirty were captured for their studies but they stubbornly refused food and died.

The scholarly chronicler, Father Lozano, recorded what he could. In *The History of the Conquest of Paraguay* he detailed their weapons and their devilish customs. There was precious little to go on. They are a small "nation," he concluded, continually attacked by jaguars and wild animals: "They are not unified and each is separated from the others, they cannot help each other and are buried in impenetrable woods, forced into them by the same wild animals who disturb their tranquillity." He was puzzled by the scarcity of women and swiftly concluded that their society was riven by little wars. He knew nothing of their rituals.

There was no further scholarship until the second half of the twentieth century. The *guajakís* remained pale spectres of the forest. Even MacDonald (who knew the Ybytyruzú well) never saw one, although he was aware that they were often hunted by the Paraguayans—and some Europeans. The skins of the *guajakí*, it was said, made the best hammocks.

He didn't even know the name by which they called themselves: the Aché—"the people."

I slept in the jeep that night, besieged by insects and dreams of the rabid white rats. Garth slept in the forest, reappearing at dawn with two infant Guaranís, dressed only in football shorts and riding a horse. They got off and approached me very carefully, entwined with fear.

"I told 'em," sneered Garth, "that you eat little kids."

I was beginning to warm to Garth. Too late, it was time to part.

Had he ever seen the Aché?

"I saw some over on the other side of the range. But they didn't want a gringo pokin' around. They had enough fuckin' problems."

It was a fair summary of their predicament. It was almost their requiem.

71

Twenty kilometres north of Villarrica, in the other direction, the people of Letter Hill were tormented by visions of rather different white men: the Vikings.

I got an old bus out there, to satisfy myself that this was insanity.

The obsession with a Viking ancestry is an old one, twinned with the delusions of treasure. Hadn't Viracocha, the Inca god, been a white man with a beard? Stories of a lost civilisation fluffed up the greed. The Jesuits reported more lost white-beards and marked their Paraguayan maps with Viking place-names. By now, the southern cone was cluttered with lost empires: El Dorado, Atlantis, the City of the Caesars, Meta, Omagua, Manoa, the Empire Puytita and—for the Guaraní—Tapuá Guazú. Even Dr. Förster took up the theme, propagating rumours of long-lost Paraguayan-Aryans at somewhere called Guanaquí.

The "runic scripts" of Letter Hill would ensure that this one ran and ran.

The village huts were scattered in the lee of Ybytyruzú. The villagers washed in a mountain stream. As we drove in, a hunter was pedalling his way home with an old Winchester slung across his shoulders. He had claws and teeth like a dog and growled as the bus passed. I got out at the village school, which was furnished with only a table, the teacher's chair and a chart of the human nervous system.

I scrambled up to the caves with the schoolmaster, Mr. Gómez. We craned our necks up at the gouges in the rock.

"It's a treasure map," said Mr. Gómez.

All I could make out were whirls and snakes, spirogyra, stickmen, Snoopy and some balloons on string. I tried to imagine what it said: today we caught eight armadillos and an extinct thing.

"We believe there's a lot of treasure," continued Mr. Gómez. "There's an Austrian living higher up the hill and he's translating it for us. We expect results any day."

We were joined by Isadora from the farm. She was on her way to feed the piglets. "The descendants of the *Vikingos* still live over the mountains," she said. "They have blond hair, green eyes . . ."

". . . and Swedish names!" added Mr. Gómez.

I noticed, with disappointment, that they were pointing in the direction of Colonia Independencia. The idea of a longship's warriors surviving a journey round the world and thirty-seven generations of disease, miscegenation and conquest—appealing though it was—now seemed irredeemably tatty.

I wished them both well with the treasure. Mr. Gómez took me back to Villarrica with him on his moped. We drank a lot of beer together. He didn't think the gold would change him.

So what had started all this, the whiteness and the elusive tribe? My feeling was that it all came back to some of the earliest and most secretive inhabitants of the continent: the Aché.

72

In August 1959, an extraordinary event happened: the Aché of Ybytyruzú simply surrendered.

The last decades had been the worst since the invasions of the Guaraní, possibly the worst in their thousands of years of existence. Their hunting grounds had been chopped away by foresters and their territory sliced in half by *Ruta Dos*. Worse, there was now an insatiable demand for *guajakí* slaves. Each savage was worth the price of a horse.

The demand was partly historical: the Guaranís' need to overwhelm their own fears, to conquer these pale, supernatural spectres and to possess them as slaves. They were expensive because the Aché were hard to track. The *montaraces*—the Indian hunters—could move right through a *guajakí* camp without knowing they were there. Even in captivity they could move as quickly and silently as an idea. Although the women were often intractably bonded by means of prostitution, the young men were more elusive. They were tormented by the prospect of never fulfilling their sexual and therefore spiritual ambitions (no *paraguaya* would ever have contemplated coupling herself to such a half-human). In a celebrated case in 1943, two braves were whipped for attempting to escape.

As soon as their tormentor was asleep, they forced a flaming log down his throat, stole his weapons and fled, back into the forest. The dead man's son joined the *montaraces*.

It was the same man who, ten years later, took part in the greatest capture of them, forty tribals herded into San Juan Nepomuceno. The leader of the hunt was a professional, Pinchín López, but his beaters were terrified Paraguayan soldiers. They believed the *guajakí* had tails, and in their panic they fluffed the ambush and shot a precious slave. The rest were corralled into a cattle pen for the night. Pinchín, a man of notable stupidity and ostentatious thirst, believed the *guajakí* could be penned up like animals. By dawn, they'd vanished, as silently as ghosts.

When news of the affair reached Asunción, it triggered the humble beginnings of outrage. For the first time, it became illegal under Paraguayan law to kill an *indigena*.

For the Aché, it was merely a stay of execution. Six years later, they padded back into San Juan and gave themselves up.

San Juan Nepomuceno sits halfway down the whip-tail of Ybytyruzú, two hours from Villarrica. It was a drowsy town of sandy streets and veterinary stores, much, I imagined, as it had been forty years before. I had lunch at the Capybara Bar, which was layered in soft pornography and the curvy white outlines of the San Marino cigarette girl. Every surface was so sticky with dust that the *estancieros* ate with their hats on, plates of knuckles and gravy. The older ones remembered the Achés.

"When he was hungry," they said, "the Aché just wandered off. He ate anything—pumas, jaguars, alligators . . ."

They remembered Pinchín López too; he shook himself to death with rum.

Where did the Aché stay?

"About ten kilometres away, at Pereira's place, on Arroyo Moroti. They may still be there."

Farmer Pereira had been only too happy to accommodate the Aché. He believed that, in time, they would lead him to the treasures of Madame Lynch.

ABOVE LEFT: The monument to the Spanish conquista of 1537. In the background,
the legislature, chewed by gunfire.

ABOVE RIGHT: The Pantheon of Heroes, Asunción. Based on Les Invalides in Paris, it took sixty years
to finish. Each of the heroes entombed there met a violent death—or endures a restless afterlife.

BELOW: The Government Palace, Asunción. Conceived by a builder from Chelsea, Captain Burton
described it as "an utter absurdity." It was completed in 1869 by slaves and children.

ABOVE LEFT: Stroessner's statue, safely encased in concrete.

ABOVE RIGHT: Lino Oviedo, the "Bonsai Horseman." He threatens to tear the Colorado Party apart and return Paraguay to the army. "Slightly mad" is the sober assessment.

BELOW: The empty plinth. With Stroessner gone, an enduring leader has yet to emerge. To date, democracy has brought only chancers, tricksters and plenty of anger.

ABOVE: Loaded with logs, an Asunción steam train awaits its orders. The railway expends millions of dollars a year and yet not a cog moves. Nowadays it employs moonlighters, Donald Ducks and other ghosts of the Paraguayan economy.

BELOW: López's navy, preserved in the slime of Vapor Cué. The *Piravevé* once served the Royal Navy as HMS *Ranger*. It was decommissioned by fire in 1869.

ABOVE: Cowboys, or *peones*, on the battlefield at Humaitá. Almost every Paraguayan has an ancestor buried in its sand.

LEFT: The ruins of the Jesuit church at Humaitá. The Brazilian ironclads pounded Humaitá at the rate of four thousand shells a day at the height of the siege.

BELOW: The "Micawbers' Shop" at Humaitá. The chain across the door once kept the Brazilian ironclads out of Paraguay.

ABOVE: An Aché woman breast-feeding a monkey. Early Europeans were quick to accuse the "rabid rats" of bestiality. However, the full horror of their society was yet to emerge.

BELOW LEFT: The Aché chief with a bow and monkey arrow.

BELOW RIGHT: Nurse Baker, providing the only help available to over eighteen thousand Chaco Indians.

ABOVE LEFT: Maria and Hein Braun, Loma Plata.
ABOVE RIGHT: Jorge Halke of Neuva Germania, with his family and his ancestors from Berlin.
BELOW LEFT: Dr. Enrique Wood, survivor of the Australian Utopia, founded in 1893.
BELOW RIGHT: "Don Nigel" Kennedy, last of the British Socialists of New London, and a veteran of the Chaco War.

ABOVE: Guaranís being led into slavery
by the Mamelucos. By 1638,
over 300,000 captives had been forced
into the São Paulo plantations.

INSET: The Basilica, Trinidad.
LEFT: From the *reducción* of Trinidad, views over
the Jesuit Republic. The arts were encouraged
but not originality.

ABOVE: The *trencito*, now abandoned in Puerto Casado.

INSET: From 1932 to 1935, the little trains carried more than 100,000 soldiers off to the brutal "War of Thirst."

LEFT: A Bolivian machine-gun nest in a bottle-tree, Boquerón.

ABOVE: The revered battleground of Boquerón today. For three weeks in 1932, the flies grew fat on the slaughter.

73

News of the Aché's surrender travelled down the anthropologists' telegraph. In Paris, Pierre Clastres, a promising young scholar, acquired tapes of their voices and taught himself their language. He read the works of Father Lozano and bought a revolver. By 1963, he was at Arroyo Moroti, eager to unravel the secrets of *guajakí*—or, as he called them, "the savages."

For a while, everything Clastres found was to his satisfaction. The Aché were a shy and secretive people whose world was finely balanced between good fortune on the one hand and poor hunting (*pané*) on the other. The imbalances were addressed by ritual, by complex ceremonies, by sacrifice and by the experience of pain through scarification, piercing and circumcision. In this balanced world, a birth portended the death of a father.

They were hunters who plucked their bodies of hair to set them apart from beasts. They had no words for "to plant" and the only cassava they ate was stolen from the Paraguayans. A man was never to eat the game he'd killed, for that offended the spirit of sharing. A woman was never to touch his arrows for that would bring *pané*.

Clastres stayed with them for a year, delving into their lives. He went hunting with them, dressed only in his boots and gun-belt. He slept in their huts and ate with them: game, forest honey and fistfuls of maggots. He missed nothing. The Aché were polyandrous and knew no sin of adultery. As the night forest was terrifying, their sex was public and unambitious. Although intrigued by some fumbled experiments with fellatio, Clastres noted (with a little Gallic *hauteur*): "They are not experts in the Art of Love."

He watched with equal detachment as his savages redressed the imbalances of their society. The unwanted child was punched from the uterus or strangled at birth. The elderly and those too sick to hunt were dispatched with the crack of a stone hatchet. Each year, his Aché met up with other groups from eastern Paraguay for the *kybairu*, the exchange of unmarried girls. The loss of women was prefaced by mock warfare. Then the war-paint was washed away and the groups play-fought for possession of a *proaa* bean. It was merely the pretext for touching each other (which, was, at all other times, repugnant), for ritual tickling and for sex and marriage.

Like Lozano, Clastres was puzzled by the shortage of women. Then, by chance, he made a discovery that he described as "terrifying": the Aché were cannibals.

Pereira knew, of course, and had done all along. He feared that if the secret of the Aché got out, he'd lose his treasure-hunters. Besides, the Aché brought other advantages: people in Asunción sent them generous parcels of food (which Pereira siphoned off and sold); he'd also found himself an endless source of unripened squaws.

He kept his counsel—and his patronage, as chief of the cannibals.

Clastres greeted his discovery not as an academic triumph but as a matter of profound despair. Cannibalism was an expression of grief. His savages, now under catastrophic environmental pressure, were quite literally tearing themselves apart and self-digesting.

He realised that they'd always eaten their dead. Father Lozano had been right after all, in giving credence to the rumours of the Guaraní ("They are like *tigres* and gorge themselves with the corpses of the dead"). Clastres also realised that they didn't eat human flesh out of nutritional necessity, though they clearly enjoyed the taste.

"It is sweet!" they told him. "And good fat!"

Their cannibalism was a religious necessity. The death of a man leaves his spirit—his *ianwe*—restless yet trapped in the living world. There is even a danger that the *ianwe* will enter the body of a living person, with fatal consequences. It can only be released by eating the dead man's carcass. When this has been picked of every scrap of flesh and tissue, the skull is then smashed and burnt and the *ianwe* is carried away west, to the Land of the Dead.

Clastres absorbed these details with a growing sense of hopelessness, not because cannibalism existed but because it was out of control. During his year at Arroyo Moroti, the number of savages fell from a hundred to seventy-five. Some succumbed to influenza. Others simply withered because they couldn't hunt and believed themselves cursed. Here was the danger: such unnatural deaths had to be attended by *jepy*, or vengeance; the *ianwe* needed a companion in his journey to the afterlife. Death therefore came in twins. As in Jesuit times, the brunt of the sacrifice was borne by the females. Women were simply cut down with the axe or crushed under a stampede of feet. Then they were eaten.

"This is the way we do it!" they'd shout as the victim's life ebbed away.

The dead were eaten with exacting rituality. Every member of the group was to be invited. Adult corpses were roasted and children boiled in a pot. Every part had to be eaten, except a woman's sexual organs— and the intestines, if they stank. The fat was soaked up on brushes and the bones were broken up and given to the older women, to lick out the marrow. Anyone could eat the body except relatives, proscribed by the same rules relating to incest.

"To eat someone," says Clastres, "is in some sense to make love with him."

Towards the end of his study, the savages ate a baby that they'd killed. Clastres found the bones afterwards, licked clean by little brushes. He was unable to remain detached any longer, feeling himself a helpless witness at the destruction of an ancient and remarkable race. Although he would return to Paraguay several times, he could never bear to return to his savages. By 1968, he'd heard, there were only thirty left at Arroyo Moroti.

Four years later, he published his treatise, *Chronique des Indiens Guajaki*. A work of compassion, it was immediately banned in Paraguay.

It was also in many ways an unfinished story.

It would remain so. In another five years, Clastres would himself be dead, killed in a car crash at the age of forty-three.

74

I couldn't expect much of my trip to Arroyo Moroti. It was simply historical curiosity, a bleak, secular pilgrimage. I hired a dilapidated taxi and a driver called Edelio, who walloped his machine out into the grasslands, trailing his sump-cover all the way. He was only twenty and had never heard of the Aché.

Pereira's farm was unrecognisable from Clastres. They were burning off the winter grass and I could just make out the last charred stumps of the trees. The rest of the forest had shrivelled back, over the horizon into the jagged Ybytyruzú.

Pereira was long dead.

We stopped at several little *chacras*. The farmers offered us *tereré* and oranges but no one remembered the Indians. Then we came upon Mr. Israel, who'd taken his tenancy much earlier than the others, in 1971.

"I remember them well. They wore animal skins, little skirts down here on their . . ." he struggled momentarily, "on their delicate bits. They had straw houses up over there, all gone now. Back then, they hunted in the forest . . ."

We gazed out over the smouldering grass.

"They ate everything!"

"Including people?" I ventured.

"Oh, yes," he said, cupping his balls absently. "But not after the War."

"War?"

"The Triple Alliance."

This was an unfruitful line. There was only one thing I wanted to know: "What happened to them?"

"They just got up and left. In 1975. They had a reserve, I think, up north."

"How many were there?"

"Fifty. Equal men and women."

Edelio ploughed me back to San Juan.

Even though finding the Aché would have to wait, I had every reason to be pleased. They'd kept their secret and the killing of women had, for the time being, abated.

75

The persecution of the Indians, however, continued.

Their rights had progressed very little since 1537, when Pope Paul III had declared them capable of salvation. By the later twentieth century, they were in the margins, making up perhaps three per cent of the population. Even there, the *Stronistas* saw them as impeding progress (or, rather, wealth) with their hunting grounds straddling vast areas of forestry. There was another problem: groups like the Aché were simply unable to fathom the concept of private property. Wherever their arrows fell was game for the taking, whether it was beef or sweet horse-meat. Sometimes they hacked their meat from living animals and then fled before the outsiders arrived with their thunder, or gunfire. The hunting of Indians was an unsurprising development.

The eradication of genocide in Paraguay was, for a long time, an over-ambitious task. But the blunting of the Indians' suffering is often credited to the work of one man: Leon Cadogan.

I met his grandson by chance in Villarrica.

Geraldo Cadogan was an evangelist preacher and a healer. He and his wife ran a clinic from a shed on the edge of town. They treated their patients with river mud and faith.

"After a month of the mud," said Christina, "uterine cancers just drop away."

The story of the Paraguayan Cadogans is one of determined tragedy.

Geraldo knew that the Cadogans were descended from Irish robber-barons who'd preyed on the Welsh. They had a square named in their honour in London. At some stage, outlawed Cadogans had wandered off to Australia, and from there they'd sailed for Paraguay, arriving in 1899 with the Utopians. Jack Cadogan declared himself a "revolutionary activist," but like his forebears, he was a nomad at heart. Three of his sons drifted back to Australia and to violent deaths: killed by a crocodile, stabbed by an Aborigine and butchered by the Japanese in New Guinea. A fourth, Hugh, was drafted into a Paraguayan revolution and died of TB. Only Leon survived, born soon after landfall and named after Tolstoy.

Leon's life took the ancestral shape, migratory and purposeless. He justified his lack of substance by declaring himself to be Irish. By 1940, he'd been a *yerba*-grower, a teacher, a detective, a father and a divorcé, and he was about to become an alcoholic.

"Then something changed," said Geraldo.

His grandfather's road to Damascus had been an encounter with an Indian he'd once defended in his police days (prosecution had never been his strength). His vocation, he suddenly realised, was the better-ment of Indians. He wrote a dictionary for the Mbyá and defended them against the more outrageous charges. After the San Juan slaving incident, he flew into litigation.

"It was my grandfather who had the killing of Indians banned, in 1957."

Stroessner thought he could contain him by appointing him Director of Indian Affairs. It was a ham-fisted ploy. From the inside, Cadogan could see for himself the army concentration camps ("Belsen for Indi-ans"), the smallpox and the rot. He denounced them all and the generals trading in slaves. In 1964, he had the honour of being fired.

Stroessner then sent the *pyragüés* in. They stole Cadogan's life's work and left him reeling under the first of several heart attacks.

"I remember him," said Geraldo, "as a tall man. White hair and thick glasses. I was rather frightened of him."

In the turmoil of his life, Leon Cadogan's family had disintegrated. His eldest son, Dick, joined the evangelists and was cut adrift by Leon. He's drifted ever since. There was only a brief interlude of stability in Dick's life, when he married a Paraguayan called Adelaida.

"I was their ninth child, born in 1966," said Geraldo. "My mother died three hours after I was born, from a haemorrhage."

Dick was inconsolable with grief. He abandoned the children for adoption and set off on his aimless wanderings around Paraguay.

"I saw him occasionally. He called by about every five years. So did my grandfather. Neither of them provided anything towards my up-bringing. I loved them but they frightened me."

"Where's your father now?"

Geraldo shrugged.

Leon Cadogan died in 1973. His work had not been in vain. *Asunceños* were appalled at the cruelty of the countryside. Foreign investigators arrived. The new Director of Indian Affairs, Colonel Infanzón, tried to buy them off with pre-pubescent Indian girls—unsuccessfully (to his surprise). Soon the world knew.

Within a year of Leon's death, the United Nations charged Paraguay with slavery and genocide. By then, the price of an Aché slave had fallen to a mere $2.

American support for Stroessner shrank back in disgust.

It was comforting to think that the suffering of the San Juan Aché had not been in vain either. In its own small way, it had contributed to the downfall of an ogre.

76

An opportunity to visit an Aché group arose some weeks later.

My friend, the soil scientist Dr. Palacios, was heading a party up into the Mbaracayú range and agreed to take me along. It was a forest five times the size of Ybytyruzú and a last refuge of jaguars, tapirs and the Aché. There were now only a thousand Aché left in the whole country.

From Asunción, we drove north-east for twelve hours in the jeep. The road, at first asphalt, turned to earth and then deep orange sludge.

"The Brazilians own everything up here," said Palacios cheerfully. "The ranches, the forests, the towns—even the cat-pits. They are the New Paraguayans."

We passed Curuguaty and Ygatimí, both capital cities for a day, during the retreat of Marshal López. Then, on the border with Brazil, we entered a dark forest, throbbing with insects and frogs.

For several days we were confined to the Biological Station as the sky chewed up the earth and violent orange storms exploded over the forest. Only the botanist wandered out into the bromeliads and epiphytes, oblivious of the watery chaos. Palacios held court at the kitchen table, eating jam with a spoon.

When the rains thundered off to Brazil, the forest warden, Silverio, led us deeper into the sopping woods. The Aché were camped five kilometres east, on a clearing of rammed earth.

The hunters had returned that week with a tapir and the tribe was replete and content. Slabs of black meat still smouldered in the fire. There were little brushes for licking up the fat.

The men were more powerful than I'd envisaged, packed with dense, unyielding muscle. Their faces were Mongoloid, sinewy, and though not white, there was a milky opacity to their skin. Their feet were broad, the toenails smashed away and the skin lacy with hookworm. All their body hair had been plucked or scorched away and tiny black-fly fed at their nicks and wounds.

Of course, there'd been adaptations—probably more in the last forty years than in the last forty thousand. The men wore shorts—shreds of charity—and the women shrugged themselves into shirts as we arrived. They spoke Guaraní and lived in stilted metal huts. They'd even started to cultivate oranges and cassava, and now kept a small larder of live animals: a sheep, an armadillo and a few coatimundis.

"They've been here since 1982," said Silverio. "Fifty families."

There was much that hadn't changed. They still had no concept of money and only the haziest notion of private property. Most potently, each man carried a longbow, two metres high with a clutch of long, spe-cialised arrows: serrated for monkeys; bladed for tapirs; a blunt punch for birds.

Palacios tried to fire one. He was unable to pull the string back and the arrow flopped uselessly into the grass. The Aché can kill at seventy metres.

"The relationship between the hunter and his game," said Silverio, "is one of love. The animal's death is a sacrifice. The Aché will raise its orphans as their own."

He showed us photographs of Aché women suckling orphaned mon-keys.

"They have," decided Palacios, "a union with the beasts."

Do they still eat the dead?

"Not in the last thirty years," replied Silverio. "Though they still think about it."

77

The Aché may well have been the savages who captured Candide on his wanderings in Paraguay: the Oreillons.

Voltaire had been educated as a Jesuit, and though he'd come to be their tormentor, he was an avid reader of the Jesuits' American adven-tures. *Candide* was written in 1758, at about the time of Father Lozano's "most barbarous" discoveries. It is not merely the fact that the naked Oreillons were cannibals "armed with arrows, clubs and stone axes" that tempts this literary connection: Voltaire was intrigued by the natives' union with beasts: "They found that the cries came from two naked girls who were tripping along the edge of the meadow, while two monkeys were nibbling at their buttocks." Candide dispatches the lewd monkeys with a few blasts of his gun. "'A pretty piece of work, sir!' said Cacambo. 'You have killed those two young ladies' lovers.'"

The European writers' presumption of bestiality was, however, too hasty. Clastres would reveal that, to the Aché, carnality with animals was well beyond the pale. His group told him that they'd once found a man with a tapir. They hacked him open with their axes, and then, of course, they ate him.

78

My journey back to Asunción was a protracted reminder of the remoteness of the Aché. I waited a day in the mud-bath of Ygatimí for a truck—or anything—to emerge. Eventually, a tiny Fiat decided to make a break for it and the boys agreed to take me. We got about five kilometres before the sludge was up at the windows. The Fiat whined for a moment, glugged and then fell silent. It was now archaeology. I completed the next four hours in a petrol tanker, a beautiful monster that churned through the slime all the way to Curuguaty.

"We stop here," said the crew. "There are too many bandits in the dark."

There was no bus until midnight. The Brazilians here were feverish and on the frontier. "Have you tried the Paraguayan girls?" they kept asking me. I booked into a hotel that had all the expectations of a whore-house except that it was derelict. I dozed on an itchy bed until I could hear the Asunción bus, raring to leave.

79

I was back in time for the Grand Caledonian Ball.

This exotic institution is the gift of the British Ladies to Asunción's rich and curious. It is held every year at the slightly foxy Golf Club. This club—in defiance of golfing convention—is one of the world's only floodlit courses. At night, it glows like a strange green planet.

Every year the tropical ballroom imagines itself to be Scottish, with banks of baronial shields and the banner of St. Andrews fluttering among the palms. Twelve pipers are flown in from the nearest little Scotland—Buenos Aires—and they arrive with all their swords and kilts, daggers and jolly Glengarrys. After 170 years in Argentina they no longer speak English, but they can still pipe a mighty *concurso de eight-some reel*. They also bring their own dancers (little pixies in tams and woolly socks) because, historically, the Paraguayans have often been unable to move, paralysed with astonishment.

We were received by The Ladies' *Presidenta*, Señora Gibson, also struggling with her English but magnificently ball-gowned in taffeta, with a sash of Hunting Campbell. All around her, waiters in brilliant drill were fighting their way into the tartan throng, with trays of frozen whisky. I joined a table of half-Britons, an Italian rancher and a *paraguaya*. She began her interrogation immediately.

"Who are these Scottish? Is it a British colony?"

We ate *piraña* soup, roasted beef and schooners of whisky mousse. The band marched in and the half-Britons marched after them, flailing and whooping. The Paraguayans barricaded themselves behind their tables and watched with unravelling perplexity. Then, at midnight, there was a distant diplomatic incident and the ambassadors rushed out in a flurry of limousines. The band carried on, wailing and marching until almost dawn.

"Where are you going next, John?" It was Rodrigo Wood, drenched with Scottishness

"To Concepción," I said, "on a little boat called *Guaraní*."

"You must visit my brother, Enrique. The last of the Australian socialists!"

Federico Robinson was more interested in the *Guaraní*.

"So they've refloated her?" he said. "She hit a cattle barge last year and sank. I lost a jeep and fifteen kilometres of plastic hose. Still, they get things back. The Río Paraguay is only shallow."

"Am I *mad*?"

"Only one man drowned."

80

Five hours later I was standing, a little unsteadily, on the quayside next to the *Guaraní*. She looked like a long wooden dish, her gunwales just out of the water. There was a stack of ugly sheds up one end.

As all the boat's food was cooked in river water, I went off to rummage the port for two days' supplies.

Asunción's docks had, it seemed, been conjured from the deeper recesses of Conrad, a place of indeterminate sex and imponderable intentions. Drinking-shops had hopeless, landlocked names like "Geneva" and "Zurich" and great finned monsters sizzled and hissed on the cobbles. The brothels were open to the street and divided up in pens, like piggeries. Stiff Imperial Prussian marines swaggered off the gunboats, ready to fill and ready to discharge.

I bought three tins of fish and boarded the *Guaraní*.

There were *pirañas* gnashing round the stern. Some of the passengers were hauling them aboard on bits of string and they lay on the deck rasping and clacking. They were only small but this wasn't the point; they ate you in their thousands. Even alligator skin is no protection; they will pile themselves on the creature and hollow it out in minutes.

"They are," wrote the writer-diplomat Cecil Gosling, "the most dangerous inhabitants of Paraguayan waters." In 1926, his friend, a police inspector, had run into a shoal; he was so badly mutilated that he swam straight back to his revolver and blew his brains out. To the Guaraní, the *piraña* is the *piraí*, which happens also to be the word for "leprosy."

This was not a comforting thought as I placed my life aboard. This skiff had already once taken the short plunge to the bottom, and judging by its load, it might easily do so again. The foredeck was heaped with cargo: a hundred crates of fizzy drinks, ten pallets of cement, a seed-drill and ninety-eight leaky drums of petrol. If we weren't barbecued first, it would be a glutinous shipwreck.

I clambered into the crumbling stack at the rear. On the lower deck was the galley and the engine room, packed to the bulwarks with eggs and sacks of oranges. The majority of passengers—a dozen Indians and *peones*—never got any higher, and after a few hours they had rattly coughs and sump-coloured skin. On the top deck was the wheelhouse and the more refined elements of upriver society: a horse-dealer, a man who dug holes in Argentina and a quack doctor.

"A storm tonight," he kept saying. "God help us."

The crew worked in bare feet. Although the mate could make engine parts with a horse-file, only the skipper had shoes. He was a slightly awesome character, lean and scrubbed and predatory. His T-shirt described him as "Foxhound."

He took my fare: five dollars to Concepción and half as much again to sleep on a mattress in a cupboard. The Indians slung their hammocks over the engine.

On time, Foxhound gave the order to leave.

The *Guaraní* clattered into the middle of the river, shivering the glassy surface. Asunción, still balmed in pink, slid down to the east. We passed through a graveyard of rotting steamers and then out under a thin white arc linking the eastern horizon with the west: the Remanso Bridge. The river widened; a vast, inert sea sliding imperceptibly south. It was like vitrified sky. In all its 1,700 kilometres, the Río Paraguay drops only thirty centimetres, maybe the length of a child's arm.

Eastern Paraguay was now way off to the right, a lustrous, smoky-blue ribbon of hills and forests. The other way, to the left, the horizon was a thin strip of bitter reeds and backwaters, swamps and stunted black trees, each hard enough to crack an axe. This was the Chaco.

After the scandalous expulsion of Cabeza de Vaca in 1546, the Spanish were never again able to muster enthusiasm for this, the western shore. To those grown fat in the sensual, undulating east, the Chaco was simply an endless, salty desert of spines and poisons. It was hardly tempting. Worse, it was infested with the most savage tribes of the Americas. These *bravos* had faces streaked in purple and ears stabbed with vulture feathers. Their lances were plumed with human scalps.

"War," it was said of the Guaycurús, "is the only occupation they consider most honourable."

When confronted with matters of native honour, the conquistadors reacted as they always did: they cheated. In 1677, they invited 300 Guaycurús to a feast and then fell on them and killed them. It was merely the low point in a struggle that hardly ever began and certainly never ended. Lacking the technology to move fast over waterless territory, the Spanish could do nothing. The Chaco was sealed off with a line of fortlets along this river. Whenever the savages came within range, they were met with enfilades of grape. Stalemate ensued.

The Jesuits played a more enterprising hand. For a while their missionaries pressed deep into the margins of the Chaco, living in dens like fortified ant-hills. However, few of the holy fathers would find beatitude or even old age. Herrera was speared; Osorio was eaten by the Payaguás; Rodríguez was sacrificed on an altar; Lizardi was pinned to a tree with arrows (it was an unhurried end; he was found with his breviary open at his own funeral service). By 1760, even their maps were suffused with despair.

"This is the land of the pagan Nogogolidis," it says, scrawled across the empty Chaco. "They are the Lengua Ocelot. There is no water in summer."

One who did survive was a German, Father Martin Dobrizhoffer. He would return to write Vienna's best-seller for 1784, in Latin. That he thrived at all is remarkable; when he first heard his Indians, he thought that they were talking in coughs and sneezes. But he persisted and, like every old freelancer, he was soon buying their souls, in his case with beads and scissors. He supplemented his report with a few sample savages. By the time he'd got them back to the mission, however, they'd died of nostalgia.

Little more was heard from the Chaco until almost the twentieth century.

After the bridge, Foxhound produced a rifle and started firing into the swamps. He was looking for capybaras.

"Or alligators," he said, leaning out of the wheelhouse and emptying a clip of bullets into the mud.

"Alligator fat makes excellent mosquito repellent," announced the Quack. "Especially when it's rotten."

The Quack had been reading the Bible all afternoon in preparation for the storm. I asked him what other medicines he prescribed. His yoke was stuffed with pills, teas, unguents, bones, herbs from the Indians and charms.

"This one is made by the Aché: cat's claw tea."

I bought a sachet. It was a cure for lung cancer, bronchitis, internal tumours, jealousy and Aids.

"Where are you going?" I asked.

"Everywhere. I am always travelling. I don't have a home."

The horse-trader came to join us. He was very pleased I had a French name.

"My ancestors were German," he said proudly.

This promising friendship only faltered when I told him that he'd need 5,500 *guaranís* to buy £1. "That's ridiculous," he said and stamped off to the galley. He returned a little later wearing the cook's glasses.

"Will you now please take my photograph?"

I did so and our friendship was back on track. The three of us spent the rest of the afternoon sitting on the wheelhouse roof, dangling our feet and staring out into our empty, silver world. Occasionally, thick rafts of water hyacinths floated past.

"Big enough," said the Quack, "to take a man to Argentina—or a jaguar."

Apart from us, there were few other boats: a cattle barge; a bulk-carrier bringing iron ore down from Brazil; a dugout and a fisherman. The *Guaraní* stopped several times at lonely *estancias* and villages of straw. Some of our Indians got off and others got on. *Peones* in thick leather armour emerged from the thorns to haul away their cement or to leave us with produce. We accumulated a large box of bearded fish.

At one village two prostitutes got on. Foxhound brushed his teeth and selected the fatter one. Her friend joined the Indians in the galley, eating boiled pumpkin and pig fat. When they'd finished, they all wiped their faces on the tablecloth. The Quack returned to his yoke and his Bible. It wouldn't be long now until the storm.

Once, all these river travellers were mere bait for the "sweet-water pirates," the Payaguás. They were far from sweet themselves; "the most pestilent Indians on the river," according to Father Dobrizhoffer, "atrocious pirates . . . more like beasts than men." They hunted by canoe, swarming out of the reeds to overwhelm merchantmen with their slaughter and cannibalism. But they fared badly in the era of gunpowder and rifling. Blasted from the water, by 1852 they were in Asunción begging and selling little birds.

The end came soon enough. After this, I'd only find them as a footnote in Thompson's *War in Paraguay*. López had conscripted them into an artillery battery. For a while they seem to have been loyal and effective bombardiers, but in time they were all blown to mincemeat and the tribe became extinct.

The storm came as the herbalist had said it would. The crew draped the decks in tarpaulins and the Indians nuzzled into shawls. All night great sheets of static exploded over the river. I thought of the petrol lashed to the foredeck.

"This," wrote Knight, as *The Falcon* was being tossed around on the river, "is the most electric region in the world."

Right or wrong, it was a bewildering display of volts. I watched it all, through the chinks in my cupboard. By dawn, the forge was spent and the day emerged shiny and brilliant, like newly minted silver.

The Quack crawled out from under his herbs.

"Drink this," he said. "It will soothe your bowels."

I politely obeyed and crossed the Tropic of Capricorn on a breakfast of tinned fish and cat's claw tea.

81

Concepción was built by the Italians in all the hope and ebullience of a new century, the twentieth. It stood with its back to the jungles of the north, confronting the Chaco—which the Italians shrewdly suspected of abundance. They built a city to receive the wealth as they reaped it in: a cathedral and a *palazzo* for the bishop, statues of Equality and Liberty, mansions—scrolled, panelled and lavishly tiled—and a post office the size of a fortress. There would be parks and walks and a club for the gentlemen. Everything would be drenched in the colours of home: the ochres of Tuscany, fruit *gelati*, fresh raspberries and the lucent blues of the Mediterranean.

The century didn't work out as planned. Concepción was always at the crucible of revolt. The first, in 1913, merely filled a mass grave. The second, the Civil War of 1947, sent nearly a third of the country into exile. The city could easily have become just a cowboy town, a frontier post and a last, jaunty drinking-hole for those about to perish in the thorns.

Surprisingly it hadn't.

I followed the pony carts up from the port. The carters rode them standing up, like charioteers. As they thundered along the arena, billowing sand, I suddenly realised we were in the centre, walled in by miniature palaces. The citizens had maintained all the aspirations of their founders; their city was as curly and fruity as it had been on the day of its eponymous conception. Even the tack shops were defiantly flashy; I could have bought a set of reins with solid-silver buckles or a gun-belt made from jaguar.

I stayed two nights, at The French Hotel.

Enrique Wood, I discovered, lived just behind the hotel. His house was typical of the street, smaller than it first appeared because from a rather promising front it tapered off like a wedge of cheese. Enrique and his wife lived there with two of everything: two children, two maids, two cats, two refrigerators and two sausage dogs. Every time their enormous front door opened, the sausages rushed out and attacked someone. The cats ate all the cake at teatime. These unrelated facts were merely the outward signs of Enrique's life; everything seems to have occurred or accumulated haphazardly, unsought and uncontrolled. It was an ancestral problem.

The Woods had arrived in Paraguay in 1894. William Wood, shearer, Queenslander and agitator, had never settled and died of the grog. His wife, Lillie, lived for the next seventy years at the breakaway colony at Cosme, wishing herself in Australia until the day she died. They'd had three sons, brought up wild and barefoot in the *campo*. Each drifted into the Great European War: Norman signed up with the Engineers; Alex joined the Black Watch in Palestine; Bill fought at Gallipoli and lost his virginity to an Arab girl. To their surprise, the brothers survived. Disowned by the countries they'd fought for, they wandered back to Cosme. Overjoyed to have them home, the colonists celebrated with rum and with fireflies in their hair. The boys said they'd never leave Paraguay again.

Then came the revolution of 1921 and they were scattered. Norman, Enrique's father, ended up in Concepción, working sometimes in tannin, sometimes in cattle. Enrique kept a photograph of him shaking hands with the Duke of Edinburgh during a rare surge in his fortunes. He made the Duke look very pale and undernourished.

Enrique was proud of his Australian origins and wore an Akubra hat. He was acutely myopic and tended to look at things with disbelief, which I soon realised was much how he felt. Like his father and uncles, his life had been carried along in the currents; he'd been a vet, a cattle-dealer and an ice-cream man. Even his socialism—for which he'd been casually beaten during the *Stronato*—was of the fluid kind.

"Who," I teased, "should be the king of Paraguay?"

It was easy. "Our goalkeeper," he said, without hesitation, "Chilavert."

He took me all over Concepción on his moped. A town of such abundant generosity and such unfulfilled expectations, it seemed to complement him perfectly. He was very popular. Every time we stopped he was surrounded and patted and ruffled.

We visited his relatives, both dead and alive. Don Norman was buried in his own zone of the cemetery between the revolutionaries and the babies. He'd held out until 1992. Of those still in the pink, Gladys Davey was a butcher and Robert Pfanl-Smith a bigot.

"You can't blame him," said Enrique. "He did well under Stroessner."

At the centre of Concepción was a steam engine, made in Leicester in 1909. The Italians had bought it for a railway that only ever happened in part. It now carried a small notice, painted with all the indignation that the city could muster: *This is not a public lavatory.*

82

I flew up to Valle Mi in a machine called a Caravan 208. The river looked panic-stricken from up there, wriggling and ox-bowing as it recoiled from the Chaco. Out on that great steaming baize, there wasn't a single river that ran the whole year round, and the temperature often scorched into the forties. I could also see the *Guaraní*, on its microscopic journey north. I would rejoin it later in the day, for the voyage back.

Valle Mi was choking in its own cement mine and so I got a boatman to take me downstream, to Puerto Casado. He lived in a mysterious and sometimes terrifying world: this river is full of two-kilo *pirañas*; here is the only rocky outcrop in the eastern Chaco; over there is a cave that is said to go down for ever.

This land was no less mysterious or terrifying for its first pioneers, at the turn of the twentieth century. It was still widely thought the Chaco would turn into a forest without light or a whirlpool that dragged men into hell. The natives drank warm blood from skulls and burnt their captives' feet to prevent them from escaping.

"It is pretty well-established," wrote the doughty MacDonald, "that there is an unknown monster here . . ."

Unsurprisingly, the first to come were men who valued their lives at less than a good adventure: Charley Kent, the old-Harrovian; George Loman, who married an Indian and sent three exotic sons to boarding school; Bob Stewart, who could drink a bottle of Scotch and still spell his name in bullet holes.

It was the Americans who arrived with the heaviest clout. Most had found that their own west was no longer wild. Tex Rickard arrived in 1912 with a gang of rednecks. He'd made his fortune promoting fights in Madison Square Garden and his men punched out 300,000 hectares of cactus. On their furloughs, they punched out the bars of Concepción, shot the bottles off the shelves and cooled their heels in the slammer.

There were plenty of others—Kelly, Lewis the Texan, and Hillman, who fought a day-long battle with the Indians all on his own.

One of the Americans surviving from this era was Margarita Kent's great-uncle, Robert Eaton. He'd invited me for coffee one afternoon, in Asunción. He was ninety-one and lived in a bunkhouse of faded photographs and anaconda skins. This is how it happened, he said:

I was born in Vermont, which is just a bunch of old rocks. I wanted adventure, cowboy stuff. You seen Will Rogers? Well, like that. Anyway, I applied for this job, $60-a-month job, working cattle in Paraguay (which I thought was the capital of Uruguay). I signed up in New York on Black Monday 1929 and bankers were jumping out of windows and all that. I was twenty and had my own saddle, lassos, a thirty-thirty and a Colt .38. That was all.

We came up from Argentina on the steamer, me and the manager, a Scottish feller called MacBain. Then we went upriver until we got to the little railway, the *trencito*. We hadn't gotten far when there was this log across the track. Next thing, MacBain has a bullet in his head and his brains were on my pants. "This is the frontier!" I thought. "It's *real*!" I was sorry about MacBain but here was a lesson: if you have a gun, always have it ready. Ours had all been in the toolbox.

The company had 4,000 *hectáreas*, eighty kilometres inland— previously unoccupied on account of hostile Indians. The Paraguayans were terrified of them—Sanapanás mostly—but I was intrigued. The *cacique* taught me to shoot a bow and arrow. They called him "Seven Germans" because he'd killed seven Germans from a survey team. It wasn't *entirely* true; they were French. I was OK with the Indians. They called me "Almost-an-Englishman" and I gave them jobs in return for corn and *yerba* . . .

In 1932 I met my wife, Charley Kent's daughter, Dorothy. She was only nineteen but she knew the Chaco well. She had no fear of the Indians and took care of all our medical problems. She had *Dr. Black's Home Medicine* and could fix broken arms and gunshot wounds. I don't know why she came with me! I was Kit Carson! Davy Crockett! She was such a pretty girl . . . She's dead now. She died in 1988.

. . . Things could get real rough. One time, we had no water for six months. The only stuff to drink was sixteen feet down. We had a lot of *tigres* too, taking the cattle. I've shot eighteen and two lions, always with the handgun. I caught two *tigres* alive and one went off to England. London Zoo! I heard they killed it when the bombing began in 1940. In case it got out, I guess . . .

I got some pictures someplace. Here. "Dorothy, 1931," "Indians hunting ostrich." Here's one of that anaconda, up there on the wall, thirty-two foot long. "Sanapanás with lungfish." "Indian puberty dance." We didn't see much of them after 1932. There was a lot of smallpox and I suppose they just ran away . . .

Then, in September, the war started. Soon, we had all the troops arriving, on the *trencito* from Casado . . .

83

The boatman left me on the wharf and I walked up a track of blinding white silt into Puerto Casado.

This was once the capital of the world's largest private property. Beyond it, the Casado family fiefdom had sprawled into the Chaco, three times the size of Switzerland; 5,000,000 hectares (or 19,200 square miles) of cattle country and *quebracho* forest. It had even had its own railway—the *trencito*—and a thousand serfs living in Casado houses. The Casados themselves lived in Buenos Aires—Argentines who'd acquired the plot (without too many questions) in the aftermath of the Triple Alliance. They'd also had holdings in Argentina, but only in Paraguay could they have been so grandiose. Even now, seventy-seven per cent of Paraguayan land was owned by one per cent of its landholders. Not only did the country have perhaps the most unequal land distribution in the world, it didn't even own itself.

I trudged through the Casados' monogrammed town.

For a while, it seemed, they'd let things prosper. Every silted street was scored with silvery lines—the rails of the *trencito*—converging on the *quebracho* factory. This had been the powerhouse of Casado wealth; where the logs were pulped into valuable tannin. Spreading out from the gates was a model village: Dutch-style houses for the managers and pretty cottages for the workers, with verandas and bougainvillaea around the door. There was even a Hotel Casado and a large red church with crow-stepped gables. I lay in there for a while, panting in the heat and drinking in the cool of Casado brick and Casado stained-glass. Here the private empire had been momentarily ethereal.

Then, suddenly, in 1996, the mighty Casados had simply closed it all down. All but fifty men were laid off. The rest were left to take their chances in a private town on the edge of a private desert. The unemployed gathered to protest, but there was no one left to shout at. Business crumbled. The hotel closed and its battlements were now powdering away. The gardens had been repossessed by feral pigs and foul birds, jays and mocking parrots. In the fountain were feral children, paddling in grey slime. Puerto Casado was disassembling itself, reverting to the scrawny Indian *tolderla* of a century ago.

I ate a plate of tripe and potatoes at the *copetín* and then walked down through the silt to the factory.

It was an enormous cathedral of rust, yawning and groaning in the hot wind. I scrambled inside, into an oily black jungle of lubricating swamps, cables, idlers and grinding teeth. At the far end was the steam shed and the mottled hulks of the *trencitos*. There were ten bantam steam engines, each named after a new, mewling Casado. Each bore an engine plate: "Berlin 1904"; "Leeds 1916"; "Percy Grant of Buenos Aires." I climbed into a miniature carriage and took a seat among the drifts of sand.

During the Chaco War, these exquisite little toys had hauled over 100,000 troops off into the thorns, 1,600 at a time. Bolivia made some attempts to disable them, popping bullets and bomblets through this great carapace of tin. Buenos Aires—and the Casado family in particular—responded with lacerating invective. Bolivia took fright and wisely pulled her aeroplanes off.

A war with Paraguay was one thing. A war with the Casados was quite another.

84

That evening, I waited on the pier for the return of the *Guaraní*.

The stevedores were waiting too, with their carts and pastries and a box of puppies. They were Sanapaná Indians. As they waited, they hunted for fish, using spears made of steel rods plundered from the factory. Soon the water was bloody and frothy and they heaved a long, sleek monster on to the decking. It had the head and teeth of a dog: the *pirá jaguá*.

"We only eat this bit," they said, and hacked its rear flanks off. The dog-head was furious and lashed about with the new, raw whip of its spine. We all watched as its courage and its life ebbed away.

I asked them if they still found anacondas.

"Plenty in the swamp here," they said, "but we don't eat them."

It was almost dusk and the swamp behind us was thrashing and croaking with reptiles. I thought of the thirty-foot specimen on Robert Eaton's wall.

"He can swallow a pig," said the stevedores, and laughed.

Doubtless this would have been less amusing to the São Paulo dentist swallowed by an anaconda in 1999. For a while, the Internet carried his portrait, taken after a month in the snake's digestive system. Father Montoya had filed equally distressing copy with the Jesuits in 1636. He'd seen an anaconda attack an Indian woman "for the purpose of violating her." "The woman was speechless with fright on seeing the huge snake so licentious, and the latter, carrying her to the opposite side of the river carried out its lascivious purpose." Maybe it was the cat's claw tea. Or perhaps Montoya had been too long on the Paraguayan rivers.

As darkness fell, I was rescued by the *Guaraní* and returned to Concepción. There were no cupboards left on the return leg. That night, I slept on the wheelhouse roof and woke under a sky as cold and silvery as fish.

85

From Concepción, I took a bus up into the northern shoulder of Eastern Paraguay. This was the Amambay Range, with a reputation for snakiness and umpteen degrees of brigandage.

To me, it unfurled like pages from *The Lost World*; dizzying parabolas of grassland, lunging forests and great purple volcanic molars embedded along the Brazilian frontier. But, like Palacios, many believed that Amambay had indeed been lost, bought out by foreigners. I could see what they meant. Americans and Brazilians had acquired big ranches along the road, with waggon-wheels on the gate and radio masts nosing up from the grass. Lyndon Johnson's cousin, Clarence, had blown his fortune on coffee ventures up here, but others, like "Rattlesnake" Matheson, had found serenity of a sort. A former rodeo rider, lumberjack, high steel worker and linebacker with the Cleveland Rams, Rattlesnake now kept 10,000 acres and a little business selling engines and dog-chews.

I went as far as I could, to the frontier and Pedro Juan Caballero.

I soon realised that it was wrong to imagine that Paraguay had been sold out. Pedro Juan had survived—and thrived—precisely because it was so doggedly Paraguayan; it was a smuggling outlet. In fact, it was more than an outlet; it was a sort of volcanic vent spewing contraband into southern Brazil. Three-quarters of Brazil's marijuana was being transshipped through Paraguay, most of it through Pedro Juan. The town was pure Paraguayan puppetry, strings pulled from above. When, in 1985, a little Pedro Juan aeroplane was impounded, wheezing under 700 kilos of pure cocaine, no one was particularly surprised to find that the pilot was one of General Rodríguez's trusties. This was, according to the old mantra, merely the "price of peace."

The price of Scotch, meanwhile, was lethally affordable. I found Pedro Juan's main drag walled in by boxes of the stuff, like a cardboard canyon. For whatever the Scotsman pays for his bottle, the Paraguayan gets five bottles and still has change for two hundred "Cowboy" brand cigarettes, a Barbie doll or a gross of Earl Grey tea-bags. Small wonder that some twelve and a half million bottles were now washing in and out of the country every year.

"Smuggling," wrote Graham Greene, "is the national industry of Paraguay."

The scale of duplicity was indeed industrial, and yet nobody called it smuggling. It was *intermediación*. These huge consignments of contraband were intermediated around town by horsemen with cloaks and trilbys and long bamboo whips. French champagne was cheap enough to bathe in, and business went on all night (with gunmen sprawled out over the merchandise). In the excitement, no thought had been given to sewers or streets, which rippled along like river beds. Even the idea of electricity had come as an afterthought, in 1974.

For a while, in spite of tropical downpours, I found Pedro Juan intriguing. I bought some whisky at a shop called "Winckler the German." I weighed up each revolver in the Mount Lebanon Gunshop. The frontier ran through the middle of the town and I wandered in and out of Brazil all morning. The two countries were separated by thirty metres of sodden red grass and they bled freely, one into the other. Even the Brazilian politicians often came blaring across the border in their loudspeaker vans. But on their side, the shops were prim and productive (shovels, gasoline tins and overalls). On our side, the merchandise was rather more disorientating.

Life, like whisky, was competitively priced if not downright cheap.

According to *Crónica*, the racketeers often sprinkled each other in machine-gun fire (and were then colourfully epitaphed across the centrefold*).* Visiting congressmen could expect to be fêted with Molotov cocktails. Journalists were faced with equally bleak prospects: be discreet or be a monument. I acquired a loyal taxi-driver, and whenever we went any distance, we had to let his daughter know where we were going. He had bad news for the victims of this casual slaughter.

"The police dump the bodies between the frontiers," he said. "It saves an investigation."

The image of corpses rotting in the red grass, of whisky canyons and crimson storm-water boiling through the streets soon took its toll. I spent more and more time in my hotel room, watching Paraguayan television: chat shows for swingers; advertisements for tarot-card readers; news bulletins read by men sucking *maté,* with "Land of Hope and Glory" rumbling away in the background. I was merely killing time, waiting for the rain to stop before I could make my next move.

Madame Lynch and her sweaty consort had re-emerged from the jungle, forty kilometres to the west, at Cerro Corá.

86

The next morning, before the lightning had abated, the loyal *taxista* drove me out to Cerro Corá. He dropped me at the bottom of a long, wet track. I walked up it, following a set of light paw-prints.

"It's a *tirica,*" said the warden at the lodge. An ocelot. "They're always here."

The warden was Wilfred Cardoso. He had a patriot's sense of history and his park was a shrine to the great Marshal-President. He also had a pet monkey that looked like Barbie in a mink trouser-suit. She climbed into my lap and fell asleep. We allowed the official version of the End of the López Era to swirl around us: "noble self-sacrifice . . . the birth of a legend . . . a path lit for posterity." Wilfred then showed me the detritus of the last fight—a few musket balls, a cooking-pot cast at Ybycuí, and a lance made by early Jesuits. When the lightning stopped, I woke the miniature monkey, thanked Wilfred and rejoined the paw-prints up to the battlefield.

Cerro Corá had probably changed little since February 1870, a swollen red haunch bulging from the jungles of Amambay. From the top, the views rolled away in all directions, from viridescence and emeralds to the pale mauves of the volcanoes. These jungles, Wilfred said, were still hunted by the jaguar—though only occasionally. This infrequency was reassuring as I plodded along in its little cousin's paw-prints. The jaguar is the third largest cat, up to ten feet from whiskers to tail, and a thunderous 300lbs of muscle. Unlike bigger cats, he's cunning and unpredictable and kills his prey by splintering its skull. The Aché were terrified of them and so was MacDonald. Only his bisexual giant antbear was a match for "Johnny Spots." The two were often to be found together, dead and enmeshed in each other's teeth and claws.

Jaguars were the least of López's problems as he blundered northwards. There were still 8,000 Brazilian cavalry hotly at his heels. His new capitals at Curuguaty and Ygatimí had lasted no more than a month. Then the scrags of his forces would set off again, possessed not so much by tactics as hunger.

These excursions were doing nothing for the Marshal's sanity. The persecutions continued. His brother, Venancio, now flogged, ulcered and caked in blood, died like a pig at Chirigüelo. As for the beauty Pancha Garmendia who had been caged up like a canary after she'd defended her virtue, she was lanced. There weren't bullets to spare for a firing squad. Three more British contractors—Hunter, Nesbitt and Alan Taylor's son—tendered their resignations. López paid them, thanked them and then had them disembowelled. Finally, at Cerro Corá, he embarked on his most ambitious persecution yet: his mother's. He had the old crone flogged and, on the eve of battle, signed her execution warrant. She was saved by the arrival of the Brazilians.

I found myself alone on the plateau where the Paraguayans had camped. General Stroessner had marked the spot a century later with an ugly fin of concrete. The plateau was still bare of trees and the storm made the red mud simmer and bubble. López's stragglers had arrived here on 8 February, perhaps a thousand of them. Madame Lynch and the children followed by carriage. The eldest boy, "Panchito," was now fifteen and a colonel. He kept a muster-sheet of the available soldiers: 409 men.

I found a thick handmade screw in the muck of the Paraguayans' camp. They'd awaited their fate for three weeks, hunting and foraging in the jungle. López designed a medal three days before the end. It was inscribed "He overcame hardship and weariness. Amambay Campaign

The death of Francisco Solano López as depicted by his great-nephew, Luis Agüero Wagner.

1870." He rejected Madame Lynch's proposal that they should break out for the Bolivian border, to the north-west. The die was already cast. He promised his men that he'd die with them, a subject he'd already given some thought to. As a student of Napoleonic France, he'd chosen his last words with care. In the end, he borrowed a taunt from Alexander of Russia, thrown in the face of Coulaincour: "I will die with my nation, sword in hand." His men sang a valedictory: *Morir por ti, patria*.

To the north of the plateau, the *cerro* sloped down to the river Aquidabán, a youthful orange torrent gnashing through the woods. In the rains, it looked impassable and ferocious, but on 1 March 1870, it had been languorous and shallow. Dawn rose, as hot and sickly as any that summer, and the Brazilian cavalry charged over the Aquidabán. López was surrounded.

In most accounts, Madame Lynch made a formal appearance at the little battle. She put on a white crinoline gown which she'd last worn to dance with the Emperor at the Tuileries. There is no saying what effect her appearance had on the troops; a middle-aged Juno, trussed into a ball-dress she hadn't worn for seventeen years. It can only have been momentary; within minutes, the skeletal Paraguayans were being crunched up under lance and sabre.

López meanwhile was effecting an equally dramatic disappearance. He clambered on to a charger and belted off south, the way they'd come. Once again he'd abandoned his fancy lady and his litter to their fate. They tumbled after him in the carriage. Six Brazilian cavalrymen also set off in pursuit. They caught up with him several hundred yards away, at a stream called the Aquidabán-Niguí.

Down by the stream, the scrub was thicker and fortified with thorns. The thickets were stippled with parrots and woodpeckers and brilliant cardinals. It was here that a Brazilian corporal called Chico Diablo ("the Little Devil") had tangled with the Monster, driving a lance deep into his belly. It sliced through peritoneum, intestines and bladder before ripping its way out again. The two men disengaged and the President then lost a slab of his forehead to a sabre. Mustering his last vestiges of cowardice, he kicked his wounded horse into the thorns and momentarily disappeared. They found him a little later, half in, half out of the dark, gingery stream.

"Give yourself up, Marshal!" bellowed the Brazilian commander. "I am the Imperial General Cámara!"

The presidential corpus bobbed in the water. He remembered his last words.

"Muero con mi patria!"

A trooper was sent to haul the Monster out of his mire. There was a brief tussle and the Brazilian blasted a ball into the bloater's chest. Blood frothed from his nose and mouth. The most vicious war of modern mankind ended with a gurgle.

The cavalrymen carried the corpse back up the slope to the Paraguayan camp. On the way, an officer hacked at its ear and tore it off.

"I promised I'd bring it home!"

In a spasm of righteousness, Cámara ordered an autopsy and his doctors immediately set about eviscerating López. Matters had concluded well. The Paraguayan dead included the President and Vice-President, nine colonels and five priests (later, each would be commemorated with a small concrete bust).

The rest of López's pups were soon rounded up, fleeing the field in their carriage. Colonel Panchito was riding escort and the Brazilians ordered him to surrender. But he'd inherited his mother's good looks and his father's arrogance.

"A Paraguayan colonel never surrenders!" he shrilled. As he fumbled for his pistol, a lance tore through his little chest. A figure in a white ball-dress clambered out of the carriage.

"Respect me!" said Eliza Lynch. "I'm English!"

Cámara regarded her with unrestrained amazement. She ordered him to take her to the body of her blubbery sweetheart, now both formally and informally mutilated. The slave-soldiers were dancing around the pieces. She found the officer of the watch, Major Peixota (who would later be president of Brazil).

"Is this the civilisation you've brought with your guns?"

In truth, she was grateful for the presence of the Brazilians. When the Little People of the Paraguayan camp heard that their president was dead, they offered to tear his whore apart—first her jewellery, then her hair, then her limbs. The Bavarian eggs were no more forgiving. They scolded their lacerated mother, Doña Juana.

"Why do you weep, Mother? He was no son, no brother. He was a monster."

Cámara took Eliza and her loot into safe custody. Though he was a shrewd man, the scale of her *bijouterie* surprised him; ninety-two pieces of jewellery, eleven gold watches, a diamond-encrusted marshal's baton, 14,000 Paraguayan dollars (now worthless) and six bars of gold. Chivalrously, he told her she could keep the lot.

That afternoon, he let her bury her son and his father.

I walked down to where Eliza had buried López overlooking the Aquidabán. I found the grave in a clearing of *kuruñais*. One of the trees bore a notice saying that it had been there during the time of these "historic events . . . of abnegation . . . the titanic struggle." It sounded like Wilfred's work. The grave itself carried a tablet dedicated to the "Unselfish Irish Comrade" who'd given a Christian burial to the Marshal-President and to Colonel Panchito "With Her Own Bare Hands."

In burying her consort, Eliza spawned what is perhaps the most enduring image in Paraguayan culture: a brilliant golden-white woman, dressed in the splendid fal-de-ral of Paris, scraping a bed for her lover in the slime of this benighted jungle.

87

Francisco Solano López's promise to die with his country came not a moment too soon. Had he left it any longer, there might have been no country left to die with.

Of an original population of around 1,300,000, only 221,079 had survived. Of these, only 29,746 were men. Nine out of every ten men had perished. It would take nearly seventy-five years to recover population levels.

"Seldom," wrote Burton, "has aught more impressive been presented to the gaze of the world than this tragedy; this unflinching struggle maintained for so long a period against overwhelming odds, and to the very verge of racial annihilation."

The apothecary Masterman gave expression to despair: "The Paraguayans no longer exist—there is a gap in the family of nations . . ."

The Allies stayed on in Paraguay for six years and fathered the next generation. The Argentines imposed their system of law and a constitution based on the United States, both of which survive. But the main interest was reparations (Brazil had spent $300 million on the war). The Allies squeezed the country to the pips but the booty was pitiful. The

Brazilians plundered what they could, including thirty-seven cases of material from the National Archive, dating from 1596 (they hauled it back to Rio, where it remains). In the end, the Allies settled for land, annexing 55,000 square miles, or a quarter of Paraguayan territory. Then they marched out.

They left the country to a half-century of penury, polygamy and political sterility. Between 1870 and 1936, there would be thirty-two presidents (two assassinated), six coups, two successful revolutions and eight failures. Women became labourers—a development that subsequent generations found hard to reverse. No one remembered how textiles were manufactured and so the industry withered away.

The only creatures to profit from this chaos were the jaguars. Knight reported that they'd become man-eaters since the war—and "the glut of human flesh"—and that they'd now wander into the towns looking for more.

In the European imagination, Paraguay, having briefly played the part of Arcadia, now took the role of Gomorrah.

88

Credit for bringing the world news of post-apocalyptic Paraguay goes to an extraordinary adventurer, Robert Bontine Cunninghame Graham.

Cunninghame Graham arrived in Paraguay in 1873, at the age of twenty-one. His life had already become a rodeo of improbable adventures. Born of aristocratic blood, both Scottish and Spanish, he had a laird's sense of honour and a hidalgo's head for idealism. Learning Spanish from his grandmother on the Isle of Wight, he was out in the New World by the age of seventeen. For four years he rode the Argentine pampas, working as a rancher, hunter, cattle-dealer, horse-breaker and poet. He learnt to throw the *boleadoras* and to hunt ostrich with the gauchos. He affected their dress (a habit that survived all his life) and fought with the rebels against Sarmiento. He survived the poison arrows of the Indians and the eager teeth of the river-fish. To the Argentines, he was (and is) Don Roberto, *el singularísimo escritor inglés*.

These adventures were merely the early rumblings of his riotous life. He met his beautiful wife in Paris by almost mowing her down with his horse. They were immediately married and set off for Texas, where their new home was enthusiastically plundered by Mescalero Indians. He be-friended Buffalo Bill and set up "Professor Bontini's Fencing School" in Mexico City. Eventually he was driven home by debts (both his and his forebears'). In Scotland, he bought an Argentine mustang that he found hauling trams through Glasgow. When, to his surprise, he was elected MP for West Lanarkshire, he rode "Pampa" to Parliament every day, arriving in the glorious manner of Don Quixote (who he now resembled from almost every angle). He was an MP for six years before setting off again on his helter-skelter travels. He went off in search of Pliny's lost treasures of Lusitania in 1892. Three years later, he was trying to reach Tarudant, the Forbidden City of Morocco (becoming instead the inspi-ration for George Bernard Shaw's *Captain Brassbound's Conversion*). With the outbreak of war in 1914, Don Roberto, now sixty-two, offered his services as a rough rider. Instead, he was sent to buy horses in South America. Typically, he was torpedoed and shipwrecked twice on the way.

But it was during his early travels in post-Triple Alliance Paraguay that Graham fomented his high-octane radicalism. Though his progres-sive ideas seem undemanding today (universal suffrage, free education, prison reform and abolition of capital punishment), in the closing stages of the nineteenth century they were seen—even by his allies—as volatile and giddy. "Graham's socialism," wrote the Labour leader Ramsay Mac-Donald, "was based on romantic ideas of freedom and his profound feeling for the bottom dog."

This was to understate his strength of feeling. Quixotic though he may have been in appearance, he was reckless in confrontation. In 1887, he got his head cracked by a policeman during labour demonstrations in Trafalgar Square and did six weeks porridge for riot. He was equally explosive in Parliament; his only contribution to the Parliamentary record is an insult to the House, followed by "I never withdraw." Once again, his friend Shaw borrowed from his life; Graham's words appear in the mouth of the Bulgarian hero of *Arms and the Man*.

What had troubled Graham in Paraguay wasn't so much the destruc-tion and cruelty of the war (which was evident all around him) but the squandering of opportunity. He found a beautiful and sensuous land but its human spirit had been crushed. He'd sensed perfection in the Paraguayans' Jesuit "Republic" of 1609–1768 (a period he'd come to regard as pure socialism), and it angered him that it had been dissipated in the years of oligarchy and absolute power that followed.

He would write about Paraguay on and off for the next sixty years. These works were often achingly nostalgic *(Vanished Arcadia)*, and in López he found the personification of human evil. His prose, always breathless, became positively anoxic on the subject:

Sadism, an inverted patriotism, colossal ignorance of the outside world, a megalomania pushed almost to insanity, a total disregard of human life or human dignity, an abject cowardice . . . joined to no little power of will and of capacity, were the ingredients of his character.

Though his passion may have impeded communication with the British at large, his idealism had a powerful effect on his contemporaries: Shaw, Keir Hardie, John Burns and Joseph Conrad. Two old comrades even went off to join the Utopians of New Australia: Smith and Kennedy. Graham was the first president of the Scottish Labour Party and was to give British socialism something it might never otherwise have had, a blast of Latin fervour. He was also a durable fighter; whether against imperialism or cruelty to animals. On various occasions he championed the Irish, the Turks, the Zulus and prostitutes. As underdogs, the Paraguayans were natural objects for his affections.

Conrad, meanwhile, was absorbing the Paraguayan story. His nightmarish political novel, *Nostromo*, emerged in 1904. It is Paraguay, seen through the prisms of his great friend's anger—Napoleonic dictators, "high sounding sentiments and supine morality," English contractors and a Great Conspiracy. There is even "a barefoot army of scarecrows" and a priest who becomes the state torturer.

After this flare of publicity, Paraguay slipped back into dark shadow.

Cunninghame Graham kept the story alive. At the age of eighty-one he finally wrote López's biography, *Portrait of a Dictator*. Three years later, he returned to South America in the certain knowledge that he'd never see Britain again. Perhaps, with all the old radicals dead, his only remaining roots were out there. He died soon after his arrival in Argentina, on 20 March 1936. His body was paraded through the streets of Buenos Aires. At the head of the procession was the President, two gauchos and Don Roberto's beloved ponies, Mancha and Gato. For underdogs everywhere, life would now be that much bleaker.

He was buried in Scotland alongside his wife, who'd predeceased him by thirty years. "A Master of Life," reads his monument, "A King among Men."

At about the time the Master was being lowered into his Scottish grave, López was re-emerging from his, at Cerro Corá.

89

Madame Lynch left the battlefield of Cerro Corá with her pride (and her loot) intact. Although the ladies of Asunción would have liked to dismantle her with their fingernails, the Brazilians were merciful. They swept her and her four surviving sons off downriver to Buenos Aires, where she was packed on a ship for Europe. She immediately began the task of restoring her reputation.

More pressing, however, was the need to restore her finances. When she arrived in Paris, she discovered that her Scottish physician, Dr. Stewart, who was meant to have salted away 220,000 gold pesos on her behalf, was now denying any knowledge of the money. With characteristic brass, she sued him in the High Court in Edinburgh. The legal establishment stood back, aghast, as the jackals fought over the booty of some awful tropical hole; both sides told spectacular lies; General MacMahon sent a deposition in support of the delicious Mrs. Lynch; she then somehow managed to produce a receipt. Dr. Stewart argued that under the law of her marriage—French law—she couldn't bring her own action. When her long-forgotten husband, Quatrefages (now bigamously remarried), entered a compearance, Stewart changed his plea to one of "force and fear." The jury found him to be the worse liar of the two, and in considering their verdicts, the judge was constrained to agree. Mrs. Lynch had won. The defender undertook to pay her the money and then promptly declared himself insolvent. She got nothing.

To add insult to injury, Dr. Stewart returned to Paraguay and to his considerable fortune. He became a pillar of the community; manager of the railways, physician to the rich, British Honorary Consul and Paraguayan citizen. MacDonald met him in 1911, in his eighties. "My only complaint," Stewart told him, "is that if I had not been exceptionally unfortunate, I might have possessed the whole territory."

His descendants—often called the *Estobartes*—still argue with the López tribe about the missing cash.

*

After the litigation, Mrs. Lynch stayed in London for a while. She had a house in Thurloe Square or Hyde Park Gate and put her boys through St. Joseph's School, Croydon. We get a last glimpse of her through Cunninghame Graham in the early 1870s:

> I saw her several times getting into her carriage . . . In her well-made Parisian clothes, she looked more French than English, and had no touch of that untidiness that so often marks the Irishwoman . . . her appearance certainly did not seem that of one who had so often looked death in the face; lived for so long in circumstances so strange and terrifying, buried her lover and her son with her own hands, and lived to tell the tale.

From then on, Eliza Lynch became ever more enigmatic. She returned to Buenos Aires in 1875 to relaunch herself as the victim and to sue her detractors. The experience of being laughed out of court merely accelerated her withdrawal from public life. She sailed up to Paraguay but was given three hours to get out or face arrest. She never went back. Instead, the Paraguayan government came after her, suing her in the Westminster County Court on a debt of $33,000. Surprisingly, she won but the Paraguayans refused to recognise the judgment. The scene of this, her last, bitter triumph, is now Brown's Restaurant on St. Martin's Lane.

After that, she reverted to inscrutability and almost disappears. She moved to Paris and sank through the strata of the seventeenth *arrondissement* as her loot ran out. Some say she was addicted to champagne. Others have her as a madam in a cat-house. It is even rumoured that she went off to the Holy Land for three years, begging for absolution. There are no clues in the photograph that survives from this period; did she have dreams or only nightmares? In the curl of her lips was there contentment or merely bitterness? Had her jowls thickened with leisure—or just the greasy slops of poverty?

One thing is clear: she died alone. It's also likely that she died in agony, with a voracious cancer of the bowel. When her neighbours had heard nothing for several days, they broke her door down. She'd died on 27 July 1886 at the age of fifty.

She was conveyed to Père Lachaise cemetery and placed in a cheap slot. Her sons erected a plaque to an "Unforgettable Mother."

Within fourteen years, another six paupers had been piled in on top of her.

90

"When I first got here, in 1929," Robert Eaton had told me, "López was still a villain."

That was all about to change.

At the precise moment that Cunninghame Graham was preparing for his poetic demise in Buenos Aires, the Paraguayan fascists were seizing control in Asunción. There was no shortage of enthusiasm for their strong-arm policies, but what the fascists lacked was a figurehead, an embodiment of Paraguayan nationalist virtues. López was hauled out of notoriety. On 1 March 1936, the sixty-sixth anniversary of his death, he was declared a national hero (the date is still a national holiday). Overnight, all laws derogatory to his memory were annulled. A historian called Juan O'Leary was contracted to sweeten up his image. Several hundred hectares of farmland later, he was able to say that López had "surrendered his cherished life on the battlefield of glory" in order that his country might be "as it remains today, a bastion of liberty and democracy."

All that was needed now was this great democrat's cherished corpse. The fascists rushed off to Cerro Corá to find it. It was a daunting task: the battlefield had long been reclaimed by the jungle; a big, well-rotted corpse buried in the leaf-litter would have been attractive to scavengers. Despite the difficulties, the fascists found it. They paraded a colourful array of witnesses, veterans and descendants who'd "remembered" the exact spot of interment. Paraguayan history was being shamelessly O'Learied.

His casket was placed in the Pantheon of Heroes. Later, Stroessner (whose wife had a touch of the López) would add his own frothy analysis: "With his sword in his hand and his country on his lips, he overcame want and exhaustion at the head of his last troops on his last battlefield."

The casket had been placed next to Dr. Francia's. That too was empty because, of course, an earlier generation had thrown his remains to the alligators.

91

From Cerro Corá, I followed the rains south. The bus driver screened a video of *Cerro Notting*, or *Notting Hill*. The passengers regarded it with bleary scepticism and hardly noticed when first the sound failed and then the picture flaked away. I got out, two hundred miles short of Asunción, at the junction for Nueva Germania. I flagged down a truck to take me the last twenty miles.

"What do you want to go there for?" said the driver. "It's dead."

He may have been right. We sludged into a great rotten forest. Wisner von Morgenstern had flogged this land to the German supremacists at a time when Paraguay itself seemed almost dead. They'd never paid and nature had long since wrestled it back. "Most of the Germans have gone now," said the driver indifferently. "Only a few are left. The Lost People . . ."

After an hour, there were palisades in the margins of the gluey track, soggy shacks and patches of vegetables. New Germany, announced the trucker. Sticky orange damp had leached out of the earth, seeping into the whitewash, the thatch and everything. Even the horses were wearily orange. The truck belly-flopped through a crust of mud and stopped at the petrol pump. I asked the attendant if there was anywhere I could stay. He looked at the goo bubbling up between his toes.

"Ask Mrs. Neuman."

It was the first glimmer of German. There were no pretty Saxon churches or *Bierstubes* here. Just thatch and orange and carts thrashing through the mud.

The undignified death of Dr. Förster in 1889 had started—or rather hastened—an end to the Germanisation of the forest. Within two years, half the colonists had wandered off to Argentina, seeking either a passage home or just a better form of poverty. The colony shares were dissipated among foreigners and with them went the stench of racial supremacy. Only a hard knot of zealots held out for their clunky principles, retreating six miles into the forest, to Tacuruty. The rest—Ercks, Sterns, Schweikharts, Fischers, Neumans and Woolfs—concentrated on survival.

Förster's squinting, steel-haired wife, Elizabeth, was among the first to leave her sinking ship. She found an excuse in the madness of her brother, Friedrich Nietzsche. Fame had left him vividly deranged; he was now kissing dray horses and calling himself Dionysus or the Duke of Cumberland. Elizabeth said he needed her. In reality, she needed him. His mind was now too curly to resist her anti-Semitism and so she was free to realign his work. She mangled his philosophy so utterly and completely that it was her, not Friedrich, that the Wagnerians put forward for a Nobel Prize—three times. In 1900, Friedrich conveniently died. Elizabeth was now someone. Her portrait was painted by Edvard Munch and she founded a swanky museum immortalising her brother (and herself). When Germans were deciding whether to fight in 1914, she puffed the little flames with ersatz Nietzsche.

Nueva Germania was temporarily forgotten.

Mrs. Neuman ran a hostelry called the Grill of Triumph. It was a low thatched building arranged around a courtyard of mud-bricks. She kept a lame pig which goose-stepped around all day, demanding food. She also had seven children. The oldest was a policeman in Asunción and the other six wandered about in bits of his uniform. There was no obvious father, but a bricklayer called Cárdenas was often around, drunk and bumping into things.

At one end of the courtyard was a rather unprivate privy. Someone had spent a long time in there carving a female torso in the cement. It was entitled "Pig Cunt." At the other end of the yard was my cell, furnished with a foam mattress, a stool and a comb. There was no glass in the window, and so, at dawn the next day, the pig thrust his head through the aperture and showered me in pig drool.

In the evening, we sat around a fire in the main courtyard roasting tufts of meat. The Neumans were hazy about their German origins. In fact, Fritz Neuman had been an enterprising man from Breslau. In 1903, he'd discovered the secret of germinating the *yerba* plant, and Nueva Germania had been briefly lifted from its economic torpor. The Neumans had even owned a piano. Within thirty years, however, prosperity had expended itself and the Neumans slithered back into penury. The next decade brought fresh tragedy. Like several New Germans, two Neuman boys volunteered to defend their unknown fatherland. They froze to death in Russia.

I had breakfast in a *copetín* run by Carlos Neuman. He was obviously having an affair. He was always cooing down the phone, and whenever he thought I was listening, he cooed in Guaraní. But in Spanish he was magnanimous and happily passed me round the remnants of the Master Race.

They were widely scattered through the *Kolonie* (Dr. Förster had believed that each house should enjoy a degree of isolation, to encourage industry). Miss Fischer lived next door, bitter and bobble-hatted. The Sterns, formerly of Frankfurt, ran the hardware store. Meni Woolf remembered his school, a gift from Hitler himself. It wasn't a success; once paratyphoid and malaria took a grip on the *Schulmeister*, he too was off down the road to Argentina.

"It wasn't Nazism," protested Meni, "just Germanism. There were many German refugees. Hitler promised to get us all home. That was what the war was all about, you know."

Only the elderly still spoke any German. No one had a view about the Försters, but they all insisted that Mengele had lived among them. It was something they wanted, not because they agreed with what he'd done, but because it indicated participation in the affairs of the outside world. Their accusations focused on a drop-out called Friedrich Ilg, who'd lived in the woods and who'd been suspiciously solvent. But from their descriptions, he was far too young. Besides, he'd killed himself in Asunción in 1985, jumping under a number 30 bus outside the Victory Cinema. I wouldn't find Mengele here.

On the second day, Cardenas killed the Neumans' pig. I returned to find a trail of blood leading from my cell, across the courtyard to a bucket of slippery blue innards. The rest of the pig had been sliced into small translucent cubes.

"Pig tonight!" squeaked the Neuman children.

It was an unappetising thought. I fumbled for an excuse.

"Where's the Försterhof?"

"Ask Jorge Halke," suggested Mrs. Neuman. "We don't know."

The Halkes lived in what had been a long manor house on the edge of the colony. The family had once owned a department store, "Bruno Halke of Berlin." Like their fortune, the Halkes' mansion had been steadily diminishing ever since their arrival in 1905. As its ends rotted, they were simply chopped away. Jorge and his family were now forced to live in the central section, a room divided into stalls. It was still just grand enough to be mistaken for the Försterhof.

Jorge had salvaged something of his ancestors' dignity. He was the

Colorado candidate and worked for the Municipality (he wore his hi-visibility council trousers even on Sundays, with a straw hat). Ten years before, he'd saved Nueva Germania from a jaguar with a brilliant bullet. He was a man for his people, limitlessly generous and humane. He was also pleased to see a European again in his amputated home. His wife and flaxen children waited on us with beans and chocolatey wine. We went through a sea-chest of old photographs.

"This is my Paraguayan grandmother, Raphaela, visiting Germany in 1929."

She was wearing a coat of jaguar pelts.

Jorge looked past her, across the mildewed Kurfürstendamm.

"I don't know why Grandfather ever left it."

Proud though he was, Jorge knew that the Halke home had never been Elizabeth Nietzsche's. The Försterhof had had stone floors, couches and cabinets of liqueurs and crystal. A lumpy Germanic script hung in the saloon: "Over all obstacles stand your ground." When Elizabeth fled, it was sold to Baron von Frankenberg. Then the Neumans owned it for a while.

"Then the Rissos bought it."

We went to see Risso after lunch in his carpentry shop. He was carving an axle out of *urunday*. His father, an Italian doctor, had lived in the Försterhof until the civil war of 1947.

"It was badly shot up by the *liberales*."

All that remained were some black stumps in a field of ragwort.

"We saved very little," said Risso. "Just some beams and this funny table."

It was mounted with a marble top and a broken mirror: Elizabeth Nietzsche's vanity stand.

Elizabeth fared rather better than her furnishings.

She survived in similar circumstances to those in which Eliza Lynch had perished. Both women had hitched themselves to men of strong words and weak will power. Both had seen their stars ascend in the capitals of Europe and crash to earth in the jungles of north-east Paraguay. Now, each returned to Europe, facing middle-age, widowhood and some dangerous scandal.

Their fates would take very different paths. Whilst Eliza had had to live on baubles looted from Paraguay, Elizabeth was busy looting her brother's literature. Eliza's assets dwindled as Elizabeth's engorged. Eliza would spend her last years struggling against lawyers, detractors and creditors. Elizabeth, by contrast, went with the flow. With the rise of Nazism, she suddenly found herself in currents that carried her thrillingly close to power.

Like Eliza, she was a courtesan at heart (though not in practice, thanks to a squint and a cast-iron face). She flattered Hitler—"Superman"—and sat through the Munich *Putsch* trial of 1923. She sent political *billets doux* to Mussolini and presents to the Führer: an anti-Semitic petition of Dr. Förster's; her brother's walking stick. None of this was going to make her the darling of the Nazi Party, but there was satisfaction in being its matriarch. There was also a fat Nazi stipend.

In these, her glory days, she didn't entirely forget Nueva Germania. Meni Woolf got his Nazi teacher. Dr. Förster's grave got its dusting of German soil. They were mostly gestures, a tilt to her faintly embarrassing past. Her dreams of a master race were now firmly bedded in Europe. Though she was intellectually turgid, Hitler and his armaments minister, Albert Speer, visited her in 1934, in a search for inspiration. Speer was moved to describe the occasion as "oddly shallow."

Within a year, Elizabeth was dead. There was no pauper's slot for her. Her body was carried by an SS guard of honour up to the church of her birthplace, Röcken near Leipzig. Stormtroopers lined the route and Hitler himself barked his way through the suitably turgid valedictories. She was then lowered into her grave, indecently close to her brother.

Though she was only eleven years younger than Eliza, Elizabeth's guile had proved the more enduring. She'd survived *La Concubina Irlandesa* by nearly fifty years. But there were still the fascist years ahead. In posterity, one would flounder, one would flourish.

"This colony failed because people took advantage of German nobility," said Jorge sadly. "We should be getting money from Germany but our negative history now makes this impossible."

Jorge had drawn up plans for a museum and a statue of Dr. Förster should there ever be a change of heart. "This should be a city."

As I got on the bus to leave, he pressed something in my hand: a jaguar's fang.

"Remember us," he pleaded. "Remember us to all your friends."

92

On my way south, I took a detour to what must be the foxiest city in the world.

It was only established in 1957, burrowed into the walls of a gorge separating Brazil and Paraguay. Through the gorge rumbles the Upper Paraná, a river that is said to carry as much water as all the rivers of Europe put together. In 1957 they found the technology to span it. The bridge was called "Friendship," although the relationship between the two banks has seldom been more than venal. When it came to pumping contraband into Brazil, the city made Pedro Juan look like an ornamental faucet. Here, the movement of materials was seismic; smuggling turned over the equivalent of five times the value of the official Paraguayan economy.

The city almost went without a name. The Paraguayans had named their other cities after the formative experiences of Christianity: Conception, Incarnation and Assumption. Here, inspiration failed them. For a while, it was named after the King of Smugglers, Port Stroessner. Now it was simply Ciudad del Este, "the City of the East." It hadn't been planned, it had just erupted. There was no cemetery because there was no older generation, and like Pedro Juan, the streets bounced around like orange rapids. Trade never stopped. Even as I watched, great ant-hills of concrete were sprouting on the banks. Others burrowed three storeys deep into the laterite, eerie fluorescent lairs of perfumes, Reeboks and sub-machine-guns. Bald dogs ate the rubbish, and liveried private armies kept the peace. Every ten minutes a bus left for Brazil, packed (as often as not) with cigarettes instead of people.

"What's there to see here?" I asked at the tourist office.

"Nothing," they said with sleepy candour. "Just shops."

I turned to leave.

"If you want any more help," they yawned, "just ask."

Obviously I'd have to find my own way around in this great twinkling rat's-nest of booty. I went underground and climbed up into the haze. I went bowling in a subterranean twenty-eight-lane bowling alley where they gave the scores in Japanese. I found a supermarket of pornography and the usual emporia of Scotch. But the most intriguing trading was always in the gutter: statues from every religion, blond wigs, "Hermès" scarves in rasping nylon, oil paintings of the *Marina Piccola* on Capri and a perfect British Army SA80, firing pink ball-bearings. Fraud was conducted with such nonchalance that the perfume cartons were often just photocopies. The traders didn't care and they didn't expect their customers to. One of them had covered herself with silk cushions and moved around like an enormous Ottoman germ. Way above her head, asleep in the plush, was a very small baby. Perhaps she didn't know it was there.

I soon realised that in its name—City of the East—there was not merely a smattering of geography but also a clue as to ownership. "CDE" was luridly Asian. It wasn't just the pagodas and the restaurants—the Osakas and the Taipeis—the Taiwanese flag actually flew from City Hall. They had, after all, paid for the place.

"In return," friends in Asunción told me, "Paraguay always votes for Taiwan at the United Nations. We are Taipei's oldest and cheapest friend. And South Africa's. And Israel's (they paid us in guns)."

Dalliances with Israel didn't seem to have worried the Arabs of the Ciudad. They regarded it as an exotic version of Aleppo and had scooped themselves a magnificent mosque from a tower block. It was widely thought that Hezbollah kept a cadre there, preying on the world's seventh Jewish community: Buenos Aires. Between 1994 and 1996, 115 *Porteños* were blown to bits by Hezbollah and Argentina rounded on the City of the East. The city responded much as it had to me: there's nothing here but shops.

93

There was a strange footnote to these bombing atrocities. One of the scrambled victims was identified by a *paraguaya* as her husband, Patricio Irala (undoubtedly a descendant of the lewd conquistador). The Argentines paid her $50,000 compensation. It was only in April 2001 that they spotted *pó-caré*, the little twisted hand of the Guaraní.

Irala wasn't mangled at all. He and his wife were back in Ciudad del Este, growing fat in their new bakery.

94

The great Paraná came boiling down from the north. I took a bus a few kilometres upstream and watched as the watery heart of the continent sucked its way south. Although, in terms of length, the Paraná is only the fourteenth river in the world, in terms of water discharged it is surpassed only by the Amazon, the Congo and the Brahmaputra. Every second, enough water passes to fill over twenty-seven Olympic swimming pools.

Then, at a place the Guaraní once knew as the "sound of rocks," the river fell strangely quiet. All that I could hear was the dull, insistent hum of turbines. The Paraná had been severed and restrained by a wall nearly eight kilometres long, comprising over eight million cubic metres of concrete. It stood a few storeys higher than London's Telecom Tower and held back perhaps the greatest man-made deluge in the world: the Itaipú Dam.

Such a construction would have been remarkable anywhere, but to find man's greatest-ever public works project in the fringes of Paraguay was eerie. Behind me was a land of ox-carts and antique cavalry, of tribes struggling with their cannibalism and of goitre and savage infant mortality. In front was hydro-electric energy sufficient to power eighteen Paraguays or the whole of New York State. At 12,600 megawatts, it had nearly twice the capacity of the Grand Coulee and six times that of the Aswan High Dam. A quarter of all Paraguayans didn't even own a light bulb.

The scale of human effort was Pharaonic (a matter of some pride to General Stroessner). The plans alone would have stacked up fifty storeys high. Forty thousand men were involved in the construction, beginning in 1973. They moved eight and a half times as much spoil as Eurotunnel (if it had been loaded in trucks, the queue would have stretched three times round the planet). They produced enough steel to build 380 Eiffel Towers and enough concrete to build 210 Olympic stadiums—or fifteen Eurotunnels. The men ate three tons of rice every lunchtime and 160 of them were crushed, ground up, electrocuted or drowned. By 1983, volts were snapping out of the turbines.

"Who *paid* for it all?" I kept asking.

People in Asunción hadn't been sure. It certainly wasn't them. Paraguay's contribution wouldn't even have covered the rice.

"It must have been Brazil."

The co-owner had paid for the lot. In return, Stroessner's men agreed to the flooding of the Guairá forests and to Paraguay paying her share from her surplus electricity. Filling their pockets with Brazilian bribes, they also agreed to sell the surplus only to Brazil and only at production cost.

"We've been robbed," most agreed.

Meanwhile Brazil was picking up the bills. From an original estimate of $2 billion, the cost rose to $26 billion. Although Paraguay won only a fraction of the contracts, $1.5 billion gushed into her tiny economy. It was like gasoline in her spluttering boilers. *Asunceños* began to eat Dutch cheese and the General began to cover his country in tarmac. Contract-fixing became wildly ostentatious. Wasmosy headed the Paraguayan consortium and underwent his revoltingly spectacular metamorphosis.

"At Itaipú," friends told me, "even the man who planted the grass became a millionaire."

Doubled up with indigestible statistics, I called at the dam reception. I found a PR man in a lacy shirt and orange plastic hat. He was surprised that I didn't know Princess Diana and told his colleagues that I was a gentleman from England who'd come to make a report. They gave me a plastic hat and attached me to a Technical Team. They would be going into the dam's bowels by van.

We took a seven-lane super-highway to the rockfill. It was the only dual carriageway in Paraguay and was completely empty and ended in a cave. We passed through, entering the dark concrete kingdom of Itaipú. It was a state as Piranesi would have dreamed it—a chasm of vertiginous gothic arches and gantries, of dripping, lifeless walkways and crushing perspectives, of the sun glimpsed through tiny trapeziums of rock and a sky of angry black waves. There were corridors two kilometres long and shafts that simply vanished into the Earth's core. Somewhere around here, up to four thousand souls were toiling away, including a little khaki army with machine-guns and double-headed eagles. We saw no one.

Eighteen gargantuan steel intestines—or penfolds—sucked the Paraná down through the rock. Each gut was big enough to engulf several buses at once, and the water thundered through it at 700 cubic metres a second. At the bottom it had to turn a turbine the weight of four hundred cars. Even the furious Iguaçu Falls would only just have managed two of these penfolds.

A brilliant silver lift darted like a fish through the darkness and we were as deep as we could go.

"The old river-bed," said the technicians.

In the gloom we scuffed through the shingle of the broken river.

"It's like a tomb," said the engineer absently.

Two hundred metres below the new river, this was an unappealing thought. The fish darted us back to the surface.

The van then zig-zagged up the rockfill on the Brazilian side. Below us, the concrete mixers, crushers and ironworks lay mouldering in the belly of the gorge. We doubled back across the lip of the dam into Paraguay. To the north, the horizon was flattened by the dark waters of its new inland sea.

The inundation had swallowed up 1,500 square kilometres of jungle. More Aché hunting grounds had been lost, drowned in deep black water. Millions of animals were driven away or perished. Some of the jaguars were rescued in a flotilla of Noah's arks and, like the Achés, they'd had to find new lives in camps and gardens and zoos. But lost for ever were the Guairá Falls. By volume, they'd been the greatest water-falls in the world.

"No white man has ever seen them in modern times," wrote Edward Knight. "The Indians say no man can dwell within thirty miles of the falls, for even at that distance, the roar is so great as to produce complete deafness in time."

Even a century later, when the exploding waters were finally silenced, they were hardly known. Thorns and heat and poison had fortified their seclusion.

However, a white man had scrambled down them, several centuries before. Had I been in Itaipú in August 1631, I would have seen him clambering over these rocks on his way downstream. He was an old acquaintance; the scribbling Jesuit, Father Montoya.

He was not alone. At his heels were 4,000 ravenous Guaranís.

95

The Jesuits had enjoyed mixed fortunes since their arrival in Paraguay forty years previously.

Already they'd established the vast *provincia* of Paraguay, covering much of modern Paraguay, Bolivia, Chile, Southern Brazil, Uruguay and Argentina. The governor had the ear of the Spanish king, and in 1608 he sanctioned their efforts to liberate the savages from their "depraved mode of life," to bring them before God and to "assure their true happiness." Indians began to drift into radical Jesuit communities, the "reductions." Here was unparalleled sanctuary: slavery was prohibited; the Spaniards, Portuguese, negroes and even the *mestizos* were barred. The Jesuit theocracy was gradually assuming its powerful form.

None of this was without its dangers. The great landowners opposed the drainage of Indian labour. The Paraguayan Church sniped at Jesuit privilege and wealth. Even the suspicions of the Guaranís occasionally erupted into bloodshed. Meanwhile, in the Chaco, Jesuits were being eaten or scalped as quickly as they could be disembarked.

The holy fathers, however, were all gristle and determination. Young men like Montoya, Brown, Stoner, Neyderdorffer and Smith represented the most muscular of Europe's adventurers. Some had ranged as far as Ethiopia, Angola and Japan. They burned with evangelism—but also with curiosity. By understanding the savages' beliefs, they hoped to infiltrate them with Christianity. If necessary, they'd meet force with force. "Go and set the world on fire" ran their motto.

In 1631 the Jesuits faced a new threat, in the eastern forests of the Guairá.

By then, Father Montoya had already been in the Guairá for twenty years, struggling to establish eight reductions. His neophytes were hunter-gatherers and cannibals. For Montoya, it was a hermit's life. His sandals were patched with fragments torn from his cassocks. He lived on cassava and wild fowl and forgot the taste of salt. "A demi-arobe of wine lasted us five years," he wrote, "for we used only what was necessary for the consecration."

This unappetising existence came to an abrupt end with a massive raid by Brazilian slavers, the *bandeirantes*.

At its best, the history of the *bandeirantes* is the scrags of an old squabble between Spain and Portugal. Ever since the signing of the Treaty of Tordesillas in 1494, the Portuguese had been nibbling loop-holes in their promise not to expand westwards, into the Spanish half of the world. In modern Brazil, the *bandeirantes* are heroes, nationalists and conquerors.

Others see them differently. Their motives were invariably acquisitive. Their appetite for slavery was leviathan (by 1638, some 300,000 Indians had been dragged off to the São Paulo plantations). They were hardly nationalists either, but a rabble of outlaws—Portuguese,

Africans, Italians, Dutchmen and Tupí half-breeds. The Jesuits hadn't witnessed such barbarity since the Levant and called them the *mamelucos*. Montoya was more forthright: "The monkey is not a Christian."

Before his eyes, the *bandeirantes* tore the eight reductions apart. Sixty thousand Guaranís were enslaved. To the slavers, their harvesting was child's play. No longer did they have to pursue the fleet savages through the forest. The Jesuits had gathered them into human dovecotes. "Of gravest concern," wrote one priest, "is that the Indians imagine that we gathered them in, not to teach them the law of God but to deliver them to the Portuguese."

As the hawks closed in for another swoop, Montoya decided on withdrawal. It was to be an exodus of biblical proportions. Like Moses, he foresaw deliverance in a far-off Promised Land. Unlike Moses, he couldn't rely on the waters parting. He and his Guaranís contemplated the deafening froth of Guairá Falls.

"In record time," he wrote, "the Indians constructed seven hundred rafts and enough dugouts to be used by twelve thousand people."

Montoya launched three hundred boats into the rapids to see if any would survive. Each one was splintered. The neophytes would have to hack their way through the thorns. On the first day they sang hymns, and on the second they began to die. *Bandeirantes* preyed on the stragglers. Two thousand perished and six thousand took their chances in the deeper forest. It took the survivors eight days to reach the end of the cataracts. Montoya conceded momentary despair: "I confess I suffered infinitely."

He rallied on the river voyage that followed. He even revived his fascination for the strange monsters that were eating his followers. "There are fish that the people call *culebras* which have been seen to swallow men entire, and throw them out again with all their bones broken as if it had been done with stones."

The Exodus drifted downstream. Eight hundred kilometres from Guairá, the exiles would find their Promised Land. It would be known simply as Misiones, or "the Missions."

Not tempted by the river route, I hurried round to see for myself the surprising developments that took place next.

96

Montoya, meanwhile, realised that to survive, the Christian Guaranís needed to be able to fight.

Here there was a problem: under Spanish law, savages were forbidden from bearing arms. In 1638, Montoya set off for Madrid to lobby for change. It took him six years to advance his arguments. He was tireless. Between submissions he wrote orations, an ethnography of Paraguay and a Guaraní dictionary.

Madrid hesitated. It was barely a century since the papacy's recognition of the Indians' human tendencies. The most powerful court in the world was now being asked to concede a savage's right to kill, even his right to kill a white man. Spain (and therefore Europe) was about to redefine her relationship with the subjugated world. Unsurprisingly, she stalled.

In the end, a decision was forced on her.

The Guaranís had been unable to bide the outcome. When the *bandeirantes* swaggered back into Paraguay in 1639, they were met by a Jesuit force under the command of Chief Ñeenguirú. A small Spanish squadron from Asunción stood by and watched in astonishment as the Christians sliced the bandits down. Two years later, São Paulo sent a powerful army to evict the Jesuits for ever. Ñeenguirú was ready for them. His artillery, comprising cannons of giant bamboo, was directed by the holy fathers.

The battle of Mhoreré lasted seven days. It would determine the frontier of the Spanish and Portuguese empires once and for all. The Guaranís fought with astonishing courage (courage that it would have served their neighbours well to heed in the centuries to come). The *bandeirantes* fled in pieces.

Madrid was unrestrained in its gratitude. With the Portuguese pressing on her frontiers, she suddenly awoke to the advantages of a Guaraní buffer-state. The court celebrated with a liturgy of thanksgiving and the Guaranís' right to defend themselves became inevitable. Ten years later, they were charged with the defence of Eastern Paraguay.

Montoya never returned to his adopted homeland but died in Peru. A cortège of forty Guaraní warriors carried his remains back over the Andes. In 1656 he was finally laid to rest in the heart of a vigorous Jesuit republic.

97

It took me two days to get down to Misiones. I stayed in Encarnación, a city of outlandish Ukrainian churches and yellow horse-drawn taxis. The Paraná had been swollen by another hydro-electric barrage and its waters now seeped into the lower streets and plazas. The citizens were gradually moving their city uphill.

Although its catch-line—"Pearl of the South"—was a little over-ornate for a town of corrugated iron and cement, Encarnación was undeniably pleasing. It was still steeped in late blossom. It also had a blatant honesty about it that had been so floridly missing in Ciudad del Este. Argentines crossed the river frontier for good cheap education. Banking was performed without commandos.

"Whenever I go there," one *Asunceño* told me, "I get a feeling of hope for Paraguay. And then I come back here . . ."

"Perhaps it's the Germans," said another. "They run it."

It could equally have been the Poles or the Czechs or the Russians. Reggie Thompson had been here when they arrived in cattle trucks between the wars. They'd named their children after the ships that saved them from Europe. *Neptunia*, he observed, was a particular favourite.

As I padded around the town, I began to wonder why I'd left Encarnación almost until last. Perhaps it was MacDonald's quips about the insects and the "Misiones itch." Or perhaps it was what Cunninghame Graham had written about the Jesuits and their "socialist utopia."

It was not a concept I was finding easy to digest.

98

I got a ride out to the reductions with a road gang. They wore their overalls tucked into their socks and knew little of the Jesuits.

"They abandoned us," said the shy one.

After an hour of sugar cane and undulating grasslands, we came to a *toldería* of crumbled shacks and rust. "Karate Lessons" said a sign.

"This is Trinity," announced the foreman. "The reduction is up the hill."

I climbed through the village to the outer defences of Trinidad. It had been the greatest of the eight reductions in Paraguay, founded in 1706. Thick red blocks of sandstone had been heaved to the hilltop and sculpted around a vast, airy plaza. Now it was empty, with no sound but the swish of grass.

The gatekeeper had silver fingernails and patent leather shoes. She was unable to embellish on the ruins.

"Don't ask me," she pleaded. "I only do the tickets."

Her ancestors had lived in stone cubicles around the square. The hard red lines of each home were considered an antidote to the promiscuity of Indian *tolderías*. Housing was identical in each of the reductions; a man could travel from one to the other and believe that they'd followed him. But the roofs were gone now and parrots nested in the joist-holes.

The shape of the reduction had however survived: a great urban experiment rising above the plains of Misiones. Here were sandstone bakeries and hospitals, cloisters, asylums, granaries, abattoirs and armouries. I found ovens and cisterns and the crimson outline of the sewers, slicing into the forest.

From up here, the Jesuit fathers could watch as their neophytes turned the estates to profit. Within two decades, there were 4,000 souls at Trinidad. Life was conducted to music and work to the rhythm of drums. The Indians wore smocks of embroidered cotton and would never know money. Whatever they produced was *tupambaé*, that belonging to God. They sang hymns as they tilled.

"On rainy days," wrote Cunninghame Graham, "they worked at other industries in the same half-Arcadian, half-communistic manner, only they sang their hymns in church instead of in the fields."

It was not easy to connect this serenity with his Scottish Labour Party, all raw-faced and tweedy. Graham, however, had been deeply affected by the ruins of the experiment.

"The laws were respected there," he went on. "Morals were pure, a happy brotherhood united every heart . . ."

This was only partly true. Although their detractors would struggle to find evidence of depravity among the Jesuits, discipline was swiftly administered with a whip. Punishments were prescribed, with some degree of stringency, in the Society's orders:

For Unnatural Acts and Bestiality . . . 3 months imprisonment, without emerging (except for Mass), and in the said 3 months they are to be given 4 whippings, 25 lashes each time, and to be the whole time in irons. In the case of other crimes such as incest and relationships with stepmothers and Mothers-in-law and contrived abortion, they are to be imprisoned two months in irons . . .

There was no death penalty, and after every flogging, the accused kissed the sleeve of his scourge, the priest. Here, perhaps, was the most telling feature of all: in each of the reductions there were seldom more than two Europeans. Whips or not, the Jesuit Arcadia was a community by consent.

I crossed to the upper end of the plaza, dominated by the magnificent shell of the basilica. It had been designed by Primoli of Milan and had once seated 5,000 Indians. Here, they'd enjoyed heaven on earth, an extraordinary stone jungle of mythical creatures and acanthus. The vaults had been leafed in gold and the apostles had beckoned with giant sandstone hands. It had taken nearly forty years to build and had barely survived the experiment. By 1800 the roof had collapsed and tropical rains were honey-combing the masonry.

I picked my way through what remained: pieces of the exotic saints, pheasants, harps, rococo ducks and a font inscribed "*Año 1720.*" Friezes of flamboyants grew around the doors and the stiff flames of Purgatory licked up the sinners. The largest statue to survive had the face of a fish and the wings of a cherub. The spirits of the forest had, it seems, mingled their seed freely among the angels.

The arts, we read, were encouraged—but not originality. The Guaranís were faithful copyists. They could reproduce almost anything: violins, harpsichords, clocks, statutes, Dürer, Bosch or Callot. Their choirs could mimic any that the holy fathers had left behind, and an old rival of Vivaldi, Father Zipoli, brought them the art of orchestral music. They absorbed it all and then they copied it. They built themselves a printing press a century before Buenos Aires. At San Cosme, they constructed an astronomical observatory and brought the world important news from Saturn. These were some of the most literate communities in the world and in a state of unceasing adoration.

Life, as one wag put it, was a perpetual Sunday.

99

News of the reductions caused a murmur of excitement in the faculties of Europe. The Italian scholar Muratori argued that in Misiones was "the perfect image of the primitive church." Here was Utopia as it had been described in the Acts of the Apostles. It was the virtuous government of Fenelon's *Télémaque*, the embodiment of an authority that had long been considered unattainable. Montesquieu urged states everywhere to adopt the model of the Paraguayan "republic" and to establish "the community of goods of Plato's *Republic*, the respect Plato asks for the gods, a separation from strangers in order to preserve morals, and a city—not the citizens—engaged in commerce."

Even Voltaire, who was never comfortable in praise of religious orders, conceded that the Paraguayan example was "unique upon the Earth" and a replica of the "ancient government of Sparta."

In the face of such dazzling praise, the Jesuits hadn't hidden their light. Father Charlevoix's *Histoire du Paraguay* confidently asserted that the Guaraní republic was founded "upon a most perfect plan," and tossed in further comparisons, with Bacon's *The New Atlantis*. There would be others. It would even be suggested that the republic was modelled on Thomas More's *Utopia* and Campanella's *The City of the Sun*.

Kind words indeed. But none of it would be enough to save the republic from treachery and the catastrophe which followed.

100

Whilst the Society of Jesus was preening its feathers, Lisbon and Madrid were conspiring to pluck it.

By 1750 the two courts were briefly and unhappily linked by marriage. For the crafty Portuguese, it was an opportunity for some creative estate management. They had a monstrous proposal: Portugal would swap the filthy River Plate colony of Sacramento for a vast swathe of modern-day Uruguay. True, Spain would gain control over a pirate's nest (which had always been a running sore in the mouth of the river), but she'd have to take with it all its pirates. Worse, she'd lose seven reductions and a quarter of the Jesuit economy. The Guaranís would be simply evicted and would receive compensation amounting to two per cent of their property's value. In the history of Spanish colonial diplomacy, the Treaty of Madrid would stand out as truly idiotic.

For the Portuguese, it was taking candy from a baby. The Spanish king's mental faculties had been eaten away by depression and chronic piety. His wife, on the other hand, was a scheming Braganza, an over-engined woman of powerful appetites. She rolled the deal through on the advice of the Marqués de Pombal (who was also Portuguese) and an Englishman (who didn't care much for either country). South America was not consulted until the ink was dry.

The Jesuits played their part in the ensuing slaughter. Intellectually, they argued that kings had no business subverting the natural rights of Indians. Disobedience was morally imperative. In the field, the holy fathers exhorted the Indians to resistance. Chief among them was an Irishman of uncertain temper and excruciating Latin: Thadeus Ennis. After four years of stalemate, he urged his Guaranís to battle.

The Guaraní army had matured beyond recognition since Mbororé. Although it had been hired by Buenos Aires to fight English and Danish corsairs, as a military force it had grown a little plump. As a pageant, it was superbly fluffy. At its head rode the officers, in red velvet doublets trimmed with lace and ostrich feathers. Then came the *alcaides*, in short breaches of yellow satin, and the sergeants in scarlet suits and silver waistcoats. The soldiers followed, soaked in colour and armed with spears, *bolas*, slings and long English guns that needed rests to fire them. They carried the standard of their patron saint before them, to protect them from evil and shot.

In Geneva, Voltaire now had his moment of mockery. *Candide* hoots at "his reverence, the colonel" who dines from gold plates and crystal goblets whilst his Indians trough in the fields. The Paraguayan Jesuits had "a wonderful system": "In this country they kill Spaniards and in Madrid they send them to Heaven. Delightful, isn't it?"

In reality, there were few delights for the Guaraní commander, Ñeen-guirú's grandson. "King Nicholas" well knew that wars were not won by fine tailoring and had a premonition of disaster. He wrote his farewells to the Society: "We are before God as we await our complete destruc-tion . . . we will resist to the end."

It was not long in coming. Father Ennis stood among the flames and whirling metal, bellowing at his Indians in Latin and Irish, but the colo-nial artillery was overwhelming. In the last set-piece, many of the

Guaranís simply crossed their arms and waited for deliverance. In one hour, 1,500 Indians were exterminated. The survivors took to guerrilla warfare, bivouacking in the trees and cutting throats. By 1756, Ennis and King Nicholas were in chains and the "Jesuit War" was over.

At the same time, the Hispano-Portuguese coupling fell apart and the Treaty of Madrid was revoked. The war had been in vain. The reductions were restored to the Jesuits. Sacramento was captured by the Spanish, using Guaraní troops. King Nicholas was spared. He would die an old man, signing denunciations of Ennis and the Jesuits. Ennis, too, survived but his journals underwent some decidedly Soviet re-editing. He then disappeared.

The literary world was less keen to forget the episode. The Brazilian poet da Gama was first, with his great epic of 1767, *O Uruguai*. Burton translated it to English and enjoyed it for all his own reasons: he thought the Jesuit Republic was a "sterile, theocratic despotism" and had no truck with the idea of a Noble Savage. Others were more generous. In the theatre, Fritz Hochwalder's *The Strong Are Lonely* awoke indignation that had been dormant for two centuries. Roland Joffé and David Puttnam brought the same outrage to the cinema screen.

The Mission emerged in the last decade of the *Stronato*. Thadeus Ennis is just recognisable in the swaggering of Robert De Niro. At the time the film was set, Paraguay's government was considered the most virtuous in the world. By the time the film was launched, it was the most diabolical. Naturally, General Stroessner had the picture banned.

A similar attack of nerves afflicted the Spanish court in the aftermath of the revolt. Hadn't the Jesuits raised their hand against the state? So far, they'd only deployed 3,000 of the 20,000 Guaraní warriors at their command. What might they do next?

101

Outside Trinidad, a man was carving a new fan-belt with a vegetable knife. In the leprosy of his car I could make out the letters "TAXI."

"Can you take me to Jesús?"

For all the turmoil of Trinidad, this was no plea for salvation. The last of the reductions was eleven kilometres away, along a bright-red cart track.

We bounced through the hills, making taxi-talk. This is where the

Germans live, in those chalets in the corn. Did we have cows in England? He had five daughters and a fruit-pulping machine. He'd been horribly mutilated when he fell in the fruit-pulper at the age of thirty-seven. Life is full of uncertainties. You can be sure of nothing.

We talked about the Jesuits. They brought these orange trees from Europe.

"We still copy things," said the *taxista*, whittling the air with his vegetable knife. "We made our own guns in the war. Even a bazooka. We copy anything. Engine parts . . ."

"Perfumes?" I suggested. "Cigarettes? CDs? Designer labels?"

He grinned. "You can be sure of nothing."

The reduction of Jesús was conceived at the height of Jesuit uncertainty.

The gatehouse was a trefoil arch borrowed from the Moors and shaped in ochre. The last fortress of God stood beyond, on a hill of *quebrachos* and palm trees. It was supposed to have been the greatest basilica in the Americas, but its walls never reached Heaven. Their empty sockets now gaped out over a Misiones that, in the end, had proved untenable.

I walked up through the copse. Apart from a cowboy filing his horse's hooves, I was the only person on the hill. There was no roof to the basilica and its transept was a meadow of campion and rye. Sacristies and vestries were scalloped into the walls and a pulpit had unfurled itself from the stone like a gorgeous orange epiphyte. But the cloisters were merely outlines and the *dormitorios* had never risen beyond ankle-height. In August 1768, the order had been given that all work was to cease. At a stroke, three thousand Indians put down their tools and Jesús was abandoned.

The end for the Jesuit Republic had been spiteful and protracted. Europe had never recovered from the spectacle of Jesuits in armed revolt. In 1759, Pombal hoofed them out of Portugal and had his revenge for Uruguay. France followed five years later. As before, Spain dithered.

For almost a century, the Paraguayan oligarchy had been besieging Madrid with their grumbles: the Jesuits paid no tax; they contributed nothing to the secular economy (but absorbed its best labour); they were sitting on a gold field; they were heretics and sodomites. Until then, Madrid had been largely unimpressed. Now she faced the possibility of an independent Guaraní state. In the spring of 1767, she gave in. The Society was expelled from all her domains. Secret orders went out to the Viceroy of La Plata, Bucareli: arrest the Jesuits, ship them to the Vatican and shut down the republic. By the following summer, Bucareli was in Paraguay with an army.

The Jesuits left without resisting. Perhaps they shouldn't have done; their sudden departure left the impression that, in the end, they lacked conviction. To others, it was abandonment. Although Bucareli gathered up nearly $30,000,000 worth of estates, he found no feathered nests. Here is his inventory of Father Zabaleta's worldly goods: ten shirts, two pillowcases, two sheets, three handkerchiefs, two pairs of shoes, two pairs of socks and a pound and a half of snuff.

As I surveyed the great orange shell of Jesús and its ankle-deep institutions, it was hard to feel pity. This vast building site had fallen victim to the Enlightenment. Perhaps it was none too soon. At every level of Jesuit administration, they'd perpetuated childhood. Initiative was stifled, and apart from the velvet majorettes, the Indians had never emerged as leaders. Not a single Guaraní became a priest. The reductions were like schools without education or—worse—without end.

I was sorry to have reached this point. My lack of enthusiasm would have horrified Cunninghame Graham. He was the last historian to witness the rituals of the Jesuit Republic, when he passed through in 1874. He found the Guaraní in the ruins of their reductions, still in their smocks and chanting in Latin. He lamented the senseless loss of idealism.

I console myself with the thought that had Graham lived to see more of the twentieth century and the epidemic of Utopias, he might have felt differently.

102

For Misiones, the Jesuits wouldn't be the last Utopians. Nearly two centuries after their rapid departure, another was on his way in. He too had been something of an experimenter. Now he was contorted with ulcers, terrified of discovery and on the run. It was Dr. Mengele, heading for Hohenhau.

It was an uninspired choice for a man who'd once sought to redesign the faces of Eastern Europe. Although it was handsome, with its orange trees and its soft green glades of sheep, Hohenhau was nothing more than agricultural. I almost missed it as my bus slewed its way east. Such tranquillity would gnaw at the doctor's anxieties.

This wasn't his only problem; Hohenhau was conspicuously German. Gemeiner Strasse was still lined with pines and the shopkeepers spoke with thick Silesian vowels. The landscape had been German since 1900 and there was a well-muscled monument to the early pioneers, dressed in the leather armour of the *montes*. Fifty-eight young Germans had died in the Chaco War and were remembered in roses and bronze. It was also the birthplace of Alfred Stroessner, who'd make this little Germany notorious. For Mengele, it was all too German, too obvious. He was right. Nazi-hunters would trawl the colony for years, long after he'd left and long after he'd died.

They would discover very little. I asked the grocer about Mengele, as she measured out sugar in an ancient balance of marble and brass. "He never lived here," she said. "We've never heard of him."

I could hardly blame her for her discretion. Hohenhau was struggling to be remembered for its heroes, its fruit and its *Kultur*—not some surly neurotic who'd skulked around in 1961.

Mengele had stayed out on a ranch belonging to the Krugs. Even today, not much happened without the Krugs. Their village house was one of the few that had survived a century of ants. It was now the *Centro Histórico* and upstairs was a wormy collection of pioneers' rifles, sewing-machines and school-books given by Hitler. Hohenhau children had repaid his generosity with a large portrait over which they'd painted the words *"El Presidente de Europa."*

The doctor would have been among sympathisers if not exactly disciples. He started to play scat and practised a little medicine. One woman told visitors that he'd often visited her hotel, that he was very polite and that he'd played the piano beautifully. Her name was Michline Reynaers. She and her husband were Belgian, and their hotel, The Tirol, was some way out, on the road back to Encarnación. I decided to pay them a visit.

I was unsure how the Reynaers would react to more questions about the Angel of Auschwitz. When Granada Television had poked a camera in his face in 1978, Armand had retorted angrily: "What was this man accused of? He was a doctor in the camps. We always hear that rubbish [the murder of Jews] that was written in the newspapers."

The Hotel Tirol was set back from the road, choked in thick, damp jungle. It was an ugly red-brick building looking down on two pools, one sludged with leaf-mould and palm husks, the other an unlikely chemical blue. Streaks of bitter smoke leaked from a boiler-house and the air was maddened with insects. I took cover in the dining room and waited for signs of life.

It had been decorated with appreciable brutality. Everything was rock, cartwheels and yokes, all slathered in dark varnish. The only decorations were the heads of a large yellow fish and a maned wolf, now almost extinct. Eventually a barman appeared and brought me *Kaffee und Kuchen*. Then there was a skittering of claws and the Reynaers came in, preceded by spaniels. As the dogs scratched themselves to sleep, the Reynaers started to play cards.

"May I ask some questions?" I ventured. "I'm writing about Paraguayan hotels."

Armand offered me Flemish, French, German, Spanish or Guaraní.

"Do you mind my tape recorder?" I asked. "I forget everything."

Michline's eyes narrowed. Armand shrugged. He was well into his eighties and his skin was loose and netted with veins. He regarded me through heavy grey hoods with what I realised was bleak suspicion.

"We arrived in Paraguay in 1950 . . ." he began. I was given a speech. They'd developed this property as a starch factory. In the summer there was no cassava so they invited people to swim in the water tanks. They built rooms and eventually they could sleep four hundred. The Brazilian consul started to call it "the Tirol."

Here goes, I thought. "What about other famous guests?"

"Sure. We had Argentine film stars, Stroessner, Rodríguez . . ."

"Dr. Mengele?"

"He was never here."

I must have looked surprised.

"We didn't have a hotel when Mengele was around."

Tiny spots of froth had erupted in the corners of his mouth. The lips were purple. I can still hear his irritation. My own voice has fallen silent.

"Perhaps," he says, "he came for a drink a few times."

I am saying nothing.

"It was very hot. A hundred and fifteen degrees. We had two drums of cold water. Our beer was always cold. I saw him here twice."

Reynaers had been lying for Mengele for almost half his life. Even in the 1970s he was feeding out nonsense to the CIA: Mengele was living in Hohenhau; he was a regular customer. Such stories came at a time of frenzied Nazi-hunting and a need to believe. One rumour had Mengele heading Encarnación's narcotics cartel. Another had him bounding round the Hotel Tirol one step ahead of the Committee of Twelve, a commando of Auschwitz survivors. Even the legendary Simon Wiesenthal fell for this one, setting it all out in a yarn that begins, "It was a hot, dark night . . ."

But Mengele had long gone. By October 1961 he was in Brazil. He spent the rest of his life in the vast, dreary suburbs of São Paulo. He suffered from shingles and depression but never remorse. The world had unfairly excluded him and had hounded him into these revolting swamps. There were moments of satisfaction (Churchill's death and Kennedy's assassination) and moments when he thought he recognised his research (the first heart transplant), but he was never happy. He lived with disgruntled misfits and drowned on a swimming trip in 1979.

Meanwhile, the world continued to search. Mengele's evasion had become a *cause célèbre*. He himself became a sort of Black Pimpernel, a villain of the silver screen with curdling tales like *The Marathon Man* and *The Boys from Brazil*. Even as he lay rotting, Congress was demanding Stroessner hand him over. The reward reached $4,000,000. Then his body turned up in 1985 and the experts satisfied themselves that the hunt was over. Not everybody was so sure. Even now, Mengele is deep in the Paraguayan jungle, or a transsexual living in Germany, dabbling in gynaecology.

As the tape finishes, I can just hear Reynaers with the last word.

"Write what you like. You can't prove it either way."

He had every reason to hope that this was true. Armand Reynaers had served out his war with a body that had modelled itself on the Jesuits, all black and discipline: the doctor's old cronies, the Waffen SS.

103

When I returned to Asunción, I told the soil scientist about the colonies I'd seen. Immigration was a playful subject.

"First," he said, "we had the conquistadors. Then the contractors—English, Americans and French. After the Big War, it was Germans, Australians and Arab traders. A 'Turk's Valise' is still a box of tricks.

"Next, there were the Italians. They've left us with our buildings and our good-for-nothing president. They had a revolution once. Paraguay was Italian for an hour!

"After 1917, we started getting Russians: generals, Jews and ballerinas. In the twenties it was Mennonites. Japanese in the thirties. Then half of Eastern Europe. Then Koreans arrived—and Taiwanese—hoping to hop into the States. Instead, they bought us up and stayed.

"Ever since, it's been people on the run: criminals jumping justice; Frenchmen escaping socialism; Germans fleeing Chernobyl; *Afrikaners* fleeing Africans. Oddballs from Norway. We became a sort of last resort.

"Now it's the Brazilians. They already own the eastern zones. They're going to drive a waterway through to the sea. Imagine that! It'll turn us inside out.

"Everything's about to change."

104

I also tracked down Gareth. We arranged to meet at Zona Urbana, a bar with a crashed car on the roof and industrial scrap riveted up the walls. I wasn't sure of anything any more. Was it a protest about industrial-isation or the lack of it?

Gareth was late, greyer and more effervescent.

"Fucking shit, this place. *Qué tal?*"

He grabbed hold of me. There were deep yellow pits scorched into his fingers. Perhaps he didn't feel pain any more.

"OK," I said. "And you?"

"Tengo ganas de vomitar."

"You want to puke?"

"All the time," he grinned, and made a sudden noise like laughter. "My money has come from Wales. *Vamos a ver Asunción!* A night cruise!"

An unpromising evening fell apart. Gareth's car was emphatically post-industrial, like the thing on the roof. The back seats were glittered in glass. First we were in the docks, driving through bonfires and ordering wedges of burnt fish. Then we were throttling up Mariscal López. Gareth drained another beer and his face seemed to liquefy.

"In Paraguay you just get a fucking truck and drive!"

Sometimes he hailed people on the pavements, as if he were crying. They regarded him with either terror or recognition, it was hard to tell which. We stopped only once, in a garden of giant concrete mushrooms. It was obviously a favourite place of Gareth's. *"Fantástico!"* he mushed. *"Es arte."*

Then we were in Plaza Independencia. A pop-star in a bikini was singing to an empty square. Gareth drove round and round the stage, shouting, *"Soy paraguayo!* I am Paraguayan!" It wasn't even true. Of all his failings, Gareth's failure to belong was his greatest.

Suddenly he said, "I'm going to see my wife."

The tour was over. Now it was my turn to disappear. I got out and walked back to The Itapuá. An absurd thought nagged me all the way.

In this great genetic soup, Gareth was like the fly, drowning.

The Chaco

The first non-Indian visitors to the Chaco soon became primarily interested in escaping from it, with life and limb intact.

—J. R. Gorham, *Paraguay: Ecological Essays*

On the Chaco shore . . . it is the utter desert as far as man is concerned, intolerable to him with mosquitoes and ague. If he penetrate it but a little way, awe seizes him to behold that gigantic network of plants that shuts him in as in a prison. In these dark depths one is oppressed by a feeling of suffocation, of restrained freedom, as in a nightmare . . .

—E. F. Knight, *The Cruise of the Falcon*

The whole landscape did look as though nature had organised an enormous bottle party, inviting the weird mixture of the temperate, subtropical and tropical plants to it.

—Gerald Durrell, *The Drunken Forest*

105

When I told the waitresses at The Lido that I was going into the Chaco, they scowled. "It's terrible. It's full of *tigres!*"

Nor was there much encouragement in anything I'd read. My guide-book said it was "interesting for two days." For an area of our planet the size of Poland, this was a bleak thought. Father Dobrizhoffer wouldn't even have given it two days; it was a "theatre of misery." Even Knight wrote it off as an "immense prison," never venturing beyond *The Falcon's* field of fire.

Most discouraging of all were the Paraguayans. For centuries, the Chaco was simply *L'Inferno Verde*, or "the Green Hell." Quite apart from blood-drinking Indians, it was a place of unimaginable thirst. In summer, the temperature reached forty-two degrees and a man could boil in his skin. Rivers vanished and the water underground was briny and foul. "Only the salty breezes of an extinct sea blow here," wrote Roa Bastos. It was hardly surprising that, though the Chaco covered two-thirds of the country, only three per cent of Paraguayans chose to live there.

"It is," said another writer, "a plain with the soul of a mountain, motionless and hard as rock." Even this was generous: there are no rocks in the Chaco, no stones for building and the wood is as hard as iron.

I studied it on the maps. Its flatness was stupefying. My bombing chart was unable to discern any change in contour at all (in fact, the Chaco was rising towards the Andes at a microscopic inch per mile). There appeared to be just one road, the Trans-Chaco Highway, bolting straight for Bolivia. Halfway along were freckles which I realised were the Mennonite colonies. I also saw that as the desert sprawled towards Bolivia, the colours changed. In the east, there was some rainfall and swamps, then there was scrub and then there was nothing. Paraguay's western flanks were defended by hot clouds of dust.

Early Europeans thought they'd find monsters in this strange, long-lost ocean. There would have been plenty to surprise them: prehistoric lungfish that survived summer by tunnelling in the dirt; three-foot gun-metal lizards and vampire bats; owls that mimicked their victims and lured them to their deaths; a wild pig believed to have vanished in Pleistocene times—until it emerged from the thorns in 1975. There were even thought to be Ayoreo tribesmen who'd never seen modern man.

In this barbarous world, the trees were pot-bellied and crooked. Gerald Durrell called it "the drunken forest" but the trees were in earnest. Almost every one was said to be plated in armour. Many had weapons— like the tuna cactus, covered in three-inch poison needles, or the algarrobo, bristling in stilettos.

Perhaps the waitresses were right. The embassy in London had shared their view of the Chaco.

"Doan go there," said the cultural attaché. "Ees only esnakes an espiders."

106

I did go—not with rifles and glass beads but in a silver Land-Rover bought on Park Lane.

"It will be the Chaco for beginners," promised my host. He was a tall, thoughtful man with a jacket full of machines. Some calculated, some trilled, some chattered to Outer Space. It was all very reassuring. Into the swamps with robo-farmer Antonio Espinoza.

There have been Espinozas at almost every momentous event in Paraguay's history: a commander with the conquistadors; a guide on the Guairá exodus; a commander under López. Antonio's father had been the Minister of Finance and had co-signed Paraguay's declaration of war with Germany. Antonio himself was widely regarded as a man of integrity, and in a moment of startling saintliness, General Rodríguez had appointed him ambassador to London.

He brushed it aside. "My mother was English."

We crossed the Remanso Bridge and I was back in Villa Hayes.

"It's the only city outside America to be named after a U.S. President."

It was hardly a flattering tribute. Villa Hayes was dust and itchy dogs.

"Welcome, Fat One," said the sign.

Perhaps Rutherford Hayes deserved no better. He is mostly remembered as the first presidential candidate to bribe a voter by telegraph (his opponent was still using the Pony Express). It served him well: he became the nineteenth president, with a majority of one. He'd be known for ever as "Rutherfraud."

His greatest moment came in 1878 when he was asked to arbitrate on

Argentina's claims for war reparations. Buenos Aires wanted the Chaco. "Hayes had never visited Paraguay and never would," said Antonio, "but he read the papers carefully and decided in her favour."

Paraguay nearly burst. Hayes became a national hero. Villa Occidental was renamed, and so eventually were streets, squares and football teams. Another senator, Huey Long, was honoured with a Chaco village, known to this day as "Mister Long." But the bunting was always for Hayes.

"In 1944," continued Antonio, "my father was at the war conference in Washington. Negotiations were at a delicate stage; the Paraguayans were still undecided. Then, one evening, they asked Roosevelt if they could pay tribute at the tomb of President Hayes."

Antonio was smiling. "White House officials searched all night."

"Did they find it?"

"Of course not. No one could remember."

Even today, the only American monument to Hayes is a plaque at his birthplace in Delaware, Ohio. It's now a gasoline station.

107

The Espinozas had a ranch the size of the Isle of Wight. There were fifteen gates in the driveway and forty-two men on the payroll. The place had its own miniature power station and the garden pond was full of alligators. Two pet rheas kept the lawns at bay.

The house was new and smelt of polish and fresh linen. There was a room full of riding boots and a Labrador that fought the alligators. The baths and sinks had arrived on a ship from England in 1955.

"Our last house," explained Antonio's wife, Diane, "was eaten by the termites. All we rescued was the plumbing. It follows us everywhere."

Diane was Texan, and sometimes she thought it all reminded her of home.

Each morning I was woken by a bat flying round my room. I assumed it wanted blood and hid under the covers until dawn. Then, at a wink from the bleary orange sun, the carnival of the Chaco would begin again. Even in their names, the revellers were exuberant and brash: limpkins, laughing falcons, pygmy tyrants, puff birds, flickers and Chaco earth-creepers.

The *estancieros* were in their saddles long before the sun had burnt the sparkle off the grass. They were magnificent men; scowling, black-faced and languid. "Half-centaurs," according to Cunninghame Graham. They wore leather aprons—*pierneras*—to protect their legs from the lash of a taut lasso, which will slice a man open. Most had revolvers and short swords. They picked up their extras killing *leones*, or pumas.

We spent the days watching the grass. To me, it seemed bountiful and lush: brilliant salads of green, endless swamps of glossy tussocks, pools, lakes and stooping caranday palms; long-horned zebus crunching through the water hyacinths; the suck and plop of hooves. To Antonio and his machines, there was only scarcity, no fat on the land and—worse—none on his cattle. He scuffed at the soil. It was powdery and white like flour.

"Hardly any nutrients," said Antonio.

We were, he explained, at the eastern extreme of Andean run-off, the interface between the Pacific west and the Atlantic east. "The silt that gets this far is just dust."

To a man who had to think in beefburgers, it was little comfort to know that he lived at the axis of the continent. Fat cows were a matter of guile. On my last day, we drove down to the southern edge of the Chaco, almost to the Pilcomayo river. We went to meet other ranchers, to roast flanks of beef and to talk grass.

108

The ranchers hacked the beef from flaming wooden skewers and threw the lungs to their dogs. On 27 January 1891, a roast like this was interrupted by the sight of Indians moving through the carandays.

Tobas! The pioneers snatched their weapons and ran for the cabin. A good lunch was suddenly bristling with guns. You could never be too wary of a Toba. He was a verminous, lank-haired thief with a flat, roasted face and cactus spines in his ears. His women were animal and tattooed with soot. In times of meat, they ate it raw. In times of want, they killed their children and turned to piracy. Their arrow-tips were made of stolen fencing wire, sharpened along all its edges to maximise haemorrhage and to allow the arrow to work loose and be re-used. They moved through the grass like whispers and took no prisoners. The killing was without end or reason: a Bolivian military mission slaughtered; the ethnologist Clevaux scalped with twenty men; Commander Page's expedition missing for eleven months.

The boys took aim.

"Let them come to us!" hissed the *ganadero*, Don Pedro Gil. He had fifteen men to fifteen *bravos*. The war-party closed in, padding like cats.

Suddenly, Gil spotted a larger shape among them. Though caked with mud and cactus-down, he wore a coat! The face was raw with the sun but there were thick side-burns and a long, thin nose. And a rifle, a .45! A waistcoat, a gun-belt, two revolvers! Gil had only fifty paces to think. Didn't his Indians talk of a wild *cacique inglés* leading savages down the Pilcomayo? Hold fire, he told his men.

"Who are you?"

Commander Page is dead, announced the rags, and his soldiers have fled.

It was Graham Kerr, undergraduate of Edinburgh University and naturalist to the expedition. He said the Indians were friends. Without them, he'd have perished.

Be good enough to let us through. We're going to Asunción.

Gil escorted the boy to the River Paraguay. In Asunción, he was met by Dr. Stewart, now sleek and long-recovered from his scuffles with Madame Lynch. An unedifying tale emerged, the gist as follows.

In February 1889, the journal *Nature* ran an advertisement: naturalist wanted for Argentine expedition up the Pilcomayo. Kerr, who was just nineteen, bought a copy on Waverley Station and applied. He was appointed and immediately went out and bought four guns and fifty litres of pickling alcohol.

The expedition appeared well organised. There was a gunboat called *Bolivia*, mounted with a maxim gun ("the very first automatic machine-gun to be taken on active service"). Fifty Argentine troopers were seconded as escorts, with splendid blue pantaloons and sabres. Comandante Page wore a golden hat and ordered that if anyone so much as stole a biscuit, he'd be shot pursuant to military law. Other than Kerr, there were only two foreigners: engineer Henderson and an Italian doctor in a bowler hat.

The *Bolivia* had hardly entered the Pilcomayo before things started to go wrong. The dried beef ran low and cockroaches ate their hair at night. *Bolivia* was grounded in the shallows and the troopers dug dams to raise the levels—and then deserted. A relief force was massacred by Indians. At night, the river glowed green and the ghostly Tobas stole their axes and clothes.

Page developed dropsy and was sent downstream by canoe, with two negroes. These boys were so terrified of persecution that when their commander died, they simply paddled on. Four days later, Page arrived at a relief post in such a state of putrefaction that he and the canoe had to be buried as one. His excitable son, Midshipman Nelson Page, took command and sliced Henderson's eyebrow off with a sabre. Everyone developed malaria. The Italian doctor died next, begging that his bones be sent home to Bologna.

His bowler hat came in useful. Kerr gave it to the Tobas he'd met out hunting. An uneasy bond began to form. Kerr shared their *luktaga*, a drink made of regurgitated locust pods, and earned their admiration. Their gifts got better and better: first, guinea pigs, then beetle grubs in honey and then lustrous naked girls. "The position was trying," admitted Kerr, "but in spite of the intimacy and friendship of my relations with the Tobas, I managed to avoid closing the gap which naturally separates the races of men."

They'd now been ten months lost. Nelson was leading raiding parties against the Orejudos' sheep. In the teeth of tribal war, Kerr decided to run for Asunción. Chief Chimaki agreed to escort him through hostile territory. They set off in full war-paint.

The end of this story is only partly happy. In Asunción, Chimaki was introduced to ice-cream, bagpipes and the Kosmos Club. Paraguayan women thought him the embodiment of masculinity and several tried to steal him. After five days, he and Kerr set off, in no particular hurry, to rescue Nelson. Meanwhile, Buenos Aires sent a brutal Indian-hunter called Bouchard to retrieve the *Bolivia* and to settle scores.

"It was a touching farewell to my Tobas," wrote Kerr. "Their lamentation at being left with the *Cristianos* and expressions of hate towards them made me feel that the future was rather doubtful."

He didn't forget them. Many years later, Sir Graham Kerr, Professor of Zoology at Glasgow, published his peculiar story as *A Naturalist in the Chaco*. Chimaki's fate is unknown (his weapons went to the Museum of

Anthropology and Archaeology in Cambridge). Perhaps he didn't survive Bouchard's revenge. Kerr always feared the worst.

The Tobas had, however, survived, though without much dignity. They couldn't compete in the age of the Mauser. Under Stroessner, they were trucked around so much that they became vapid and disorientated. By chance, I saw a small group as we drove north from the Pilcomayo.

They were squatting by the highway; spears and roasted faces. Hanging in the thorns were the carcasses of armadillos, peccaries and deer—meat for sale. In their old lands, the Tobas were now poachers and outlaws.

109

At exactly the same time as Kerr was hacking his way out of Toba territory, a neighbour of his from Edinburgh was hacking into Lengua territory, a hundred miles to the north.

He was Wilfrid Barbrooke Grubb, six years older than Kerr but made of the same stuff. Among his ancestors were Tudor pirates and Jacobite rebels, and his grandmother had escaped from the Paris rebellion of 1830 dressed as a boy. He was sinewy and powerful (the Lengua called him "Bull-neck") and wore linen suits and bandoliers of bullets. When the suits were burnt, he wore Indian dress, feathers and necklaces. Everything about him was indomitable. Even his cat killed snakes.

Unlike Kerr, his enthusiasm for the continent was spiritual. He'd been recruited by the South American Missionary Society during the same thunderstorm that killed the Earl of Lauderdale. By 1886, he was among the Yaghans of Keppel Island, living on mutton and penguin eggs. Three years later, he proposed to Mary Bridges of Harberton, Tierra del Fuego, and left for Paraguay. He wouldn't see Mary again for twelve years.

His foray into Lengua country was the first of many. He set off with little water and no languages. His guides usually lost heart and deserted him; no one had ventured this far since the Jesuits' gruesome adventures. Grubb would travel perhaps a hundred miles without seeing a soul, surviving on venison, fox-meat and insects. Then, when he did meet the Lenguas, his problems would begin.

The term *"Lengua"* was Spanish (they were "Guaycurús" to the Guaraní). It derived from their lip-plates, which made them look as if they had long, lolling tongues. There was virtually no sense in which they could be compared to other humans, so adapted were they to life in the cactus. They had no concept of private property; the greatest sin was not to share the meagre resources of the wild. Nor had they any concept of obligation; there was no word for "must" in their language and there were no punishments. There was never an opportunity to store resources and so the idea of capital accumulation had long been lost. Not only could "things" not be owned or accumulated, they couldn't be worked; art and manufacture were an affront to nature.

All that a man could call his own was his name. Even this changed regularly and was never addressed to his face. The name usually described an attribute: Monkey, Rat-face, Alligator-stomach or Stinking-water. In all other respects, the language was stripped to the essentials: just seventeen "sounds" articulated in pops and clicks. They used no more than a thousand words, often hitched together to express more complex needs.

Scarcity was at the heart of their existence. It determined not only how they lived but who should live. Every pregnancy prompted an enquiry: are we able to feed another mouth? If not, the foetus was beaten from the womb or, if the mother was unable to endure the pain, the pregnancy continued and the newborn was choked with sand. Even after birth, a child had to be sustainable; if it became ill or lost a parent, it was clubbed to death with a bone-axe. If its mother died in childbirth, it was buried with her, alive.

Intervention in this state of Eden was, as Grubb knew, dangerous. Lenguas lived in perpetual fear of magic. Their terror was supervised by the *wiskis*, who'd earned their authority through gruelling weeks of initiation: eating raw snakes and bats and swallowing poisons (if they vomited, they had to start again). These shamans were seldom keen to yield such hard-won power. "The wizards," wrote Grubb to Mary, "are evil and must cease to exist. I must declare open war on them."

War it nearly was. He was often threatened and occasionally fired on. He developed his own rules for survival: respect Lengua taboos; give no presents; laugh at danger. It wasn't always enough to save him. In 1897, a convert called Poet shot him in the back with an arrow. The head passed beneath his shoulder-blade, smashed a rib and penetrated his lung. Alone and over a hundred miles from the Mission, he excavated the arrow-head and collapsed. He was found by other Indians and taken to their *toldería*, but his problems weren't over; Lenguas believe that if a man dies during darkness, his spirit will haunt them for ever. They decided that Grubb wouldn't survive and that he should be buried before sunset. Grubb was now laughing for his life. He offered them an ostrich hunt and bought a reprieve. Two days later, in foundry heat, he threaded back to the Mission. Poet was less fortunate. After a fortnight, he was caught by the Lenguas, and in an unusual gesture, they decided to kill him. He was given an opiate and clubbed to death.

The spiritual conquest of the Lenguas was a daunting task never completed. Unlike the Guaraní, their beliefs wouldn't easily interbreed with Christianity. Theirs was a terrifying world, created by a beetle. There was no god—only vampires, spirits, holy dogs and magic. Man had four souls, and in death, the fourth—his evil *jangaoc*—could only be liberated by burning his shelter and his animals. The corpse's bones were then smashed up, to prevent him walking as a ghost.

Grubb never fully recovered from his wounds but declared it his duty to rescue the Indian from the torture of magic. Others joined him in this blistering effort and suffered: Hunt was "covered with boils from head to foot," Major Rapin of the Swiss Army died of malaria and William the Cook drowned crossing the Paraguay. Like the Jesuits, they recognised the need for settlement and sustenance. They taught the Indians horticulture and ranching and built mission stations, the most enduring at Makthlawaiya. Photographs of this time depict a life of uncomplicated pleasure: capybara hunts; the brick church; the chief wearing deerskins and a silk top hat.

In 1921, Grubb retreated home to Edinburgh. The cold killed Mary, but Grubb survived another nine years, keeping goats and digging coal from his own little seam. His party trick was to get one foot up on to the mantelpiece, and at the age of sixty-four he took up driving lessons. He achieved 40mph on the Biggar Road, which was considered a good speed for a man who'd been attacked by Redskins. He died the following year, surrounded by his pelts and magic charms.

Response to the Missions' work has always been mixed. To the Paraguayans, Grubb was *el Pacificador de los Indios*. To his fellow-countrymen, he was "the Livingstone of South America," though his fame was surprisingly transient. However, to a contemporary German traveller, Hans Tolten, the missionaries lived a "Robinson Crusoe existence, as if on some wild forgotten island" (he himself preferred to conduct relations with the Sanapanás at a more sexual level). Others objected to evangelism in any form. This is the line Burton would have taken. To him, shamanism, like slavery and cannibalism, "had its uses": it was the first step from savagery; it created a "comparatively learned class"; it taught the art of governing. Christians, he thought, tended to regard it "with childish and unreasonable horror."

In the end, the Burtonian view prevailed. The missions survived until the 1990s and the arrival of social science. Perhaps they'd served their purpose, providing the Lenguas with a glimpse of their inevitable fate: of property, ownership, law, fencing and retribution. The next glimpses would be much harder, without top hats and vicarage teas. Anthropologists declared Makthlawaiya to be a relic and it was abandoned. The missionaries and doctors were dispersed.

Just one had stayed on, resisting witch-doctors and anthropology.

"She lives on the Trans-Chaco," people told me. "Just ask the bus driver to drop you at the English nurse."

Her name was Beryl Baker.

110

Two hours up the highway, the carandays began to thin, leaving only the winter swamplands. The persistence of nothingness was bewildering. After a while, it was hard to recall any other world but this: the blue, the indefinite grasses and the desolate punctuation of thorns. No wonder that the Lengua believed that a dead man's spirit wandered this earth for ever; there was nowhere else, no hiding, no shadow. A man could stand here and see everything there had ever been and ever would be: watery nothing in winter, dusty nothing in summer. I imagined that it made him a little mad, a king of infinite space.

After four hours, the bus shuddered and stopped.

"The English nurse!" announced the driver. He pointed at a brittle nest of aromitá and yuqueri. Beyond it, there was a small lagoon speckled with ibis and storks. In a moment of enchantment, I got off the bus and let it crash away into the void.

There were huts among the trees. In the first, there was a small dispensary, a living room and a washhouse. The sink was piled with ten dog-bowls and a Union Jack teacup.

"Miss Baker is out," said the girl sweeping the porch, "visiting the Indians."

Though no one was expecting me, visitors are rare and valuable in the Chaco. She took me to her father, the *estancia* foreman, Miguel. He was a big, leathery man in pantaloons and home-made boots. He had his own chameleon and a weakness for alligators. We drank a few horns of bitter *tereré* and stood on the edge of the lagoon, watching them thrash and squabble.

"This *estancia* belongs to a very good man," said Miguel. "He lets Miss Baker keep her clinic here. He is from Texas (near the United States) but now he lives in Asunción. His name is Rhett Butler, which always makes foreign people laugh. I am not sure why."

We walked back through the huts. A baby was asleep in a hammock.

"All my men are Sanapanás," said the *capataz*.

"No Lenguas?"

He shook his head. "You can't have both. They won't work together. They have different ways. Some won't eat eggs, others believe their dogs are holy. The Lengua thinks he's superior."

Suddenly, there was noise up by the gate: engines, barking dogs, thundering horses and a wild pig whistling round in a deep, tight groove. A blaze of sparkling birds hurried to the scene.

"Miss Baker returns," said Miguel.

She was smaller than I'd envisaged. I knew that her work covered hundreds of square miles and I'd made her much larger; she was light and fragile, like a bird. I'd also expected someone shot with colour and acerbity; she was calm and pale. She wore a print dress and rubber shoes and had a crest of ashy hair. She was nearly sixty and had been in the Chaco almost half her life.

"You're from London? So was I." There was still a trace of an accent. "How about a pot of tea? Peppermint or ordinary?"

She busied herself with ordinary. The house was being eaten by termites and had sagged to one side. She hopped nimbly across the slopes, put the kettle on and washed her syringes. Her animals were now sounding a crescendo of demands. She sent a shovel of birdseed out among the cardinals and mashed some offal for the dogs.

"They all sleep in here at night, to keep me warm. There was a puppy," she said absently, "but the rattlesnakes killed it."

She made some toast and listened to the radio messages, first in Spanish, then Lengua and Sanapaná. ("Ramón Gonzáles, your tyres are ready"; "Sepe of Zalazar South, your mother has tuberculosis . . ."). She then warmed the teapot and sent me off to feed Ping, the wild pig.

Ping was a white-collared peccary that Miguel had rescued from the Indians. Despite all my potato peelings, our friendship didn't flourish. Every time he saw me, his bristles swelled up and the air was suddenly gassy with concentrated jockstrap and vomit. As I fled, retching, he whistled in triumph.

Beryl had laid the table. "I hope you'll stay. The tractor driver's hut is free."

I thanked her. "As long as it's not with Ping."

We sat down to tea and a large brown head appeared at the window and whinnied.

"This is Eldorado. I'll tell you about him. He once saved my life."

When they closed Makthlawaiya, I brought Eldorado with me. There was no other way to visit patients. I rode everywhere.

I got my first job working in a government place, down the road in Pozo Colorado. It meant working for Stroessner, but what choice did I have? Pozo is a trucking stop and pretty rough. The so-called doctor ran the clinic as a brothel, and eventually, he just disappeared. After that, I ran a clinic in the middle of nowhere—by myself. It was very dangerous. The nearest house was five kilometres away and all I had was my horse.

Then, one Saturday night, some men came up from Pozo in a jeep. They were very drunk and were stripped down and very excited. "Let us in!" they shouted. "We're sick." I told them that the clinic was closed. "Come back in the morning," I said. They started to throw themselves at the door, to get me (I was younger then . . .). I must have screamed.

Then I heard Eldorado, somewhere in the darkness. He was stamping and snorting and I could hear him charging towards us. Suddenly, he appeared, rearing and bucking. He grabbed one of the men by the ear and flung him to the ground. They were terrified. I could hear them screaming, "It's a beast! A beast!" They ran for their jeep with Eldorado kicking and biting at them. He chased them all the way down the road. I never saw them again.

The Chaco is a dangerous place. Drifters end up here. And criminals. Eldorado makes me feel safer. Although I don't ride much any more, Eldorado is always around. He can sense danger. If someone starts to raise their voice at me, Eldorado pushes between us and shoves them out of the way.

He knows when I'm afraid.

III

The next day, the Lenguas came to the dispensary. Some had walked all night and were hunched under the trees, chalky and exhausted. Their clothes were cheap and their faces blank and taut, as if the skin had been stretched too tight. No one spoke. The children were just weeping miniatures of their parents. For 18,000 Indians in the eastern Chaco, Nurse Baker offered the only prospect of medical treatment.

All morning, the dispensary rattled with tuberculosis.

"I could cure the TB," said Beryl, "but they go to the *wiski* first. He takes their money and sucks the evil spirits out. Six months later, they come to me with a chronic condition."

She was prising cattle ticks off her arms.

"But when the *wiski* is ill," she went on, "he comes to me. And he can pay!"

"So things are back to where they were?"

"Yes," she said, "I suppose they are. The *wiskis* are very powerful. They have all sorts of tricks—drinking snake venom and finding money in people's ears. But it's not just conjuring; it's vocational. It's also terrifying. To be cursed by the *wiski* is to die. I have seen Lenguas simply curl up in their blankets and will themselves to death. It takes surprisingly little time."

That afternoon, Beryl took the children back to their *tolderías* in the Land-Rover. They were overwhelmed by the experience and fouled the seats.

"I have to be everything," she said. "Nurse, orderly, gynaecologist, midwife, dentist (I'm good at pulling teeth). I see a lot of gunshot wounds and stabbing. And cancer. There are hard decisions to be made every day."

"I don't suppose the money grows on trees."

"Dear Rhett does what he can. The British Embassy bought me the Land-Rover. A church in England pays for the petrol. It's always a struggle."

I asked Beryl if she was angry at what had happened. She thought about this.

"Yes," she admitted, "I am. What did the anthropologists think would happen? They were here for no time. They stayed in the *tolderías* and made themselves ill and then they went back home. Did they think the Lengua was a Noble Savage best left to his own devices? This is not a museum. These people are entitled to progress. Did they think the Chaco could be happy hunting grounds again? It's impossible; like turning ham back into pigs. Anyway, Lenguas want radios and motorbikes. There is no going back. Yes, I am angry. In their 'kindness,' they've trapped the Indians between two worlds. They're condemned to a life of witchcraft and manipulation."

On my last afternoon, Beryl told me a story that gave me little hope for her and even less for the Indians.

Three weeks before, the Indians brought her a badly wounded man. He was a good man, a Paraguayan who'd often helped them. He'd also witnessed two thugs from Concepción stealing cattle. They attacked him with knives at a wedding. It was a professional job; the blades sliced through his liver, kidneys, intestines and lungs. There was nothing that could be done for him. They set off for the Mennonite Hospital but he died a few miles up the highway.

What happened to the killers?

They were arrested and released the next day. The police won't touch them. The Indians are frightened and give them money and food. Sometimes the thugs come round here, asking for work. Rhett says he'll put a bullet in them if he has to. Miguel's got a rifle and so has the tractor driver. We don't know what will happen.

As to the Indians, it seems that now they're on their own.

112

I continued up the highway into the Kolonie Menno.

On the map, it was a large white rectangle lightly freckled in the north. I had a friend in Asunción who was born up here. "Go and see my parents," she said. "Just ask for Heinrich and Maria Braun. I'll tell them you're coming."

The Brauns lived in a clapperboard cabin on the edge of Loma Plata. It was a small town with a streak of red sand running through the middle. The townsfolk had yellow hair and dungarees and lived to a simple code: *Tod, Not und Brot* ("Death, Need and Bread"). There were three churches and a *Bibelschule* but no bar, no cinema and no restaurant. It was as if the Wild West had been won by German Anabaptists, which in a sense it had: this was the heart of the peculiar state-within-a-state, the theocracy of the Mennonites. Here, Paraguay was momentarily on hold: no tax, no national service, no *colorados*, no whisky. A million hectares of land fell under this Mennonite *privilegium*, divided into three colonies: Menno, Fernheim and Neuland.

The colonies, and Menno in particular, did not encourage frivolity. Abstention was administered by pastors and *Oberschulzes* and there was a police force of beefy pink puritans called the *Ordnungsmänner*. Their beliefs forbade them guns, but after careful debate, they'd agreed to flashing red lights on their cars. Loma Plata fell silent at dusk and there was never dancing. If the Jesuits had created the perpetual Sunday, Menno had refined it to Sunday Evening without End.

The Brauns welcomed me with pickles, cold chicken and guava tart.

They were like grandparents from a children's story. Their cabin was surrounded by tamarind trees and bedded in sand. There was always an Indian asleep in a deckchair on their porch. They even had a dog with its head on upside-down and an earth closet and a cage full of parrots. There were canvas shutters on the windows, and when sand-storms blew, they buttoned themselves in and made rag carpets.

I adored them, but I wasn't sure what the Brauns made of me. They saw my little camera and thought I was filming them for television (which they didn't have). Heinrich had lost all his teeth on one side and so looking askance had become anatomical. He was small and crumbly and his hair was tufted into a soft white question-mark. He could speak a German version of Canadian but he couldn't understand my English and usually answered the questions I should have asked.

"Where was your farm, Heinrich?"

"The porridge was from Canada. We've eaten it every day for seventy-seven years."

There was more of Maria but she wasn't able to understand me at all. She'd had thirteen children and was well known for her Mennonite cooking. She spoke only the language of the colonies, *Plattdeutsch*, but said all she wanted to in soups and fruit pies. A knobbly tract was nailed over her sink: *Ich aber und mein Haus wollen dem Herrn dienen*. At dawn, I could hear her rustling barefoot to the kitchen, muttering prayers and recipes in the dialect of eighteenth-century Danzig.

The Brauns lived mostly in a large hallway, next to a wood-stove. They kept their knives and forks in old jam tins and the doors were trimmed with frilly pelmets that they called "gardines." There was no other decoration, just things children had brought them, reminders of their farm; an armadillo shell; an oven-bird's nest; a wool-comber. In my room, there was a large ochre trunk where the family linen was stored. It had giant brass hinges and was lined with prayers and old labels peeled from salmon tins.

Menno was the oldest of the *Kolonies* and the Brauns had been there since the start. Their story is written in the footnotes of the Mennonites' endless wanderings.

113

Jacob Braun was only a child when, in 1789, his father decided to hitch up the horses and leave the Mennonite heartlands for ever. Danzig had turned against them since the imposition of Prussian rule. Lutherans spat on them in the streets and broke up their assemblies. New taxes were bringing the farm to its knees, and even if they'd managed to save, they weren't allowed to buy more land. When the Russian tsar offered them plots in the Black Sea basin, the Mennonites accepted and with them went Jacob's family.

The Mennonites called their time in the Ukraine "a golden era," which was a sure sign of trouble to come. They built bible schools and *Strassendörfs*, villages with streets as long and wide as the Champs-Elysées. The Brauns had farms on the lush black shores of the Chortiza and grew wheat and maize and beets as big as your head. Jacob married and had a son, also Jacob. They learnt the ways of the steppes and hung gardines around the doors. They made soup with beetroot and sour cream, and on special days there were fruit pies and baked *pirozhnyes*, stuffed with meat and spice. The Brauns seemed happy, as if it had always been that way.

Then, in 1861, the wind changed. The serfs were freed and the air was chilly with Pan-Slavic nationalism. Mennonites were no longer welcome. Then the Brauns ran into fresh disaster: Jacob the Younger had died in 1863, leaving a son, Abram, aged four. These were bitter winters for the foundling and the resentment never left him. His chance to escape came in 1873, when Tsar Alexander II threatened to draft the Anabaptists into his army. Pacifism and the abhorrence of all violence went to the heart of Mennonite beliefs. At the age of fifteen, Abram ordered the family's belongings into the great ochre trunk and they joined the exodus for North America.

The journey should have earned Abram a promised land: Hamburg, Grimsby (where they were confined as "pestilent"), Liverpool, shipwrecked off Quebec City, Dakota and—finally—Altona, Manitoba. For a while, the Brauns were satisfied. The trunk was unpacked at Eigengrund and, with their neighbours, they rebuilt the steppes on the prairies. Then the Great War came and the Mennonites were first accused of being German and then conscripted into the Canadian army. Some went, like Klippenstein, Heinrich's uncle (who survived with shrapnel wounds and an English wife and lived out his days as a ticket-collector on British Railways). Others, like the Brauns, dug their heels in. They refused to study English (though some spoke it) and refused to raise the Union Jack in their schools. Abram died, refusing everything, at the end of the war. It would be left to his son, Hein, to load up the ochre trunk and move the Brauns on.

Three years later, the Mennonite elders announced that they'd found the ideal place: Paraguay. They'd negotiated the *privilegium* and had bought 138,000 acres of land at $5 an acre, with more to come. It was to be a home for 60,000 Mennonites. In the meantime, 1,765 volunteers would do. Among them, of course, was Hein, with the trunk, his wife and his first five children (there were another ten to come).

"I remember very clearly the day we left Altona," Heinrich told me. "April the thirteenth, 1927. I was four and a half."

A beautiful spring day turned into a murderous summer. The immigrants arrived in stinking Puerto Casado in temperatures of 110 degrees and were held up for a year. In their photographs, the Braun children are dressed in pinafores and straw bonnets, but typhus was soon among them. Johann died in the second month, and a new baby, Abram, died within a day of life. In all, nearly 168 perished and 335 said that enough was enough and went home.

When the survivors were allowed to move inland to Menno, most were unable to choke their disappointment. The Brauns settled at Schöntal—or "Nice Valley"—a wistful name for a place without contours. Hills were not all that was missing; nearly all the wells were salty, the grass was too bitter for cattle and there was no stone for building. There were no doctors and the only cure for snake-bites was a poultice of gunpowder which was then ignited. Mrs. Derksen performed the colony's first amputation without any previous experience and on a leg ravaged by jiggers. When the north wind blew, the new arrivals were lashed with scalding sand.

"My father didn't say much," said Heinrich. "We got down to work."

Strassendörfs were once again strung out across the plains. The thorns were hacked back for buffel grass and an ox-track was carved through to the *trencito* stop, eight days away (the Trans-Chaco Highway didn't come until 1961). Hein Braun and his children planted oranges, guavas and lemons and all seemed well until 8 November 1936, when locusts ate everything and they had to start again.

"*Tod, Not und Brot*," said Hein and little else.

The girls wore aprons and scarves and the boys went barefoot. In a snapshot from this time, the Braun children are skinning a pig. On Sundays, they went to the *Komitee* house and sung hymns under the huge, spiky words GEMEINNUTZ VOR EIGENNUTZ ("The common good above self-interest"). They learnt arithmetic and the catechism at school and then left. The girls were forbidden to cut their hair and were married off at sixteen. Hein made them wear black on their wedding days.

A picture of Hein has also survived. The experience of photography obviously displeased him and he is buttoned up and dark. His wife died in 1966, and the next year he made his first trip back to Canada. For a man who believed that neckties and moustaches were the outward signs of human weakness, it was an even more remarkable journey than the one he'd made forty years before. As usual, he said nothing, but those who knew him realised that, despite all, he was satisfied with the path he'd taken. He died in the old people's home in Loma Plata in 1980, and the trunk passed to Heinrich.

114

I'd arrived in the Mennonite colonies with two preconceptions. The first (from the writer Richard Gott), that Mennonites were "fearsome religious maniacs with limitless funds," never really caught the breeze. The second, that they had appalling table manners, found full and colourful expression at the table of Heinrich Braun.

It was only when he was slurping up his *borsch* that I realised that Heinrich did have a dental plate after all. Having until then been conspicuously ineffective, it now started thrashing around, mulching up gherkins, chicken *pirozhnyes* and fruit pies, sometimes in and sometimes out. To work effectively, everything had to be soggy, and so it was shovelled into milky tea, mashed up and then scooped into the thrasher. Heinrich lingered over these rituals, prolonging them with lavish belches and lots of spitting on the floor. When the worst was over, he polished his dental plate in tea, planted his elbows in the chaos and burped.

"Let's go to Osterwick and see my old farm!" he said after the third ransacked lunch.

I hadn't noticed Heinrich's car before. It was a tiny Toyota Starlet, slipped in among the parrots. Heinrich, however, was suspicious of its intentions and never took it up beyond second gear. He'd also filled it with cushions so that my face was now crushed up against the ceiling. My first view of the Mennonite farmlands would be rather squashed, like Alice's view of Wonderland after too many *"Eat Me's."* We bunny-hopped out of Loma Plata, very sedately and at the head of a long and angry caravan of tractors.

It was a sad journey in many ways. For me, because I would soon be leaving these warm, essential people with their peculiar Ukrainian ways. For Heinrich, because he caught a glimpse of his past and saw it crumbling away. Despite all the snakes and smallpox and heat, he couldn't remember a time that wasn't happy, and in his mind, every detail was still fresh and brilliant. Osterwick meanwhile had faded.

We arrived in the late afternoon, when the grass was yellow and sleepy. The *borachos* were in bloom and the air was warm and fluffy with their down. A tractor was ticking along the great sandy drift that stretched through the village, gathering milk-churns. Most of the little farms were abandoned now, their orchards and white picket-fences feathered in weeds; their land engulfed by the *Kooperativs*. Heinrich stared at the debris of his farm in disbelief.

"I had sixty acres of cotton and we picked it all by hand!"

We walked through the old yard. It had been home until 1984, a two-room mud-brick farmhouse with earth floors and a shed for the thirteen children. There were always rattlesnakes under this tree, said Heinrich, and this was the first cistern in Osterwick. The rainwater trap had now almost collapsed and the shutters were unbuckling themselves from the house. Funk, recalled Heinrich, was a useless builder.

Proximity to his old earth triggered other recollections. Heinrich remembered the first appearance of the Lenguas in 1929, wearing deer-skins and bringing melons and meat for the hungry Mennonites. He remembered how the Chulupís arrived soon afterwards, threatening the Lenguas and their *Lencos*—their "whites"—with war. Then war itself came in 1932 with bi-planes and roads "green with soldiers marching." The pacifists now found themselves crushed between two desperate armies.

"We gave the Paraguayans eggs and bread. Occasionally, they stole from us."

Surprisingly, only one Mennonite died. Abram Giesbrecht was shot by a trooper whose reasoning had been splintered by gunfire. The army hunted the soldier through the *montes* and executed him.

"Poor Giesbrecht," said Heinrich, with startling, involuntary clarity. "The bullet entered his shoulder and burst out of his face."

115

Osterwick has provided us with a riddle.

In 1975, Heinrich's neighbour, Siemens, was digging his plot when a thick coin flopped out of the soil. It depicted Maximilian I in the year of his election as Holy Roman Emperor and was dated 1493. It wasn't a valuable coin; a copper "hollow penny," embossed on one side, indented on the other. Nor was Siemens' coin the only one; two more *Hohlpfennigs* would be unearthed in different parts of the colonies. Eventually, they all found their way to the Filadelfia Museum, where they now sit on tussocks of cotton wool.

Here's the puzzle. How did these coins, minted in Augsberg five years before the discovery of South America, find themselves here, over four hundred kilometres into this desert? Even Asunción, which would become the nearest civilisation, was still nearly forty years off. Perhaps it was a hoax. But by who? The Mennonites held their land by contract and had no wish to advance a fanciful German "inheritance" claim.

Perhaps the Indians brought them here, the fruits of trade or plunder? This still didn't explain the fact that they were German. Why had no Spanish coins been found?

There's no obvious answer, but in the annals of Maximilian's family there's a trail of clues. The Emperor's son, Philip, married Juana the Insane of Madrid, uniting the courts of the Habsburgs and Spain in a formidable alliance. They produced a son, Charles V, whose adventures included the launch of Cortés and Pizarro. In 1536, he dispatched the massive River Plate expeditionary force, and among the ships was a company of his old countrymen, eighty *Landsknecht*s from Nuremberg. Some of these squires, it seems, had embarked with pocketfuls of old *Hohlpfennig*s.

After the foundation of Asunción, the path becomes less clear. Some of the Germans stayed on. Ulrich Schmidel of Straubing was one of those who joined Irala's last attempt to punch through the Chaco to Peru, and he provides us with energetic accounts of the ambushes and slaughter. Perhaps the pennies were lost on these Spanish routs.

Or perhaps the *Landsknecht*s had launched excursions of their own? It is an intriguing thought: German conquistadors stumbling towards Osterwick and an imponderable fate.

116

I left Menno and went to the Fernheim colony and its main town, Brotherly Love, or Filadelfia.

Despite its cuddly name, Filadelfia was an unloved crust of a place, torn into strips by avenues: Unruh, Hindenburg and Industry. It was much as I imagined North Dakota towns had been before the arrival of asphalt and welfare: a wooden church, porches of tin, trucks ploughing the sand. The dust was like gas, bitter and excoriating, and was every-where: in food, folded into plaid, tattooed into boots, creased into raw yellow faces. By noon, the *Hauptstrasse* was a long, wide welt of hot vapours, great feathers of dirt fretting up and down, mad for air. The Indians, always hovering for work, now hunched in thorny shade.

I soon realised that the colony was more than unloved, it was a source of perpetual reproach. Even in the name Fernheim—or "Distant Home"—there was the constant reminder that "home" was merely rela-tive and that it wasn't here. The Fernheimers were unable to understand the contentment of the Menno colonists and accused them of simplicity and a *lange Leitung,* a circuitous wiring system. They said that, over in Menno, they were just *Strooheed* or "strawhatters" (and, for their airs and sophistication, they themselves were the *Schiltmetze,* or "visorcap-pers"). Even now, the *Oberschulzes* were forced to admit that, given the choice, every Fernheimer would up sticks tomorrow and head off for Canada or, better still, Germany. They'd never wanted Filadelfia and had never loved it.

I tried to find someone who could remember why they'd ever come here. I was taken to Cornelius Neufeld, water-diviner and slaughterman at the abattoir. Although he was in his seventies, his face was full and red, like a parcel of knuckle and brisket, and every day he unzipped and dismantled a dozen cows. I watched as his Chulupís worked around him, impressive in all their blood and knives and growling at each other in *Plattdeutsch.*

A cold pink hand steered me through slaughter soup and cartridge cases to the office. Cornelius' white rubber aprons squeaked as he packed himself into a chair.

"I left the Ukraine seventy-one years ago . . ." he began. His Spanish, like his meat, had been jointed and filleted. It was easy to follow.

It seems the Brauns had been right to leave Russia when they did. For the 100,000 that remained, the screw tightened. The Bolshevik Revolu-tion of March 1917 brought the threat of collectivisation. The Kerensky regime was briefly sympathetic to Mennonites, but by October 1917, that too was swept away. From then on, the Mennonites were kulaks and the killing began. Some of the villages organised *Bürgerwächter,* or self-defence, but their departure from scripture only opened wounds that have festered ever since. It also brought revenge. In the early days, a few found escape routes, but when collectivisation caught on, these bridges were burnt.

"I was born in August 1929," said Cornelius. "Two months later my parents took me to Moscow."

Thirteen thousand families undertook the same quest, to plead for deportation. All that winter, the Mennonites camped outside Moscow, tormented by the ice and secret police. Some died; most were herded back to the Ukraine. Only four thousand were given exit visas, including the Neufelds. They were moved to Leningrad and then by ship to Kiel. But despite the efforts of President Hindenburg, there was no home for them in Germany and they were forced on. There was only one place they could go.

Six months later, the Neufelds were riding the *trencito* to the end of the line. It moved so slowly that the children ran alongside. It then took several more weeks to get to their allotted land, "Fernheim," where the naked Lenguas built them homes from mud and sticks.

"The Indians called me Big Watermelon," recalled Cornelius, his laughter crashing away through the slaughterhouse.

Then came the *grosse Sterben*, the "Big Death," a typhus epidemic that killed ninety-seven of them. At last the Anabaptists found a use for the pot-bellied *boracho* trees: as coffins.

"That's how we came to Paraguay," finished Cornelius. "We had no choice."

As the Fernheimers had never abandoned the hope that their town was only temporary, it had an artless, transitory feel, like a vast dressing-station in a long war. There were two colours, brown and clay, and no gardens. Some of the outlying hamlets didn't even have names, just numbers like "Village Number Eight" or "Freedom Field Five." The town's lumpy aspirations were carved into the town cross: *Arbeit, Eintracht, Glaube!* Work, Unity, Faith! Anywhere else, this might have sounded like hubris. In a town where everyone wanted to be elsewhere, it smacked of desperation.

"The Nazis promised to get people home," recalled Cornelius. "My father led the resistance." In June 1944, the two factions fought an unedifying punch-up under the town cross. Order was only restored two days before the Normandy landings, with the arrival of the Paraguayan army.

The Nazis were expelled to Nueva Germania, and with them went the last hopes of an exodus.

Against all its inclinations, Filadelfia had put down roots and institutions.

The Mennonite Hospital was the best outside Asunción, even though it was only wood and tin. A museum preserved all the hopes of the early settlers, their roubles and felt boots and Red Army hats. There was a library and a church hall, where weddings were celebrated, soberly, in coffee and pickles. There were bleak huts for the *Gemeindekomitee*—the council of elders—and tax machinery to punish the childless and indulge the fruitful. A radio station scattered announcements through the *montes*: prayer meetings, petrol pump times or the minutely prosaic.

"Mr. Duerkson has lost his watch on the road to Number Five . . ."

Of all their institutions, the one most eloquent of the Fernheimers' beliefs was their sparkling supermarket. It was a co-operative, expressing not socialism but a community of capitalists: a man is valued by his efforts on Earth (although he must never excel, for that's ostentation). It exemplified the rejection of the State; Mennonites could pay in scrip, not money. As in heaven, they could store up credit (although if they fell in debt it caused the till-alarms to ring).

But the guiding hand of the *Gemeindekomitee* was at its most insistent in the choice of merchandise. Alcohol was strictly forbidden. So too were any toys that offended pacifism: guns, Action Men, police cars, rockets, spacemen and even dinosaurs. Childhood was distinguishable from adolescence only by smaller seed-drills and bulldozers. Shelves were piled high with sobriety and godliness. There were pyramids of Bibles and barbed wire, bolts of canvas, spades, hymns on CD, charcoal irons, biblical tracts and dungarees. Other stuff was more marginal and I wandered the aisles pondering the theological debates that had raged over each new product. Who'd let "Froot Loops" in? And Barbie's Garden Party set? When I found "007" aftershave, I began to wonder how long it could all last.

I walked on, to the edge of town.

Out there was another *Krankenhaus*, for lunatics and alcoholics. The grounds were patrolled by tapirs captured in the wilds. They were pink and hairy and curiously officious, a *Komitee* of buttocks.

117

Bobby and Eva Frick were Swabians and had been on the run from reality ever since abandoning their various marriages. They'd had an apple farm in Australia and had lived in a cabin on an ice-field in Alaska. Jack London was their inspiration. In 1984, they'd seen an advertisement in a German newspaper: *"Settlers wanted, Fernheim, Paraguay."* They arrived three months later, shot all their neighbours' dogs and waited to see where fortune's currents would carry them next.

I stayed with them for much of my time in the colony, at Village Number Three.

Bobby was pleased that I was there because I might have an affair with Eva and then he could kill me. It wasn't that he disliked me (he was less sure about Eva), he simply wanted to make a magnificent gesture. He was a powerfully built man covered in reddish bristles and scars gouged out by motorbikes and wild animals. He made a living as a plumber to the Mennonites and yet somehow the opportunities for expansive gestures kept eluding him. Most of this he blamed on the CIA. A loaded shotgun and Winchester Repeater always hung over the mantelpiece, in case things changed.

Eva's world was less straightforward. A large quantity of seventies clothing had survived her wanderings, and she changed several times a day, as if she were several simultaneously disenchanted teenagers. She was angular and lean but more hungry than alluring. She kept four hundred cattle and visited them in heels and lip-gloss. No wonder Bobby suspected her itinerary, but Eva was simply living in her parallel world. Despite the long search for wilderness, she'd yet to admit that she was just lonely. I imagined that that was why she took in lodgers.

"Fifty dollars a day," she said but by the end of the week it was free.

The Fricks' cabin was set in a deep tuft of *quebracho* trees and yellow blossom. I was surprised by how much I liked it and spent hours sitting on the veranda, book-ended by two giant dogs. I was vaguely aware of four children who came scavenging at mealtimes and who regarded their parents with deep scepticism. Most of the time they were out in the thorns, hunting parrots and ripping up the cactus with a tractor. There was virtually no water and the lavatory was only flushed three times a week. In the evenings, the family took long hikes into the *montes*, armed with crossbows.

Once I'd established the outer limits of the Fricks' eccentricity, I became strangely fond of them. Every night we sat up drinking, first rum and then cartons of blackcurrant pig-wash. The first casualty was usually my command of English, but the Fricks babbled on. Sometimes I could even sense them talking to each other, using me as a sort of inert conduit of communication. At other times, Bobby's stories of grizzly bears were so violent that they broke the chairs.

By then, I was having problems of my own. My jaw was now flapping around uselessly and hot, pyroclastic flows of alcohol and sauerkraut were billowing up from within. I gathered myself just enough to discover that the Fricks had found a common enemy.

"The Mennonites are bastards . . ."

"*Shlursh . . . ?*"

". . . they don't let us buy land, they charge us higher rates of interest . . ."

". . . they're ignorant. Never been beyond Asunción . . ."

"*Thatsh shrurely . . .*" It was hopeless. Acute pig-washing had robbed me of forensic skills. The Fricks were now unstoppable.

"They breed like cats . . ."

". . . *inter* breed . . ."

"They drink . . ."

"And fuck the Indians . . ."

"Hypocrites."

"Cranks."

By the morning, Eva had either mollified or thought of fresh lines of contempt.

" . . . and I had the *first* pair of high heels in Filadelfia!"

I often accompanied her to the co-operative to buy provisions. She wore jeans and white stilettos and the Mennonites and their baggy wives regarded her with unrestrained fascination.

"I have a bit of a reputation," said Eva needlessly.

I shrank away, terrified that, in the gossip that trickled through Filadelfia's plumbing, Bobby would be a cuckold and I would be a lover—and a target.

I felt happier when we went out to Eva's *estancia*, way off in the hinterlands. The foreman was an old Paraguayan, who wore pin-stripe trousers and lived in a wooden crate. He seemed to survive on rum and sugar and shot armadillos with his catapult.

"Come in," he cooed. "My wife's overslept."

In fact she was long dead and the foreman was enjoying a joke. But he wasn't pleased to see me. Eva was the only human being left in his world and he liked to have her all to himself. Instead, she made him get the horses. They had blood pouring down their necks and I must have winced.

"*Vampiros*," grinned the foreman. Bats.

We rode out into a furnace of violet blossom and needles. The armoured trees closed in around us and their cusps tore at my skin. In time, the rips would become raw and infected. Meanwhile, Eva had more unnerving news.

"I lost four calves in here. Killed by the pumas."

For the next hour, I was deeply troubled by the loss of little snags of meat but comforted by the thought that it could be worse. Then the vicious forest parted and we were before a long, wooden cabin.

"This used to be our home."

There were still skulls and snow-shoes nailed up on the veranda and books in the shelves, drifted in cobwebs. The sink was full of dirty dishes. A loyal fridge still hummed.

"What *happened*?" I asked.

"Bobby brought his mistress back here. I could never come back."

Once again, the Fricks had simply jumped out of their lives.

Eva drove back to Number Three in silence. I made foolish attempts at jollity.

"He beats me," she said softly. "With a club."

There was a pause.

"I've been to the *Ordnungsmänner*. Can you imagine telling those shit-heads that your husband is beating you? They look at me as though I am a witch."

118

The relationship between the Indians and the Mennonites was more complicated than the blackcurrant blasts had suggested.

"When we arrived," Heinrich had said, "we were very surprised to find Indians on the land."

The Lenguas were no less surprised. Who were these very old people? Hard work seemed to have turned them completely white. They had faces like pineapples and voices loud enough to scare off a man's "innermost." But they were also gentle and had music and molasses. The nomadic Lenguas halted.

For the Mennonites this created a dilemma. They'd sought isolation and now found themselves beginning again among the most primitive people on Earth. The irony of fleeing persecution only to become invaders hadn't escaped them. But what were they to do? There was little guidance in the scriptures: they were not to exploit or evangelise. On the other hand, doing nothing wasn't an option. All around them were starving, naked wretches, drowning babies in sand and eating poison frogs. The Mennonites' instinctive reaction was to employ them.

Initially, the results were satisfying. Infanticide was abandoned (except for runts, twins and deformities) and the Lenguas took to clothes. Then the numbers proliferated and the Chulupís marched up from the Pilcomayo, demanding their share of the providence. In seventy years, the indigenous population rose to 25,000, twenty-five times what it had been in 1926. Suddenly, Filadelfia had its own vast, helpless *Lumpenproletariat* packed ten-to-a-shack in the so-called labour camps.

Eva enjoyed driving me out to these places. It was the only time that she felt self-righteous.

"Black Filadelfia," she announced.

Lives lay in components: sticks, cardboard, plastic, dust, turds, rags, bones. Nothing was attached or possessed. Things just fluttered in the grit. There weren't even paths between the tribes: Chulupí, Lengua, Toba, Sanapaná. Each one had its own grit and refused to cross into another's. The only language they had in common was *Plattdeutsch*.

One tribe refused to settle at all: the Ayoreo. The others said they were scalp-hunters and lived only in the thorns. Before the *Lencos* came, there had been a war, lasting thirty years. The Ayoreos hadn't been forgiven for their savagery. They hate us and we hate them. They even attacked some *Lencos* and killed them with their clubs. That was ten years ago but the *Lencos* still watched it on their videos.

One day, a farmer pulled up outside the hospital with a truck of Ayoreos. He was a giant in giant tractor-boots and overalls. I've brought them for their vaccinations, he said.

"Is it true," Eva asked him, "what the other tribes say?"

The Mennonite looked over his charges thoughtfully. They had bright nutmeg skin and glossy black hair like horse-tail. They gurgled up at him, tiny teeth in thick purple gums.

"They're very emotional," he said. "Yes, traditionally their first response was always to kill. That's how they've survived."

The Chaco War provided the occasion for a revised approach to the Indians.

Both sides had regarded *indigenas* as spies and had them machine-gunned like pigs. The Lenguas were almost exterminated and those that survived scattered deep into the needles. After the ceasefire, a teacher called G. B. Giesbrecht went off in search of them. He found them out at Armadillo Pond—or Salve Yange. From now on, he insisted, the Indians would no longer be vagrants and scavengers but would themselves be farmers. He began to organise the purchase of land and a new initiative: settlement.

After his death, his work was continued by his son. Helmut Giesbrecht had silver temples and a gold filling but his office was painted Filadelfia sludge. He agreed to take me to the settlements, but as he spoke only *Plattdeutsch* and dialects, I persuaded Eva to come as translator. She wore slingbacks and something small and mauve.

A long road lanced into the haze.

We stopped at the farm of a small, shrivelled Lengua called Lorenzo Brillante. His tribal name was "One Boy" because his mother had smothered all his siblings. He remembered the Ayoreo war: they took away babies on their spears, as if they were going to roast them. He was a hunter before he came here. Now he had two hectares of beans, a hut, three chairs and a wife.

"He didn't burn the house down when his father died. These days, they paint the door a different colour. That's enough to confuse the ghosts."

Even though Helmut Giesbrecht was filtered through Eva, I recognised commitment and perseverance. He knew his work could never be finished. Sometimes it couldn't even be understood.

"The Lengua must never show emotion. Whatever he wants is a secret."

"Do they get divorced?" enquired Eva.

"They separate. The children go to the grandparents."

"Sounds good," she muttered, in English.

"Nicht gut," corrected Helmut, *"aber natürlich."*

The distinction between what was good and what was natural had persisted at Armadillo Pond. It was like a preliminary sketch of Filadelfia except that the blossom was yellow, not khaki, and grapefruits grew in the street. There was a Lengua supermarket and a Chulupí school. The British Embassy had donated a college to teach girls ironing and showering and the other advances of the last ten thousand years. The nurses at the *Krankenhaus* were crisply starched Lenguas.

"Did they train in Asunción?" we asked.

"No," said Helmut, "here. If Lenguas leave their territories too long, their people won't ever let them back." He smiled. "Progress is slow. We can't force the pace."

Not everybody shared Helmut's enthusiasm for settlement. His brother had run away to join the anthropologists.

They said that the destruction of nomadic institutions was disastrous. Women, who'd once selected those who'd live from those who'd die, had become disenfranchised. Worse, mimicking the patriarchal Mennonites had made women merely chattels. In every other sense, the Indians were still unable to grasp the concept of ownership. They were unable to use what they had and yet they'd lost the ability to share. Manufacture seemed generations away.

Some thought it was all a waste of time. As soon as the Mennonites turned their backs, everything fell apart. "If an Indian's cold," said Bobby, "he'll just pull his front door off and throw it on the fire."

On any view, the rate of settlement lagged behind vagrancy.

My last day in Filadelfia, Bobby took me to the tip. Indians poured down the slopes of smouldering rinds and husks to meet us. This infuriated Bobby, but as usual, his anger was unleashed without direction.

"Thousands of Indians!" he snarled. "Living on the surplus of a few hundred Mennonites!"

The Indians tore into the fresh garbage.

Helmut had said, "I believe they were sent by God. They force us to confront ourselves, our embarrassment of riches."

119

Rembrandt knew all about the embarrassment of riches. He was married to a Mennonite and the marriage brought him lucrative commissions. In *Cornelis Claesz Anslo and Aeltje Gerrits Schouten* or "The Mennonite

Preacher and his Wife" (1641), a young couple pose in black. They want to celebrate their thrift and so Rembrandt has included a candle and scissors in the foreground. Cut the taper and save the fat. On closer examination, the couple's collars and cuffs are exquisitely embroidered. Thrift has rewarded them well.

They seem only remotely aware of the presence of the artist. The preacher is admonishing his wife with hard words from the catechism. He wants to be remembered for his piety. She wants to be remembered for her suffering. They are good people though unlovely. They have found the love of God.

Finding some for their fellow man will prove a little harder.

120

They say that the trees in the Chaco are so specifically adapted that nothing introduced can survive. I discovered that there was an exception. Its introduction was almost as gruelling as its survival.

The journey began in Siberia on 17 December 1930.

As black day turned to white night, fifty sledges set out for the frozen Amur. The riders, two hundred of them, were the remnants of one of the Mennonites' bleaker attempts to find isolation in the world. For some years, they'd farmed the frosted earth between the Zeya and Bureya. Then Stalin had found them and had determined that what was theirs should become The People's. The settlers waited for the "River of Peace" to harden, and then, on a night as heartless and propitious as any, they slipped away.

There were Soviet guards posted at every mile along the banks. Parents smothered the cries of their children. One infant choked on over-caution. They quickly buried her body in the snow and hurried on. Shortly before dawn, they dropped on to the petrified currents, which popped and rattled like gunfire. Most were terrified, some were scorched by the ice. Abram Unger was so badly frost-bitten that they had to hack his feet off.

At sunrise, the frozen Israelites stumbled off the water into China. But Manchuria was not a Land of Milk and Honey. For thirteen months, they lived twenty to a room in Harbin, working as servants. A new home was sought but nobody wanted the stateless "Harbiners." In the end, they set off through the Chinese countryside for Paraguay.

From the coast, they caught fishing boats to Shanghai and then travelled "freight" through the South China Sea. In Saigon, they bought seeds for their unquantified future. Then they hitched onwards, west: Singapore, Suez, Marseilles, Le Havre, Lisbon, Rio, Buenos Aires, Asunción, Casado, "Kilometre 145." The old hands rode out to meet them off the *trencito*, amongst them the Brauns. They built the Harbingers their first mud homes and the Siberians thanked them with all they had: the seeds.

The strange pods were folded into sand. Within a short while, the Chaco had a new flavour: tamarind.

121

Although the first Unger arrived in the Chaco without feet, they've never settled. Wandering was now in the blood.

Even Abram refused to settle. He abandoned the other Harbingers and went roaming with the Indians. He was an adept hunter, and in later life he became an enthusiastic taxidermist, visiting deformity upon his prey for ever. The Filadelfia Museum is still haunted by his crooked sloths and cats and weirdly contorted foxes.

I'd met his grandson, Jakob, walking in Eastern Paraguay and now I went to visit him. There was much of his grandfather about him. He was temperamentally restless and wore his beard like Solzhenitsyn, which—I imagined—made him feel Siberian. He'd ducked much of his formal education and had spent the time exploring the *montes*, usually barefoot. He knew the names of all six hundred Chaco birds and could give them in English, Latin and Guaraní. At the age of forty he was the *éminence grise* of Chaco wildlife. Was it enough?

"No," he'd say. "This place is finished. Time to move on."

This I expected, but there was another side to Jakob which was harder to place. It wasn't just that he kept a revolver and a house full of computers, all whirring and chirping like the forest; he was incongruously sceptical. By now, I'd developed superior antennae for detecting atheism, and in the presence of Jakob, they began to twitch.

"My mother was from Neu-Halbstadt," he said and, little by little, I realised that this was an explanation.

One day, we drove out to the Neuland Colony. The Neulanders had arrived on the third and last of the waves of Mennonite migration. They were living proof of the wisdom of earlier departures. They were lucky to be living at all. Stalin's collectivisation had proved more vicious than any had imagined. Then, in October 1941, the Ukrainian colonies were "liberated" by Panzer Divisions. For almost exactly two years, their lives were eerily German. Then the Russian front burst and 30,000 Mennonites were swept backwards towards the west. They buried their dead by the roadside as they went. Nearly 20,000 others were recaptured by the Soviets, who committed them to an uncertain fate.

It was no better for those who made it to Germany. Any man who could carry a rifle was thrown a uniform and marched back into the inferno. By the end, the survivors' options were skinny. In 1947, the last few thousand were shipped to Paraguay (which was in the grip of civil war).

Although the old hands welcomed them with mud huts and chicken *pirozhnyes*, the Neulanders showed no inclination to flourish. Half the families were without fathers. Friedensheim would be a village comprised entirely of widows. Worse, the spirit was gone. They'd not been allowed to use churches for fifteen years. For many, if God had ever existed, he'd died in all the lice and sleet and burnt flesh of the war. The Neulanders were imbued with a deep sense of futility. By the seventies, half of them had drifted away.

Jakob took me to a "widow village."

"This is where my mother grew up."

One of the original houses had been preserved. The table was laid as if for tea, with Red Army mess-tins and butter-knives impressed with swastikas.

Jakob and his wife, Maria, kept a little zoo out in Toledo. The Unger family had been gathering specimens in the Chaco ever since their wanderings began.

"My grandfather sent seeds to the Botanical Gardens in Berlin," said Jakob. "I believe they still have his bottle-tree."

Jakob kept some brocket deer and armadillos, but at the heart of his collection were the Pleistocene pigs. I tried to look impressed, but they reminded me of Ping, except twice the size and steeped in rotting farts. They looked like giant sabre-toothed hedgehogs and were known as Wagner's Peccary, a name they thoroughly deserved. Inexplicably, they were also in great demand. Jakob had bred seventy and dispatched them round the world. San Diego is a hotbed of these brutes.

I realised that Jakob held them in real admiration.

"I've had them in captivity for four generations," he said, "and yet they refuse to be tamed. They are deeply wild."

Nobody else lived in Toledo. There was nothing there but a clearing of blank white crosses. On 28 July 1932, the forest had ignited and all that day a squall of metal had ripped backwards and forwards through the cactus. It had lasted until dusk, when there was a new and stranger sound: the sound of Aymará, guttural in triumph. The Guaranís melted away, into the undergrowth.

It was the Chaco War, now taking its ominous shape.

122

Amongst my friends, I found rare unanimity as to the causes of the war.

"Black gold," they said. "Oil."

"Standard Oil supported Bolivia. Royal Dutch supported us."

It was a convenient theory because it put the blame for this crazy, fatuous war beyond the boundaries of the continent. But there was never any oil. The subject wasn't even raised until the fighting was over (when Bolivia used it as an excuse to seize Standard's assets).

I preferred the idea that war was geographically inevitable. It was a theory propagated in the early thirties by a Chaco man called Sir Christopher Gibson. The Gibsons had had long associations with Paraguay (and still run the Highland Ball). Old Herbert Gibson was the first man to be knighted for endeavours outside the British Empire. When the First World War began, he returned to Europe to fight and his Lenguas put on war-paint and set off after him. The Gibsons were generally reckoned to know which way was up.

Sir Christopher saw the Chaco as a great void. On the Pacific side were the Children of the Sun, with their cities and social order, infallible priests and a history recorded in "stelas, ideographs and mnemonic quipus." On the Atlantic side were Arawaks, Caribs and Guaraní, "builders of the long house, botanists and herbalists, cannibals by ritual." In between them lay a vast no-man's-land, which the Incas called the *chacu*, "the place of abundant game." It would only be a matter of time before the warring parties poured into the vacuum.

If this all sounded a little frilly, there was a stout reason why war hadn't come sooner: technology, or rather the lack of it. Neither side had the means to move an army fast over this desiccated ocean-bed, to drill for water and tanker it to the troops. By the twentieth century, the Bolivians thought they had the machines in place. All they needed was a spark. Ironically, it was provided by the pacifists; Asunción's land deal with the Mennonites provoked howls in La Paz. Sir Christopher's offers of mediation were swept aside.

"Is *even* Paraguay going to push us around?" snorted the Bolivian president, Salamanca. "War should be an adventure for Bolivia! Let us go to the Chaco—not to conquer or die, but to conquer!"

Such bluster portended disaster. By close of play, almost one in every thirty Bolivians was lost in the Chaco's dirt. More would die of thirst than wounds. For years afterwards, whole columns of sun-bleached troops would be found in the thorns, turned to salt in the flight for home. It was true: the war would prove an unforgettable adventure.

The first campaigns were fought in postage stamps. Bolivia depicted itself sprawling up to Asunción. Paraguay, meanwhile, perched itself in the Andes. In reality, the warring parties were still a month's journey apart.

By 1932, they'd expended their philatelic urges and the shooting began. Bolivia had already reached the Mennonite colonies and was picking off Paraguayan outposts, like Toledo. Asunción responded with a fearsome display of poverty. The city buses were commandeered and there was a collection of wedding rings to buy rifles. There were only two significant military assets, the Italian gunboats, *Humaitá* and *Paraguay*. Though they would never fire a shot in anger, they ferried the army up to Puerto Casado. From there, the soldiers took mini trains out to the front.

By early September, the two ancient races were face to face in the thickets of Boquerón. *La Guerra de la Sed* ("the War of Thirst") was about to flare, uncontrolled.

"We'll drive you over there," said Jakob. "It's a strange place."

123

We drove south along narrow channels, or *picadas,* cut through the spiny growth. It was a beautiful day of lemon-yellow paratodo trees and cactus jewelled with birds. Jakob called out their names as we passed, like pieces of a lost orchestra: piculets, horneros and undulated tinamous. Maria said the weather was "unseasonably fresh"—quite unlike the spring of September 1932, which is said to have blazed.

Despite the years of dust-storms, floods and armadillos, we could still trace the outline of the trenches. We followed them into a dark tangle of bottle-trees. The bunkers had collapsed but the marks of Bolivian hatchets were still sharp in the stumps and shorings. They'd had a month to defend their water-hole and had dug a giant kidney fortified with barbed wire, stakes and interlocking fields of fire. In the middle was the prize. Nowadays, it is a succulent lagoon of lilies and whistling herons. Then, it was the only water for sixty kilometres. Already, men were fighting about water, not oil.

I tried to picture the defenders: khaki uniforms, caps with leather visors, rich brown boots called *choclateras*. Weren't they already Chaco veterans? They'd marched 450 miles from their railhead in Bolivia, surviving on hard tack and jingoism. They were used to hardship and had good reason to believe that victory would be theirs: Bolivia was a giant against puny Paraguay, three times as rich; she had tanks and flamethrowers and a splendid German commander called General Kündt (he was a veteran of the Russian Front and would lick these savages in days). The enemy didn't even have boots.

But beneath the bravado was anxiety. The soldiers were mostly Indians from the Altiplano and had neither affection nor loyalty for their white officers. Everything they'd learned about this lowland hell they hated: the sickly heat, the barbs that tore their uniforms and skin, the voracious ants, the endless diarrhoea.

It was a different story thirty metres away through the scrub. True, the Guaranís would fight in bare feet, but they saw a different war ahead. It wasn't an adventure but a matter of survival. The very existence of Paraguay was threatened and they responded as their grandfathers had— with stealth, guile and ferocity. The *patas peladas*—The Unshod—would move fast through the scrub, carrying only ponchos, canteens and rifles. The last stages of battle were often fought on their terms, concluded with machetes.

The Chaco would be no kinder to them, but it suited their purposes perfectly.

*

We followed a tapir's footprints round to the west side, where the forest hadn't grown back. It was still an open space, sprayed with tiny yellow flowers. Along the edge of the clearing, the bottle-trees had been hollowed out to make nests for Bolivian guns. It was here that the Paraguayans tried to force their way in.

For three weeks the two sides poured fire into each other's faces. The orchestras stopped and the forest wailed. The earth began to boil. Young men were vaporised in shell-bursts and their shreds pinned up in trees. Others were unexpectedly lopped and pruned and died in the open, peeled alive by ants. At midday the field was covered in butterflies, licking up the moisture from the dead. Then came the flies who, as the weeks passed, grew fat and blue and bloated.

It wasn't long before thirst began to kill. In that heat, each man needed ten litres a day just to function. The Paraguayans couldn't deliver it and a form of madness evolved; men wandered off into the scrub to look for fountains or to ambush their own water trucks. Sanity was restored summarily and without blindfolds.

It was worse for the Bolivians. The enemy had aligned their weapons on the lagoon and any movement was spattered with fire, even at night. At first the water was merely filmy and meaty, but then the pond was crusted over by the dead. The Bolivians ate their mules and then their beautiful boots. After dark, they crawled into the wasteland to pick the carrion clean of bottles and bullets.

Maria found one they'd missed, a bright green cartridge.

"This stuff turns up everywhere," she said. "It's endless."

Veterans of these battles believe that they are indeed endless. They say that the whistle and crunch of shells bounce through the ether for ever. The rest of us hear only the ant-shrike and the sleepy whirr of insects.

But this battle did end, although not with a boom. The last Bolivian positions were overrun by the writer Arthur Bray. He was a scholarly man, an Anglo-Paraguayan who'd served on the Western Front and who'd lost the facility for pleasure. The experience of Boquerón would render him permanently sinister. Both sides had lost nearly two thousand men. Both had fought with alarming obstinacy. Bray's captives were men reduced to gristle and maggots. Some had lost their minds and believed that the pot-bellied trees had eaten their comrades. When they heard this, the Guaranís wept.

We headed back to Toledo.

124

Boquerón didn't end the war, as it should have done. It proved to be merely an overture. The Paraguayans had also rushed back, along these *picadas*, to Toledo. They were off to meet the counterattack.

The trenches burrowed outwards from Jakob's zoo. They'd lasted better than Boquerón's. But for the snakes, I could have climbed through the bunkers and awaited bombardment.

The fort was built by General Belaieff, the anthropologist. He wasn't the only White Russian on the Paraguayan side; there were sixty others in gold braid. It was a war much to their liking; Major Chirkoff would cut down an entire Bolivian company with his machine-gun and Captain Kassianoff was to die in a magnificent cavalry charge. They are remembered in a popular drink: *tereré ruso* (*tereré* with sugar and muddy water). Of course, it's coincidence that—once again—Kündt, the Russians and the Fernheimers all faced each other across the same battlefield, but it gave Toledo a certain symmetry.

In all other respects the battle was grotesque.

It started with a tiny Bolivian aeroplane straying into small-arms fire. First, the observer jumped out without a parachute, and then the pilot smeared himself across the Paraguayan lines. Both were buried with full honours and the Bolivians sent a wreath and a fly-past. With the funerals over, the killing began.

It lasted two weeks. The Bolivians eventually got just near enough to the Paraguayan trenches to be caught up in the thorns and barbed wire. The Guaranís then finished them off with home-made grenades and bayonets.

The Mennonites have gathered up a thousand carcasses. They kept a skull for their museum and buried the rest in a pretty spot beneath the paratodos.

"Why do men do these things?" they ask, and then life reverts to Sunday.

125

After Toledo, the war moved west and out of sight.

It was a curious war. Some have described it as a dress rehearsal for the

Second World War, but in the field it was its own show, picaresque and surreal. The last bi-plane dogfight in aviation history was enacted over Ballivian. At *Campo de Los Muertos*, the Guaranís played dead and then jumped up for a devastating curtain-call. At Nanawa, their line was held by kitchen boys and cooks, and at Strongest, the armies tried to blast each other out with music and obscenities. Often the Paraguayans bombed their thirsty troops with ice-cubes. Often the Bolivians just bombed themselves. The show ground west.

A pattern emerged. The Bolivians would be separated from their water and then the Guaranís would cut round the back to offer them dehydration or surrender. Behind these moves was a man with chilly blue eyes who played the war like chess, not theatre. General Estigarribia is often credited with genius, and later he would stand for presidency. Had his propeller not come off over Altos, he might have spared Paraguay the *Stronato* and the uncomfortable years ahead.

Meanwhile, Paraguay was rounding up the enemy. She captured 21,000 soldiers and 10,000 civilians, or one per cent of Bolivia's population. They were marched back east and set to work in gardens and farms. Many stayed on after the war and their descendants are still affectionately referred to as *Los Bolivianos*. There was booty too: 28,000 rifles, 2,300 machine-guns and $10,000,000 worth of ammunition. It would be enough to meet Paraguay's military requirements for the next forty years. Even a decade ago, the artillery was still trundling round Asunción with Schneider mountain-guns, made in 1927.

Bolivian morale slithered. The myth of Paraguayan invincibility took shape: the Guaranís lived on palm hearts and thin air, fought like wild-cats and were everywhere. For some, the solution was *izquierdismo*, blowing the left hand off and walking home with the wounded. Others swam across the Pilcomayo into Argentina. Ten thousand deserted and more would have gone if only they'd had compasses.

Kündt was constantly amazed by the collapse of his strategy. Why weren't his machines grinding up the savages? At the height of his aston-ishment, he was fired. He returned to Germany, where failure finally killed him. His flame-throwers hadn't worked and the tanks had lurched around like ovens before being captured by barefoot Guaranís. The planes and artillery had proved useless; they could never find their tar-get—until too late. They were added to Asunción's armoury.

As the war moved into its third year, manpower faltered. The Chaco was entombing men faster than they could be recruited. Soon, there'd be more people buried in its dust than had ever lived there. The war would claim 88,000 men, 36,000 of them Paraguayan. Asunción responded to such losses with all it could; the police force was mobilised; the age of conscription was lowered to seventeen.

Both sides used mercenaries, although all they could offer them was thrills. Some found them. Thomas Wewege-Smith flew Junker K43s for Bolivia and would later set pulses racing with his saucy log-book: *War, Planes and Women, the Enthralling Story of an Airman's Adventures in Love and War*. Paraguay meanwhile received unwelcome assistance from Argentina's "Machetemen of Death." After some embarrassing looting, they were asked to leave. The quality of the freebooters was never high. Here is another one, who pops up in *Waugh in Abyssinia*:

> The German driver—an adventurous young airman who had come to look for good fortune after serving in the Paraguayan War—kept a rifle across the wheel and inflicted slight wounds on passing farmers at point-blank range.

Surprisingly, Paraguay's new arrivals rallied to the call to arms (even though they could have sought exemption). There were the Russians, of course—but the roll of honour would also contain Germans, Poles, Americans, Italians and Arabs. New Australia sent its share, men like Rod MacLeod, Sid Apthorpe and the Wood brothers—veterans of Gallipoli and Palestine. The English socialists provided Ricardo Smith and the Kennedy boys; Nigel served as a water-carrier and Douglas died in captivity on the Altiplano, where he's buried. Plenty of others were sacrificed; Shepperson, a young American, died of typhoid and Walter Gwynn was killed in a dogfight. Each of the newcomers seems to have found in Paraguay something precious, something worth preserving.

"Paraguay was the way it was," said Don Nigel, "but we liked it that way."

Most of the immigrants emerged transformed. Some were empowered: Arthur Bray became Chief of Police and Stroessner became president. Others were just less foreign. Charley Kent the trapper became an army guide and Robert Eaton ended up with a prison camp. He watched in horror as the war hacked across his ranch.

"The Bolivian was outclassed," he told me. "Not everyone died a hero's death."

Elsewhere, the world regarded the slaughter with only mild interest. The thirties was a busy time. The League of Nations protested and then collapsed under its own weightlessness. *The Morning Post* dispatched a reporter to see if there was a story. It was Reggie Thompson. He bought a Winchester Repeater, like Bobby Frick's, and stamped around the Chaco looking for the front line. He never found it and was appalled by whisky at 2/6 a shot. After a month, he prematurely announced the Paraguayan victory and then went off sightseeing to Iguaçu Falls.

Eventually, Estigarribia's brilliant moves ended in the foothills of the Andes and in stalemate. Bolivia didn't have the ferocity to throw the Paraguayans off and Paraguay didn't have the strength to deliver the *coup de grâce*. They agreed a truce for noon on 14 June 1935. In the last half-hour of the war, the antagonists opened up on each other with almost everything they had. No one knows how many widows and orphans were created in the final minutes of this senseless conflict. At twelve, the guns fell silent and men climbed out of their trenches from east and west and met in no-man's-land. It was now only a short walk between the two sides of the continent. The men are said to have wept and embraced and then the two armies turned and began the long march home.

It seems hardly right to talk of a victor. Both countries were left ragged and exhausted and neither has ever fully recovered. Within years, both would turn in on themselves, self-digesting in civil war. But in the short term, Paraguay had achieved all she'd needed to: she'd fought for survival and she still existed. Along the way, she'd secured 20,000 square miles of empty, greenish desert. That's two Paraguayan and three Bolivian lives for every dreadful square.

The victory parades in Asunción were muted. Not even Reggie Thompson came out to watch.

126

One Sunday, the Ungers took me up the Trans-Chaco Highway to where the tarmac ran out.

"They *had* promised to pave it all the way to Bolivia . . ." said Jakob ruefully.

As we drove westwards, it got drier, as I'd expected, and the trees shrivelled into claws. More surprisingly, the weather changed and an icy *surazo* was whipped in from the south like a ghostly orange cavalry. As the sand kicked and whinnied at the windows, I could sense Jakob's mood cloud over. He spotted a red flag in the cactus.

"The Swiss colony," he said. "Most of them are pensioners. They were told this would be a sweet retirement. Hospitals and swimming pools! They hardly have enough water to wash . . ."

Jakob's treasured desert had turned to broken promises.

"And all this," he said, gathering up the northern horizon in his grimace, "is owned by a thief. Did you ever hear of the Süd Milch scandal in Germany? The shareholders of a dairy were fleeced of millions and millions of dollars. It all ended up here."

"Is crime the new cash crop?" I asked.

"You need to ask the army about that. They've been at it for years."

Suddenly, there, at the end of the tarmac, was the army. They'd taken over the old Bolivian garrison, Camacho, and renamed it "Mariscal Estigarribia." It was a parade of cement and dust-devils and not much else. A concrete banner had been hauled up over the road: "Third Army Corps." It was guarded by three old men, dressed for an old war: green fatigues, floppy green hats, machetes and blankets slung from the shoulder.

"They're the best soldiers," said Jakob. "Recruited from the western tribes, the Guaraní-Nandeva."

As for the rest, few Paraguayans held them in affection. The heroes of the Chaco War had been tidied away in the *Stronato,* when the army became the Ministry of Theft. Mariscal Estigarribia itself had developed a reputation as a pit-stop for the army's stolen cars, bound for Bolivia. The Colorados' sultans even enjoyed a little slavery, with a ready supply of puppyish conscripts.

"Look at them," said Maria. "Some are only thirteen or fourteen!"

A squad of shaven children were dabbing whitewash on the guardhouse.

"Sometimes these kids learn too much," said Jakob. "I expect you've heard what happens?"

Everyone knew. The over-curious were boxed up and sent home with their cards marked "leukaemia," "rabies" or "accidental gunshot wound." Such misfortune hadn't ended with the departure of Stroessner; in the last decade, a hundred and three conscripts had met improbable deaths. I'd often seen their parents marching around Asunción. Murderers! they shouted. Clean up the army!

Many *Asunceños* agreed, although saying so in public was still considered a little unhealthy.

We drove out to a stadium on a plain of giant craters.

It was sports day for the children of the Chaco. The Indians sent drummers and the army sent a captain in jackboots and mirrors, a reminder that youth is not always fun and games. The Germans won the football and the Lengua won the long barefoot dash through the grit. I asked Jakob about the craters.

"The Americans dug them. To build their runway."

"They have an *airbase*? Here?"

"People say it's huge. Deep tunnels under the desert."

"But we're five hundred kilometres out of Asunción. Why *here*?"

Jakob shrugged. "On the map, it's almost the centre of the continent."

"Well, yes, but it's not exactly its heart."

"No," said Jakob, looking around bleakly, "not exactly."

Maria had another idea. "I heard it was their fuelling stop for the South Pole."

This was quite a thought: the crossroads of two plump armies, one heading south with Froot Loops and atomic clocks, the other heading west in stolen cars. I was surprised by the amount of secrecy that seemed to be thriving in this enormous, empty wilderness. Perhaps openness merely encourages grander distortion.

We returned to the cement village and ate at "The French Hotel." Whatever chain of events had brought them here had left the owners in a state of stubble and deep shock. All they could remember of their former lives was *gratin dauphinois*.

What happens after the tarmac? I asked the Frenchmen.

"Rien," they said. *"Pas d'eau. Pas d'essence. Seulement des épines."*

I'd reached an extremity. It was time to turn round and head for home.

Epilogue

"In this blessed land of Paraguay," Mr. Visconti spoke as though he were adding a moral to the story, "there is no income tax and no evasions are necessary."

—Graham Greene, *Travels with My Aunt*

I had begun, not only to dimly understand, but to enthusiastically fall in love with the brutal and tender land of Paraguay.

—Ariel Dorfman, foreword to *Son of Man*

127

In Asunción, I had lunch with the soil scientist, Dr. Palacios. We talked about the places I'd been to.

"You probably think you understand us now," he said, "but you won't. You *can't*. We don't even understand ourselves. You think I'm joking? Remember that three-quarters of all Paraguayans were born during the *Stronato*, which was one long lie. It's been no better since then. We're still ruled by liars. We live in a state of deception. What intrigues me is that we've always been this way."

He poured himself some beer and it foamed down the glass, on to the table.

"I've thought about this a lot," he went on. "I call it *Paraguay oculta*. I learnt history at school but I now realise that most of it was lies. That leaves me wondering who we are. Was our Jesuit *provincia* really an enlightened republic or just another state of delusion? Who was Dr. Francia? Was he black? No one seems to have exploited our confusion better than Francia. He ruled Paraguay for years and years and then vanished. There's hardly a trace of him."

"What about the López era?" I asked.

"It was a fantasy which we all shared, then regretted, then rebuilt. What was the war all about? What happened to the treasure? Was there any?"

The last century, said Palacios, had been just as elusive.

"You can see why we became a hideaway for Nazis. For them, it was like running deep into a forest. We didn't even know what our own people were doing. What happened in the civil war? It was a war as catastrophic as the Chaco but it's never mentioned. A third of our people disappeared but there isn't a single memorial to them, not even a plaque."

A waiter appeared with flanks of beef and maize cake. Palacios waited until he'd moved away and then continued his theme.

"Stroessner. He called himself 'The Luminous Lighthouse.' It sounded good (none of us had ever seen the sea), but it just meant we'd be dazzled. Even now he's gone, we're still frightened that his people are out there, in the dark." He paused, chewing thoughtfully. "*Paraguay oculta*. It's a good name, isn't it?"

I mentioned the airbase.

He shook his head. "We don't know who runs this country. Or who owns it. Our politics is just a sleight of hand. Who killed Professor Argaña? Did *anybody* kill him? Our politicians seem unable to lead us without trickery, without filling their pockets first. It's as if there's no tomorrow. Only today counts. That's the way the *Indians* think."

The scientist sighed. "That's it, I suppose. Although we don't know it, deep down we're still Indians."

128

I have never found departures easy but I'd never imagined that leaving Paraguay would be so difficult. This was partly because Asunción was now smothered in summer and many of those I'd come to know had fled the city. Without the goodbyes and the rituals of departure, my journey seemed frayed and incomplete. I spent a whole morning punching numbers into my telephone but all I got back was my own trills or, worse, the irritation of servants.

"They're away until next March. May I take a message?"

Or: "Miss Yegros has gone to a wedding for two months."

Or: "I'm sorry, he's in São Paulo having his bowels examined."

I even called Gareth but the phone just rang and rang. Some months later, I got a card from his wife saying that Gareth had taken a turn for the worse and that they'd taken him to the alcoholics' home in Filadelfia. It was hard to imagine Gareth with a German God and all those tapirs but at least he'd found a form of surrealism that wouldn't drown him. As usual, I had a feeling that I'd probably never see him again. More than ever, I hoped I was wrong.

I didn't call everyone. I didn't have the stomach for the lactating girl with her strawberry shakes and I didn't have the guts for another rocket-tour with Fluff.

The other difficulty with leaving was that I'd contracted a bout of bereavement. I'd always suspected Asunción of underlying melancholy and I began to wonder if I wasn't somehow tainted. Dr. Palacios had done nothing to allay my fears. "We've been in mourning since the *Grande Guerre*," he'd said. "It overwhelms us like sleep."

I realised I was being ridiculous. I simply didn't want to leave. I'd settled back into the rhythm of the city: my room at the old skin clinic;

the delicious torpor of the evenings; *piraña* soup at The Lido; lancers in uniforms of cobalt and silver. On the day of my return to Asunción, the gunboat *Humaitá* had been decommissioned and I'd climbed aboard with a commando of schoolchildren. *Humaitá* had seen seventy-three years' service, two wars and thousands of layers of slaty paint. She still had her hammock-hooks and Genoese guns and a bloom of hot diesel still wafted up from the hatches. I was entranced and would have yelled and blubbered down the speaking-tubes except that—fortunately— words now completely failed me.

Palacios was right, of course; the city bore its loss like sleep. In the squares, *Asunceños* wore a dazed, confused expression and life was glimpsed in a series of inexplicable dreams: a pink palace, a man carrying a stuffed lion, the giant bronze frogs. What would the citizens find when they awoke? Perhaps they never would and this would always be the Republic of Regret, the antithesis of Eldorado. I had no doubt what lay at its centre. All roads led there. I often found myself outside and now I went there again: the Panteón de Los Héroes.

As far as I could tell it was a faithful and sturdy replica of Paris except that it was rendered in cement. It had taken sixty years to complete and had sat out two wars in its scaffolding trusses. The result was bluntly secular and would have delighted Voltaire (who is walled up in the original); in here, even the Virgin Mary had to wear her medals. Everything smelt of gun-oil and boot polish. The Napoleonic guards were hunched in a corner with their Coca-Colas and cheese *empanadas*. Beneath the dome was a large round nest, clustered with caskets. These were the caskets of heroes: Estigarribia, Caballero, Carlos López, Francisco López (empty, eaten by leaf-mould), Francia (empty, eaten by alligators) and poor General Díaz (now all in one box, reunited with his leg). It was a sobering thought that, of Paraguay's greatest figures, only two had gone quietly to their graves. Perhaps it was no surprise that her people seemed to regard death as a virtue and bereavement as hereditary.

Perhaps too there really was a contagious aspect to it all: I now had a powerful urge to slow things down. I decided to buy some souvenirs. It wasn't that I wanted anything elaborate, just a few hostages to slow the pace of departure. It was a hopeless strategy. Most of the stuff was made of scooped-out armadillos or other harmless animals and was offered up as ashtrays and handbags. Other things were only tangentially

Paraguayan (like the statues of Napoleon) or just odd (like the masturbating goblins). I settled for a tape describing itself as the *Himno Nacional*, but when I got it back, all I could hear were some old men, singing their way home on the bus.

My efforts to wrap things up and say goodbye were going dismally. In the absence of living company, I decided to go off and visit the dead.

129

Marshal López had carved off a corner of Recoleta for his dead contractors.

It was supposed to be a *British* cemetery, insisted Robert Eaton.

"It was not just for any Protestants," he'd said. "My wife, Dorothy, was most indignant when they let the Germans in."

Poor indignant Dorothy was now packed down among the erstwhile Germans. There was a vase of fresh roses on her tomb and, in breach of her own rules, she'd left a space at her side for a foreigner, the American who'd never stopped adoring her. Nearby were her family—her mother, Constance Kent, and her father, Charley the trapper. Charley had seen action in three wars: Boer, Great and Chaco. At the age of seventy, even he had realised that he was too old for his fourth. He died a few days after the liberation of Naples, in October 1943. Infuriatingly, he'd been outpaced by his old classmate and enemy, now leading the embattled Britons: Sir Winston Churchill.

There were other names I recognised among all the gothic and frangipani: the Australians—Woods, McLeods and Apthorpes—and the socialists—Stanleys, Kennedys and Smiths. But there were also many missing. I couldn't find any sign of the great *Yanqui* rednecks; perhaps all this nicety hadn't suited them. Nor could I see the English barristers; perhaps "the Land of Women" had proved more than gentlemen could handle.

Leon Cadogan was there. His tomb was not that of a wandering Irish poet, which was how he saw himself, but a liberator, which was what he became. Many thousands of Indians owed him their lives and they'd repaid him with an altar of black granite and a title—Dragonfly—in silver letters: *Tupá kuchuvi vevé*.

I walked on, to the far end, to the wreckage of the English contractors. Many of the tombstones were missing or had been prised apart by the slow dentistry of roots. Those that remained told a painful story. Here lay the little Nesbitts, none of whom had reached the age of one. Mary Watts had lived just long enough to see her husband win the Order of Merit, for heroism at the naval skirmish of Riachuelo. They weren't to be reunited in death: John fell foul of López's paranoia, was shot by firing squad and was buried in the southern marshes.

Here too was John Muir, driven to drink at the age of twenty-six. On 11 May 1863, he'd cut his own throat and then hanged himself, astonishing the doctors with a self-decapitation. At the time, his death was blamed on the bullying of Newton and Grant, the same men who'd driven Whytehead to suicide. Mrs. Newton was here (Mr. Newton had escaped on a British gunboat), but where was Grant?

As I eased between the fragments, a flock of parrots suddenly exploded from the canopy. They spiralled madly upwards, hung for a moment and then dropped, falling somewhere beyond the wall, in Catholic Recoleta. The noise woke the grave-digger, who burrowed out of the shade and sniffed the air for news.

"Yes," he said sleepily, "we have Señor Grant."

We set off through the marble forest. He said his name was Celso. After a while we came to a bench.

"Here he is."

The last monument to Alexander Grant, native of Forfarshire, sometime foundryman of Ybycuí, drunk, misanthrope and bully, had been wrenched out of the ground, upended and was now a repository for bottoms. Celso and I lay on the ground and looked upwards at the inscription. Grant had survived Whytehead by only two months.

I hardly dared ask what had happened to the Chief Engineer.

"Ah," said Celso, apologetically, "they put this road through here in 1985. Some of the graves got bulldozed."

Poor Whytehead. Paraguay's greatest architect had been ground up to make a cul-de-sac. Perhaps the ambitious Dr. Stewart had also been powdered by a Caterpillar, but somehow I doubted it. I preferred to think he'd always fancied something grander—a Parthenon, perhaps— and had defected to the Catholic side.

Celso sensed my disappointment. We set off again.

"This one was our great hero. He killed hundreds of Brazilians."

It was George Thompson, buried with full honours: "Civil Engineer. Fellow of the Royal Geographical Society, Lieutenant-Colonel of the

Paraguayan Army Engineers." *Teach us to number our days that we may apply our hearts unto wisdom.*

We walked back towards the gate.

"Celso, are you sure there are no others?"

He thought about it a moment. "Wait," he said. "There's a very great lady. She's over the wall with the Catholics." He hesitated. "They call her *La Concubina Irlandesa.*"

Madame Lynch was back from Père Lachaise.

130

Things had not gone quietly for Eliza's last remains. Just as death had intruded so colourfully upon her life, so now did life intrude upon her death. Whether she'd have wanted it or not, she was about to make her second and probably final trip to Paraguay.

There had been a brief period of quiet after 1900, when the Parisians had stopped pouring corpses into her little grave. The last of her fellow tenants, a Madame Martin, had sealed herself in with a massive lump of granite, and for a while, Eliza would rest in cramped but bearable peace. The López children didn't think it necessary to provide a flashy monument. Instead, they'd attached a simple and inexpensive plaque that described their mother as "Unforgettable."

She might have proved that even this was a lie but for the rise of Paraguayan fascism. Madame Martin and friends were about to have their peace imploded. First, the fascists came over and riveted the Paraguayan State Seal into Madame Martin's granite flanks, and then they planted a flagpole. There was then a pause whilst they repaired to Asunción to plan their next move, or rather Eliza's.

Meanwhile, her image underwent some restoration. The problem was that there was little agreement about what she should be like. The artists made her a strapping warrior-queen with biceps like frozen turkeys. The writers, on the other hand, saw her as the Princess of Love, a sugary popsy who overflowed with tenderness and honey. It wasn't easy to reconcile the two. Stroessner didn't bother; he didn't understand art and had little time for women. A good woman was one who was barefoot, at heel and festooned with babies. That's how Madame Lynch would be. In 1961, her return was sought.

The task of returning Eliza fell to a Paraguayan-Syrian called Teófilo Chammas. He'd already impressed the government with his aptitude for smuggling and was considered equal to a daunting mission: Eliza had to be extracted from French bureaucracy, from under a ton of granite and from the remains of Madame Martin and a dozen other well-wormed *défuntes*. How he did it was his secret—and it wasn't his only one: Eliza Lynch arrived back in South America packed with four kilos of best Lebanese hashish.

For a while, she languished in the docks in Buenos Aires. The Argentines were troubled not so much by the weed as by the fact that she'd returned at all. Eventually, according to the official version, the *Humaitá* was sent to collect her. In Chammas' version, he tipped her into a suitcase and flew her back to Asunción in a seaplane. Either way, the day of her return to Asunción, 25 July 1961, became a Day of National Homage. It was also the seventy-fifth anniversary of her death.

On the quayside, leading the mourners, was Stroessner himself, sobbing manfully and dressed in the style of a Ruritanian Air Chief Marshal. "Our National Heroine," he sniffed. "Our National Martyr." In an impressive display of grief, he carried the casket up to the Panteón and laid it next to that of Mariscal López. But, even though no one could be sure that either were in their boxes, the bishop had forbidden the unmarried couple to lie together in perpetuity. So, once the gnashers of teeth had dispersed, Eliza was spirited out through the back door and off to the Ministry of Defence. There she stayed for the next nine years, in her own little shrine, among her last bits of crockery and her lover's enormous underpants.

Finally, on the centenary of Paraguay's emasculation, she was on the move again, this time to join the gentry at La Recoleta. All her life they'd tried to exclude her. Now she was to be implanted among them.

I was surprised by Eliza's latest tomb. It was rudely modern, like some public lavatories under full sail. There were little china swans as tokens of breeding, and pebbledash for Ireland. Her bronze casket was identical to that of Marshal López (which, of course, was identical to Napoleon's). It was a curious setting for the unearthed Parisians; Madame Martin and friends must have wondered where their eternity was all going to end.

Most surprising of all was the statue on the roof. It was Eliza designed by a junta. All I recognised was the ball-gown, now clinging as deliciously as possible to the body of a ploughman. She was carrying a shovel, and at her feet were two tiny graves into which she'd just tossed the scrags of her family. Underneath, General Stroessner's sniffles had turned to brass: "Eliza Alicia Lynch, who selflessly accompanied the Greatest Hero of the Nation to his Immolation at Cerro Corá." In fleeing a shortage of potatoes, the girl from Cork had become an Olympian.

A few doors down from the Temple O'Lynch was the Tomb O'Leary. As historian and poodle to the Court of Don Alfredo, O'Leary had provided the last, loyal howls.

> Like Joan of Arc [he wailed], she died the death of a martyr, content in the belief that history would vindicate her noble name, would restore her stolen reputation and would enshrine her in the uppermost reaches of that region of heaven reserved for the spiritual remains of the greatest woman South America has ever known.

Goodbye, I mused, Eliza Lynch, Empress of Paraguay.

131

Right to the end I continued to bombard the atmosphere with phone calls. There was now a note of distress about them, because the old skin clinic, which until then had served me so well, was beginning to eat me. Where once skin had been soothed and creamed and healed, it now boiled and buckled into welts the size of golf balls. Summer had brought a blaze of bedbugs.

I showed Miriam my bed, scattered with cracked carcasses and threads of blood. She was unimpressed.

"They're all dead."

"They are *now*," I protested. "But they have friends."

Miriam switched to denial. "There are no *chinches* here."

She would not be moved, but I would. For my last night, I decided my pelt needed sanctuary and so I started to pack. At that moment, the Francos answered my calls. Come up and stay with us, they said. Although it meant moving up to Legoland, their intervention was heavenly. A cloud lifted and with it a plague of controversial bedbugs.

I took a last walk through the old squares. It was a beautiful, silent day, a soldier-blue sky tufted in white. The *Guaraní* was at her quay, ready to renew her cycle. I could see Foxhound on his exercise bike, pedalling sedately nowhere. On the Plaza de Los Héroes, the Ladies who Lunch were gathered under a banner: Amnesty International (Paraguay). They were stacking up signatures to loose off at Colombia and Yasser Arafat. Injustice, they trilled, End the Injustice.

"What about here?" I asked. "The gangsters of the *Stronato* are still up there, in their palaces in Villa Morra. What about them?"

But they wouldn't have it. It was like accusing them of bedbugs. They swooned with denial.

"The big houses were built after Stroessner."

"Those days are over."

Were they? True, Stroessner was in Brasília, unthreading himself with senility (Doña Eligia had finally abandoned him and Freddie junior was dead, leaving only Gustavo to shoo away the paparazzi and the curious). But the other big players were still out there, dispensing malice: Wasmosy, bricked up in his fortress; President Macchi, driving round in a stolen BMW; Lino Oviedo, pulling strings from his foreign jail. Sometimes Paraguay seemed like one of Estigarribia's brilliant chess matches, grotesquely mutated. One bishop, five and a half million hapless pawns, twelve *faux*-castles and three kings, all in checkmate. In one sense the game was over, but all it would take was one false move and all would be back in play.

The Francos' house was in an advanced state of subtlety. It had been so quietly tiptoed into its square of jungle that now I can remember nothing about it, except that it was newish and that all the portraits were of cows. As always, José only ever said half of what he might have said and his children said even less. But they were kind and solicitous and observed me very closely before submitting their reports to Virginia: "John hasn't had any breakfast yet" or "John has just fallen down the stairs with all his luggage." It was like finding myself among miniature *pyragüés*, now mysteriously copper-coloured and benign. The only member of the household to produce any volume was the parrot, who sang the national anthem all through dinner.

"Here's something that'll please you," said Virginia, and gave me a newspaper cutting. It was Pastor Coronel, oozed across a slab of marble. "He died whilst you were in the Chaco. Heart attack."

The Grand Inquisitor was dead. Virginia was right; I did feel a certain satisfaction. I thought of her parents' maid and Leon Cadogan who'd been unravelled by his cruelty. And Chase Sardi who'd lost his eardrum and the union man who was sawn into pieces. There were plenty of others. Coronel, by comparison, had enjoyed a comfortable retirement. Though he'd never left his air-conditioned oubliette, he died among his suitcases, still packed with dollars.

"Everyone was at the funeral."

"You didn't go, did you?"

José and Virginia looked at each other, puzzled.

"This is a village," said Virginia. "He was part of our life. That's how it is."

Afterword

LINO OVIEDO was released from prison in Brazil in December 2001 after the Brazilians wearied of his extradition proceedings. He has started his own party which will inevitably tear the Colorados apart after fifty-four years of rule. Right now, he hovers on the Paraguayan frontier, threatening the country with his own peculiar brand of redemption.

My friend, JAKOB UNGER, gave in to his nomadic instincts and, in late 2001, he left Paraguay forever. He now works in a furniture factory in Winnipeg, Canada.

The BRAUNS decided that they could no longer cope in their little cabin and they moved closer to the *Krankenhaus* in Loma Plata. They are now back in the heart of the colony that they helped to found seventy-four years ago.

NURSE BAKER wrote with news of terrible floods in the Chaco. After that, her letters stopped.

Things looked better on the football field. During the toughest World Cup 2002 qualifiers, Paraguay's goalkeeper-who-would-be-king, CHILAVERT, somehow scored four extraordinary goals and the Guaranís advanced on Japan. They eventually lost to the finalist, Germany.

Meanwhile, ex-President RAUL CUBAS decided that he couldn't stand another moment in exile and, in February 2002, he returned to Paraguay in a taxi. He was immediately arrested and faces up to twenty-five years in prison for conspiracy to murder Vice-President Argaña.

Two months later, another ex-president finally received his deserts, at least in part. After years of convoluted litigation, JUAN WASMOSY was convicted of defrauding the state of $6 million. Although he is the first president to have been convicted in modern times, no one is seriously predicting the beginnings of change. He was sentenced to four years imprisonment.

At about the same time, Paraguayans were given a grisly view of their past. A TV crew picked up two left-wing politicians outside a covert police house, both men naked and lavishly tortured. Although the police protested that the men were dangerous kidnappers, Paraguayans would not fall for this one again. Cabinet ministers resigned in droves and in panic. President MACCHI responded as he always did, with unnerving sloth.

VIRGINIA FRANCO still writes. José has decided on action and has thrown his weight behind a new political party, Paraguayan Solidarity. Though Virginia still sees her country in glorious ochre and vermilion, her letters are ever more threaded with anxiety. The future, as much as the past, is riven with uncertainty.

Chronology

1866 Allies cross into Paraguay (April); Paraguayans massacred at Tuyutí (May); Allies defeated at Curupayty (September)
1868 López flees Humaitá (March); Humaitá surrenders (August); Paraguayans routed at Lomas Valentinas (December)
1869 Capture of Asunción (January), Ybycuí (May) and Piribebuy (August); Paraguayan fleet burnt at Vapor Cué
1870 Battle of Cerro Corá

Arcadias and Utopias

1881 The visit of *The Falcon*; foundation of San Bernardino
1886 Foundation of Nueva Germania
1889 Death of Dr. Förster

The Green Hell

1927 First Mennonites arrive at Menno
1932 Chaco War begins; Bolivians capture Toledo (July); Battle of Boquerón (September)
1935 War ends in stalemate

Fascism and More War

1936 Fascists assume power
1937 Jews are prohibited from entering Paraguay
1945 Paraguay declares war on Germany (2 February)

The Stronato

1954 Stroessner seizes control
1959 Dr. Mengele arrives from Buenos Aires
1989 Stroessner ousted in Rodríguez's *coup d'état* (2 February)

Democracy of Sorts

1996 Lino Oviedo accused of plotting a *coup d'état* (April)
1999 Assassination of Vice-President Argaña (23 March); nine demonstrators shot
2000 Attempted *coup d'état*; *Congreso* shelled (May); *liberales* win their first election victory in over fifty years (August)

Further Reading

Jesuits

Abou, Selim—*The Jesuit Republic of the Guaranis (1609–1768)* (Crossroad Herder, New York, 1997)

Cunninghame Graham, R. B.—*A Vanished Arcadia* (William Heinemann, London, 1901; Century Classics, London, 1988)

Cunninghame Graham, R. B.—*Brought Forward* (Duckworth, London, 1916)

Hochwaelder, Fritz—*Sur la Terre comme au Ciel* (or *The Strong are Lonely*) (Samuel French, Inc., New York, 1954)

Voltaire—*Candide*, Chapter xiv (trans. Prof. John Butt, Penguin, London, 1947)

Dr. Francia

Rengger, J. R. and Longchamp—*The Reign of Dr. Francia* (London, 1827, a translation of the French translation of the German original)

White, Edward Lucas—*El Supremo* (Dutton, New York, 1934)

The War of The Triple Alliance

Baillie, Alexander, FRGS—*A Paraguayan Treasure* (Simpkin Marshall, London, 1887)

Bourgarde La Dardye, Dr. E. de—*Paraguay: The Land and the People* (George Philip & Son, London, 1892)

Burton, Richard—*Letters from the Battlefields of Paraguay* (London, 1870)

Cunninghame Graham, R. B.—*Portrait of a Dictator* (William Heinemann, London, 1933)

Masterman, George Frederick—*Seven Eventful Years in Paraguay* (London, 1869)

McLynn, Frank—*From the Sierras to the Pampas* (Century, London, 1991)

Robertson J. P. and W. P.—*Letters on Paraguay* (London, 1839, 2 vols.)

Thompson, G.—*The War in Paraguay* (London, 1869)

Washburn, Charles Ames—*The History of Paraguay* (Boston, 1871, 2 vols.)

Eliza Lynch

Barret, William E.—*Woman on Horseback* (Modern Literary Editions
　　Publishing Company, New York, 1938; Peter Davies, London, 1938)

Brodsky, Alan—*Madame Lynch and Friend* (Harper and Row, New York, 1975;
　　Cassell, London, 1976)

Varela, Héctor—*Eliza Lynch* (Editorial Tor, Buenos Aires, 1933)

Law Reports: IX Macpherson 860, *Stewart-v-Anthony Gelot and William Mason*

Young, H. L.—*Eliza Lynch: The Regent of Paraguay* (Anthony Blond, London,
　　1966)

The Mennonites

Redekop, Calvin—*Strangers Become Neighbors* (Herald Press, Ontario, 1980)

Stoesz, Edgar and Stackley, Muriel—*Garden in the Wilderness* (CMBC,
　　Manitoba, 1999)

Warkentin, Abe—*Strangers and Pilgrims* (Die Mennonitische Post, Manitoba,
　　1987)

Utopians, Immigrants and Colonists

MacDonald, A. K.—*Picturesque Paraguay* (Kelly, 1912)

MacIntyre, Ben—*Forgotten Fatherland* (Farrar Straus Giroux, New York, 1992)

Mulhall—*Handbook of the River Plate Republics, 1875* (p.400, "Lincolnshire
　　farmers")

Plá, Josefina—*The British in Paraguay 1850 to 1870* (Richmond Publishing, 1976)

Thompson, R. W.—*Germans and Japs in South America* (Faber, 1940)

Whitehead, Anne—*Paradise Mislaid* (University of Queensland Press, 1997)

Chaco War

Farcau, Bruce—*The Chaco War, Bolivia and Paraguay 1932–35* (Praeger, 1996)

Hagedorn, D. and Sapienza, A. L.—*Aircraft of the Chaco War 1928–1935*
　　(Schiffer, 1997)

Thompson, R. W.—*An Echo of Trumpets* (George Allen and Unwin, 1964)

Wewege-Smith, Thomas—*War, Planes and Women, the Enthralling Story of an
　　Airman's Adventures in Love and War* (Hutchinson, London, 1938)

Zook, David H.—*The Conduct of the Chaco War* (Bookman Associates, New Haven, 1961)

The Stroessner Years

Alegría, C. and Flakoll, D.—*Death of Somoza* (Curbstone Press, 1996)

Aren, Richard—*Genocide in Paraguay* (Temple University Press, Philadelphia, 1976)

Chippindale, P. and Harriman, E.—*Juntas United* (Quartet, 1978)

English, Adrian—*Regional Defence Profile Latin America* (Jane's, 1988)

Hilton, Isabel—*The General* (Granta No. 31, 1990)

Lewis, Paul—*Paraguay Under Stroessner* (University of North Carolina Press, Chapel Hill, 1980)

Niedergang, Marcel—*The Twenty Latin Americas, Vol. 1* (Penguin, London, 1971)

Nazis

Astor, Gerald—*The Last Nazi* (Weidenfeld and Nicolson, London, 1985)

Posner, Gerald—*Mengele* (Cooper Square Publications, 1999)

Seiferheld, Alfredo—*Nazismo y fascismo en el Paraguay* (Asunción, Editorial Histórica, 1986)

Thomas, H.—*Doppelgängers* (Fourth Estate, London, 1995)

Natural History

Attenborough, David—*Zoo Quest in Paraguay* (Lutterworth, 1959)

Durrell, Gerald—*The Drunken Forest* (Penguin, London, 1956)

Kerr, Sir John Graham—*A Naturalist in The Gran Chaco* (Cambridge University Press, Cambridge, 1950)

Travel and Exploration

Clastres, Pierre—*Chronicle of the Guayaki Indians* (Faber, 1998)

Dobrizhoffer, Martin—*An Account of the Abipones: an Equestrian People of Paraguay* (London, 1784)

Gibson, Sir Christopher—*Enchanted Trails* (Museum Press, London, 1948)

Grubb, W. Barbrooke—*A Church in the Wilds* (Seeley Service and Co. Ltd, 1914)

Hunt, R. J.—*The Livingstone of South America. The Life of W. Barbrooke Grubb* (Seeley Service and Co., 1932)

Iyer, Pico—*Falling off the Map: Some Lonely Places of the World* (Black Swan, London, 1994)

Knight, E. F.—*The Cruise of the Falcon* (Sampson Low, Marston, Searle and Rivington, London, 1887)

Mansfield, C. B.—*Paraguay, Brazil and The Plate* (1856)

Meyer, Gordon—*The River and the People* (Methuen, 1965)

Tolten, Hans—*Enchanting Wilderness, Adventures in Darkest South America* (Selwyn and Blount, 1936)

Walker, J.—*South American Sketches of RBC Graham* (University of Oklahoma Press, 1978)

Paraguayan Literature

Roa Bastos, Augusto—*Son of Man* (Monthly Review Press, 1988)

Roa Bastos, Augusto—*I the Supreme* (Faber, London, 1986)

English Literature

Conrad, Joseph—*Nostromo* (Penguin Popular Classics, London, 1994)

Greene, Graham—*Travels with My Aunt* (The Bodley Head, London, 1969)

Greene, Graham—*Ways of Escape* (Vintage, London, 1999)

Kingsley, Charles—*Westward Ho!* (Macmillan & Co., 1889)

Southey, Richard—*A Tale of Paraguay* (Longman & Co., 1825)

General

Kirkpatrick, F. A.—*Latin America* (1938)

Lambert, P. and Nickson, A.—*The Transition to Democracy in Paraguay* (Macmillan, London, 1997)

Las Amigas Norteamericanas—*The Land of Lace and Legend* (6th ed., 1983)

Pendle, George—*A History of Latin America* (Penguin, London, 1963)

Zago, Manrique—*Paraguay, Land of Marvels* (Asunción, Zago, 1997)